Lecture Notes in Computer Science 14290

The series Lecture Notes in Computer Science (LNCS), including its subseries Lecture Notes in Artificial Intelligence (LNAI) and Lecture Notes in Bioinformatics (LNBI), has established itself as a medium for the publication of new developments in computer science and information technology research, teaching, and education.

LNCS enjoys close cooperation with the computer science R & D community, the series counts many renowned academics among its volume editors and paper authors, and collaborates with prestigious societies. Its mission is to serve this international community by providing an invaluable service, mainly focused on the publication of conference and workshop proceedings and postproceedings. LNCS commenced publication in 1973.

Alessandro Cimatti · Laura Titolo
Editors

Formal Methods for Industrial Critical Systems

28th International Conference, FMICS 2023
Antwerp, Belgium, September 20–22, 2023
Proceedings

Springer

Editors
Alessandro Cimatti
Fondazione Bruno Kessler
Povo, Italy

Laura Titolo
NASA Langley Research Center
AMA-NASA LaRC
Hampton, VA, USA

ISSN 0302-9743 ISSN 1611-3349 (electronic)
Lecture Notes in Computer Science
ISBN 978-3-031-43680-2 ISBN 978-3-031-43681-9 (eBook)
https://doi.org/10.1007/978-3-031-43681-9

This Springer imprint is published by the registered company Springer Nature Switzerland AG
The registered company address is: Gewerbestrasse 11, 6330 Cham, Switzerland

Paper in this product is recyclable.

Preface

The International Conference on Formal Methods in Industrial Critical Systems (FMICS), organized by ERCIM, is the key conference at the intersection of industrial applications and formal methods. The aim of the FMICS series is to provide a forum for researchers and practitioners who are interested in the development and application of formal methods in industry. FMICS brings together scientists and engineers who are active in the area of formal methods and interested in exchanging their experiences in the industrial usage of these methods. FMICS also strives to promote research and development for the improvement of formal methods and tools for industrial applications.

This volume contains the papers presented at the 28th International Conference on Formal Methods in Industrial Critical Systems (FMICS 2023), which was held during September 20–22, 2023. The symposium took place in Antwerp, Belgium, and was organized under the umbrella of CONFEST, alongside the 34th International Conference on Concurrency Theory (CONCUR 2023), the 20th International Conference on Quantitative Evaluation of Systems (QEST 2023), and the 21st International Conference on Formal Modeling and Analysis of Timed Systems (FORMATS 2023).

This year we received 24 paper submissions. We selected a total of 14 papers for presentation during the conference and inclusion in these proceedings with an acceptance rate of 58%. The submissions were reviewed by an international Program Committee (PC) of 29 members from a mix of universities, industry, and research institutes. All submissions went through a rigorous single-blind review process overseen by the Program Committee Chairs. Each submission received at least three review reports and was actively and thoroughly discussed by the PC. Additionally, the authors were given the possibility to write a rebuttal.

The program of CONFEST 2023 included two FMICS invited keynotes: one by Joost-Pieter Katoen, from RWTH Aachen University, on fault tree analysis via formal methods, and one by Anna Slobodova, from Intel, about the application of formal methods in electronic design automation.

We are grateful to all involved in FMICS 2023. We thank the authors for submitting and presenting their work at FMICS 2023 and the PC members and sub-reviewers for their accurate and timely reviewing. We also thank the invited speakers, session chairs, and attendees, all of whom contributed to making the conference a success. We are also grateful to the providers of the EasyChair system, which was used to manage the submissions, to Springer for sponsoring the Best Paper Award and for publishing the proceedings, and to the Steering Committee of FMICS for their trust and support. We thank the General Chairs of CONFEST, Guillermo A. Pérez and Jean-François Raskin, for providing the logistics that enabled and facilitated the organization of FMICS 2023.

August 2023

Alessandro Cimatti
Laura Titolo

Preface

Organization

Program Committee Chairs

Alessandro Cimatti	Fondazione Bruno Kessler, Italy
Laura Titolo	AMA-NASA LaRC, USA

Steering Committee

Maurice ter Beek	CNR-ISTI, Italy
Alessandro Fantechi	University of Florence, Italy
Hubert Garavel	Inria, France
Tiziana Margaria	University of Limerick and LERO, Ireland
Radu Mateescu	Inria, France
Jaco van de Pol	Aarhus University, Denmark

Program Committee

Jasmin Blanchette	LMU München, Germany
Supratik Chakraborty	IIT Bombay, India
Pedro D'Argenio	Universidad Nacional de Córdoba, Argentina
Jennifer Davis	Collins Aerospace, USA
David Deharbe	CLEARSY, France
Alexandre Duret-Lutz	LRDE, France
Alessandro Fantechi	University of Florence, Italy
Alessio Ferrari	CNR-ISTI, Italy
Hubert Garavel	Inria, France
Pierre-Loïc Garoche	ENAC, France
Klaus Havelund	NASA Jet Propulsion Laboratory, USA
Jean-Baptiste Jeannin	University of Michigan, USA
Barbara Jobstmann	EPFL, Switzerland
Laura Kovács	TU Wien, Austria
Tiziana Margaria	University of Limerick and LERO, Ireland
Paolo Masci	AMA-NASA LaRC, USA
Stefan Mitsch	Carnegie Mellon University, USA
Rosemary Monahan	Maynooth University, Ireland
David Monniaux	VERIMAG, France

Sergio Mover	École Polytechnique, France
Yannick Moy	ADACORE, France
Jorge Navas	Certora, USA
Dejan Ničkovič	Austrian Institute of Technology, Austria
Kristine Yvonne Rozier	Iowa State University, USA
Cristina Seceleanu	Mälardalen University, Sweden
Martina Seidl	Johannes Kepler University, Austria
Jaco van de Pol	Aarhus University, Denmark
Alicia Villanueva	Universitat Politècnica de València, Spain
Virginie Wiels	Onera, France

Additional Reviewers

Davide Basile
Pamina Georgiou
Rong Gu
Michael Rawson
Philipp Schlehuber-Caissier

Contents

Experimenting with Formal Verification and Model-Based Development in Railways: The Case of UMC and Sparx Enterprise Architect

Davide Basile(✉), Franco Mazzanti, and Alessio Ferrari

Formal Methods and Tools Lab ISTI – CNR, Pisa, Italy
{davide.basile,franco.mazzanti,alessio.ferrari}@isti.cnr.it

Abstract. The use of formal methods can reduce the time and costs associated with railway signalling systems development and maintenance, and improve correct behaviour and safety. The integration of formal methods into industrial model-based development tools has been the subject of recent research, indicating the potential transfer of academic techniques to enhance industrial tools. This paper explores the integration of an academic formal verification tool, UML Model Checker (UMC), with an industrial model-based development tool, Sparx Enterprise Architect (Sparx EA). The case study being analyzed is a railway standard interface. The paper demonstrates how formal verification techniques from academic tools can be integrated into industrial development practices using industrial tools, and how simulation in Sparx EA can be derived from traces generated by the UMC formal verification activity. From this experience, we derive a set of lessons learned and research challenges.

Keywords: umc · sparx enterprise architect · formal verification · uml

1 Introduction

The adoption of formal methods and railway standard interfaces has been identified as crucial in reducing the time for developing and delivering railway signalling systems, as well as decreasing the high costs associated with procurement, development, and maintenance [12,15,47]. Formal methods tools are essential to ensure correct behaviour, interoperability of railway interfaces, and safety. Formal methods are mainly used and developed by academia, and their uptake in the railway industry has been the subject of recent studies [10,17,31,33,36,38,41,55].

Model-based development is an industrially adopted software engineering technique that supports the creation of models to represent a system's behaviour and structure. These models are used to generate code, documentation, test cases, system simulations, and perform other tasks. Examples of commercial tools are PTC Windchill Modeler SySim [5], Sparx Systems Enterprise

The original version of chapter 1 has been revised: two authors' names and the publication year in Reference [36] have been corrected. A correction to this chapter can be found at https://doi.org/10.1007/978-3-031-43681-9_15

A. Cimatti and L. Titolo (Eds.): FMICS 2023, LNCS 14290, pp. 1–21, 2023.
https://doi.org/10.1007/978-3-031-43681-9_1

Architect [6], Dassault Cameo Systems Modeller [2]. These tools are often based on the Unified Modeling Language (UML) OMG standard [49,50], which is considered a semi-formal method. Semi-formal methods owe their name to their lack of a formal semantics. The semantics of semi-formal methods is informally described in natural language documents (e.g., [51]). This informal semantics suffers either from semantic aspects intentionally left open by the standards or unintentional ambiguities [9,21,26,27]. As a result, the same semi-formal model executed on different simulators may behave differently.

There is a growing body of literature on the integration of formal methods techniques into model-based development tools (e.g., [13,19,20,23,34,40,52,54, 56,59]), and the formalization of UML state diagrams has been recently surveyed in [9]. This integration shows how techniques developed in academia—typically formal—can be transferred to enhance current industrial tools—generally semi-formal.

This paper explores the combination of an academic formal verification tool with an industrial model-based development tool to develop a railway interface. The formal verification tool used is the UML Model Checker (UMC), while the selected model-based development tool is Sparx Enterprise Architect (Sparx EA). The models developed using the two tools are related, with the Sparx EA model used for model-based development activities and the UMC model used for formal verification, in particular model checking.

This paper builds upon previous activities carried out during the Shift2Rail project 4SECURail [7]. The case study being analyzed is a fragment of the UNISIG Subset 039 [61] and Subset 098 [60] standard interface called the Communication Supervision Layer (CSL). It is borrowed from the first release of the "Formal development Demonstrator prototype" of the 4SECURail project [43,53] and is specifically dedicated to the control of the communication status between two neighboring Radio Block Centre (RBC). The paper aims to demonstrate how formal verification techniques from academic tools can be integrated into industrial development practices using industrial tools. In particular, [9] reports that "counterexamples are rarely mapped back to the original models" and more specifically that "UMC could be used to verify UML models". We use UMC to formally verify the UML state diagrams of Sparx EA and the traces generated by the UMC verification phase are reproduced as simulations in Sparx EA.

The contributions of this paper are: i) a set of UML notation constraints oriented towards maintaining the correspondence between Sparx EA and UMC models; ii) a set of actionable rules to map the two notations; iii) the mapping of traces generated by the UMC formal verification into simulations in Sparx EA; iv) a set of lessons learned and challenges derived by applying the proposed methodology to a case study from the railway industry.

Structure of the Paper. We start with the related work in Sect. 2. Background on the used tools is in Sect. 3. Section 4 discusses the methodology for connecting the semi-formal and formal models. A concrete example showing how the methodology is applied to a case study is in Sect. 5. The lessons learned, limitations and challenges are discussed in Sect. 6. Section 7 concludes the paper and discusses future work.

2 Related Work

Several works have been carried out in the railway domain concerning the usage of formal and semi-formal notations to represent a wide diversity of systems [31], according to the formal model-based development paradigm [28].

Among them, Chiappini et al. [25] consider a portion of the ERTMS/ETCS system as case study and propose an approach to manually translate natural language requirements into an enhanced UML language. The UML representation is then translated and verified by means of the NuSMV model checker.

Ferrari et al. [29,32] start from requirements expressed by means of UML component diagrams, and use Simulink/Stateflow, with the aid of Simulink Design Verifier, to verify the model behaviour of an automatic train control system. Similar to us, the authors also define a set of modelling guidelines and notation restrictions to remove ambiguities from the models, with the goal of achieving clearer models and generated code.

In [48] Miller et al. report their infrastructure to translate Simulink models into different formal languages, including SPIN and NuSMV, to perform formal verification. Model translation is also the target of Mazzanti et al. [46], who also report a method to increase confidence in the correctness of the transformation. The method starts from UML state machines, which are translated into multiple formal notations.

Still on the translation from UML-like models to other formal notations, recent works have focused on transforming these models into mCRL2 [20,59]. Many studies also focus on the translation from UML into the B/Event-B notation [57,58], with formal verification performed by means of Atelier B and ProB [22].

A recent set of works by Mazzanti and Belli [18,47] focuses on the incremental modelling of natural language requirements as UMC state machines, and associated formal validation. Initially, a UML state machine modelling the set of requirements under analysis is created. This initial model is not targeting any specific tool and it contains pseudo-code. Once consolidated, the state machine model will eventually be written using the UMC syntax. In [18,47] it is showed how, under certain notation restrictions, it is possible to automatically translate the state machines from UMC to other verification tools such as ProB and CADP [35], where the models are formally verified to be equivalent. In [18] it is discussed how the formal verification of UMC state machines can be used independently to transform natural language requirements into formally verified structured natural language requirements.

Similarly to [18,47], in this paper we use a preliminary version of the same case study and a relaxed version of the restrictions imposed on the UML state machines. Moreover, our work complements [18,47] by showing how the developed UMC models can be imported into Sparx EA to enable various tasks other than formal verification, including generating diagrams, documentation, code, and interactive simulations. More details on the rationale for the choice of the case study of 4SECURail, the tools, and the prototype architecture are in [43–45,53].

3 MBSD, Sparx Enterprise Architect and UMC

Model-Based Software/System Development (MBSD) is a methodology for creating software and hardware artifacts using models expressed as graphical diagrams. Models are used throughout the development cycle. The development process is guided by a model of the software architecture, which represents a semi-formalization of the system's abstract level without implementation details. Semi-formal models can be complemented by their formal specifications, enabling formal techniques like model checking or theorem proving. Early detection of errors is possible by verifying the model against requirements using techniques such as model checking.

UML, an OMG standardised notation [49,50], is the standard for many MBSD environments. Models support modular design by representing different views of the system at distinct levels, such as requirements definition, implementation, and deployment. Code and test generation ensures that the implementation is derived directly from the models with traceability. In this paper, we will focus on a specific subset of UML, detailed in Sect. 4.

In UML, a model consists of multiple classes, each with its own set of attributes. Objects are created by instantiating these classes and assigning values to the attributes using the object-oriented paradigm. A classifier behaviour can be assigned to a class in the form of a UML state machine. A state machine can be triggered by events, e.g., signals. The state machine includes various states and transitions connecting them. Transitions have labels of the form `trigger[conditions]/effects`, where the conditions are on the variables of the class and the trigger arguments, and the effects can modify these variables and generate outgoing signals. Two examples of state machines, accepted by the tools UMC and Sparx EA, are in Fig. 1 and Fig. 2.

3.1 Sparx Enterprise Architect

Sparx Enterprise Architect is an MBSD tool based on OMG UML [49]. It was selected after an initial task was conducted during the 4SECURail project to test and gather information about factors such as licensing costs, customer support, and training [43]. The most desirable feature was the modelling and simulation of state machine diagrams.

MBSD tools differ in the way in which UML state machines can be composed. Different MBSD tools provide different solutions. Sparx EA [6] is an MBSD tool that offers an Executable State Machine (ESM) artifact specifically designed for simulating the *composition* of different state machines. These machines can interact through a straightforward instruction for sending an event, and do not require excessive notation. An example of ESM for composing the state machine in Fig. 2 with other state machines is depicted in Fig. 3. ESM provide all the necessary elements for easy translation to/from a formal specification amenable to verification and graphical display of an informal specification, as well as simulation.

In addition to simulating a composition of state machines, the standard simulation engines of Sparx EA can be used to interact with each machine individually. Source code is automatically generated from such ESM models, which is then executed/debugged. It is possible to generate source code in JavaScript, Java, C, C++ and C#. The source code also contains the implementation of the behavioural engine of state diagrams, for example the pool of events for each state machine, the dispatching method and so on. Once designed, a system composed of several interacting state machines can be simulated interactively, by sending triggers, to observe its behaviour. The ESM is used for generating code, and the simulation gives an interactive graphical animation of the system being debugged. In this paper, we used Sparx EA unified edition version 15.2 build 1559.

3.2 UML Model Checker

The UML Model Checker (UMC) [8,16,39] is an open-access tool explicitly oriented to the fast prototyping of systems constituted by interacting state machines. UMC allows the user to design a UML state diagram using a simple textual notation, visualise the corresponding graphical representation, interactively animate the system evolutions, formally verify (using on-the-fly model checking) UCTL [16] properties of the system behaviour. Detailed explanations are given when a property is found not to hold, also in terms of simple UML sequence diagrams. With UMC it is possible to check if/how a given transition is eventually fired, if/when a certain signal is sent, if/when a certain variable is modified, or a certain state reached.

The formal semantics of UMC models is provided by an incremental construction of a doubly labelled transition system [16]. In addition, for a restricted set of UMC notation this can be given through the automatic translation into the LOTOS NT language [24,37,42] described in [18,45,47]. The strong bisimilarity of source and target models can be proved with, e.g., mCRL2 `ltscompare` [3] or CADP `bcg_cmp` [1]. Note that UMC is an academic tool that is primarily utilized for research and teaching. We used UMC version 4.8f (2022).

4 Methodology

In this section, we present the methodology used to connect the UMC and Sparx EA models. It is worth noting that the proposed methodology works in both directions. It is possible to use a forward engineering method by analyzing the model in UMC first and then translating it into Sparx EA for development. Alternatively, it is possible to use a reverse engineering approach, and if the Sparx EA models meet the specified condition described below, they can be translated into UMC for formal verification. The rationale is that the two tools are complementary and their features shall be used jointly. While Sparx EA supports typical MBSD activities, such as interactive simulation and code generation, UMC supports formal verification.

UMC supports a subset of UML State Machine Diagrams, polished from some syntactic sugar notations, and each construct can be mapped one-to-one to a construct in Sparx EA, if the Sparx EA model follows the same restrictions. Relating the UMC model and the Sparx EA model is almost straightforward when notation constraints are enforced. The following adopted restrictions on the model are exploited to keep the notation light and as much independent as possible from UML technicalities. Indeed, many of the constructs that are discarded are syntactic sugar that can be expressed using a lighter notation.

Syntactic Restrictions on UML State Machines

- no `entry`, `exit`, or `do` behaviour is present in the states of the model (these behaviors can be equivalently expressed in state transitions),
- interaction happens using only *signals*, and no operation calls are used,
- only one-to-one interactions are used, i.e., no signals broadcast,
- conflicts in enabled transitions are only allowed in the environment,
- no timing behaviour is present (time elapsing is explicated using a TICK event), no internal and local transitions are used, no hierarchical states are used, no history, fork, join and choice nodes are used.

Environment. In Sparx EA interactive simulations the human user acts as the environment. Consider, for example, a system composed of two components C1 and C2. When only one of the two components (e.g., C1) is fully modelled, then events from C2 can be considered part of the environment of C1 and manually triggered. In model checking tools like UMC a (possibly non-deterministic) environment needs to be explicitly modelled to obtain a fully closed system on which the verification is automatic.

Semantics of Sparx ESM and UML Models. In the context of UML State Machine models, certain aspects of the model's behaviour are left unspecified by the ISO standard [49]. For example, the order in which events occur is left open to interpretation. As a result, it is difficult to formally verify the accuracy of a translation from a formal to a semi-formal model and vice-versa, from the semi-formal to the formal one. Indeed, the Sparx EA models do not have a formal semantics and Sparx EA does not have the ability to exhaustively generate the state space of the model. In our case, the correctness of the translation (i.e., the correspondence between the formal and semi-formal model) has been validated informally, and by translating traces derived from UMC proofs into simulations in Sparx EA (cf. Section 5).

The UML state diagrams in both UMC and Sparx EA are avoiding the presence of aspects with ambiguous semantics. Sparx EA provides a way to inspect and review the code generated by an ESM to disambiguate the semantics choices left open by the UML standard. Thus, a code review has been performed to check that the semantics of Sparx EA and UMC state machines are aligned. Regarding how events are ordered in each pool of events, both UMC and Sparx EA use a first-in-first-out policy. In Sparx EA, the scheduling of state machines and the dispatching of messages are fixed, with each state machine completing its run-to-completion cycle before another one starts. Conflicts in enabled transitions are not present in the Sparx model (i.e., the model is deterministic), so there is no need to specify a choice strategy. However, UMC allows for all orders of scheduling, it interleaves all run-to-completions steps of different state machines, and permits all possible behaviours obtained by fixing a specific strategy for selecting one among many enabled transitions (UMC models only allow conflicts in the environment, which is not translated in Sparx EA). Thus, the semantics of UMC includes the semantics of Sparx ESM, as well as all semantics obtained by changing the scheduling order. If a safety property holds in the UMC model, it will also hold in the Sparx model.

The effects of each transition contain Java code, limited to performing arithmetic operations on variables, sending signals, and reading values. These restrictions on Sparx models are necessary to disambiguate the semi-formal semantics and proceed in external formal verification using model checking.

Rules for Relating the UMC Model with the Sparx EA Model. We now describe the rules to relate a UMC model with a Sparx EA model. An example of application of the rules is in the next section, where Fig. 1 and Fig. 2 show how the state machines of Sparx EA and UMC are related.

1) Each class in UMC corresponds to a class in Sparx EA.
2) Attributes of a class in UMC correspond to attributes of the corresponding class in Sparx EA.
3) Each Object in UMC, with its variables' instantiation, is mapped into a Property of an ESM (i.e., an instantiation of class), to where the values of the attributes can be instantiated.
4) Both UMC and Sparx EA classes have a relation "has-a" with other classes, in such a way that every object has a reference to other objects to whom it is interacting with.
5) Each class in UMC is specified as a state machine. Similarly, in Sparx EA a classifier behaviour will be assigned to each class in the form of a state machine.
6) States and transitions of a machine in UMC are in one-to-one correspondence with those of a machine in Sparx EA.
7) Signals that are attributes of each class in UMC are in correspondence with global trigger events in the Sparx model, accessible by each state machine. These events are of type `Signal` and have the same parameters as in UMC.
8) In UMC the sending of a signal with, for example, two parameters, is performed using the instruction `Object.Signal(value1, value2)` where `Object` is the receiver object argument, `Signal` is the signal invoked in that object, and `value1` and `value2` are the values to be passed as arguments. In an ESM, the objects are connected by connectors typed with the relation "has-a" coming from the class diagram. Each end of a connector identifies the partner of a communication.

The above send operation is performed in Sparx EA with the macro `%SEND_EVENT("TRIGGER.sig(value1,value2)",CONTEXT_REF(RECIPIENT))%;` where `sig` denotes the specification of the signal assigned to the trigger (i.e., names and types of the parameters), `TRIGGER` corresponds to `Signal` in UMC, and `RECIPIENT` corresponds to `Object` in UMC. `RECIPIENT` is the identifier provided in the corresponding connector end of the ESM. In case values of signals must be accessed inside the guard or effect of a transition, in UMC this can be done by simply accessing the parameter with its declared name. In Sparx EA values of signals are accessed as follows. In the effect of a transition, the instruction `signal.parameterValues.get("arg")` is used, where `arg` is the name of the parameter of the signal. If the value is accessed in a condition, the above command becomes `event.signal.parameterValues.get("arg")`. We also note that this syntax is specific to Java code generation.

5 Case Study

The chosen case study is a subset of the RBC/RBC handover protocol borrowed from the 4SECURail project [43,53]. This protocol is a crucial aspect of the ERTMS/ETCS train control system, in which a Radio Block Centre (RBC) manages trains under its area of supervision. An RBC is a wireless component of the wayside train control system that manages the trains that can be reached from its assigned geographical area (i.e., the area of supervision). When a train approaches the end of an RBC's area of supervision, a handover procedure with the neighbouring RBC must take place to manage the transfer of control responsibilities. Since neighbouring RBCs may be manufactured by different providers, the RBC/RBC interface must ensure interoperability between RBCs provided by different suppliers. The selected subset of the RBC/RBC protocol is the Communication Supervision Layer (CSL), responsible for opening/closing a communication line between RBCs and maintaining connection through life signs. The CSL's functional requirements are specified in UNISIG SUBSET-039 [61] and UNISIG SUBSET-098 [60]. In particular, two sides are identified: the Initiator CSL (ICSL), and the Called CSL (CCSL). The initiator is the RBC responsible for opening the connection. The layers above and below the CSL are called, respectively, RBC User Layer and Safe intermediate Application sub-Layer (SAI). In this paper, these other layers are treated as external environment and thus are not specified. All models and other artifacts are available in [11].

Formal and Semi-formal Models. We now describe some aspects of the CSL model, focusing on the ICSL. The state machine modeling the ICSL is provided both as a formal model in UMC (see Fig. 1) and as a semi-formal model in Sparx EA (see Fig. 2). Each transition is labeled with a name (e.g., R1) to keep track of the correspondence between the two models.

The ICSL state machine is composed of two states `NOCOMMS` (the two RBC are disconnected) and `COMMS` (the two RBC are connected). The ini-

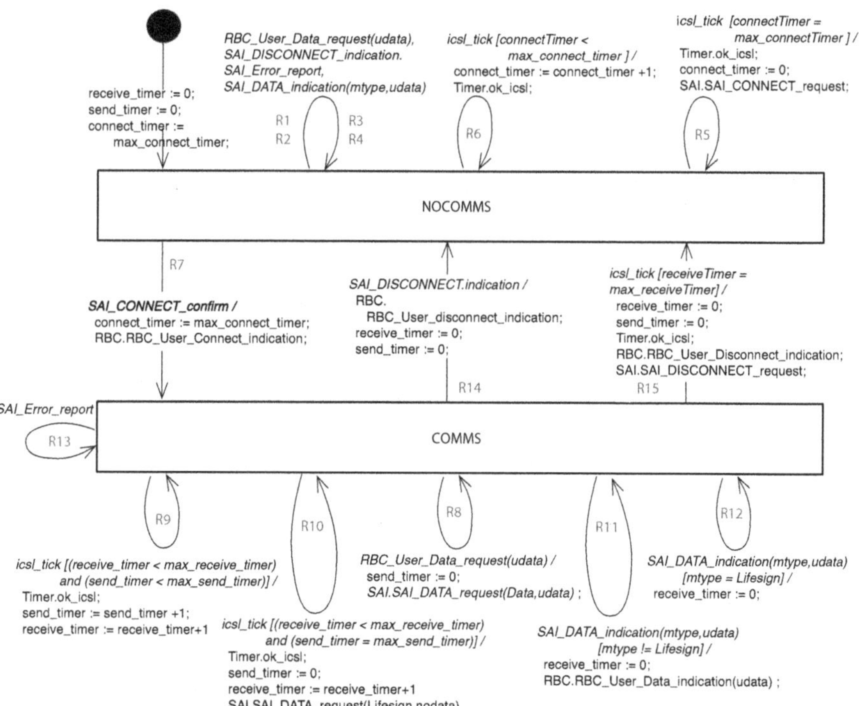

Fig. 1. The Initiator Communication Supervision Layer State Machine of UMC

tial state is NOCOMMS. From state NOCOMMS, a counter `connect_timer` is incremented at each reception of a TICK signal from the clock (R6). If the threshold `max_connect_timer` is reached, a request for connection SAI_CONNECT_REQUEST is signaled to the SAI (which will be forwarded to the CCSL), and the counter is reset (R5).

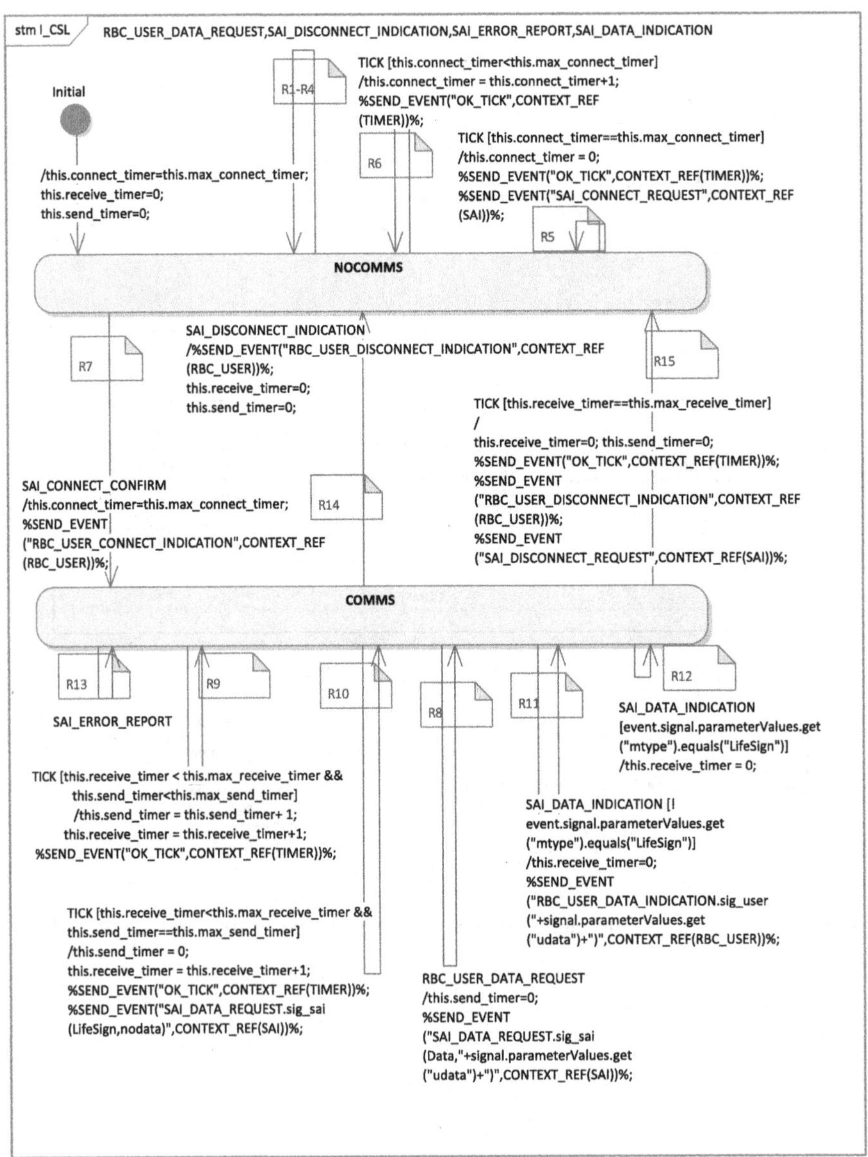

Fig. 2. The Initiator Communication Supervision Layer State Machine of Sparx EA

The signal of connection SAI_CONNECT_CONFIRM (signaling the connection of the CCSL) coming from the SAI triggers the transition to state COMMS (R7). In state COMMS two counters are used. A counter receive_timer is used to keep track of the last message received. A counter send_timer is used to keep track of the last time a message was sent. These counters are incremented at the reception of a signal from the clock (R9). Each time a message is received from the SAI, the receive_timer is reset (R11,R12). Moreover, if the message is not of type LifeSign, it is forwarded to the user (R11). Similarly, if a message is received from the user, it is forwarded to the SAI (R8), and the send_timer is reset. Whenever the threshold max_send_timer is reached (R10), a LifeSign message is sent to the SAI (which be forwarded to the CCSL) and send_timer is reset. This message is used to check if the connection is still up. Whenever the threshold max_receive_timer is reached, the connection is closed because no message has been received within the maximum allowed time. In this case, a signal of disconnection is sent to both the user and the SAI (R15). If the message of disconnection is received from the SAI (R14), then it is only forwarded to the user and the connection is closed.

Mapping. We now discuss how the rules from Sect. 4 have been applied to provide a correspondence between the two models in Fig. 1 and Fig. 2. The class diagram (not displayed here) contains the classes I_CSL, C_CSL, SAI and RBC_User. An additional class TIMER is used to model the elapse of time, and it is part of the environment. These classes and their attributes are the same for both Sparx EA and UMC, according to rule 1 and rule 2. Following rule 4, the classes I_CSL, C_CSL both have relations "has-a" with TIMER, RBC_USER and SAI.

We recall that in Sparx EA the environment classes TIMER, SAI and RBC_USER are just stubs with a dummy behaviour assigned to them.

The ESM artifact is displayed in Fig. 3. The ESM illustrates the composition of different class instances. There are two instantiations of the environment classes RBC_USER and SAI, one for each CSL. There is one instantiation of the environment class TIMER for both CSL. The objects C_CSL and I_CSL are instantiating their respective classes, and they are initialising their attributes. These objects are the same in Sparx EA and UMC according to rule 3.

Moreover, following rule 4, each CSL will refer to its RBC_USER, SAI and TIMER using the context references RBC_USER, SAI and TIMER, respectively, as depicted in the ends of the corresponding connectors in Fig. 3.

According to rule 5, the behaviour of the classes I_CSL and C_CSL is specified by state machines in both UMC and Sparx EA. The states and transitions of these state machines are in correspondence according to rule 6. Following rule 7, the signals with their parameters are also in correspondence.

Finally, we use the transition R11 as an example for showing how rule 8 is applied. In UMC, SAI_DATA_indication(mtype,udata) is the trigger of R11. In Sparx EA, the trigger SAI_DATA_INDICATION does not report its parameters, which are declared separately in the type of the signal associated with the trigger. The parameters have the same name in both Sparx EA and UMC. In UMC, the condition of R11 is `mtype != LifeSign`. Indeed, it checks whether the type of the received message is not a life sign. In Sparx EA, the condition of R11 is `!event.signal.parameterValues.get("mtype").equals("LifeSign")`. We remark that Sparx EA uses Java as code for the conditions and the effects (other languages are also supported, e.g., C++). The code present in the effects and conditions (with the exception of the macros) will be injected into the generated source code as is. Finally, `RBC.RBC_User_Data_indication(udata)` and `receive_timer:=0` are the instructions of the effect of R11 in UMC. Basically, the message received by the SAI is forwarded to the user and the timer is reset. In Sparx EA, the effect of R11 also contains two instructions. The timer is reset with the instruction `this.receive_timer=0;`. The signal is forwarded with:

```
%SEND_EVENT("RBC_USER_DATA_INDICATION.sig_user("+signal.
parameterValues.get("udata")+")",CONTEXT_REF(RBC_USER))%;
```

we note that the macro is mixed with Java code. Indeed, it uses the code `signal.parameterValues.get("udata")` to read the field `udata` of the signal received by the SAI. The signal `sig_user` only contains one parameter (`udata`) and is assigned to the trigger `RBC_USER_DATA_INDICATION`.

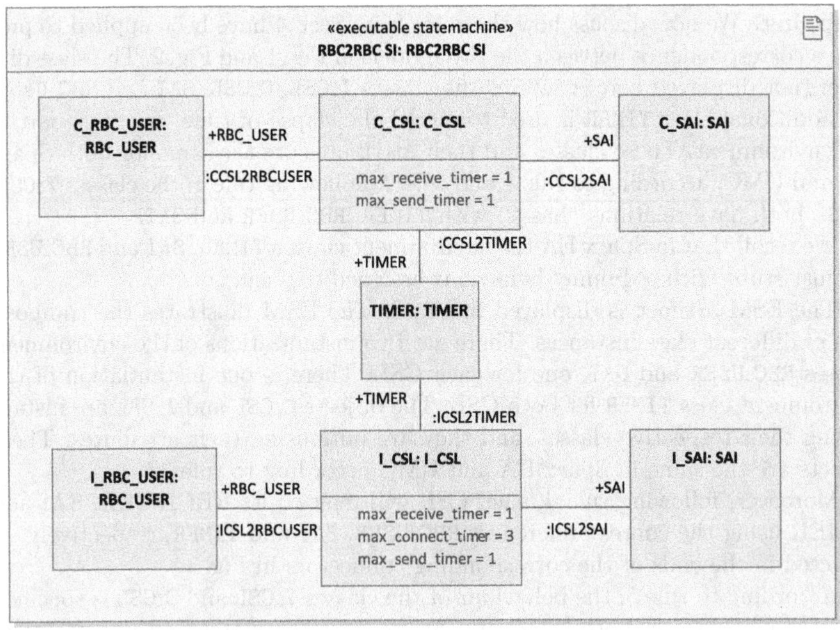

Fig. 3. The Executable State Machine of Sparx EA, showing the composition of the various instantiations of the state machines

5.1 Model Checking Sparx EA Models

We now show one of the benefits of our approach, i.e., the formal verification of semi-formal models. We remark that, generally, MBSD tools such as Sparx

EA are not equipped with facilities for performing formal analyses. Through the mapping described in Sect. 4, it becomes possible to perform model checking of Sparx EA models by exploiting the connection with UMC. The model checking of a formal property produces a trace showing that the property holds or is violated. We show below how the produced trace is simulated in the Sparx EA semi-formal model.

Reproducing UMC traces in Sparx EA has two main benefits. Firstly, it allows the reproduction of the detected issues in Sparx EA. This is generally desirable for interacting with stakeholders that are only knowledgeable of the used industrial tool but are not aware of the underlying formal verification that has been carried out. The second goal is to validate the correspondence between the semi-formal and formal models presented in this paper. Indeed, if the trace is not reproducible in Sparx EA then we have detected a misalignment between the semantics of the formal and semi-formal models. Even if the correspondence is sound, this is still possible since UMC overapproximates all possible behaviours of Sparx EA. Therefore, an issue signalled by UMC might not be detectable by only relying on the interactive simulation capabilities provided by Sparx EA. Indeed, the simulation engine shows only a subset of all behaviours that the real system may have because, e.g., it fixes the order in which state machines are executed.

We now provide an example of a temporal property formally verified with UMC, using the models in Fig. 1 and Fig. 2. We need to mutate the models to cause the violation of an invariant, in such a way that a trace showing the violation is generated by UMC. This is typical of model-based mutation testing [14], where mutations are applied to the model to measure the effectiveness of the validation. We apply a mutation changing the condition of transition R9 from a conjunction to a disjunction. The mutated condition becomes (in UMC) `(receive_timer < max_receive_timer) or (send_timer < max_send_timer)`. The introduced mutation enables a scenario where `send_timer` exceeds its maximum threshold `max_send_timer`. This violation can be detected, for example, by verifying the property `EF sendTimer_Error` where `EF` is a temporal operator stating that something will eventually happen in the future, and `sendTimer_Error` is defined by the instruction `Abstractions {State: I_CSL.send_timer > I_CSL.max_send_timer -> sendTimer_Error}` as a state property holding when the `send_timer` has a value greater than `max_send_timer`.

Figure 4 (left) shows a fragment of the sequence diagram automatically generated by UMC after model-checking the property (the full sequence diagram is in [11]). The sequence diagram graphically depicts a trace proving that the property holds in the model with the current set-up of variables (displayed in Fig. 3). This means that the counter exceeds its maximum allowed value. Figure 4 (left) only highlights the necessary environment interactions that are needed in Sparx EA to reproduce the trace. The first `TICK` event received causes `I_CSL` to request a connection (R5), which is confirmed by `I_SAI` (R7), causing the switch to state `COMMS`. At the reception of the second `TICK`, the transition R9 is

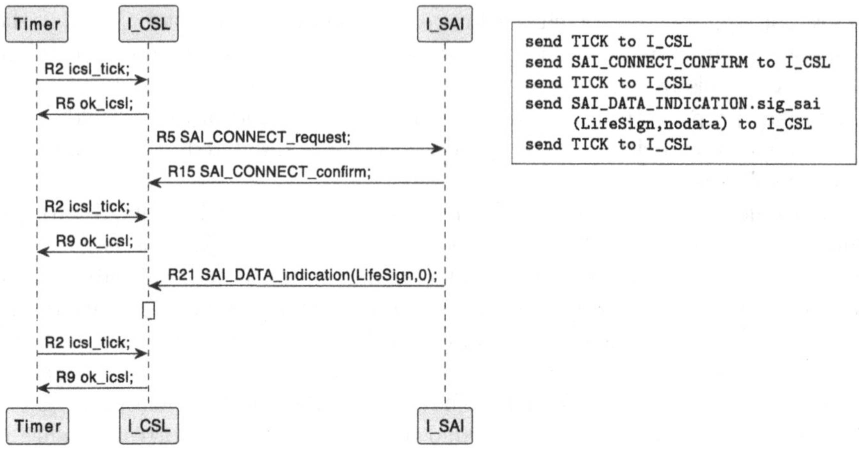

Fig. 4. On the left, a fragment of the sequence diagram generated by UMC showing that the property `EF sendTimer_Error` holds. On the right, the instructions needed to reproduce the trace in Sparx EA interactive simulation

executed, which increments both `send_timer` and `receive_timer` to their maximum allowed value (i.e., `1`). A life sign is subsequently received, which causes the reset of `receive_timer` (R12). After that, another tick is received, triggering again the mutated transition R9, causing `send_timer` to exceed its maximum allowed value.

To reproduce the trace in Sparx EA, the interactive user assumes the role of the environment. In particular, all signals sent from the environment to one of the machines will be replicated by the interactive user. Indeed, Sparx EA simulations permits sending these signals from the simulation console. As showed in Fig. 4 (left), all signals sent to the `I_CSL` are coming from the environment components, and thus will be replicated by the interactive user. In particular, the instructions inserted at console during the simulation are displayed in Fig. 4 (right). Each instruction causes all machines in the model to execute their run-to-completion cycle. After all instructions are executed, the simulation reaches a state where `I_CSL.send_timer = 2` (see Fig. 5), proving the error. A short video reproducing this experiment and the logs of the simulation are in [11].

6 Lessons Learned and Limitations

The experience of connecting the UMC formal model and the Sparx EA semi-formal model led to a set of lessons learned, which are reported below.

Modelling Restrictions. The introduction of modelling restrictions was fundamental to avoid ambiguities that are present in the informal semantics of UML state machines. The adoption of the proposed restrictions enabled the connection of Sparx EA semi-formal models with UMC formal models. Moreover, thanks to a limited and simple set of notation constraints, not only the translation process

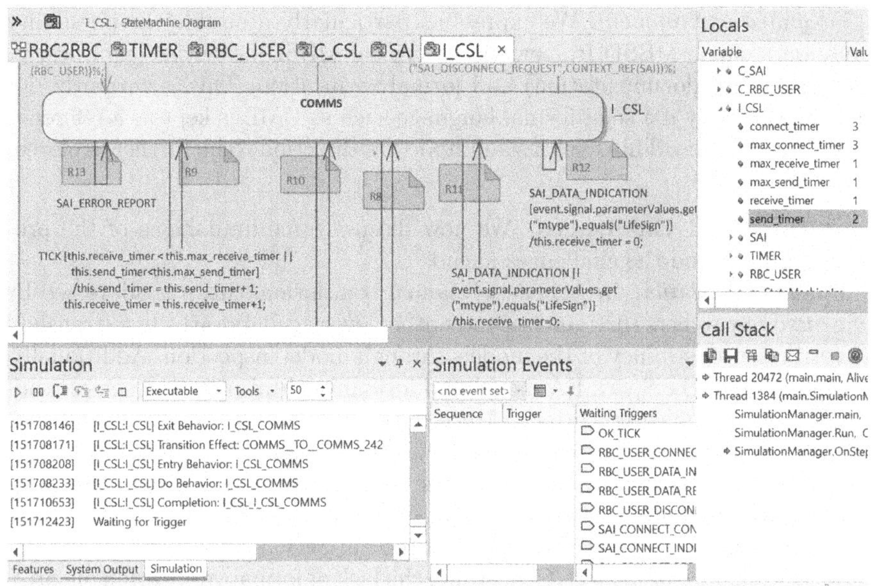

Fig. 5. A portion of the Sparx EA simulation where `sendTimer_Error` is true

was straightforward, but the models appeared cleaner and easier to inspect. Our notation constraints are stricter than those used in [29,32], therefore, we conjecture that our restricted UMC state machines could also be easily modelled as Simulink/Stateflow state charts.

Complementary Tools. UMC and Sparx EA played complementary roles in this experience, and have been developed in academia and industry, respectively. Their combined usage allows the cross-fertilization of academic techniques and industrial practices. This allowed us to check fine-grained temporal properties that were hard to verify by only using the simulation capabilities offered by Sparx EA. On the other hand, the Sparx EA model represents the starting point of the model-based development activity (including visual simulation) that will eventually lead to the final product.

Bidirectional approach. Whilst generally the literature proposes unidirectional approaches (cf. Section 2), our methodology supports both forward and reverse engineering. This is also helpful in maintaining aligned the formal and semi-formal artifacts during the evolution of the system to newer versions.

Tool Competence. The researchers involved in this experience have complementary expertise in the two tools considered. This was fundamental to achieve a sufficient degree of confidence in the correctness of the developed models, as full control of the used notations is needed to prevent misrepresentations. Together with other works [30,33], we argue that similar case studies shall involve a diversity of experts to successfully carry out the process described in this paper.

Integrated environment. We express as particularly desirable the possibility to rely on a single MBSD framework for typical MBSD activities (e.g., design, code generation, documentation) and formal verification. This is currently out of reach, especially if a semi-formal language such as UML is kept as a reference underlying notation. This remains an important direction to be further explored.

Limitations and Challenges. We now discuss some limitations of the proposed approach and the challenges ahead.

Manual Translation. In regards to manual translation, this was addressed by having two researchers (first and second author) work collaboratively to translate and verify the consistency of the models through model inspection. Additionally, the simulation of the Sparx EA model and formal verification of the corresponding UMC model increased the confidence in the accuracy of the correspondence. This was achieved by demonstrating how traces from the formal verification process can be replicated by simulating the semi-formal model. Moving forward, we intend to fully automate both the translation process and the verification of model conformance to the restrictions outlined in Sect. 4.

Correspondence of Models. Concerning the lack of formal verification of correspondence between formal and semi-formal models, it is worth noting that this is an inherent limitation of semi-formal approaches. These methods, by definition, lack formal semantics, and as a result, formal verification of behavioral correspondence is not feasible. In fact, while inspecting the semantics of Sparx EA models, in particular the code generated from the ESM, we ran into corner cases that needed interactions with the support at Sparx Systems. The next released version (15.2) fixed the issues detected in our experiments [4].

Generalisability. Concerning representativeness and generalisability of the results, it should be noticed that the restrictions on the notation and the translation process have been evaluated in reference to our specific case study from the railway domain. In other domains, and for other systems, different needs may emerge that require additional restrictions, or the relaxation of existing ones. In particular, in the current case study the two modelled state machines are not directly interacting. Each machine (ICSL and CCSL) is only interacting with the surrounding environment components. Further case studies are needed to extend the scope of validity of the proposed constraints and implemented process.

Partial Representation and Scalability. The verified Sparx EA model only provides a partial representation of the final product, as the code generated from the ESM is utilized for simulation purposes. Thus, further development is required to refine the generated code and produce the final implementation. This raises the challenge of ensuring that the verified properties are maintained during the refinement process. A possible solution is to minimize the difference between the verified Sparx EA model and the final implementation. Formal verification may become challenging if the size of the models increases significantly. It should also be noted that the complete implementation of an industrial system requires significant resources, which may not be readily available for a research activity like the one described in this paper. Therefore, substantial involvement of practitioners from both academia and industry is required. In this case, the issue of non-disclosure and confidentiality must also be considered, particularly when the intention is to make the models publicly available, as in this paper [11].

7 Conclusion

This paper has presented an investigation into the combination of an academic formal verification tool, UMC, with an industrial semi-formal model-based development tool, Sparx EA. The integration has been achieved through the definition of a set of notation restriction rules and rules for relating semi-formal and formal models. We have demonstrated how the output of the UMC formal verification can be connected to Sparx EA interactive simulations. The presented approach has been experimented on a case study from the railway domain. From this experience, we have derived a set of lessons learned and limitations driving future research challenges.

In the future, we plan to investigate how much the UML notation constraints presented in this paper can be relaxed to allow more freedom in the design of the models whilst preserving formality. We would also like to fully implement an application that is formally verified using the proposed methodology.

Acknowledgements. This work has been partially funded by the 4SECURail project (Shift2Rail GA 881775). Part of this study was carried out within the MOST - Sustainable Mobility National Research Center and received funding from the European Union Next-GenerationEU (Piano Nazionale di Ripresa e Resilienza (PNRR) - Missione 4 Componente 2, Investimento 1.4 - D.D. 1033 17/06/2022, CN00000023). The content of this paper reflects only the author's view and the Shift2Rail Joint Undertaking is not responsible for any use that may be made of the included information.

References

1. CADP: bcgcmp man page, https://cadp.inria.fr/man/bcg_cmp.html
2. Dassault Cameo Systems Modeler, https://www.3ds.com/products-services/catia/products/no-magic/cameo-systems-modeler/, Accessed Apr 2023
3. mCRL2: ltscompare man page, https://www.mcrl2.org/web/user_manual/tools/release/ltscompare.html
4. Multiple improvements to executable state machine code generation, https://sparxsystems.com/products/ea/15.2/history.html, Accessed May 2023
5. PTC Windchill Modeler SySim, https://www.ptc.com/en/products/windchill/modeler/sysim, Accessed Apr 2023
6. Sparx Systems Enterprise Architect, https://sparxsystems.com/products/ea/index.html, Accessed May 2023
7. The Shift2Rail 4SECURail project site, https://projects.shift2rail.org/s2r_ip2_n.aspx?p=s2r_4securail, Accessed May 2023
8. UMC project website, https://fmt.isti.cnr.it/umc

9. André, É., Liu, S., Liu, Y., Choppy, C., Sun, J., Dong, J.S.: Formalizing UML state machines for automated verification-a survey. ACM Comput. Surv. (2023). https://doi.org/10.1145/3579821
10. Basile, D., et al.: On the Industrial Uptake of Formal Methods in the Railway Domain. In: Furia, C.A., Winter, K. (eds.) IFM 2018. LNCS, vol. 11023, pp. 20–29. Springer, Cham (2018). https://doi.org/10.1007/978-3-319-98938-9_2
11. Basile, D., Mazzanti, F., Ferrari, A.: Experimenting with Formal Verification and Model-based Development in Railways: the case of UMC and Sparx Enterprise Architect - Complementary Data (2023). https://doi.org/10.5281/zenodo.7920448
12. Basile, D., et al.: Designing a Demonstrator of Formal Methods for Railways Infrastructure Managers. In: Margaria, T., Steffen, B. (eds.) ISoLA 2020. LNCS, vol. 12478, pp. 467–485. Springer, Cham (2020). https://doi.org/10.1007/978-3-030-61467-6_30
13. Basile, D., ter Beek, M.H., Ferrari, A., Legay, A.: Modelling and Analysing ERTMS L3 Moving Block Railway Signalling with Simulink and UPPAAL SMC. In: Larsen, K.G., Willemse, T. (eds.) FMICS 2019. LNCS, vol. 11687, pp. 1–21. Springer, Cham (2019). https://doi.org/10.1007/978-3-030-27008-7_1
14. Basile, D., ter Beek, M.H., Lazreg, S., Cordy, M., Legay, A.: Static detection of equivalent mutants in real-time model-based mutation testing. Empir. Softw. Eng. **27**(7), 160 (2022). https://doi.org/10.1007/s10664-022-10149-y
15. Basile, D., Fantechi, A., Rosadi, I.: Formal Analysis of the UNISIG Safety Application Intermediate Sub-layer. In: Lluch Lafuente, A., Mavridou, A. (eds.) FMICS 2021. LNCS, vol. 12863, pp. 174–190. Springer, Cham (2021). https://doi.org/10.1007/978-3-030-85248-1_11
16. ter Beek, M.H., Fantechi, A., Gnesi, S., Mazzanti, F.: A state/event-based model-checking approach for the analysis of abstract system properties. Sci. Comput. Program. **76**(2), 119–135 (2011). https://doi.org/10.1016/j.scico.2010.07.002
17. ter Beek, M.H., et al.: Adopting Formal Methods in an Industrial Setting: The Railways Case. In: ter Beek, M.H., McIver, A., Oliveira, J.N. (eds.) FM 2019. LNCS, vol. 11800, pp. 762–772. Springer, Cham (2019). https://doi.org/10.1007/978-3-030-30942-8_46
18. Belli, D., Mazzanti, F.: A case study in formal analysis of system requirements. In: Masci, P., Bernardeschi, C., Graziani, P., Koddenbrock, M., Palmieri, M. (eds.) SEFM Workshops. LNCS, vol. 13765, pp. 164–173. Springer (2022). https://doi.org/10.1007/978-3-031-26236-4_14
19. Bougacha, R., Laleau, R., Dutilleul, S.C., Ayed, R.B.: Extending SysML with refinement and decomposition mechanisms to generate Event-B specifications. In: Ameur, Y.A., Craciun, F. (eds.) TASE. LNCS, vol. 13299, pp. 256–273. Springer (2022). https://doi.org/10.1007/978-3-031-10363-6_18
20. Bouwman, M., Luttik, B., van der Wal, D.: A Formalisation of SysML State Machines in mCRL2. In: Peters, K., Willemse, T.A.C. (eds.) FORTE 2021. LNCS, vol. 12719, pp. 42–59. Springer, Cham (2021). https://doi.org/10.1007/978-3-030-78089-0_3
21. Broy, M., Cengarle, M.V.: UML formal semantics: lessons learned. Softw. Syst. Model. **10**(4), 441–446 (2011). https://doi.org/10.1007/s10270-011-0207-y
22. Butler, M., et al.: The First Twenty-Five Years of Industrial Use of the B-Method. In: ter Beek, M.H., Ničković, D. (eds.) FMICS 2020. LNCS, vol. 12327, pp. 189–209. Springer, Cham (2020). https://doi.org/10.1007/978-3-030-58298-2_8
23. Cavada, R., Cimatti, A., Griggio, A., Susi, A.: A formal IDE for railways: Research challenges. In: Masci, P., Bernardeschi, C., Graziani, P., Koddenbrock,

M., Palmieri, M. (eds.) SEFM Workshops. LNCS, vol. 13765, pp. 107–115. Springer (2022). https://doi.org/10.1007/978-3-031-26236-4_9
24. Champelovier, D., et al.: Reference manual of the LOTOS NT to LOTOS translator (2023), https://cadp.inria.fr/ftp/publications/cadp/Champelovier-Clerc-Garavel-et-al-10.pdf, Accessed May 2023
25. Chiappini, A., et al.: Formalization and validation of a subset of the European Train Control System. In: Proceedings of the 32nd International Conference on Software Engineering (ICSE). pp. 109–118. ACM (2010). https://doi.org/10.1145/1810295.1810312
26. Cook, S.: Looking back at UML. Softw. Syst. Model. **11**(4), 471–480 (2012). https://doi.org/10.1007/s10270-012-0256-x
27. Derezińska, A., Szczykulski, M.: Interpretation Problems in Code Generation from UML State Machines: A Comparative Study. In: Kwater, T., Zuberek, W.M., Ciarkowski, A., Kruk, M., Pekala, R., Twaróg, B. (eds.) Proceedings of the 2nd Scientific Conference on Computing in Science and Technology (STI). pp. 36–50. Monographs in Applied Informatics, Warsaw University of Life Sciences (2012)
28. Ferrari, A., Fantechi, A., Gnesi, S., Magnani, G.: Model-based development and formal methods in the railway industry. IEEE Softw. **30**(3), 28–34 (2013). https://doi.org/10.1109/MS.2013.44
29. Ferrari, A., Fantechi, A., Magnani, G., Grasso, D., Tempestini, M.: The Metrô Rio case study. Sci. Comput. Program. **78**(7), 828–842 (2013). https://doi.org/10.1016/j.scico.2012.04.003
30. Ferrari, A., Mazzanti, F., Basile, D., ter Beek, M.H., Fantechi, A.: Comparing formal tools for system design: a judgment study. In: Proceedings of the 42nd International Conference on Software Engineering (ICSE). pp. 62–74. ACM (2020). https://doi.org/10.1145/3377811.3380373
31. Ferrari, A., ter Beek, M.H.: Formal methods in railways: a systematic mapping study. ACM Comput. Surv. **55**(4), 69:1–69:37 (2022). https://doi.org/10.1145/3520480
32. Ferrari, A., Fantechi, A., Bacherini, S., Zingoni, N.: Modeling guidelines for code generation in the railway signaling context. In: Denney, E., Giannakopoulou, D., Pasareanu, C.S. (eds.) Proceedings of the 1st NASA Formal Methods Symposium (NFM). NASA Conference Proceedings, vol. CP-2009-215407, pp. 166–170 (2009), https://ntrs.nasa.gov/citations/20100024476
33. Ferrari, A., Mazzanti, F., Basile, D., ter Beek, M.H.: Systematic evaluation and usability analysis of formal methods tools for railway signaling system design. IEEE Trans. Softw. Eng. **48**(11), 4675–4691 (2022). https://doi.org/10.1109/TSE.2021.3124677
34. Filipovikj, P., Mahmud, N., Marinescu, R., Seceleanu, C., Ljungkrantz, O., Lönn, H.: Simulink to UPPAAL Statistical Model Checker: Analyzing Automotive Industrial Systems. In: Fitzgerald, J., Heitmeyer, C., Gnesi, S., Philippou, A. (eds.) FM 2016. LNCS, vol. 9995, pp. 748–756. Springer, Cham (2016). https://doi.org/10.1007/978-3-319-48989-6_46
35. Garavel, H., Lang, F., Mateescu, R., Serwe, W.: CADP 2011: a toolbox for the construction and analysis of distributed processes. Int. J. Softw. Tools Technol. Transf. **15**(2), 89–107 (2013). https://doi.org/10.1007/s10009-012-0244-z
36. Garavel, H., ter Beek, M.H., van de Pol, J.: The 2020 Expert Survey on Formal Methods. In: ter Beek, M.H., Ničković, D. (eds.) FMICS 2020. LNCS, vol. 12327, pp. 3–69. Springer, Cham (2022). https://doi.org/10.1007/978-3-030-58298-2_1

37. Garavel, H., Lang, F., Serwe, W.: From LOTOS to LNT. In: Katoen, J.-P., Langerak, R., Rensink, A. (eds.) ModelEd, TestEd, TrustEd. LNCS, vol. 10500, pp. 3–26. Springer, Cham (2017). https://doi.org/10.1007/978-3-319-68270-9_1
38. Gleirscher, M., Marmsoler, D.: Formal methods in dependable systems engineering: a survey of professionals from Europe and North America. Empir. Softw. Eng. **25**(6), 4473–4546 (2020). https://doi.org/10.1007/s10664-020-09836-5
39. Gnesi, S., Mazzanti, F.: An Abstract, on the Fly Framework for the Verification of Service-Oriented Systems. In: Wirsing, M., Hölzl, M. (eds.) Rigorous Software Engineering for Service-Oriented Systems. LNCS, vol. 6582, pp. 390–407. Springer, Heidelberg (2011). https://doi.org/10.1007/978-3-642-20401-2_18
40. Horváth, B., et al.: Pragmatic verification and validation of industrial executable sysml models. Syst. Eng. (2023). https://doi.org/10.1002/sys.21679
41. Huisman, M., Gurov, D., Malkis, A.: Formal Methods: From Academia to Industrial Practice. A Travel Guide (2020), https://arxiv.org/abs/2002.07279
42. Leduc, G.: Information technology-enhancements to LOTOS (E-LOTOS). ISO/IEC International Standard (2001), https://www.iso.org/obp/ui/#iso:std:iso-iec:15437:ed-1:v1:en
43. Mazzanti, F., Basile, D.: 4SECURail Deliverable D2.2 Formal development Demonstrator prototype, 1st Release (2020), https://www.4securail.eu/pdf/4SR-WP2-D2.2-Formal-development-demonstrator-prototype-1st%20release-CNR-3.0.pdf, Accessed May 2023
44. Mazzanti, F., et al.: 4SECURail Deliverable D2.1 Specification of formal development demonstrator (2020), https://www.4securail.eu/pdf/4SR-WP2-D2.1-Specification%20of%20formal%20development%20demonstrator-CNR-1.0.pdf, Accessed May 2023
45. Mazzanti, F., Belli, D.: 4SECURail Deliverable D2.5 Formal development demonstrator prototype, final release (2021), https://www.4securail.eu/pdf/4SR-WP2-D2.5-Formal-development-demonstrator-prototype.final-release-CNR-1.0.pdf, Accessed May 2023
46. Mazzanti, F., Ferrari, A., Spagnolo, G.O.: Towards formal methods diversity in railways: an experience report with seven frameworks. Int. J. Softw. Tools Technol. Transf. **20**(3), 263–288 (2018). https://doi.org/10.1007/s10009-018-0488-3
47. Mazzanti, F., Belli, D.: The 4SECURail formal methods demonstrator. In: Dutilleul, S.C., Haxthausen, A.E., Lecomte, T. (eds.) RSSRail. LNCS, vol. 13294, pp. 149–165. Springer (2022). https://doi.org/10.1007/978-3-031-05814-1_11
48. Miller, S.P., Whalen, M.W., Cofer, D.D.: Software model checking takes off. Commun. ACM **53**(2), 58–64 (2010). https://doi.org/10.1145/1646353.1646372
49. Object Management Group: Unified Modelling Language (2017), https://www.omg.org/spec/UML/About-UML/
50. Object Management Group: OMG Systems Modeling Language (OMG SysML) (2019), https://www.omg.org/spec/SysML/1.6/
51. Object Management Group: Precise Semantics of UML State Machines (PSSM) (2019), https://www.omg.org/spec/PSSM
52. Peres, F., Ghazel, M.: A proven translation from a UML state machine subset to timed automata. ACM Trans. Embed. Comput. Syst. (2023). https://doi.org/10.1145/3581771
53. Piattino, A.: 4SECURail Deliverable D2.3 Case study requirements and specification (2020), https://www.4securail.eu/pdf/4SR-WP2-D2.3-Case-study-requirements-and-specification-SIRTI-1.0.pdf, Accessed May 2023

54. Salunkhe, S., Berglehner, R., Rasheeq, A.: Automatic Transformation of SysML Model to Event-B Model for Railway CCS Application. In: Raschke, A., Méry, D. (eds.) ABZ 2021. LNCS, vol. 12709, pp. 143–149. Springer, Cham (2021). https://doi.org/10.1007/978-3-030-77543-8_14
55. Seisenberger, M., et al.: Safe and Secure Future AI-Driven Railway Technologies: Challenges for Formal Methods in Railway. In: Margaria, T., Steffen, B. (eds.) ISoLA. LNCS, vol. 13704, pp. 246–268. Springer (2022). https://doi.org/10.1007/978-3-031-19762-8_20
56. Sheng, H., Bentkamp, A., Zhan, B.: HHLPy: practical verification of hybrid systems using Hoare logic. In: Chechik, M., Katoen, J.P., Leucker, M. (eds.) FM. LNCS, vol. 14000, pp. 160–178. Springer (2023). https://doi.org/10.1007/978-3-031-27481-7_11
57. Snook, C.F., Butler, M.J.: UML-B: formal modeling and design aided by UML. ACM Trans. Softw. Eng. Methodol. **15**(1), 92–122 (2006). https://doi.org/10.1145/1125808.1125811
58. Snook, C.F., Butler, M.J., Hoang, T.S., Fathabadi, A.S., Dghaym, D.: Developing the UML-B modelling tools. In: Masci, P., Bernardeschi, C., Graziani, P., Koddenbrock, M., Palmieri, M. (eds.) SEFM Workshops. LNCS, vol. 13765, pp. 181–188. Springer (2022). https://doi.org/10.1007/978-3-031-26236-4_16
59. Stramaglia, A., Keiren, J. J. A.: Formal verification of an industrial UML-like model using mCRL2. In: Groote, J.F., Huisman, M. (eds.) FMICS. LNCS, vol. 13487, pp. 86–102. Springer (2022). https://doi.org/10.1007/978-3-031-15008-1_7
60. UNISIG: RBC-RBC Safe Communication Interface - SUBSET-098 (2012), https://www.era.europa.eu/system/files/2023-01/sos3_index063_-_subset-098_v300.pdf, Accessed May 2023
61. UNISIG: FIS for the RBC/RBC Handover - SUBSET-039 (2015), https://www.era.europa.eu/system/files/2023-01/sos3_index012_-_subset-039_v320.pdf, Accessed May 2023

The 4SECURail Case Study on Rigorous Standard Interface Specifications

Dimitri Belli[1], Alessandro Fantechi[2(✉)], Stefania Gnesi[1], Laura Masullo[3], Franco Mazzanti[1], Lisa Quadrini[3], Daniele Trentini[3], and Carlo Vaghi[4]

[1] ISTI-CNR, Via G. Moruzzi 1, Pisa 56124, Italy
[2] DINFO, University of Florence, Via S. Marta 3, Firenze, Italy
alessandro.fantechi@unifi.it
[3] MER MEC STE, via Bombrini 11, Genova 16149, Italy
[4] FIT Consulting, Via Sardegna 38, Roma 00157, Italy

Abstract. In the context of the Shift2Rail open call S2R-OC-IP2-01-2019, one of the two work streams of the 4SECURail project has pursued the objective to corroborate how a clear, rigorous standard interface specification between signaling sub-systems can be designed by applying an approach based on semi-formal and formal methods. The objective is addressed by developing a demonstrator case study of the application of formal methods to the specification of standard interfaces, aimed at illustrating some usable state-of-the-art techniques for rigorous standard interface specification, as well as at supporting a Cost-Benefit Analysis to back this strategy with sound economic arguments.

1 Introduction

In an increasingly competitive market as the railway one, the application of Formal Methods (FM) within the process of developing standard interfaces between signaling sub-systems is believed to be a winning strategy for the construction of high-quality, safe, and reliable signaling infrastructure, gaining in this way the interest by the infrastructure managers (IMs). Such a trend is fostered by economic and technical reasons. Economic reasons can be found, besides the market competition, in the reduction of both vendor lock-in effect and costs caused by change requests due to requirements inconsistencies. Technical reasons concern the reduction of interoperability problems and the fact that clear, rigorous specifications of standard interfaces are well suited to exploit formal methods within the development of signaling systems.

In the context of the Shift2Rail open call S2R-OC-IP2-01-2019, one of the two work streams of the 4SECURail project [24] has pursued the objective to corroborate how a clear, rigorous standard interface specification can be designed by applying an approach based on semi-formal and formal methods.

The work stream was intended at defining (and prototyping) a demonstrator of the use of state-of-the-art formal methods for the development and analysis of standard interfaces, with measured cost/benefit ratio for the industrial application of the demonstrated process. The activity of the project included

A. Cimatti and L. Titolo (Eds.): FMICS 2023, LNCS 14290, pp. 22–39, 2023.
https://doi.org/10.1007/978-3-031-43681-9_2

hence i) the specification of the demonstrator for the use of formal methods in railway signalling by identifying, selecting, and composing appropriate formal methods and tools for industrial application; ii) the identification of a railway signaling system to be used as a test case, composed of subsystems that should interoperate by means of standard interfaces, to exercise the formal methods demonstrator, iii) use the developed test case as an information source to base a Cost-Benefit Analysis of formal methods usage in the railway signalling domain.

In this paper we show the main results of the relevant workstream of the 4SECURail project, both in terms of recommended techniques for the specification of standard interfaces (Sect. 2) and of a Cost-Benefit Analysis of the adoption of formal methods in the railway industry (Sect. 3). Section 4 draws some conclusions.

2 The Demonstrator Case Study

The current trend in the direction of clear and rigorous specifications of standard interfaces is to complement the use of natural language requirements with graphical SysML/UML artifacts - see, e.g., EULYNX [7]. However, the unrestricted use of SysML/UML as a specification language for "Systems of Systems" (SoS) can be problematic because of its genericity and the lack of precise semantics. SysML/UML conceals many hidden assumptions that may have a strong impact on the expected behaviors of the modeled system. Formal models that can be rigorously analysed need instead to be mechanically associated with the semi-formal SysML/UML-based designs. The goal of our work is to show a possible approach and highlight the pros and cons of the application of formal methods for the specifications of standard interfaces.

The adopted methodology is fully described in Deliverables D2.1 [18], D2.2 [17], and D2.5 [19]) of the 4SECURail project, and is exemplified with the development of a demonstrator that illustrates the application of formal methods to a selected case study. Deliverable D2.3 [22] describes the details and rationale of the selected case study, which is based on the RBC/RBC communication layer that supports the execution of the RBC/RBC handover protocol.

2.1 The 4SECURail Case Study

The European Train Control System (ETCS) acts as an automatic train protection system which continuously supervises the train movements on a line to ensure their safe speed and distancing. To this purpose, a Radio Block Centre (RBC) communicates with all the trains in its supervision area. The transit of a train from an area supervised by a Radio Block Centre (RBC) to an adjacent area supervised by another RBC occurs during the so-called RBC-RBC handover phase and requires the exchange of information between the two RBCs according to a specific protocol. This exchange of information is supported by the communication layer specified within the documents: UNISIG SUBSET-039 [25], UNISIG SUBSET-098 [26], and UNISIG SUBSET-037 [27], and the whole stack

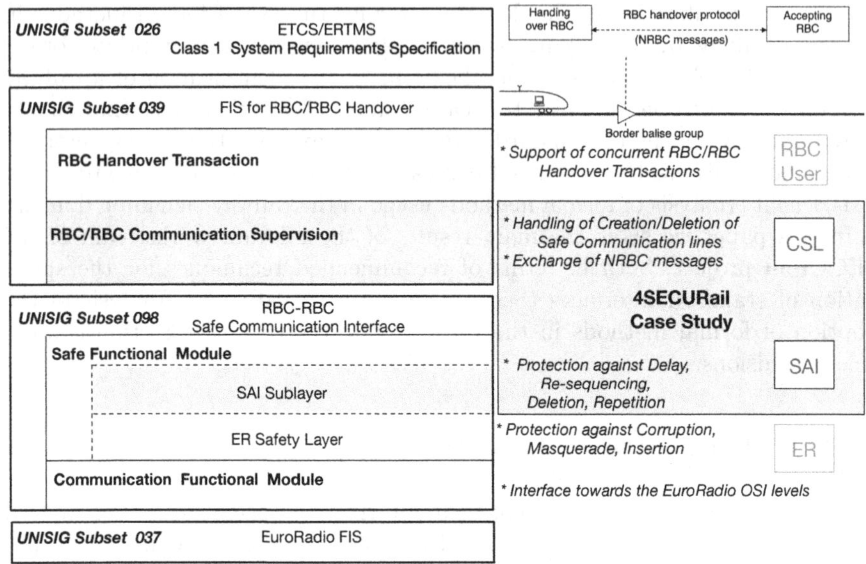

Fig. 1. Overall structure of the 4SECURail case study

is implemented by both sides of the communication channel. Figure 1 summarizes the overall relation between the components of the UNISIG standards, supporting the handover of a train. The components considered in the case study are the Communication Supervision Layer (CSL) of the SUBSET-039 and the Safe Application Intermediate SubLayer (SAI) of the SUBSET-098. These two components are the main actors that support the creation/deletion of safe communications and protect the transmission of messages exchanged. In particular, the CSL is responsible for requesting the activation – and in the event of failure, the re-establishment – of the communications, for keeping controlling its liveliness, and for the forwarding of the handover transaction messages. The SAI is responsible for ensuring that there are no excessive delays, repetitions, losses, or reordering of messages during transmission. This is achieved by adding sequence numbers and time-related information to the RBC messages. The RBC/RBC communication system consists of two sides that are properly configured as "initiator" and "called".

With respect to the SUBSET-098, the 4SECURail case study neither includes the EuroRadio Safety Layer (ER), which is responsible for preventing corruption, masquerading and insertion issues during the communications, nor the lower Communication Functional Module (CFM) interface. With respect to the SUBSET-039, the 4SECURail case study does not include the description of the activation of multiple, concurrent RBC-RBC handover transactions when trains move from a zone supervised by an RBC to an adjacent zone supervised by another RBC. From the point of view of the CSL, the RBC messages are forwarded to/from the other RBC side without the knowledge of their specific contents or the session to which they belong.

2.2 The Formalization of the Case Study

The goal is to demonstrate how formal methods provide an even more efficient requirements definition, reducing development problems related to residual uncertainties, and improving interoperability of different implementations.

The overall approach followed during the modeling and analysis process is incremental and iterative. About 53 versions of the system have been generated, each one widening the set of requirements of the case study modeled, and each one passing through the steps of semi-formal and formal modeling and analysis. During this iterative process, four kinds of artifacts have been generated and kept aligned:

1. An abstract, semi-formal UML state machine design of the components under analysis.
2. A more detailed executable version of the same UML state machines.
3. A set of formal models derived from the executable UML state machines.
4. A natural language rewriting of the requirements based on the designed and analysed models.

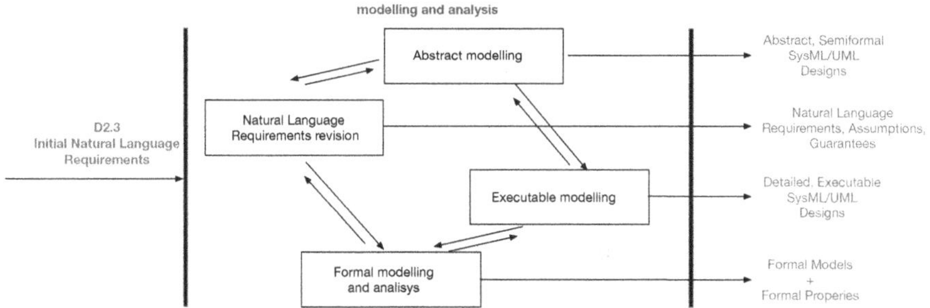

Fig. 2. The 4SECURail demonstrator generated artifacts

Figure 2 depicts the relationship between these artifacts. The activity of generating and elaborating most of the shown artifacts (currently) requires a human problem understanding and solving activity, apart from the generation of the formal models starting from the UML executable ones, that can be (and has been in part) automated.

The natural language requirements describe the system at a high abstraction level, omitting all the details related to irrelevant implementation issues. On the contrary, during the executable modeling, which is the base for formal modeling and analysis, we need to specify these details as well.

In fact, we found it useful to introduce an intermediate level of "abstract modeling" where the logical structure, interfaces, and the expected main control flow of the system are modeled in a rigorous notation, while irrelevant implementation issues are still described in an abstract way using natural language. These abstract models need to be further refined into executable models prior to the formal modeling activity.

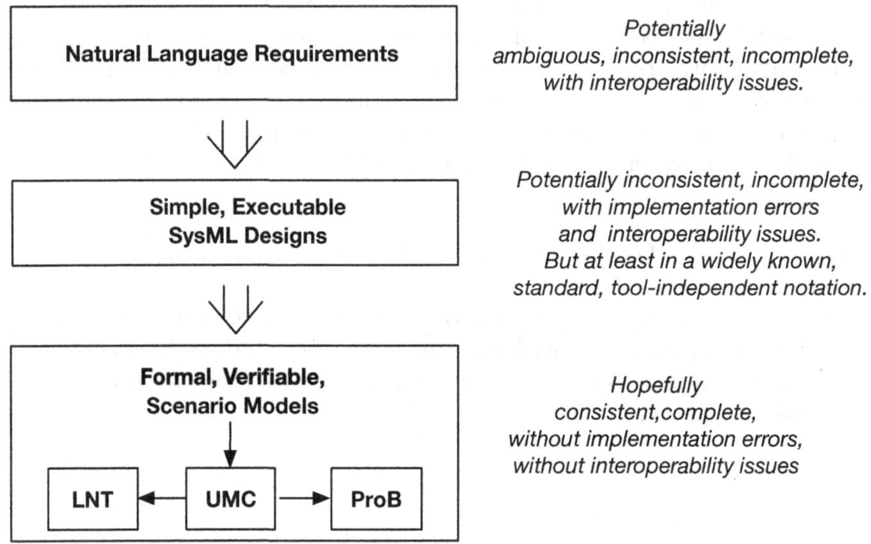

Fig. 3. From natural language to formal models

As a first formal modeling step, the executable UML system diagrams corresponding to a given scenario are translated into the notation accepted by the UMC tool[1], chosen as the target of the initial formal encoding because it is a tool natively oriented to fast prototyping of SysML systems. At the beginning of the project, the possibility of designing the SysML system using a commercial MBSE framework - namely SPARX-EA[2] - has been evaluated. But implementing a translator from the SPARX-generated XMI towards UMC would have been a significant effort and it would have tied the whole analysis approach to a specific commercial tool, a fact which was not considered desirable.

Therefore, our initial SysML models have the structure of simple graphical designs; their role is just to constitute an intermediate, easy-to-understand documentation halfway between the natural language requirements and the formal models. A detailed description of these SysML models is presented in [3,19,21]. The translation of the SysML designs in the UMC notation constitutes a step towards a full formalization: UMC supports a textual notation of

[1] https://fmt.isti.cnr.it/umc.

[2] https://sparxsystems.com/products/ea/index.html.

UML state-machine diagrams that directly reflects the graphical counterpart[3], allows fast state-space exploration, state- and event-based (on-the-fly) model checking, and detailed debugging of the system. However, UMC is essentially a teaching/research-oriented academic tool and lacks the maturity, stability, and support level required by an industry-usable framework.

So, we have planned the exploitation of other, more industry-ready, formal frameworks and further formal models have been automatically generated in the notations accepted by the ProB[4] and CADP/LNT[5] tools (Fig 3). ProB has been selected as the second target of formal encoding because of its recognized role - see [9] - in the field of formal railway-related modeling. It provides user-friendly interfaces and allows LTL/CTL model checking, state-space exploration, state-space projections, and trace descriptions in the form of sequence diagrams. CADP/LNT has been selected as the third target of the formal encoding, because of its theoretical roots in Labelled Transition Systems, that allow reasoning in terms of minimization, bisimulation, and compositional verification. CADP is a rich toolbox that supports a wide set of temporal logic and provides a powerful scripting language to automate verification runs.

There are indeed several ways in which SysML/UML designs might be encoded into the ProB and LNT formal notations. In our case, we made the choice to generate both ProB and LNT models automatically from the UMC model. The translation implemented in our demonstrator is still a preliminary version and does not exploit at best all the features potentially offered by the target framework. Nevertheless, the availability of automatic translation proved to be an essential aspect of the demonstrated approach. Our models and scenarios have been developed incrementally, with a long sequence of refinements and extensions. At every single step, we have been able to quickly perform the lightweight formal verification of interest with almost no effort. This would not have been possible without an automatic generation of the ProB and LNT models. This approach based on the exploitation of formal methods diversity allows us to take advantage of the different features provided by the different verification frameworks.

In Fig. 4 we present a table reporting the main verification features supported by the three formalization frameworks, highlighting in purple those features that require more advanced knowledge of the underlying theory and tools, while the list of features colored in black represent features that do not require a specific advanced background in formal methods to be used (e.g., analysis that can be carried out by just pushing a button). Another important advantage of our "formal methods diversity" approach is that it allows us to verify the absence of errors in the frameworks and in the translators by checking the equivalence of the formal models and the verification results. In all three frameworks,

[3] actually, often it is a graphical representation that is automatically generated from the UMC encoding.

[4] https://prob.hhu.de/.

[5] https://cadp.inria.fr/.

in fact, the underlying semantic model is a finite automaton whose transitions from state to state correspond to a single run-to-completion step of one of the state-machines that constitute the system. To show the equivalence of the UMC, ProB and LNT models we exploit the UMC feature that allows to decorate the semantic LTS of the system in a custom way, and export it in the Alderabaran ".aut" format. When comparing the ProB and UMC models, the UMC LTS is decorated with the transition labels of the UML model. These labels actually correspond to the names of the ProB "Operations" that trigger in ProB the system evolution. The LTS corresponding to the ProB evolutions is automatically generated with custom-developed translators, still in the ".aut" format, from state-space description generated by the tool itself. The two LTS can be formally proved to be strongly equivalent. When comparing the LNT models and the UMC models, the UMC LTS is this time decorated with the communication action occurring during a run-to-completion step (or with the transition label if no communication occurs). On the LNT side, the semantic LTS, which can be exported in the ".aut" format by default, is decorated with the synchronization actions of the various processes (or with an internal action identical to UMC transition label if no communication occurs). Again, the two LTS can be proved to be strongly equivalent using standard equivalence checkers working on LTS in the ".aut" format. Since the same UMC semantic model, even if differently labelled, has been proven to be strongly equivalent to the other two semantic models, we can conclude that the three models are actually equivalent. In fact, even without performing all the transformations and equivalence checking, just observing the number of states and edges of the LTS in the three models gives immediate feedback on the presence of translation errors or differences in the three execution engines.

For more details on the case study see [22], while for a detailed description of the generation process and the generated models, we refer to [19,20].

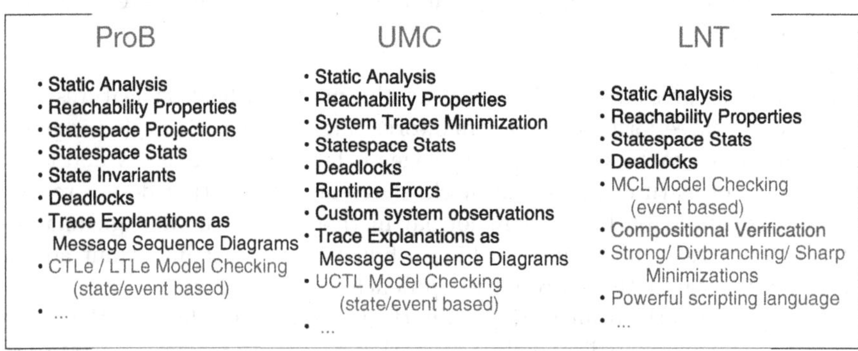

Fig. 4. Push-button (black) and advanced features (purple) of the three adopted formalization frameworks.

Summarizing, the demonstrator has provided explicit evidence about the advantages and difficulties associated with the introduction of formal methods in the standardization of specifications of railway systems, in particular in relation to their SoS nature. Furthermore, it has shown how the application of formal methods can provide useful feedback for improving the process of writing specifications, and how formal methods can detect and help to solve ambiguities and uncertainties introduced by natural language and semi-formal descriptions.

3 Cost-Benefit Analysis

A further objective of the 4SECURail project has been to perform a Cost-Benefit Analysis (CBA) of the adoption of formal methods in the railway industry. The final result of the analysis can be found in the 4SECURail Deliverable D2.6 [30]. We are not aware of any existing fully-fledged CBA applied to cases of formal methods adoption in the railway sector.

The 4SECURail CBA was developed taking the point of view of the Infrastructure Manager (IM), which bears the costs of the manufacturer/developer as prices. Thus, while the 4SECURail demonstrator experience has allowed us to directly observe and evaluate the potential costs of a rigorous approach in requirements specification and analysis, the quantitative evaluation of the future benefits of the approach cannot be performed by observing just the activity carried on in the project. The literature survey in [29] reports some examples of assessment of benefits of adoption of formal methods in the railway sector, but only in a limited number of cases some partially usable quantitative data are available (e.g., see [4,5,8,10–14,16,23,31]).

The CBA presented in this section includes two main contributions: on one side, a methodological framework to conduct the analysis is set up, with the definition of cost/benefit categories tailored to the case study (but reasonably adaptable to different formal methods application case studies) on the other hand, the instantiation of the framework is carried out by a careful assessment of actual values of cost and benefits per each category.

The adopted CBA methodology follows the guidelines set in the European Commission Guide to Cost-Benefit Analysis reported in [6], and is composed of (i) Financial Analysis, which includes the assessment of additional costs borne and additional savings accrued by an IM faced by the choice to use formal methods, and costs/benefits for suppliers, e.g., savings in terms of shorter time needed for software development, that is reflected in the price paid by IMs to purchase a RBC (of which the RBC/RBC handover interface, addressed in the 4SECURail demonstrator, is a key component); (ii) Economic Analysis, which considers benefits for users, i.e., passengers of train services, and for the "society" at large. Relevant categories of costs and benefits for the CBA have been identified (Fig. 5), such as additional costs for learning Formal Methods and for developing, by means of FM, tender specifications for the procurement of a railway signaling component, as well as savings in software development, verification, and validation, benefits for rail users due to higher maintenance efficiency, higher service availability and time saved for a lower probability of service disruption.

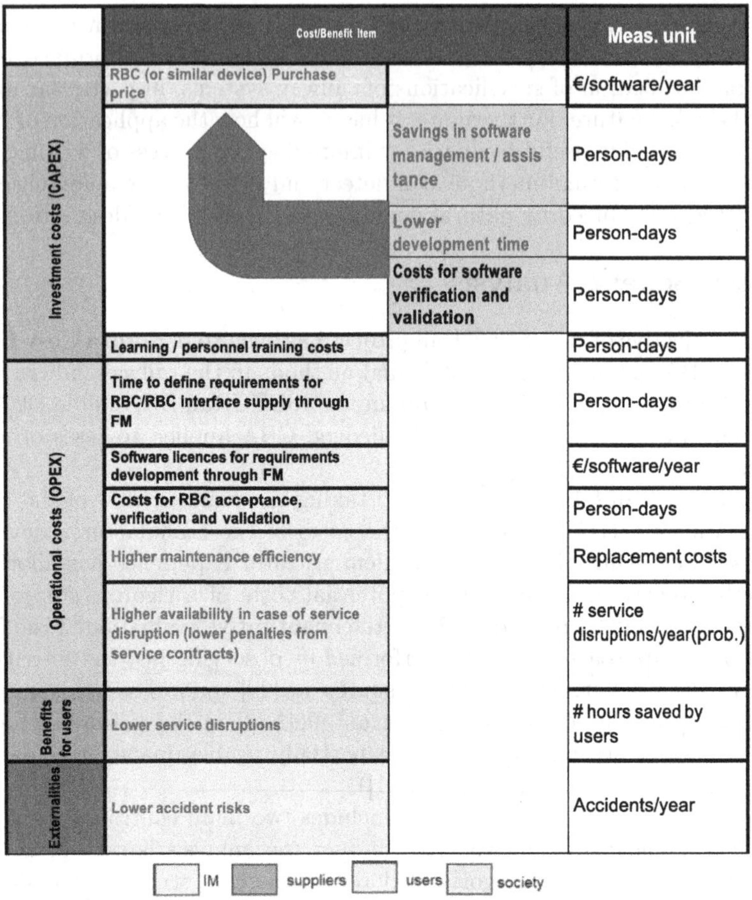

	Cost/Benefit Item		Meas. unit
Investment costs (CAPEX)	RBC (or similar device) Purchase price		€/software/year
		Savings in software management / assis tance	Person-days
		Lower development time	Person-days
		Costs for software verification and validation	Person-days
	Learning / personnel training costs		Person-days
Operational costs (OPEX)	Time to define requirements for RBC/RBC interface supply through FM		Person-days
	Software licences for requirements development through FM		€/software/year
	Costs for RBC acceptance, verification and validation		Person-days
	Higher maintenance efficiency		Replacement costs
	Higher availability in case of service disruption (lower penalties from service contracts)		# service disruptions/year(prob.)
Benefits for users	Lower service disruptions		# hours saved by users
Externalities	Lower accident risks		Accidents/year

IM suppliers users society

Fig. 5. Cost/Benefit matrix representing the structure of relevant cost/benefit categories. In the item columns, costs are written in black and benefits in green. The respective loser/beneficiary stakeholder is indicated by the background colour, according to the bottom line. (Color figure online)

As it is evident from Fig. 5, a major part of the cost/benefit items are borne/gained by IMs (or, more properly, to one single IM), from which point of view the CBA is developed. However, the scheme identifies also cost items assumed to be borne by the suppliers (i.e. by one developer, supplying one IM) and paid out by the IM through the SW purchase price. The latter is assumed to decrease with respect to the Baseline scenario, as a result of the savings accounted for by the supplier.

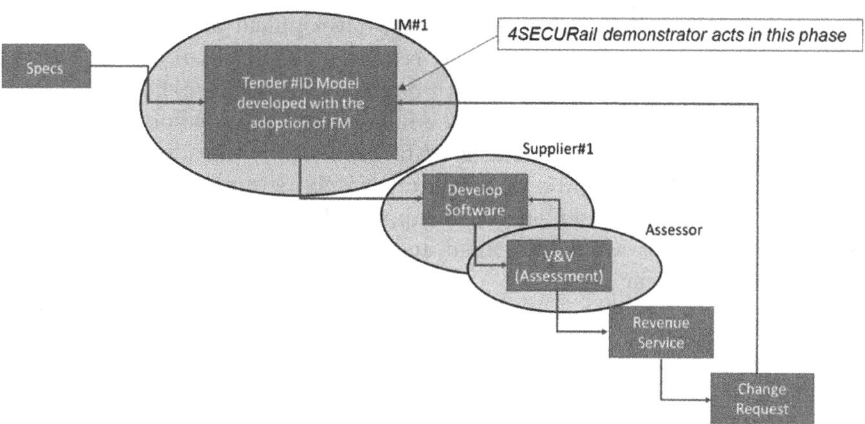

Fig. 6. "Semi-formal methods development" business case. Each oval represents the competence area of the indicated stakeholders, i.e. the activity in which IMs, suppliers and assessors bear costs.

A micro, bottom-up case study for CBA was set-up to assess costs and savings borne by an IM faced with the choice to use FM in the development of specifications for the provision of RBC-RBC handover interfaces, vs. the baseline scenario, that is the development with no use of FM. This allowed a proper assessment of actual values of cost and benefits per each category set in Fig. 5. The business case of "semi-formal methods development" (mirroring the parallel business model proposed in the X2RAIL-2 project reported in [1]) assumes the adoption of a "tender model", in which tender requirements are developed with the use of FM (Fig. 6).

The quantitative assessment of cost and benefit categories was possible by integrating the outcome of the demonstrator developed in 4SECURail, and by assumptions based on literature and on Consortium's knowledge and experience, so overcoming the lack of fully comparable case studies, data confidentiality of software developers, and low availability of quantitative cost data about FM adoption. The assessment of effort per process and related costs made in 4SECURail [30] led to the calculation of the total cost of learning and specifications development, as borne by the IM during the 15-year time horizon. Table 1 summarises such calculations, covering all cost items assumed to be borne by the IM each year, except learning costs and software licenses, that are assumed to occur every 5 years. Unit staff costs for juniors and trainees are assumed to increase every year of a 5-year cycle, after which the staff turnover applies. As per Table 1, costs for the development of specifications (one + change requests per year) range from nearly 80,000 €/year, at the beginning of the time horizon, to 160,000 €/year at the end of the learning cycle, i.e. in the year characterized by the highest cost of juniors/trainees. Additional costs and potential savings brought by FM to the development of RBC/RBC interface (and RBC software) by IM's suppliers (i.e. software developers) are assumed to be reverted to software purchase price: if the supplier saves on development and verification and validation (V&V) costs, such savings determine a proportional decrease of the purchase price of the software ordered (through a tender process) by the IM. This assumption is once again in line with the fully-competitive perspective adopted in 4SECURail, made possible - or at least facilitated - by the adoption of FM in the development of specifications, which ultimately determines a lower dependence of an IM from a single long-term supplier. In the CBA 20% time savings were assumed for software development and V&V, leading to a financial saving of Euro 21,000 per year.

Table 1. Learning and specification development - annual costs

Additional staff (senior)	#	1
Additional staff (junior/trainee)	#	2
Unit staff cost (senior)	€/y	70,000
Unit staff cost (junior/trainee)	€/y	27,000
Staff costs-IM	€/y	124,000
Learning-general case	PM	**2.6**
Learning costs	€/y	**26,867**
Development effort (single specification)	PM	7.0
Development effort (single specification)-BASELINE	PM	2.0
Specification development cost	€/y	51,667
Specifications/year	#	5
Potential specification development cost	€/y	*258,333*
Development effort (change request)	PM	4.0
No. change requests/year	#	1
Specification development cost (spec.+change requests)	€/y	**51,667**
SW Licences	€/y	1,800
Total cost of learning and spec. development	€/y	**80,333**

The convenience for the IM to adopt FM is connected to the economies of scale generated by the replication of savings in software re-development in reply to change requests, issued by the IM through further tender processes. Since such economies of scale are likely verifiable but not easily quantifiable, the analysis has followed up with the identification - entailing a sensitivity analysis - of the optimal scale for which the additional resources deployed by the IM generate enough savings in software development to balance the additional investment and operational effort needed. In other words, the sensitivity analysis aimed at detecting what is the business scale for which the higher effort borne by the IM is balanced by savings in the development of the interface, and how much suppliers should save in the development of interfaces in reply to change requests, to ensure a competitive purchase price.

As evidenced in Fig. 7, according to 4SECURail assumptions, the break-even between additional costs borne by IM and savings is verified if the purchase price of software upon change requests is -40% vs. the baseline.

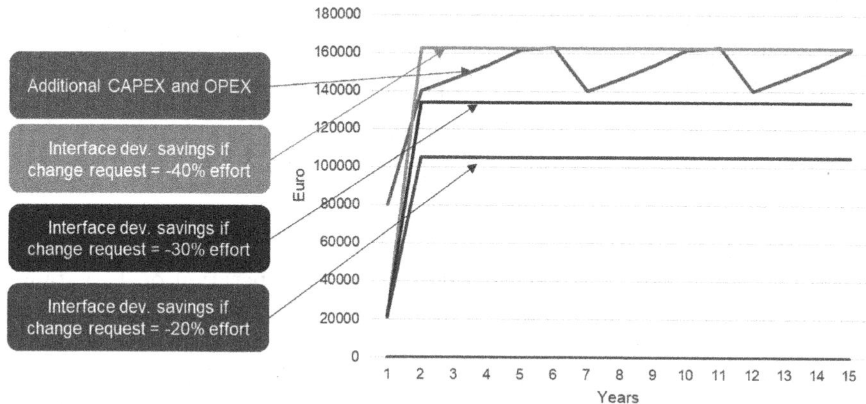

Fig. 7. Computation of break-even between additional costs and savings

In this scenario, the total annual savings for suppliers are 162,600 Euro/year, which overcome additional costs borne by IMs every year except the ending learning cycle one, i.e. when the labour cost has increased to the maximum assumed during the learning cycle. The calculation process is shown in Table 2, which covers the first two years of the time-horizon (i.e. the first one, with no change requests, and the second one, having a cash flow identical to all other years in the period).

Table 2. Calculation of savings in software development and V&V

	year	*1*	*2 and onwards*
Time savings interface development	PM	2.4	2.4
Time savings V&V	PM	0.6	0.6
V&V costs (Assessor) savings	Euro	3,000	3,000
Assumed PM time saving development change request	40%		
Time savings interface development (change request)	PM	4.8	4.8
Staff cost supplier	Euro/PM	6,000	6,000
Development and V&V cost savings (single interface)	Euro/year	21,000	21,000
Development and V&V cost savings (single change request)	Euro/year		35,400
Potential cost savings (5 interfaces)	*Euro/year*	105,000	105,000
Assumed cost savings (interface + change requests)	**40%**	**21,000**	**162,600**
	30%	21,000	133,800
	20%	21,000	105,000

The Financial Analysis performed on the case study demonstrated that, if cost savings enjoyed by suppliers are passed on to prices, the IM faces net cash flow savings over a multi-annual time horizon (assumed 15 years): comparing additional investment and operating costs with savings, the Net Present Value (NPV) of the adoption of FM is 50,917 Euro, with a 17.9% Internal Rate of Return[6]. Such values demonstrate the financial feasibility of the adoption of FM from the point of view of a single IM. The definition of NPV commonly used in CBA has been adopted. NPV, indicating the value of an investment as discounted to present time's values, is defined as:

$$NPV = \sum_t B_t(1+i_t)^{-t} - \sum_t C_t(1+i_t)^{-t} - K$$

where B indicate benefits, C costs, discounted with the rate i every year t of the project's lifetime, and K the initial investment.

Four scenarios were built considering the current operation on two Italian lines (a high-speed line and a highly congested node) to assess benefits for users in case cancellations or delays are avoided due to higher maintenance efficiency generated by FM. The simulation has assumed a service disruption causing 60' delay or train cancellation during one day on both reference Italian lines, for which a daily traffic of 116 trains (Milano-Melegnano) and 109 trains (Firenze-Bologna HS) is reported in the Network Statement [15].

The Economic Analysis has assessed the benefits due to higher maintenance efficiency, higher service availability, and time saved for a lower probability of service disruption. The assessment was based on the quantification of service disruptions that may happen on a rail line due to failure of RBC/RBC handover interface, and in particular those due to ambiguity of specifications. They are very rare according to 4SECURail Consortium's knowledge (0.1% of total cases). The calculation of penalties has been based on the Performance Regime in force on the Italian rail Network, issued by RFI (Italian IM) and valid until 2023 [15]. Values are the following:

- Delay 60 min: 4.5 € per minute = 300 € (applied both on HS lines and rail nodes).
- Train cancellations: 120 € (applied both on HS and regional services). The related amount saved by the IM is taken into account as net benefit in the CBA. Moreover, avoided service disruptions mean avoided delays for passengers, which can be monetized applying the appropriate Value of Time (VoT), defined in [6].

According to assumptions and calculation made, the service disruptions avoided have a value ranging from nearly 13,000 €/event in case of cancellations, 32–34,000 €/event in case the service disruptions cause 60' delays.

The annual value of time saved thanks to higher maintenance efficiency brought by the use of FM is estimated to range between 112,000 €/year in

[6] IRR is defined as the discounting rate necessary to obtain NPV=0. The indicator is adimensional and represents the expected return of the investment over the project's lifetime.

case of 60' delay on regional services, to 581,000 €/year in case of HS services cancellation. Those values rise to 562,000 €/year and 2.9 M€/year respectively, if change requests are taken into account. Figure 8 shows the order of magnitude of the annual (not discounted) value of each benefit category compared to costs. Not surprisingly, benefits from time saved for passengers are by far the most relevant benefit category (Fig. 8). Indeed, expected benefits for users, although computed using many (realistic) assumptions, justify the adoption of FM and the necessary investment.

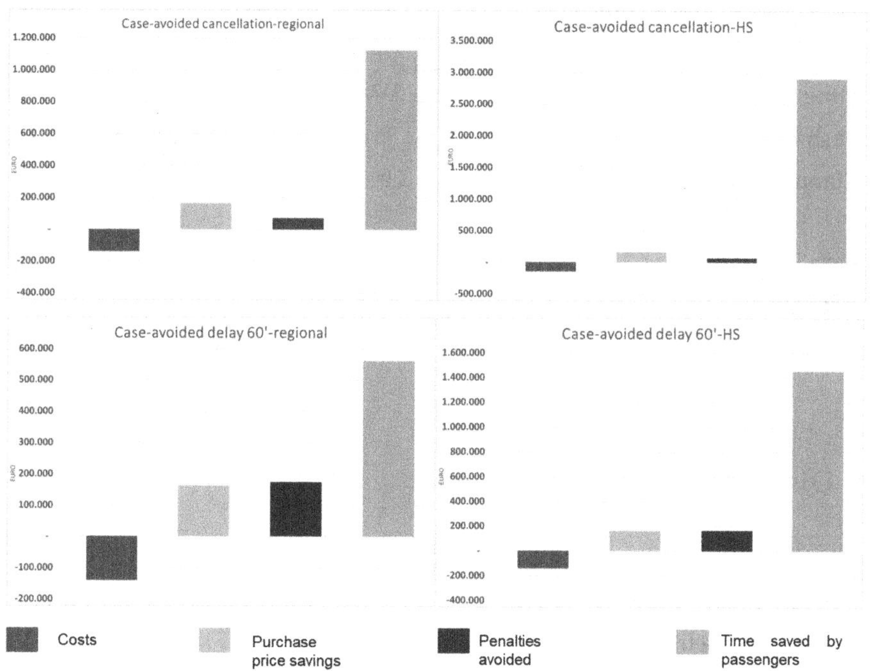

Fig. 8. Value of benefit categories per scenario (Euro/year)

The Economic analysis has demonstrated the net convenience of the FM adoption for the society as a whole (IM, users and all other involved stakeholders), since the net positive cash flow of benefits vs. costs during the 15-year period is about 9 MEuro. Indicators of the Economic analysis are highly positive: NPV is 7.067 MEuro and the Benefit/Cost Ratio (BCR) is 5.05, i.e., the process generates (actualized) benefits 5 times higher than cost borne by the IM. Such benefits are likely higher if FM are applied on a EU-27 scale. The net benefits for users and society may justify public granting of the adoption of FM in the railway safety domain. The definition of BCR is given as:

$$BCR = \frac{\sum_t B_t (1+i_t)^{-t}}{K + \sum_t C_t (1+i_t)^{-t}}$$

where variables have the same meaning as for the definition of NPV.

Cash flows of the Economic Analysis for relevant years are reported in the Table 3.

Table 3. Cash flow (kEuro/year) and Economic Analysis indicators

	year	*1*	*7*	*10*	*15*
CAPEX and OPEX for IM		-80.33	-140.18	-161.48	-161.48
Savings in SW development		21.00	162.60	162.60	162.60
Avoided penalties		13.08	65.40	65.40	65.40
Time saved for passengers		112.52	562.60	562.60	562.60
Cash flow		66.27	650.42	629.12	629.12
Cumulated cash flow		66.27	3904.70	5814.70	9002.72
NPV	**7.067 M€**				
B/C Ratio	**5.05**				

4 Discussion and Conclusions

The goal of the 4SECURail demonstrator was to show a possible way to use formal methods to improve the quality of System Requirement Specifications of signaling systems, using this experiment as a source of information on which to base a Cost-Benefit Analysis.

The outcomes of the project (see in particular [17]) have shown that the creation of an easy to understand and communicate, graphical but also executable, SysML model is an intermediate step that already allows to detect possible weaknesses in the natural language requirements, but that formal modeling and analysis is needed to detect and remove less trivial errors.

The results of the project have also shown how a "formal methods diversity" approach can be successfully exploited to gain more confidence in the correctness of the formalization and analysis, and to gain access to a rich set of options for performing the analysis of the system. Even without using advanced formal verification techniques, e.g., involving bisimulations and complex temporal logic formulas, we have experienced that many easy-to-use analysis (e.g., static checks, invariants, deadlocks, reachabilities) can be performed without any specific advanced background.

This lightweight use of formal methods is not aimed at full system verification/validation (which would not be possible anyway due to its parametric nature), but remains a very important aid for the early detection of ambiguities in the natural language requirements and in errors in their rigorous specification.

The Cost-Benefit Analysis developed on the 4SECURail demonstrator suggests that efforts and costs for formal analysis of system requirements are likely to be distributed among the various entities supporting the standard itself, and not to a single IM. Benefits are spread over the entire supply chain, including suppliers, if economies of scale are activated among IMs and suppliers in software development. The "multi-supplier" mode enabled by FM is likely to generate time and cost savings for rail safety industry.

The numeric cost/benefits results shown in the previous section are produced by the application of the Cost-Benefit Analysis procedure on data collected within the 4SECURail demonstrator test case, from the experience of the industrial partners, and from relevant literature (more details in [28]).

Although the compliance with the European Commission Guide to Cost-Benefit Analysis guidelines enhances methodological solidity, the input values used for the cost/benefit categories are derived from a limited basis of available data for such categories. This undermines the ability to generalize results to different case studies. Such threat to the *external validity* of the approach can only be addressed by enlarging the basis of available data by further experiments covering a wide spectrum of case studies, addressing different systems and employing different formal methods and tools. This would require greater attention of the formal methods community to the quantification of costs and benefits parameters (e.g., as given in [2]) since the evidence of the beneficial effects of formal methods is mostly given instead in the literature in a qualitative way. On the other hand, the analysis of the scarce literature where some cost quantification is given has shown how different the values of some cost categories can be in different formal methods frameworks (e.g., the software licenses when using commercial, qualified tools vs. using open-source ones). Nevertheless, we believe that the approach followed in the 4SECURail project can be taken as a first example of fully fledged Cost-Benefit Analysis, developed according to internationally accepted standards, on the application of Formal Methods in the rail signalling industry, that can be taken as an example on which to base further efforts in this direction.

Acknowledgements. This work has been partially funded by the 4SECURail project. The 4SECURail project received funding from the Shift2Rail Joint Undertaking under the European Union's Horizon 2020 research and innovation programme under grant agreement No 881775 in the context of the open call S2R-OC-IP2-01-2019, part of the "Annual Work Plan and Budget 2019", of the programme H2020-S2RJU-2019. The content of this paper reflects only the authors'view and the Shift2Rail Joint Undertaking is not responsible for any use that may be made of the included information.

References

1. Aissat, R., Boralv, A.: X2RAIL-2, Deliverable D5.3 Business Case (2020)
2. Basile, D., Fantechi, A., Rosadi, I.: Formal analysis of the UNISIG safety application intermediate sub-layer. In: Lluch Lafuente, A., Mavridou, A. (eds.) FMICS 2021. LNCS, vol. 12863, pp. 174–190. Springer, Cham (2021). https://doi.org/10.1007/978-3-030-85248-1_11
3. Belli, D., Mazzanti, F.: A case study in formal analysis of system requirements. In: Masci, P., Bernardeschi, C., Graziani, P., Koddenbrock, M., Palmieri, M. (eds.) SEFM 2022. LNCS, vol. 13765, pp. 164–173. Springer, Cham (2022). https://doi.org/10.1007/978-3-031-26236-4_14
4. Bibi, S., Mazhar, S., Minhas, N.M., Ahmed, I.: Formal methods for commercial applications issues vs. solutions. J. Software Eng. Appl. (2014)
5. Burroughs, D.: SNCF develops new-generation interlockings with a 1bn Argos partnership (2018). https://www.railjournal.com/signalling/sncf-develops-new-generation-interlockings-with-e1bn-argos-partnership
6. van Essen, H., et al.: Handbook on the external costs of transport, version 2019 1.1. Delft: European Commission, Directorate-General for Mobility and Transport (2019)
7. EULYNX. Eulynx Project site (2021). https://eulynx.eu/
8. Ferrari, A., Fantechi, A., et al.: The metro Rio case study. Sci. Comput. Program. **78**(7), 828–842 (2013)
9. Ferrari, A., Mazzanti, F., Basile, D., ter Beek, M.H., Fantechi, A.: Comparing formal tools for system design: a judgment study. In: Proceedings of the ACM/IEEE 42nd International Conference on Software Engineering, pp. 62–74 (2020)
10. Fitzgerald, J., Bicarregui, J., Larsen, P.G., Woodcock, J.: Industrial deployment of formal methods: trends and challenges. In: Romanovsky, A., Thomas, M. (eds.) Industrial Deployment of System Engineering Methods, pp. 123–143. Springer, Heidelberg (2013). https://doi.org/10.1007/978-3-642-33170-1_10
11. European Union Agency for Railways. Report on railway safety and interoperability in the EU (2018). https://data.europa.eu/doi/10.2821/205360
12. Garavel, H., Beek, M.H., Pol, J.: The 2020 expert survey on formal methods. In: ter Beek, M.H., Ničković, D. (eds.) FMICS 2020. LNCS, vol. 12327, pp. 3–69. Springer, Cham (2020). https://doi.org/10.1007/978-3-030-58298-2_1
13. Gleirscher, M., Marmsoler, D.: Formal methods in dependable systems engineering: a survey of professionals from Europe and North America. Empir. Softw. Eng. **25**(6), 4473–4546 (2020). https://doi.org/10.1007/s10664-020-09836-5
14. Hall, A.: Realising the benefits of formal methods. In: Lau, K.-K., Banach, R. (eds.) ICFEM 2005. LNCS, vol. 3785, pp. 1–4. Springer, Heidelberg (2005). https://doi.org/10.1007/11576280_1
15. RFI Rete Ferroviaria Italiana. Prospetto Informativo della Rete, updated December 2021, with relevant annex "Gradi di Utilizzo dell'Infrastruttura: infrastruttura a capacità limitata e infrastruttura satura" (2021)
16. Krasner, J.: How product development organizations can achieve long- term cost savings using model-based systems engineering (MBSE) (2015). https://docplayer.net/18566603-How-product-development-organizations-can-achieve-long-term-cost-savings-using-model-based-systems-engineering-mbse.html
17. Mazzanti, F., Basile, D.: 4SECURail Deliverable D2.2 "Formal development Demonstrator prototype, 1st Release" (2020). https://www.4securail.eu/Documents.html

18. Mazzanti, F., et al.: 4SECURail Deliverable D2.1 "Specification of formal development demonstrator" (2020). https://www.4securail.eu/Documents.html
19. Mazzanti, F., Belli, D.: 4SECURail Deliverable D2.5 "Formal development demonstrator prototype, final release" (2021). https://www.4securail.eu/Documents.html
20. Mazzanti, F., Belli, D.: Formal modeling and initial analysis of the 4SECURail case study. EPTCS **355**, 118–144 (2022). https://doi.org/10.48550/arXiv.2203.10903
21. Mazzanti, F., Belli, D.: The 4SECURail formal methods demonstrator. In: Collart-Dutilleul, S., Haxthausen, A.E., Lecomte, T. (eds.) RSSRail 2022. LNCS, vol. 13294, pp. 149–165. Springer, Cham (2022). https://doi.org/10.1007/978-3-031-05814-1_11
22. Piattino, A., et al.: 4SECURail Deliverable D2.3 "Case study requirements and specification" (2020). https://www.4securail.eu/pdf/4SR-WP2-D2.3-Case-study-requirements-and-specification-SIRTI-1.0.pdf
23. Ruiz, A., Gallina, B., de la Vara, J.L., Mazzini, S., Espinoza, H.: Architecture-driven, multi-concern and seamless assurance and certification of cyber-physical systems. In: Skavhaug, A., Guiochet, J., Schoitsch, E., Bitsch, F. (eds.) SAFECOMP 2016. LNCS, vol. 9923, pp. 311–321. Springer, Cham (2016). https://doi.org/10.1007/978-3-319-45480-1_25
24. Shift2rail. 4SECURail (GA 881775) project site. http://www.4securail.eu
25. UNISIG. FIS for the RBC/RBC Handover - SUBSET-039 (2015)
26. UNISIG. SUBSET-098 - RBC/RBC Safe Communication Interface (2017)
27. UNISIG. Subset-037, euroradio fis v3.2.0, December 2015
28. Vaghi, C.: Table of CBA related bibliografy. https://zenodo.org/record/8174266
29. Vaghi, C.: 4SECURail Deliverable D2.4: "Specification of Cost-Benefit Analysis and learning curves, Intermediate release" (202). https://www.4securail.eu/Documents.html
30. Vaghi, C.: 4SECURail Deliverable D2.6: "Specification of Cost-Benefit Analysis and learning curves, Final release" (2021). https://www.4securail.eu/Documents.html
31. Woodcock, J., Larsen, P.G., Bicarregui, J., Fitzgerald, J.: Formal methods: practice and experience. ACM Comput. Surv. **41**(4), 2009 (2009)

Statistical Model Checking for P

Francisco Durán[1], Nicolás Pozas[1], Carlos Ramírez[2], and Camilo Rocha[2(✉)]

[1] Universidad de Málaga, Málaga, Spain
[2] Pontificia Universidad Javeriana, Cali, Colombia
camilo.rocha@javerianacali.edu.co

Abstract. P is a programming language equipped with a unified framework for modeling, specifying, implementing, testing, and verifying complex distributed systems. This language is based on the actor model, and its framework includes a compiler toolchain for code generation, bounded randomized testing, and reachability analysis. This paper presents an extension of P's framework to include statistical model checking of quantititive temporal logic formulas. The distributed statistical model checking for discrete event simulators MultiVeStA has been integrated into the P framework for Monte Carlo validation of P programs against QuaTEx quantitative temporal logic formulas. For this, P's compiler has been modified to generate instrumentation code enabling the observation of a program's attributes without direct, manual intervention of the code. As a result, distributed incremental statistical model checking is now available for P via probabilistic sampling. As the experiments show, some of them reported here, these new verification capabilities scale up and complement the ones already available for P.

Keywords: P programming language · Statistical model checking · MultiVeStA · QuaTEx

1 Introduction

P is an asynchronous event-driven domain-specific programming language. A P program defines a collection of interacting state machines that communicate with each other using events. Overall, it provides primitives to capture protocols that are inherent to communication among components. P is being used in, e.g., Amazon (AWS) for analysis of complex distributed systems and protocols [11]. One main advantage of P lies in its testing and validation capabilities. They can be extended to support several analysis engines to check that the distributed system programmed in the language satisfies the desired correctness specifications. For instance, it currently ships with randomized bounded state-space search for bug finding and symbolic space exploration. Given the inherent complexity of distributed systems, reasoning about different correctness aspects of their interleaving semantics can always benefit from other formal methods approaches to face such a challenging task. Furthermore, the execution of current available tools for P cannot be distributed, which limits their scaling.

This paper reports on new statistical model checking capabilities made available to P. These capabilities are contributed by integrating MultiVeStA [12] inside

A. Cimatti and L. Titolo (Eds.): FMICS 2023, LNCS 14290, pp. 40–56, 2023.
https://doi.org/10.1007/978-3-031-43681-9_3

P's execution and verification environment. Quantitative temporal logic formulas of the form "what is the expected number of times a resource is available before it stops working?" and "what is the probability that a resource will be available after x many uses?" expressed in the QuaTEx [1] language can now be verified: their statistical correctness is checked with Monte Carlo simulations using probabilistic sampling. This is possible because the usual non-deterministic behavior, due to concurrent computation and all other sources of non-determinism in P (such as those tied to specific language constructs) are made purely probabilistic. This is achieved by ensuring that the scheduler provides a deterministic ordering of messages (see, e.g., [3]), which are the basic communication means in the actor model [2,10] implemented by P.

MultiVeStA is a tool for distributed statistical model checking that can operate on different discrete event simulators. In order to integrate P with MultiVeStA, specific functions were implemented to observe a program's state and to coordinate the Monte Carlo simulations, including new functionality in P's compiler to automatically generate code for any given program. The overall result of this effort is that the P simulator can still be run independently or under the control of MultiVeStA, which now can set a random seed for sampling, perform step-by-step execution, and query state observation on P programs. For its checks, MultiVeStA will run as many independent simulations as needed to respect a user-specified confidence interval. Moreover, MultiVeStA offers a client-server architecture to distribute simulations, which allows their concurrent execution and scale up of the analysis.

The use of the tool is showcased with the help of the running example of a bike sharing system. The example is inspired in a case study originally presented in [13], based on a real public system. Quantitative properties, such as those given above, are analyzed in experiments well beyond the reach of current techniques and tools available to P. This paper also reports on how the approach scales up: it presents information on how the tool works on a local machine and on a configuration of AWS instances.

Outline. This paper is organized as follows. Section 2 overviews P and introduces the bike sharing system example. Section 3 explains how statistical model checking is possible for P programs, and how it can be done with the help of MultiVeStA and QuaTEx. Sections 4 and 5 present, respectively, details about the integration and validation efforts of the proposed approach. Section 6 concludes the paper.

2 An Overview of P

P is a domain-specific language designed for programming asynchronous event-driven systems [6,11]. In P, a system is programmed as a collection of interacting state machines that communicate using events. P programs are compiled into executable code, which can then be checked with state exploration techniques to identify design bugs.

2.1 An Overview of P and its Semantics

The underlying model of computation in P is the actor model [2,10], a classical model for concurrent computation. The actor model has received interest during the past decades, mainly because of its simple message-passing semantics, the proliferation of multi-core and cloud computing, and the creation of new programming languages based on it such as Scala and P. In this model, an actor is a concurrent object operating asynchronously and interacting with other actors by asynchronous message-passing. Each actor has a queue of messages waiting to be processed, which are stored and served in the order they arrive. An actor's response to a message can include performing local actions, creating other actors, and sending new messages. Their own private state can be modified, but can only affect each other indirectly through messaging. An actor model execution can be non-bounded and it ends once all message queues are empty.

P's approach to system implementation has the key advantage of keeping the code in sync with the model. It can be recompiled as many times as needed, i.e., the maintenance of the implementation directly happens on the state machine diagrams implementing the actor model. The working assumption is that the properties checked on the state machine diagrams must also hold on the code automatically generated from the model. P has been used to implement and verify significant industrial applications. Some of its war stories include the implementation and verification of the USB device driver stack core in Microsoft Windows 8, formal reasoning about the core distributed protocols involved in the strong consistency launch in Amazon S3, and formal model creation of the OTA protocol and the validation of its correctness in Amazon. The interested reader may check [11] for details on these case studies.

P's language design ensures that a program can be checked for its responsiveness, i.e., its capacity to handle all events in a timely manner. Of course, being able to model complex distributed systems, the language provides the means for specifying different types of machines, states, actions, events, etc. For testing purposes, the programmer can simulate the environment in which the system is to be executed by programming nondeterministic *ghost* machines, which are later eliminated during the compilation process. The interested reader may check [11] for a complete account on the language.

A P program is comprised of state machines that communicate through events. Each machine has a set of states, actions, and local variables. The states and actions contain code statements for reading and updating local variables, sending events to other machines, raising local events, or invoking external functions to handle data transfer. When a machine receives an event, it executes transitions and actions, causing the aforementioned code fragments to run.

When verifying P systems, handling every event at every state can lead to combinatorial explosion in the number of control states, rendering its use impractical. To alleviate this situation, in addition to its compiler, P provides a tool for explicit-state bounded model checking. Several different model checkers have been used associated to different versions of P (see [4,5,11]).

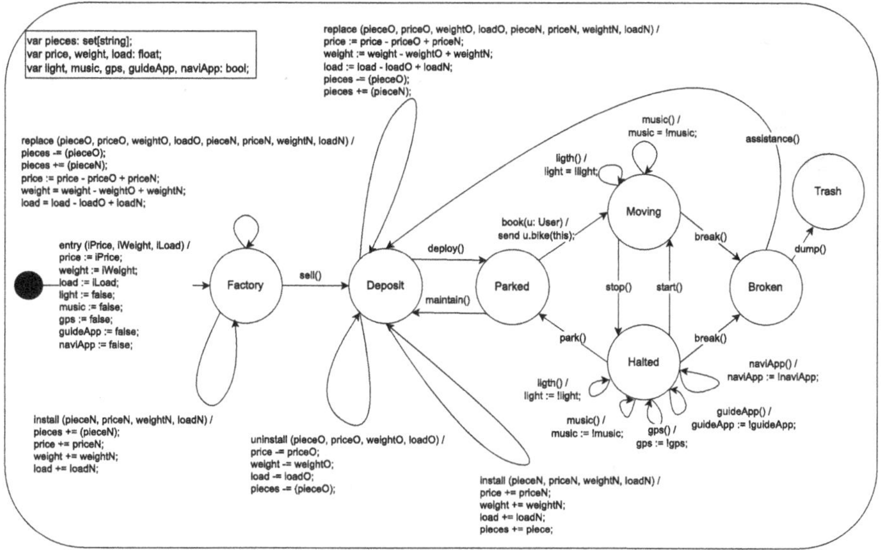

Fig. 1. The Bike state machine

2.2 A Case Study: A Bike Sharing System

To illustrate some of the main features of P, a case study based on a bike sharing system is showcased. The example is inspired in a case study originally presented in [13], based on a public system operating in Pisa, Italy.[1] The model consists of a state machine for a bike and four ghost machines representing its environment. The Bike machine is shown in Fig. 1 and the environment machines in Fig. 2. The state machines cover the lifecycle of any bike, including its manufacturing, maintenance, and use. Even though P programs are entered in its textual form, the example here is introduced with the help of a diagram. To get a flavor of its actual syntax, the code of the auxilіry function Handle is shown in Listing 1.

Starting from a base bike, a number of optional devices can be installed during its manufacturing, and later be replaced, removed, or added during its maintenance at the deposit. As available components, there are different types of wheels (Winter, Summer, and AllYear), Light, different forms of energy source (Dynamo and Battery), Engine, different applications (MapsApp, NaviApp, GuideApp, Music), GPS, Basket, and different frames (Diamond and StepThru). Each one of these components has a price and a weight, and consumes certain amount of energy. Starting with values for these attributes already installed in the base bike configuration, the total price of a bike depends on the prices of its components. Nevertheless, bikes are subject to constraints so that not all feature combinations yield valid products. For example, bikes may not be more expensive than a given price or consume energy beyond a certain threshold.

[1] In [13,14], the example was used to illustrate the feature-oriented language QFLan.

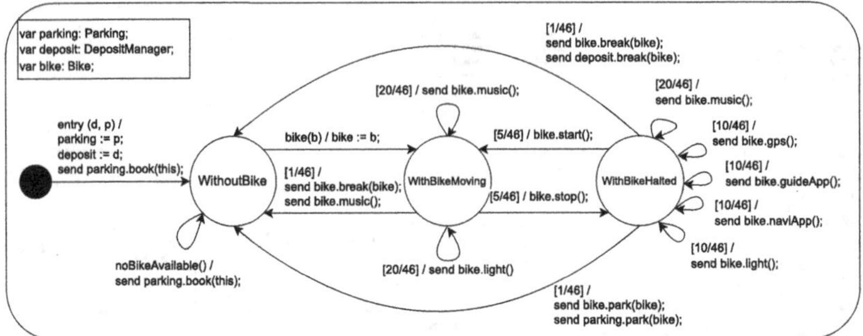

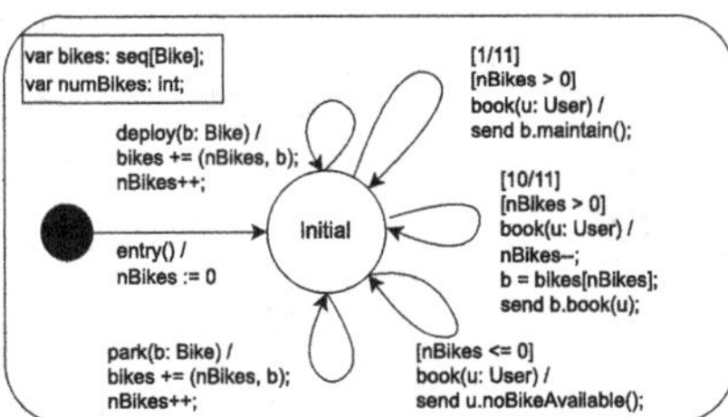

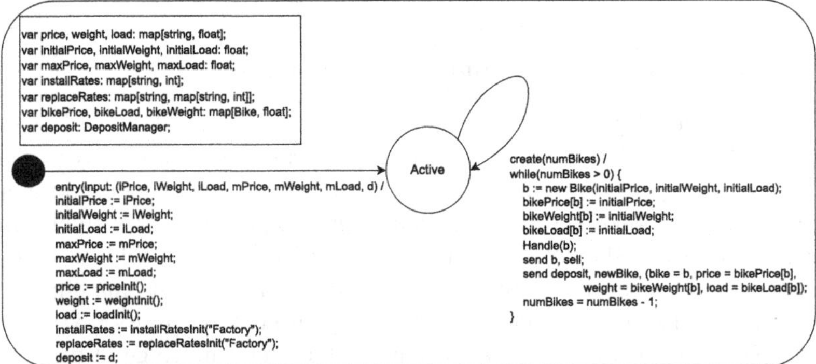

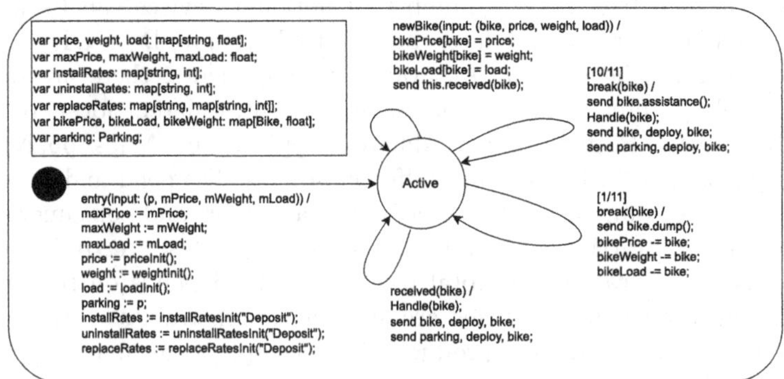

Fig. 2. Ghost machines

The example uses several data structures and illustrates many of the different features of P. For example, a bike keeps its components in the pieces variable, of type set[string], and a factory manager keeps information on bike components in the variables price, weight, and load, all of type map[string,float].

The different behaviors of ghost machines may be described as the specification of any possible behavior. In this case study, they have been modeled as a probabilistic system, so that all decisions are quantified. The example illustrates how, while some actions depend on the reception of given events, other are probabilistic, with fixed probabilities or with probabilities that depend on the state of the machines with respect to the given constraints.

- For example, in accordance to the state machine of the user, when in the WithoutBike state, it can receive a noBikeAvailable() or a bike(b) event, with a bike b, firing one transition or the other: the decision only depends on the event that is received.
- Upon the reception of an event, or even spontaneously without the need for an event, multiple transitions may be fired depending on a probability value. For instance, a user can do several things at the WithBikeMoving state: with probability 20/46, it can send a music() event to the bike (to turn the music on or off); with probability 5/46, it can send a stop() event to the bike; etc.
- There can also be conditions associated to transitions, so that an event may fire one or the other depending on the evaluation of the condition. For example, in the Parking state machine, the reception of a book() event in the Initial state will result in one transition or another, executing the corresponding actions, depending on whether there are bikes available or not ([nBikes > 0] or [nBikes <= 0]).
- In the case of the FactoryManager and DepositManager state machines, the probabilities depend on the state of the bikes under operation and the given constrains. As stated in the original papers by ter Beek et al. [13,14], the installation, removal, and replacement of each component has an associated *rate*. The probability of a transition is then calculated as the fraction between the rate of the installation, removal, or replacement of a component, and the summation of the rates of all possible actions. For example, if only three actions A, B, and C are possible in a certain state S, with respective rates 3, 7, and 9, the corresponding probabilities would be 3/19, 7/19, and 9/19. These probabilities are calculated in the Handle(Bike) auxiliary function invoked from the state machines of both managers.

The code of the Handle(Bike) function is shown in Listing 1. It uses the predefined operation choose(int) to return a random number in the range $[1..n)$, for n its argument, and uses the auxiliary function Out(Bike) to calculate the summation of rates of active transitions. It also uses predicates ValidInstall(Bike,string) and ValidReplace(Bike,string) to check, respectively, the installation and the replacement of the given component on the given bike. The entire code of the case study and the properties to be checked (as presented in Sect. 5), is available at https://github.com/PST-P/p-pst.

```
fun Handle(bike: Bike) {
  var piece, replacement: string;
  var outv, current, chosen: int;
  var done, actionDone: bool;

  done = false;
  outv = Out(bike);
  while (!done) {
    current = 8; // deploy rate
    chosen = choose(outv);
    if (chosen < current) {
      done = true;
    } else {
      actionDone = false;
      foreach (piece in keys(installRates)) {
        if (!actionDone && ValidInstall(bike, piece)) {
          current = current + installRates[piece];
          if (chosen <= current) {
            actionDone = true;
            send bike, install, (piece = piece, price = price[piece],
                       weight = weight[piece], load = load[piece]);
          }
        }
      }
      if (!actionDone) {
        foreach (piece in keys(uninstallRates)) {
          if (!actionDone && ValidUninstall(bike, piece)) {
            current = current + uninstallRates[piece];
            if (chosen <= current) {
              actionDone = true;
              send bike, uninstall, (piece = piece, price = price[piece],
                         weight = weight[piece], load = load[piece]);
            }
          }
        }
      }
      if (!actionDone) {
        foreach (piece in keys(replaceRates)) {
          foreach (replacement in keys(replaceRates[piece])) {
            if (!actionDone && ValidReplace(bike, piece, replacement)) {
              current = current + replaceRates[piece][replacement];
              if (chosen <= current) {
                actionDone = true;
                send bike, replace, (pieceOld = piece, priceOld =
                  price[piece], weightOld = weight[piece], loadOld =
                  load[piece], pieceNew = replacement, priceNew =
                  price[replacement], weightNew = weight[piece], loadNew =
                  load[piece]);
              }
            }
          }
        }
      }
    }
    outv = Out(bike);
  }
}
```

Listing 1. Handle function

3 Statistical Model Checking with MultiVeStA

Quantitative properties of concurrent systems, such as P programs, are usually specified in logics that enable querying expected values on simulations. This is possible, for instance, whenever such systems exhibit the so-called *no-unquantified-non-determinism* property. It means that the usual non-deterministic behavior due to concurrent computation and all other sources of non-determinism, such as those tied to specific language constructs, need to be made purely probabilistic. This property can be nontrivial to meet when different components perform local transitions concurrently. As explained in [7], there are two well-studied ways for guaranteeing the absence of unquantified non-determinism: by introducing a scheduler that provides a deterministic ordering of messages (see, e.g., [3]), or by relying on continuous probability distributions with message delays and computation time (see, e.g., [8]).

For P, there are exactly two sources of non-determinism, both considered in this work: one due to the concurrent behavior natural to the actor model it implements and the other associated with non-deterministic choice (e.g., P's $ and choose operators). In the proposed approach, the first source of non-determinism is dealt with by modifying P's scheduling algorithm. Both sources of non-determinism are then guarded by probabilistic distribution functions that are sampled for simulation.

Quantitative aspects of P models can be computed with the Quantitative Temporal Expressions language (or QuaTEx in short) [1]. Formulas in this language can query the expected value of state or path expressions, including simple state probabilities such as the ones expressible in PCTL [9]. QuaTEx formulas are given path-based semantics in the following sense: starting at a state s, a formula φ is evaluated against all paths $paths(s)$ starting at s, which is a measurable set with associated probability measure because of the no-unquantified-non-determinism assumption. Operationally, to compute the value of a path expression from a given state, QuaTEx supports a framework for parameterized recursive temporal operator definitions using a few primitive non-temporal operators and the 'next' ($\bigcirc$) temporal operator: it takes an expression at the next state and makes it an expression for the current state.

QuaTEx formulas are defined on values of the system under analysis s that are queried using the rval function. This function takes a string as argument and returns a numerical value. There are two predefined queries to the s.rval(string) function, namely steps and time, which return the number of steps taken by the simulator and the current simulation time, respectively. The # character represents the temporal next operator, which is used by MultiVeStA to advance a simulation in one transition (i.e., one-step execution). In addition, the integration automatically adds support for querying the following values on the model at hand with rval:

- alive.*MACHINE.INDEX* evaluates to value 1 if the machine *MACHINE* with index *INDEX* has been created and 0 otherwise.
- state.*MACHINE.INDEX.STATE.EVENT* evaluates to value 1 if *EVENT* within state *STATE* was the last event called for machine *MACHINE* with index

```
1   BikeIsUsed(counter) =
2     if( s.rval("steps") > 5000 )
3     then counter
4     else if ( s.rval("alive.Bike.0") == 1.0 )
5          then if ( s.rval("state.Bike.0.Moving") == 1.0 )
6               then #BikeIsUsed(counter + 1)
7               else if ( s.rval("state.Bike.0.Broken.dump") == 1.0 )
8                    then counter
9                    else #BikeIsUsed(counter)
10                   fi
11              fi
12         else #BikeIsUsed(counter)
13         fi
14    fi;
15
16  eval E[ BikeIsUsed(0) ];
```

Listing 2. Number of times a bicycle is used before breaking down

INDEX and 0 otherwise. If an *EVENT* is not specified, then it will check that *STATE* is the last state visited by the machine.
- *MACHINE.INDEX.PROPERTY* evaluates to the value of *PROPERTY* in machine *MACHINE* with index *INDEX*. Recall that these properties can only refer to numerical values. Boolean values are represented as 1 if they are true and as 0 if they are false.

To illustrate the use of QuaTEx, consider the function BikeIsUsed(int) in Listing 2: it recursively computes the number of times a bicycle is likely to be in motion before it completely breaks down (or the iteration reaches 5 000 execution steps, whichever comes first). The argument counter is incremented in one unit each time the simulation enters the Moving state. If the dump event of the Broken state has been reached (or the simulation reaches the indicated step limit), then the accumulated value will be returned. The function has two base cases and three recursive calls. The base cases correspond to the situation in which the number of steps has exceeded 5 000 (line 3) and the bike is broken (line 8). The recursive cases correspond to the situation in which the bike is moving (line 6), the bike is not moving and has not broke down yet (line 9), and the bike is not alive (line 12). In the first case the recursion step is called by increasing the function's argument in one unit, while in the other two cases the argument is unchanged. The value of interest is computed by evaluating the expected value of the call BikeIsUsed(0) (line 16). The evaluation of this expression is presented in Sect. 5.

The model checking problem for probabilistic P models with respect to quantitative properties is then solved by simulating the system of interest for finitely many runs, and by using hypothesis testing to infer whether the samples provide a statistical evidence for the satisfaction or violation of the property. This is achieved by the usual Monte Carlo simulations, which are a powerful scalable alternative to numerical probabilistic model checking techniques (which may suffer from state space explosion issues). MultiVeStA carries out Monte Carlo simulations without fixing up front the number of simulations. Instead, it estimates the expected value of the QuaTEx expression with respect to two parameters provided by the user, namely, δ and α. The parameter δ defines a stopping criteria to the sample generation; this task stops when the confidence interval, computed using the Student's t-test, is less or equal than $\delta/2$. The parameter α is the additive inverse of the probability of the result reaching its mean. When the value of the mean is within that interval with probability $(1 - \alpha)$, the experiment will end. A batch size and a maximum number of simulations may also be given as parameters. To speed up the execution in distributed environments, the simulations may be requested in batches, so that the results of the simulations are collected and sent together to reduce the communication time. If the maximum number of simulations is reached before the confidence interval is met, which depends on δ and α, the experiment is ended. See [12] for additional details.

4 Integration of P and MultiVeStA

MultiVeStA has already been integrated with different discrete event simulators; guidelines for its integration with simulators are available in [12]. To launch, coordinate, and analyze Monte Carlo simulations, MultiVeStA requires the definition of a Java class extending the base class `NewState`. This new class is required to override methods for establishing the seed of the pseudo-random number generator, starting the simulation, performing one step of simulation, executing the entire simulation, and observing the program's state.

Figure 3 depicts the overall architecture of the integration between MultiVeStA and P. The white dotted rectangles represent the components that were added for enabling the tools to work in tandem. The original P simulator takes as parameter the `dll` file obtained from compiling a program's source code. This file contains the state machine definitions of the actors involved in the simulation. There are two main components in the P simulator, namely, the runtime and the scheduler. The *runtime component* disassembles and executes the code for creating the objects associated to the actors in the model simulation. The *scheduler component* receives the pending tasks from each actor and randomly selects the next task to execute, if any. A simulation is executed until a bug is found or no messages are pending. The output of the simulation is then a trace of events that leads to a bug or statistical data of a successfully ended execution.

The class required by MultiVeStA is called `PState`, a subclass of `NewState`. MultiVeStA takes this class, the QuaTEx query, and some additional information, and generates the result associated to the query. The operations required by MultiVeStA include the ability to explicitly set up and manage the P simulator. The P simulator is run independently, continuously processing messages from the MultiVeStA process, for setting the random seed, performing one simulation step, or querying a state observation. Each overridden method in the class `PState` outputs the corresponding messages. For this purpose, a new component `PMultivesta` was added to the P simulator.

To process requests from MultiVeStA, two main modifications to the simulator were implemented:

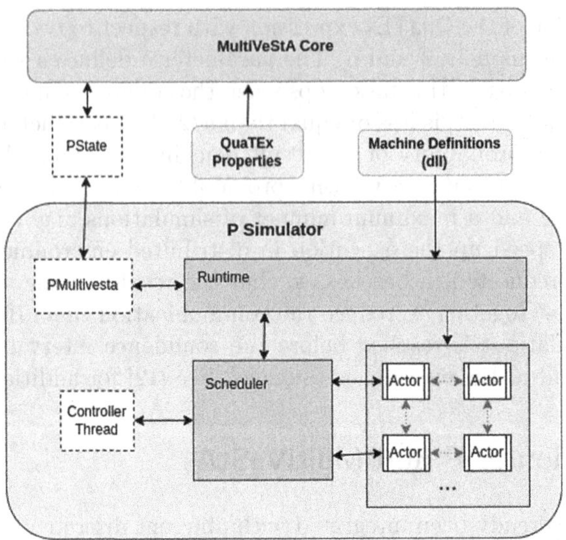

Fig. 3. P-MultiVeStA Main Components and Integration Architecture

- To enable the step-by-step execution of the simulation, a lock was added to the scheduler to control the execution of tasks. The lock control is carried out by a new thread (`ControllerThread`) in the P simulator.
- To enable state model querying during simulations, the P compiler was instrumented with auto-generated code so that specific elements of the model's state can be directly accessed. Moreover, mechanisms to verify if a machine has been created, and to check if a machine is in a specific state were added.

By combining these elements, the execution can be controlled by MultiVeStA. It takes as input the file with the QuaTEx formula to be analyzed and uses it to control the execution of the P program. Specifically, MultiVeStA can request the execution of a simulation step or query the value of a specific element of the state machine associated to some actor in the model. MultiVeStA collects the statistical information of each Monte Carlo simulation to determine the value of the quantitative formula contained in the given QuaTEx file. Once each Monte Carlo simulation is completed, a plot with the results and a CSV file with the recollected data are automatically generated.

5 A Case Study

This section illustrates the sort of quantitative property analyses that are now enabled for P programs thanks to its integration with MultiVeStA. It uses the bike example presented in Sect. 2. Since the execution of the Monte Carlo simulations may be run concurrently, results illustrating the scalability of the approach by running experiments in Amazon's cloud are also presented. The experiments reported in this section consider 10 users and 100 bikes. Different numbers of users or bikes may be considered for further experimentation.

To run the experiments as fairly as possible, a Docker image was created and used. It downloads and installs .Net 6.0, downloads the modified version of the MultiVeStA library and the modified version of P, exposes the port on which the MultiVeStA server will be listening, and runs MultiVeStA in server mode on that port. Using this scheme, QuaTEx properties can be both verified locally or on a configuration of distributed machines. The results presented suggest that the proposed integration between P and MultiVeStA scales up in distributed scenarios such as Amazon's cloud.

5.1 Verifying Quantitative Properties of the Bikes Example

As explained in Sect. 4, the integration between P and MultiVeStA takes as arguments the actors' definitions resulting from the compilation of the P program (given as a C# `dll` file) and a file with the QuaTEx properties to be verified. Since the simulations may be run remotely, the size of the batches can also be specified as a parameter (in addition to the parameters δ and α, see Sect. 3). Three different verification tasks showcase the different sort of properties and results that can be handled by the reported integration.

In addition to the property specified in Sect. 3, two additional properties will be considered. Specifically, the following questions will be answered: how likely is it that a bicycle is used more than a given number of times before it breaks down?, and how much time will a bicycle be used before being discarded?

Property 1: How Many Times Will a Bicycle Be Used Before Breaking Completely? The property presented in Listing 2, in Sect. 3, was run with parameters $\alpha = 0,05$, $\delta = 0,2$, batch size 20, and simulation bound 1 000. This is a property with a high variability due to the small probability of occurrence of the dump event. Thus, it reaches the maximum number of steps before converging. The result shows that the bike is used an average of 380,02 times, with a Confidence Interval (CI), computed using the Student's t-test, of 57,57.

Property 2: How Likely Is It that a Bicycle Is Used More Than a Given Number of Times Before It Breaks Down? The property shown in Listing 3 measures the probability that a bicycle will be in use more than a given number of times before it breaks down. The parametric execution of the QuaTEx property is analyzed for values in a given range and increment: as it can be seen in line 16, the BikeIsUsed(x) function is invoked with values of x in the range $[0, 400]$ and with increments of 20 units. In this property, a countdown is performed using the variable counter. Each time it enters the Moving state, the counter variable will be decremented by one unit. When this variable reaches 0 or the step limit is reached, the value 1 is returned indicating that the bike has not broken down yet. Alternatively, if the bike reaches the dump event of the Broken state, the value 0 is returned indicating that the bike has broken down. Since

```
BikeIsUsed(counter) =
  if ( counter <= 0 || s.rval("steps") > 5000 )
  then 1
  else if ( s.rval("alive.Bike.0") == 1.0 )
       then if ( s.rval("state.Bike.0.Moving") == 1.0 )
            then #BikeIsUsed(counter - 1)
            else if ( s.rval("state.Bike.0.Broken.dump") == 1.0 )
                 then 0
                 else #BikeIsUsed(counter)
                 fi
            fi
       else #BikeIsUsed(counter)
       fi
  fi;

eval parametric(E[ BikeIsUsed(x) ], x, 0.0, 20.0, 400.0);
```

Listing 3. Probability that a bicycle is used more than x times before breaking

MultiVeStA takes the average of this value, the final result is the probability that the bike has not broken. Figure 4 shows the value of BikeIsUsed(x) plus/minus the Confidence Interval (CI), computed using the Student's t-test, divided by 2. The chart shows how the probability of the bike being able to make the given number of movements decreases as the number of movements increases. The analysis was performed with parameters $\alpha = 0,05$, $\delta = 0,1$, and batch size 20.

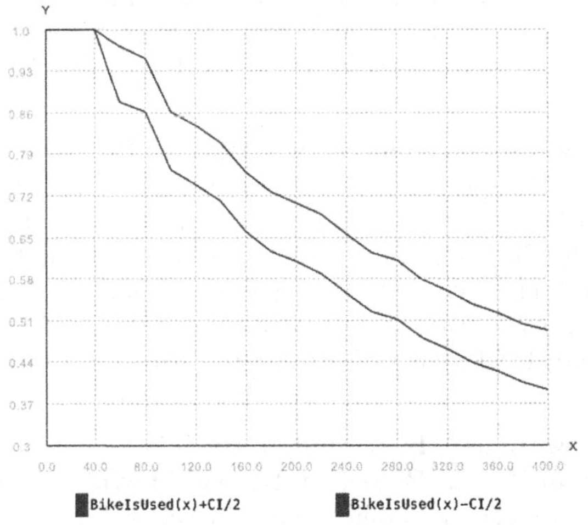

Fig. 4. Results for the property in Listing 3

Property 3: How Much Is a Bicycle Used Before Being Discarded? The property in Listing 4 measures the percentage of use of a bicycle before it needs to be discarded, calculated as the fraction between the number of steps in which the bike is alive and not broken, and the total number of steps. The analysis was

```
PercentageBikeUsed(counter) =
  if ( s.rval("steps") > 5000 )
  then counter / s.rval("steps")
  else if ( s.rval("alive.Bike.0") == 1.0 )
       then if ( ( s.rval("state.Bike.0.Moving") +
                   s.rval("state.Bike.0.Halted") +
                   s.rval("state.Bike.0.Parked") ) > 0 )
            then #PercentageBikeUsed(counter + 1)
            else if ( s.rval("state.Bike.0.Broken.dump") == 1.0 )
                 then counter / s.rval("steps")
                 else #PercentageBikeUsed(counter)
                fi
            fi
       else #PercentageBikeUsed(counter)
       fi
  fi;

  eval E[ PercentageBikeUsed(0) ];
```

Listing 4. Percentage of use of a bicycle before discarded

performed with parameters $\alpha = \delta = 0,05$ and batch size 20. The PercentageBikeUsed function also uses a counter variable as an accumulator. When the step limit is reached or the dump event of the Broken state is reached, the accumulated steps in the counter divided by the total steps given by the simulator are returned, resulting in the percentage of bike usage before it breaks. The analysis returns a value of 38,29% with a CI of 4,9%.

5.2 On the Scalability of Statistical Model Checking

To get a glimpse on how the analysis carried out on P programs using MultiVeStA scales up, Property 3 has been executed in different scenarios, and time information has been recorded and summarized in this section. Its verification has been executed in a local machine (local), and on AWS using instances of two machines with different computational power (t2.small and t2.2xlarge). The local machine is a *Macbook Pro* with an M1 processor, 8 CPUs, and 8GB of RAM; the AWS t2.small machine has 1 vCPU and 2GB of RAM; and the AWS t2.2xlarge machine has 8 vCPUs and 32GB of RAM.

Figure 5 presents the execution times (in seconds) of some experiments. For each type of machine (local, t2.small, and t2.2xlarge), 1, 4, and 8 instances where used (x axis); the total execution time (on the left) and the average interaction time (on the right) are also shown. As explained in Sect. 3, for the evaluation of QuaTEx formulas, MultiVeStA controls the execution of the P program by requesting one step of execution or querying on the state of the actors in the simulation. Since the duration of the simulations may differ significantly, the time taken is a measure that may complement the total execution time, in average, by these interactions. In this way, it can be better seen how time accumulates because it is possible that a larger number of messages are sent, although the indicated execution time may be high.

As shown in Fig. 5a, when running locally, as the number of processes increases, both the total time and the interaction time worsen considerably

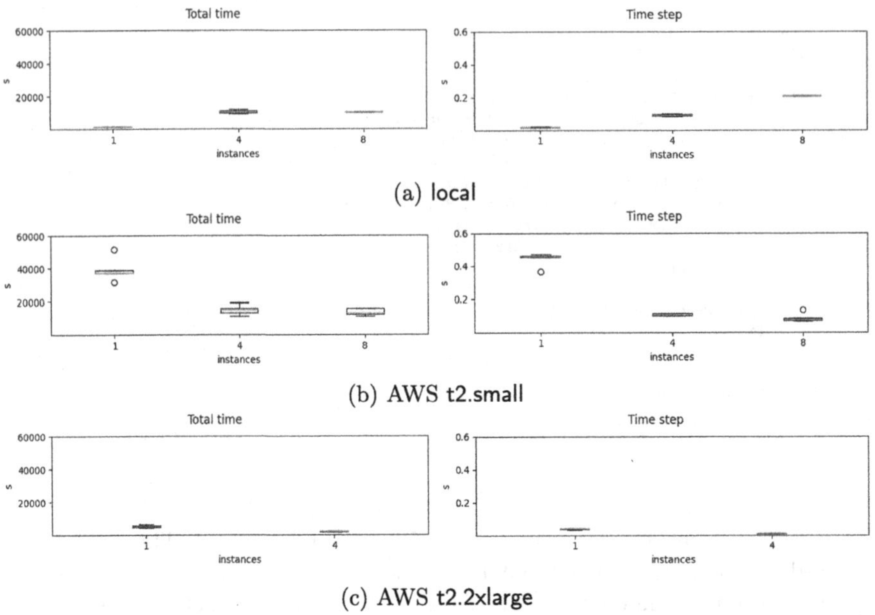

Fig. 5. Performance results executing locally and in the cloud

(although the executions are very fast individually). For example, for 8 processes the execution had to be stopped due to taking an excessive amount of time. This is why the execution time for 8 instances appears low despite the much higher time per interaction: each of the processes had to synchronize and the processor with only one process was already at 100% capacity. In consequence, when more processes were added, they competed for CPU usage and ended up increasing execution time.

The results presented in Fig. 5b for the execution in the cloud show that for 4 instances the execution time is approximately 4 times less than the execution time for a single instance. However, for 8 instances there is no significant improvement. This is likely due to how the workload is divided among the servers in MultiVeStA. For this property, the executions need an average of 100 iterations. Therefore, when dividing it between 4 instances, each machine executes 25 iterations, but for 8 instances each machine performs about 15 iterations as they are distributed more or less uniformly. This is why the time per message is reduced to about half that of 4 instances, but not in the overall execution time, as more executions are performed ($8 \times 15 = 120$).

In Fig. 5c, it can be observed that both the total execution time and the time per message decrease as more powerful machines are used. This setting was tested with 1 and 4 instances because AWS has a default usage limit of 32 vCPUs.

6 Concluding Remarks

This paper presented a development to enable statistical model checking for P programs. It was achieved by integrating the MultiVeStA model checking tool with the P framework. As a result, QuaTEx quantitative temporal logic formulas can be automatically analyzed using statistical inference based on Monte Carlo simulations. The integration effort adapted P's compiler to automatically generate code to observe the state of a program, add new functions at the C# level to control the Monte Carlo execution of P programs, and return values that may be part of the formulas to be verified. A case study was presented to illustrate the main features of the P programming language, explain how probabilities are understood and used in the proposed approach, and to showcase three verification tasks of quantitative properties that can be done automatically with the help of the tool. Results of extensive experimentation were also presented, where different machine configurations in Amazon's cloud are used. One major advantage of the approach is that it can scale up in distributed settings.

In the future, the plan is to pursue several research directions. One of them corresponds to adding the developed integration to P's toolchain so that programmers can automatically launch verification tasks with the help of a single click in their programming environments. Other endeavor is related to the extension of P's language and semantics with explicit probabilistic constructs. This goal will bring a broader wealth of probabilistic modeling and verification capabilities (e.g., by using other PDFs in addition to the uniform one). It is important to note that the effort reported in this paper does not introduce explicit probabilistic constructs in P's language for enabling probabilistic behavior. On the contrary, the full P language is supported, with no change at all. The extension of the language with explicit probabilistic constructs may require the extension of the actor model to a more general probabilistic setting. Finally, a formal semantics of the language may help in mathematically understanding different language design decisions such as the ones just mentioned. Moreover, if a formal semantics of the language is developed, then new formal analysis techniques and tools may become available to verify temporal properties of P programs, including quantitative ones.

Acknowledgments. The authors would like to thank D. Giannakopoulou and C. Muñoz for fruitful discussions on these ideas, and the anonymous referees for their very helpful comments that helped in improving the paper. This work was partially supported by Amazon Research Awards (Fall 2021) Project "Probabilistic and Symbolic Tools for P Program Verification", and projects TED2021-130666B-I00 and PID2021-125527NB-I00 funded by the Spanish government.

References

1. Agha, G., Meseguer, J., Sen, K.: PMaude: rewrite-based specification language for probabilistic object systems. Electron. Not. Theoret. Comput. Sci. **153**(2), 213–239 (2006). Proceedings of the Third Workshop on Quantitative Aspects of Programming Languages (QAPL 2005)

2. Agha, G.A.: Actors: a Model of Concurrent Computation in Distributed Systems (Parallel Processing, Semantics, Open, Programming Languages, Artificial Intelligence). Ph.D. thesis, University of Michigan, USA (1985)
3. AlTurki, M., Meseguer, J., Gunter, C.A.: Probabilistic modeling and analysis of DoS protection for the ASV protocol. In: SecReT@LICS/CSF 2008, Electronic Notes in Theoretical Computer Science, vol. 234, pp. 3–18. Elsevier (2008)
4. Andrews, T., Qadeer, S., Rajamani, S.K., Rehof, J., Xie, Y.: Zing: a model checker for concurrent software. In: Alur, R., Peled, D.A. (eds.) CAV 2004. LNCS, vol. 3114, pp. 484–487. Springer, Heidelberg (2004). https://doi.org/10.1007/978-3-540-27813-9_42
5. Deligiannis, P., Senthilnathan, A., Nayyar, F., Lovett, C., Lal, A.: Industrial-strength controlled concurrency testing for C# programs with coyote. In: Sankaranarayanan, S., Sharygina, N. (eds.) TACAS 2023. LNCS, vol. 13994, pp. 433–452. Springer, Cham (2023). https://doi.org/10.1007/978-3-031-30820-8_26
6. Desai, A., Gupta, V., Jackson, E.K., Qadeer, S., Rajamani, S.K., Zufferey, D. : P: safe asynchronous event-driven programming. In: ACM SIGPLAN Conference on Programming Language Design and Implementation, PLDI 2013, Seattle, WA, USA, June 16–19, 2013, pp. 321–332. ACM (2013)
7. Eckhardt, J., Mühlbauer, T., Meseguer, J., Wirsing, M.: Statistical model checking for composite actor systems. In: Martí-Oliet, N., Palomino, M. (eds.) WADT 2012. LNCS, vol. 7841, pp. 143–160. Springer, Heidelberg (2013). https://doi.org/10.1007/978-3-642-37635-1_9
8. Eker, S., Meseguer, J., Sridharanarayanan, A.: The Maude LTL model checker. In: WRLA2002, Electronic Notes in Theoretical Computer Science, vol. 71, pp. 162–187. Elsevier (2002)
9. Hansson, H., Jonsson, B.: A logic for reasoning about time and reliability. Formal Aspects Comput. **6**(5), 512–535 (1994)
10. Hewitt, C., Bishop, P.B., Steiger, R.: A universal modular ACTOR formalism for artificial intelligence. In: Proceedings of the 3rd International Joint Conference on Artificial Intelligence, Standford, CA, USA, 20–23 August 1973, pp. 235–245. William Kaufmann (1973)
11. P Developers. P's web site (2023). https://p-org.github.io/P/. Accessed 10 May 2023
12. Sebastio, S., Vandin, A.: Multivesta: statistical model checking for discrete event simulators. ValueTools 2013, pp. 310–315, Brussels, BEL, 2013. ICST (Institute for Computer Sciences, Social-Informatics and Telecommunications Engineering)
13. ter Beek, M.H., Legay, A., Lluch-Lafuente, A., Vandin, A.: Statistical analysis of probabilistic models of software product lines with quantitative constraints. In: Proceedings of the 19th International Conference on Software Product Line, SPLC 2015, Nashville, TN, USA, 20–24 July 2015, pp. 11–15. ACM (2015)
14. ter Beek, M.H., Legay, A., Lluch-Lafuente, A., Vandin, A.: A framework for quantitative modeling and analysis of highly (re)configurable systems. IEEE Trans. Software Eng. **46**(3), 321–345 (2020)

Pattern-Based Verification of ROS 2 Nodes Using UPPAAL

Lukas Dust(✉), Rong Gu, Cristina Seceleanu, Mikael Ekström, and Saad Mubeen

Mälardalen University, Västerås, Sweden
{lukas.dust,rong.gu,cristina.seceleanu,mikael.ekstrom,saad.mubeen}@mdu.se

Abstract. This paper proposes a pattern-based modeling and UPPAAL-based verification of latencies and buffer overflow in distributed robotic systems that use ROS 2. We apply pattern-based modeling to simplify the construction of formal models for ROS 2 systems. Specifically, we propose Timed Automata templates for modeling callbacks in UPPAAL, including all versions of the single-threaded executor in ROS 2. Furthermore, we demonstrate the differences in callback scheduling and potential errors in various versions of ROS 2 through experiments and model checking. Our formal models of ROS 2 systems are validated in experiments, as the behavior of ROS 2 presented in the experiments is also exposed by the execution traces of our formal models. Moreover, model checking can reveal potential errors that are missed in the experiments. The paper demonstrates the application of pattern-based modeling and verification in distributed robotic systems, showcasing its potential in ensuring system correctness and uncovering potential errors.

Keywords: Robot Operating System 2 · Pattern-Based Modeling · Model Checking

1 Introduction

Robotic systems are often distributed systems consisting of sensors, actuators, and controllers. Communication among these components involves buffers and job scheduling, which demand an elaborate design and extensive testing to ensure the correctness of the system. To provide the foundation and standardize the design of distributed robotic systems, the Robot Operating System (ROS) [13] has been developed as an open-source middleware, which allows fast prototyping for robotics. Since 2015, ROS has been upgraded, and ROS 2 [12] has been released consequently. ROS 2 utilizes Data Distribution Service (DDS) and supports real-time execution and communication. Both generations of ROS have drawn increased interest in academia and industry in recent years [1]. However, the consortium of developers decides to end the support of ROS in 2025 [10]. Hence, robotic systems using ROS need to be updated to ROS 2, with potential

A. Cimatti and L. Titolo (Eds.): FMICS 2023, LNCS 14290, pp. 57–75, 2023.
https://doi.org/10.1007/978-3-031-43681-9_4

behavioral consequences that have not been investigated enough in the community. In order to improve the real-time capability of ROS 2, research on response-time analysis of processing chains [5,7] and end-to-end timing analysis [16] has been conducted. These proposed analytical methods facilitate the verification of ROS 2 systems, but require manual and intensive computation that varies from system to system. When implementing a ROS 2 system, many options for system configuration are presented to the developer, such as the buffer sizes of DDS communication. Without tool-supported automation, these analytical methods are hard to employ.

Another difficulty of analyzing ROS 2 systems is due to the multiple versions of ROS 2 [11] and the lack of documentation. For instance, ROS 2 comes with an inbuilt module, called executor, which conducts the internal scheduling of functions (a.k.a. *callbacks*) that are triggered on the arrival of data or timers. Every main component of a ROS 2 system (i.e., *node*) consists of at least one such executor, and every communication channel has a configurable size of input and output buffers. In ROS 2 versions up to *Dashing*, timers are scheduled independently from other kinds of callbacks (e.g., publishers and subscribers), whereas in ROS 2 *Eloquent* and *Humble*, timers are scheduled together with other callbacks [5]. These give rise to two different ROS 2 executor semantics.

The different scheduling mechanisms in ROS 2 have been discovered, but not sufficiently regarded in the literature, which hinders ROS 2 developers from predicting the execution order of callbacks. As a result, they may exhibit abnormal phenomena, such as *instance misses* of timers and unexpected *latency* of callbacks. Instance misses occur when a buffer overflow leads to instances being skipped, while the latency of a callback describes the maximum time between the release of a callback instance and the time of completing its execution. Furthermore, although robotic systems, as a type of cyber-physical systems [4], are mostly safety-critical, trial-and-error approaches are dominant in verifying and testing them [14]. Such methods are not systematic, are hard to automate and error-prone.

Formal methods, such as *model checking*, are well-known for providing mathematical and rigorous analysis of complex systems. Model checking enables an automatic exploration of the system's state space, based on which an exhaustive verification is conducted to check if the system satisfies its specification. However, one of the drawbacks of using model checking is the complicated process of formal modeling, especially when the system is distributed and complex. To overcome such a difficulty, we propose a *pattern-based* modeling approach for ROS 2 systems. Additionally, ROS 2 systems are often real-time, which means that they are subjected to timing requirements such as scheduling a periodic callback every 2 ms within a certain level of jitter. Consequently, we employ *timed automata* (TA) [2] as the modeling language and UPPAAL [9] as the model checker in this paper, due to their ability of expressing and verifying such requirements, respectively.

We report our experimental results on ROS 2 systems, which reveal problems of scheduling in different versions of ROS 2. In addition, we present our pattern-based modeling of ROS 2 systems, and demonstrate the capability of model checking in the automatic verification of ROS 2 systems. Our TA models are experimentally validated, as the behavior of the ROS 2 systems shown in our experiments are also presented in the verification of the TA models. Moreover, we show that our UPPAAL-based verification can even reveal potential errors that are not detected via experiments.

In summary, we answer the following research questions. **RQ1**: Given the two behavioral semantics of single-threaded executors in ROS 2, how to ensure the correctness of a design of ROS 2-based systems with respect to the behavior of timer callbacks, callback latency, and the sizes of input buffers of callbacks? **RQ2**: What are the patterns for modeling ROS 2 systems, which can be reused in verification? **RQ3**: Can model checking find the errors of ROS 2 systems, which are shown in experiments, but also reveal potential errors that are not discovered via experimental evaluation? Our contributions are as follows:

- We demonstrate the difference in callback scheduling and the potential errors in different versions of ROS 2, through experiments and formal verification, which has not been addressed in the literature.
- We design patterns for modeling ROS 2 systems, which simplify the complex construction of formal models that require configuration of parameters.
- Our formal models of ROS 2 systems are validated by experiments. The behavior of ROS 2 presented in the experiments is also exhibited when model-checking our formal models. Moreover, we show that model checking is able to reveal potential errors that are missed in the experiments.

2 Background

To make the remainder of the paper comprehensible, this section introduces the concepts in ROS 2 first, including the internal scheduling mechanism. Next, Timed Automata and UPPAAL are briefly overviewed.

2.1 ROS 2

ROS 2 is an open-source middleware that enables fast prototyping and developing distributed robotic systems. ROS 2 is continuously updated, and distributions are released as stable versions that do not change.

ROS 2 System Model. ROS 2 systems are composed of the so-called *nodes* representing the core elements in the system that are communicating with each other. An example of such a system is given in Fig. 1, where two nodes, represented by green ellipses, communicate with each other over defined communication channels of ROS 2. There are two types of communication, *publisher-subscriber* and *service-client* communication, represented by the red and blue boxes in Fig. 1, respectively.

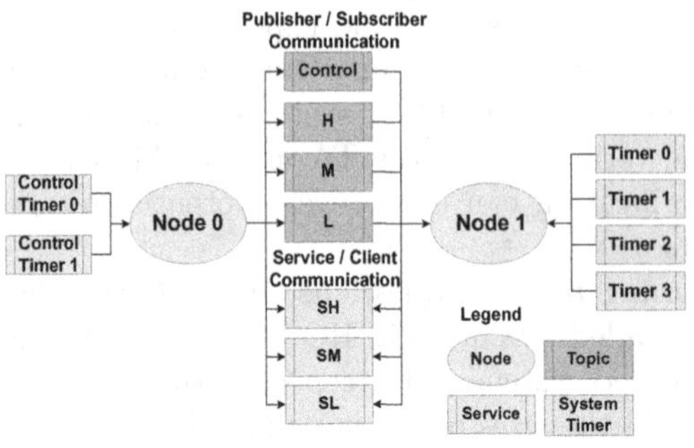

Fig. 1. Schematic example of a ROS 2 system containing two nodes communicating with each other.

The publisher-subscriber communication is unidirectional: a sending node sends data, by utilizing the so-called *publisher*, to all nodes that subscribe to the specific communication channel called *topic*. The event of incoming data in the receiving node triggers a subscription-specific function called *subscription callback*. The second kind of communication, is the service-client communication. This kind of communication is bidirectional. A directed request is sent from the requesting node (Node0) to the receiving node (Node1). Triggered by that request, a *service callback* starts executing in Node1. The response of the *service callback* triggers a *client callback* on arrival in the requesting Node0. Every registered access to a communication channel where data is received (Subscriber, Service, Client) has an individual FIFO input buffer, whose size is configurable. Besides communication, there is another method of triggering callbacks in ROS 2, via the system *timers*, denoted in yellow in Fig. 1. Timers can be configured as periodic or sporadic, whereas in the latter case, timer callbacks are triggered several times sporadically (i.e. when given a set of wall times).

ROS 2 Scheduling and Execution. The execution of ROS 2 relies on a host operating system that assigns resources to each node that executes the ROS 2 internal scheduler module, called *the executor*. The executor's task is to schedule the execution order of the presented four types of callbacks (subscriber, service, client, timer). The default executor operates on a single thread in the host operating system. The scheduling performed by the executor is non-preemptive and polling-point based, meaning that a callback cannot interrupt an other callback's execution, and only the callbacks that have been released before the time when the executor polls are considered for scheduling. Furthermore, an instance of polling is performed when only one instance of every released callback from the previous polling instance has finished its execution. While ROS 2 has evolved, the executor has changed so that there exist two versions of the executor (ExV1 [7] and ExV2 [5]). The main difference between the two versions is that timers are polled continuously after each execution of a callback in ExV1, while in ExV2, timers are polled after all the callbacks from the previous polling instance have finished their execution. Specifically, in ExV2, timers are polled together with any other types of callbacks.

2.2 Timed Automata and UPPAAL

In this subsection, we introduce the formal definitions of Timed Automata (TA) and the semantics as well as a TA-based model checker UPPAAL. In the interest of space, we refer to the literature [2,9] for detailed and precise introduction of these concepts. Understanding the theory of Timed Automata and the mechanism of model checking in UPPAAL is not required for this work.

Definition 1. *A Timed Automaton (TA) [2] is a tuple:*

$$\mathcal{A} = < L, l_0, C, \Sigma, E, Inv >, \tag{1}$$

where L is a finite set of locations, l_0 is the initial location, C is a finite set of non-negative real-valued variables called clocks, Σ is a finite set of actions, $E \subseteq L \times \mathcal{B}(C) \times \Sigma \times 2^C \times L$ is a finite set of edges, where $\mathcal{B}(C)$ is the set of guards over C, that is, conjunctive formulas of constraints of the form $c_1 \bowtie n$ or $c_1 - c_2 \bowtie n$, where $c_1, c_2 \in C$, $n \in \mathbb{N}$, $\bowtie \in \{<, \leq, =, \geq, >\}$, 2^C is a set of clocks in C that are reset on the edge, and $Inv : L \rightarrow \mathcal{B}(C)$ is a partial function assigning invariants to locations. □

Definition 2. *Let $< L, l_0, C, \Sigma, E, Inv >$ be a TA. Its semantics is defined as a* labelled transition system *$< S, s_0, \rightarrow >$, where $S \in L \times \mathbb{R}^C$ is a set of states, $s_0 = (l_0, u_0)$ is the initial state, and $\rightarrow \subseteq S \times (\mathbb{R}_{\geq 0} \cup \Sigma) \times S$ such that:*

1. *delay transition: $(l, u) \xrightarrow{d} (l, u \oplus d)$, where $d \in \mathbb{R}_{\geq 0}$, and $u \oplus d$ is a new evaluation of clocks such that $\forall d' \leq d, u \oplus d' \models Inv(l)$, and*
2. *action transition: $(l, u) \xrightarrow{a} (l', u')$, if there exists $e = (l, g, a, r, l') \in E$ such that $u \in g$, $u' = [r \mapsto 0]u$ is a new evaluation of clocks that resets $c \in r$ and keeps $c \in C \setminus r$ unchanged, and $u' \models Inv(l')$.* □

UPPAAL [9] is a tool that supports modeling, simulation, and model checking of an extension of TA (*UTA*). In UPPAAL, UTA are modeled as *templates* (see Fig. 2) that can be instantiated. UTA extends TA with data variables, synchronization channels, urgent and committed locations, etc. In UPPAAL, UTA can be composed in parallel as a *network* of UTA (NUTA) synchronized via *channels*.

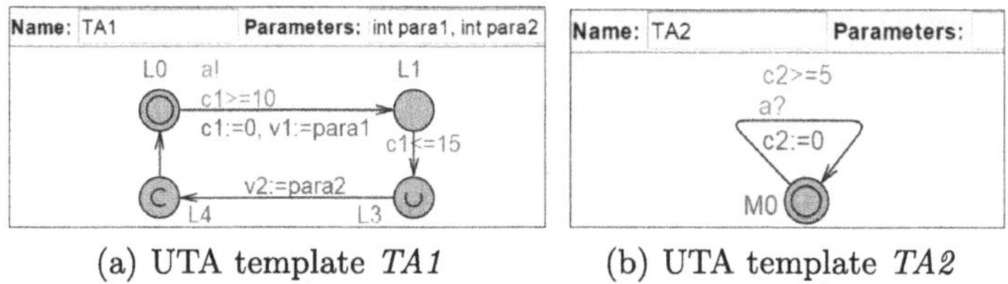

(a) UTA template *TA1* (b) UTA template *TA2*

Fig. 2. An example of UTA templates in UPPAAL

Figure 2 depicts an example of a NUTA in UPPAAL, where blue circles are *locations* that are connected by directional *edges*. Double-circled locations are the *initial* locations (e.g. `L0`). Encircled "u" denotes *urgent* locations (e.g. `L3`), and encircled "c" denotes *committed* locations (e.g. `L4`). UTA require that time does not elapse in those two kinds of locations and committed locations are even stricter, that is, the next edge to be traversed must start from one of them. On the edges, there are assignments resetting clocks (e.g., `c1:=0`) and updating data variables (e.g., `v1:=para1`), guards (e.g., `c1` >= `10`), and synchronization channels (e.g., `a!` and `a?`). At location `L1`, an invariant `c1` <= `15` regulates that clock `c1` must never exceed 15 time units. In UPPAAL, templates of UTA can have parameters (e.g., `para1` in TA1) that are assigned values when the UTA are instantiated.

The UPPAAL queries that we verify in this paper are of the form: (i) **invariance**: `A[] p` means that for all paths, for all states in each path, `p` is satisfied, and (ii) **supremum evaluation**: `sup{con}:list` evaluates the supremum of the expressions in the `list` only when the condition (i.e., `con`) is *true*.

3 Modeling and Verification of ROS 2 Nodes in UPPAAL

In order to answer RQ1 and RQ2, this section explains our modeling approach. UPPAAL is the tool for modeling and verification in this paper. In order to derive the needed features of ROS 2 and explain the level of abstraction to understand the conducted modeling, this section starts by defining the constructs and representation of all elements that are needed for the verification of *timer blocking*, *callback latencies*, and *callback input buffer sizes* in ROS 2 systems. Furthermore, the verification should be conducted in a way that allows a simple configuring of models. Therefore, a template-based approach of modeling is followed, and the implementation of the templates is explained.

ROS 2 Feature Selection and System Abstraction. As denoted in Sect. 2.1, a ROS 2 system is composed of multiple nodes communicating with each other over different communication channels, which generates various configurations of parameters, such as buffer sizes, distribution of communication channels and Quality-of-Service (QoS) settings for the communication. Nevertheless, verification in this paper involves only a part of a ROS 2 system, which means that irrelevant components and parameters can be removed or represented as abstract elements of our formal model.

We verify three features of ROS 2 systems, that is, the *latency* and *input buffer sizes* of callbacks, respectively, and the behavior of *timer* callbacks. Next, we introduce the modeling of these three features.

- *Callback latency.* The latency of a callback describes the maximum time between the release of a callback instance and the time of completing its execution. In order to verify the latency of a callback, all components and parameters that influence its execution need to be modeled. In ROS 2, those components and parameters include the scheduling algorithm of the executor, as well as the release and execution mechanisms of all callbacks in the

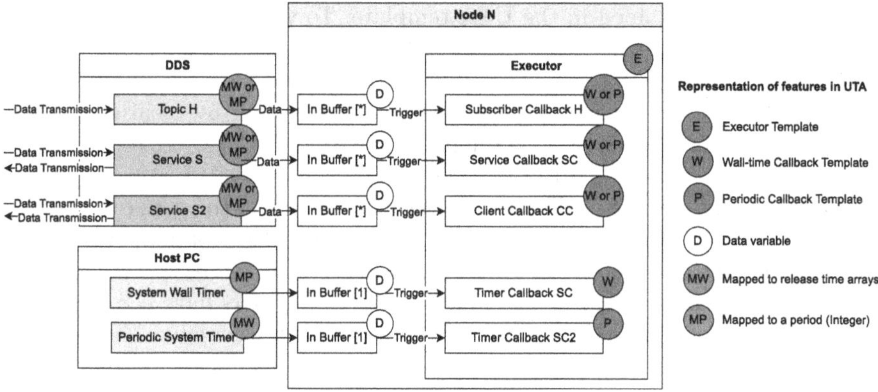

Fig. 3. Selected ROS 2 component features and their abstraction in the UTA model

same executor. Overall, in order to generalize the modeling to fit all types of callbacks, it is important to find modeling patterns that can be easily configured without changing the model. The patterns include the modeling of the callback execution, the scheduling of callbacks, which is an abstraction of the executor, and the events triggering the releases of callbacks, which are the arrival of messages and system timer events. An example of a ROS 2 node containing two timers, one subscriber, one service, and one client is shown in Fig. 3. The figure reduces components that are irrelevant to our verification of ROS 2, e.g., all sending communication channels. Attached to the corners of rectangles that represent the ROS 2 components, circles show the corresponding UTA templates. In particular, callbacks and executors are modeled as UTA templates, i.e., encircled E and W.

Specifically, every callback is released on a specific event that is unique for that callback. The event can be either an arrival of data in the input buffer of the callback or an event triggered by an active system timer, called timer event. The arrival of data is dependent on the execution of the sending nodes, which are not included in our verification. Instead, we model the arrival times as integers or multiple parameters of UTA templates, depending on the frequency. Concretely, for representing the periodically arriving data, it is sufficient to pass the length of the period as a parameter of the UTA template of callbacks. Sporadically arriving data can be modeled as an array of integers representing the specified arrival times relative to the global time. Therefore, only two different templates of callbacks are needed. Other specifications that are callback specific and that influence the scheduling and execution are passed as parameters to the UTA template of that particular callback. Such parameters include the type, the ID, and the execution time of a callback. Only the execution time but not the function of a callback is relevant, as the ROS 2 features that we select for verification do not concern the functions of callbacks. Furthermore, the input buffer of a callback also affects its execution and is contained in the UTA template. To verify callback latency, we also need to model the executors of ROS 2. Since there are two versions of the single-threaded executor, we need to design the model to allow simple switching between these two versions. This is achieved by creating a UTA template for each version accordingly. Furthermore, the UTA templates of the callbacks are designed to work with both templates.

- *Callback input buffer size.* The second verification goal of the paper is to verify if the designated input buffer size is sufficient for the data communication and scheduling of callbacks. In the UTA templates of the callbacks, the size of a buffer is passed as an input parameter. Note that timers have a fixed buffer size, which is one, while other callbacks' buffer sizes are configurable. In UTA, we model the actual utilization of a buffer as a counter instead of modeling the buffer itself. From the perspective of verification, actual data in the buffer is irrelevant, but the utilization of the buffer matters. When a callback is released, it is inserted into a buffer, waiting for being scheduled. In our UTA, the corresponding variable of buffer utilization increases, representing the callback being inserted into the buffer. At the beginning of each instance of execution of the callback, the variable is decreased, representing removing the callback instance from the buffer. Therefore, the counter always represents the actual number of elements in the buffer at any point during execution. This allows to perform queries to check if a specific utilization is reached during execution.
- *Timer behavior.* ROS 2 timer callbacks have the highest priority of all callback groups. Nevertheless, the buffer size is statically set to one and cannot be changed by users. This means that, if a timer is released two times before it is executed once, an overflow occurs, where one instance of execution is skipped. In ExV1 (Executor Version 1), timers are considered for scheduling after each callback execution. Therefore, the maximum blocking time of callbacks is the sum of execution time of its previous callback and higher priority timers. In ExV2, timers are only considered for scheduling when all callbacks polled before it have finished their execution, leading the worst-case blocking time to be the sum of the execution time of all callbacks in the system and plus the execution time of timers that have higher priority. Therefore, ExV2 is more vulnerable to blocking, leading to buffer overflow and skipped timer instances. Nevertheless, instance misses caused by buffer overflow can still occur in ExV1. The overflow detection for buffers, which we model in the UTA callback templates, can be used to detect such instance misses.

To summarize, to model and perform verification on latency and buffer sizes for callbacks, only two types of callback templates and an executor model template are needed. The following sections show the modeling approach of the callback and the executor templates.

Modeling of Callbacks. As stated in the previous section, our model consists of two UTA templates representing callbacks. The first UTA template models the periodic callbacks. The second UTA template models sporadic callbacks released at specified time points defined in an array. In the following, the general model for both types is derived, and later, the differences in the templates are presented. A simplified version of the UTA templates for the periodic and sporadic callback is presented in Fig. 4, where guards, updates, and invariants are partially shown[1] Generally, each callback type has four components, the `Waiting`, `Released`, `InReadySet` and execution components, represented by the blue boxes in Fig. 4. The initial location is location `Waiting`. The callback is not ready to be scheduled at that location, as it is waiting for an event to arise, which triggers the callback. At location `Released`, the triggering event has occurred, and the callback is ready to be polled by the executor, meaning that it is to be scheduled. This polling is modeled as an edge from location `Released` to location `InReadySet`, labeled by a broadcast channel `poll` that synchronizes the callback UTA with the executor UTA. Traversing this edge models ROS 2's behavior of including a callback into the so-called ready set in the executor. The executor only considers callbacks included in such a ready set for scheduling. A callback being scheduled is modeled by the edge from `InReadySet` to `StartExecution`, where the execution component of the UTA template starts.

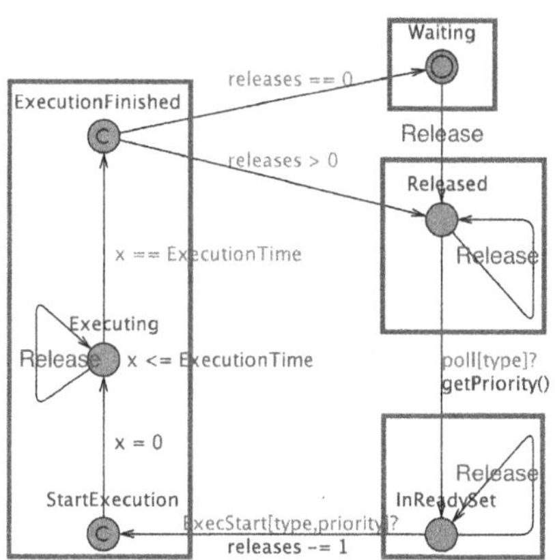

Fig. 4. UTA template overview representing callbacks.

A callback being executed is modeled as the execution component of the UTA template. The component contains three locations for the sake of facilitating the verification. Location `StartExecution` is where the execution starts. At location `Executing` and its outgoing edge to `ExecutionFinished`, we have an invariant and a guard, respectively, meaning that the callback model is forced to stay at location `Executing` for `ExecutionTime` long. This models the execution time of the callback. Finally, the execution finishes when the UTA can go back to location `Waiting` or location `Released`, depending on the availability of releases.

The type of callback is essential for the scheduling of callbacks. Therefore, the callback type is passed as an input parameter to the template. Furthermore, the priority of a callback is important to determine the execution order among all other callbacks of the same type. The priority is determined by the callback registration time, where the earliest registered callback has the highest priority. In our model, priorities are passed to the callback template as input parameters, where 0 is the highest priority, representing the callback that is initialized first. Priorities must be unique within each group with the same type of callbacks.

[1] The complete model is published: https://sites.google.com/view/pbvros2nodes.

To check the utilization of the input buffer of callbacks, the UTA contains an integer named *releases* representing the number of elements contained in the buffer that stores callback instances. With a model parameter representing the maximum buffer size, those two elements are sufficient to model the input buffer of a callback. When a callback instance is released, the callback input buffer is checked before the instance is stored in a buffer and waiting for being scheduled. When the number of instances waiting in the buffer exceeds the maximum buffer size, an overflow happens. Our verification of the buffer size checks whether the value of *releases* ever exceeds the maximum buffer size. Therefore, a designated boolean variable *NoOverflow*, true by default, is set to false when an overflow occurs. Therefore, it can be used as a property in the verification, indicating buffer overflow, and generating counterexamples of cases where an overflow occurs.

In the callback UTA (Fig. 4), every location has a self-loop edge because a new instance of a callback can be released at any point during the life cycle of an existing callback. We label the self-loop edges with red `Release` statements. The `Release` edges are guarded by the next releasing time, meaning that callbacks can only be released when the releasing time comes. While transferring via the `Release` edge, the variable *releases* is increased, representing the filling of the buffer, and the subsequent release time is calculated. Furthermore, a timer, specific to the instance and contained in the array *ReleaseTimers* is reset.

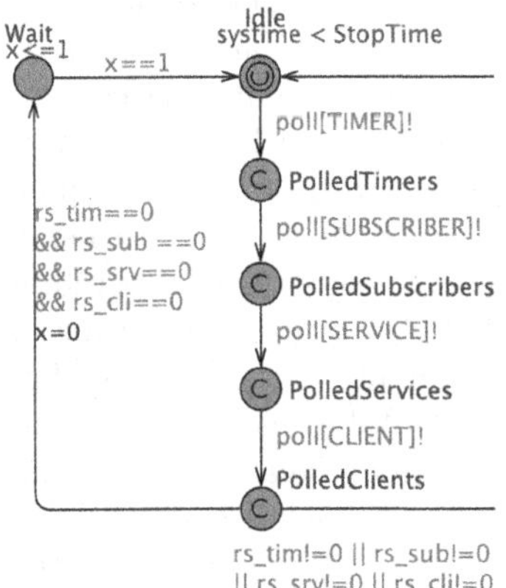

Fig. 5. UTA template extract showing the polling of callbacks in the executor

ROS 2 Executor. The executor model is needed to schedule the callbacks following the ROS 2 executor algorithm. As explained in Sect. 2.1, two versions (ExV1 and ExV2) of the single-threaded executor exist, which are specific to ROS 2 distributions. The executor versions differ in their approach to polling callbacks. Both executors are provided as a template in this section so that the executor can be chosen in later systems configurations by instantiating the template of the desired version.

In both versions of the executor, the model consists of two main components. The idle component presented in Fig. 5 is valid for both versions of the executor. The execution component differs between ExV1 (Fig. 6(a)) and ExV2 (Fig. 6(b)). In the Idle component in Fig. 5, at initial location `Idle`, we have an invariant constraining the system time and the UTA input parameter *StopTime*. This invariant forces a deadlock after reaching the stop time and is used to reduce the model's state space. When reaching location `Idle` in Fig. 5, both executors use broadcast channels to poll the released callbacks. One broadcast channel is used for each callback type, where the final locations are committed for the polling not be interrupted. Global variables are included in the model to track the number of released callbacks for each type. The variables are increased by each released callback that is using the polling channel (*rs_tim*, *rs_sub*, *rs_srv*, *rs_cli*). If all sets are zero after the polling, the UTA goes to location `Wait`. At location `Wait` and its outgoing edge to `Idle`, we use an invariant and a guard, respectively, meaning that the callback model is forced to stay at location `Wait` for one time unit. That allows the model to progress in time while the executor is idle.

After the polling of all callbacks (location `PolledClients`), if any of the sets is not zero, the UTA continues with the execution component. The execution component is shown in Fig. 6(a) for ExV1 and in Fig. 6(b) for ExV2. In the execution component of both versions of the executor, the execution of callbacks is performed, ordered by the group and the priorities of callbacks. Timers are executing first, followed by subscribers, services, and clients. This is modeled by the executor component starting at location `FetchTimer`. At this location, if any timer is contained in *rs_tim* the synchronized channel `ExecStart` is used to model the beginning of the execution of a callback. The implemented channel logic only allows one callback (of the corresponding type) at a time to use the channel. The order is determined by the priority of the callback. Triggered by the callback UTA, in ExV1 (Fig. 6(a)), once the execution time has passed, the channel `ExecDone` is decreasing *rs_tim*. The target location is leading to another channel `poll[TIMER]` that performs the polling of timers only, leading back to location `FetchTimer`. In ExV2 (Fig. 6(b)), once the execution time has passed, the channel `ExecDone` leads back to `FetchTimer` immediately, such that no polling of timers is carried out. When *rs_tim* is empty, the next group is executed following the same process. In ExV1, if the variable *rs_tim* is increased under the polling of timers, the UTA goes back to `FetchTimer` in order to execute the obtained timer first.

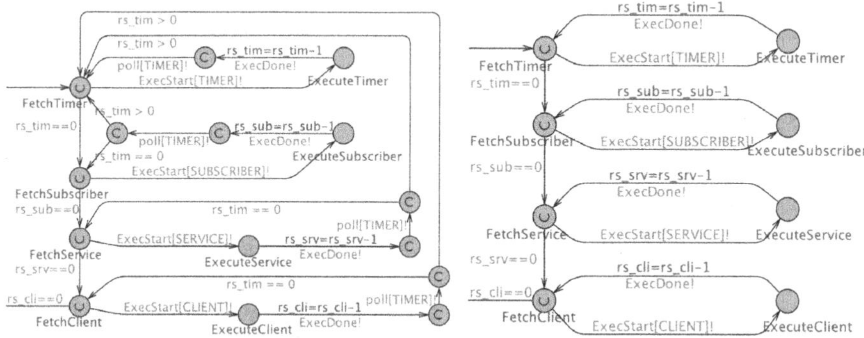

(a) UTA template extract showing the execution component of ExV1

(b) UTA template extract showing the execution component of ExV2

Fig. 6. Execution component of the executor UTA templates

System Declaration. When modeling a ROS 2 node, the created UTA templates are instantiated in the system declaration. Every system model consists of one executor and one or many callbacks. In our system model, assigning the executor the lowest priority of all system components is essential to generate the right results and allow progression in time while the executor remains idle.

Verification. To simplify the verification of occurring buffer overflow, the model of each callback contains the variable `NoOverflow`, which is true as long as no overflow occurs. Hence the absence of a buffer overflow is confirmed when the following invariance holds, where `cb` stands for any callback in our UTA model, and A[] means for all states in every possible path:

```
A[] cb.NoOverflow
```
(2)

A buffer overflow is always equivalent to a missed callback instance. Furthermore, it can be verified if a specified amount of releases in the buffer of any callback is reached at any time during execution. This is achieved by checking the variable `releases`, as shown in the following example query (Query (3)). Nevertheless, given the model implementation approach, the value of the variable `releases` will never exceed the defined buffer size. Hence, only values smaller than the configured parameter `bufferSize` can be verified using that approach, showing if a smaller buffer size would be sufficient.

```
A[] cb.releases <= 5
```
(3)

When the query passes, the buffer of the verified size (e.g., 5 in Query (3)) is sufficient, and the buffer size can be adapted.

The latency of a callback is defined as the maximum time from the release of any instance of a callback until the end of execution of that specific instance. The latency of any callback instance can be determined by reading the value of the instance-specific timer contained in `ReleaseTimers` at location `ExecutionFinished`. Using the following supremum evaluation in UPPAAL, the longest latency of a callback is determined.

```
sup{cb.ExecutionFinished}:cb.releaseTimers[cb.instance]
```
(4)

4 Evaluation of Pattern-Based Verification

To evaluate the proposed model templates, we compare the simulation and verification of the model to system traces gained by system execution. The evaluation is performed on two scenarios of ROS 2 message passing between two nodes, utilizing the ROS 2 system shown in Fig. 1. The first scenario (SC1) focuses on sporadic callbacks only, while the second scenario (SC2) combines sporadic and periodic callbacks. In SC2, using ExV2, a buffer overflow occurs, leading to instance misses. The experimental system and the scenario composition are explained briefly, followed by the comparison of model-based verification with the execution trace of one system execution.

Experimental System. The experimental ROS 2 system (Fig. 1) consists of two nodes that communicate. `Node0` is the control node used to control the experiment by sending sequences of messages and service requests to `Node1` at the defined times, and `Node1` is the system under verification. Communication channels are named after the priority of the callback in `Node1`, which they belong to. The topics are called *H, M, L* (High, Medium, Low) and services *SH, SM, and SL* (Service High, Service Medium, Service Low), respectively. Furthermore, one control topic exists to control the experiment by setting the timers in `Node1`. Each callback in `Node1` is programmed to execute 500 ms, for simplifying evaluation. Moreover, each callback records its execution information in the ROS 2 log when execution is started and finished. By using this information, we can compare the execution trace of our model to the actual execution of callbacks in a real ROS 2 system. The system is set up on a single computer using docker to create a controlled environment and enable simple switching among the different ROS 2 distributions. The selected distributions for the experiments are ROS 2 *Dashing* (the last distribution that contains ExV1), *Eloquent* (the first distribution that contains ExV2), and *Humble* (the latest long time stable distribution that contains ExV2). In this evaluation, each scenario comprises different message sequences. The specific sequences and the resulting execution traces from one actual execution are shown in the following.

Scenario 1 (SC1): Sporadic-Callbacks. The first scenario is taken from the experimental evaluation of the scheduling algorithm of ExV1 conducted in Casini et al. [7]. The scenario utilizes four timers, three subscribers, and three services. All callbacks in `Node1` can be modeled as sporadic callback UTA, each executing a defined number of times. This scenario transmits two message sequences (*S0, S1*). The first sequence *S0* is released at time 0, triggering the following callbacks: *<L; M; H; SH; SL; L; M; H; SH; SL>*. The second sequence *S1* triggers $< SM; SM;\ H >$ and is sent at 1.5 s. Timers T0 and T1 are configured to release after 0.2 s, while T1 and T2 release after 2.3 s. Figure 7 shows the resulting execution traces when executing the scenario with ExV1 and ExV2. There are significant differences in execution. After timers are released (e.g., T0 and T1), ExV1 (upper trace) schedules them immediately after the execution of the cur-

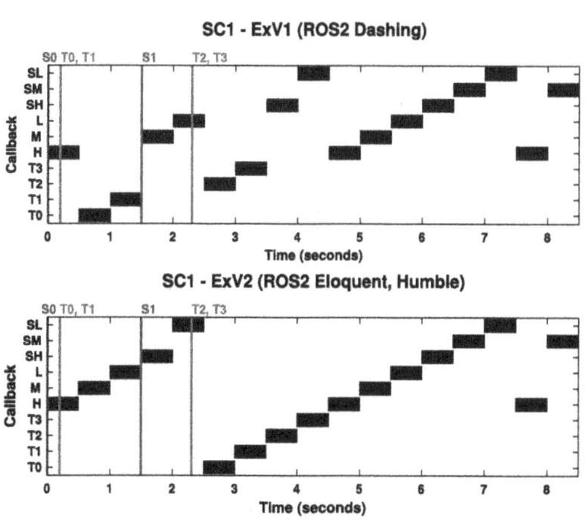

Fig. 7. Execution diagram of Node1 executing SC1 on different ROS 2 distributions. Sequence releases are marked in blue and releases of timers in red.

rent callback, whereas ExV2 (bottom trace) schedules timers after all the callbacks remaining in the ready set are finished.

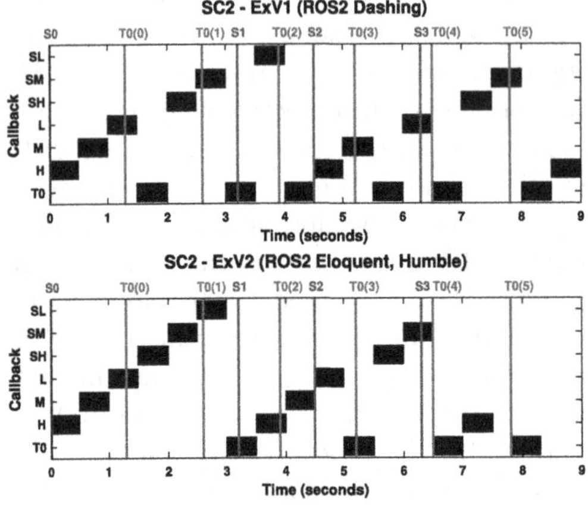

Fig. 8. Execution diagram of Node1 executing SC2 on different ROS 2 distributions. Sequence releases are marked in blue and releases of timers in red.

Scenario 2 (SC2): Periodic Timer and Buffer Overflow. SC2 utilizes only one timer (`T0`) in `Node1`, releasing periodically every 1.3 s. Four sequences (*S0, S1, S2, S3*) are contained in SC2. *S0* is released at time 0, triggering the following callbacks in `Node1`: $< H; M; L; SH; SM; SL >$. *S1* at 3.2 s triggers $< H; M; L >$. *S2* is released at 4.5 s, triggering $< SH; SM >$ followed by *S3* triggering $< H >$ at 6.3 s. Figure 8 shows the resulting execution traces of one real execution. Differences in execution can be seen. For SC2-ExV2, it is visible that even though the timer `T0` is released six times during the experiment, only four instances are executed. This is caused by the timer getting blocked over consecutive releases and the input buffer overflowing. In SC2-ExV1, instead, `T0` is executed for every release instance and is scheduled during the next scheduling action after its release.

UPPAAL Model Configuration. The proposed UTA templates are instantiated to model the created scenarios. For example, to model the execution of `Node1`, the model must contain one executor and all included callbacks. An excerpt of instantiated templates can be found in Tab. 1. The initialization of callbacks `H` and `T0` are shown. Release time arrays and other variables such as *releasesH* and *StopTime* are declared at the beginning of the system configuration. The given example shows the initialization of ExV1. One time step in the created model is chosen to be equivalent to 100 ms, as it is the greatest common divisor of all release and execution times. Sporadic callbacks are instantiated with the following parameters: the ID, the execution time (5, representing 500 ms), the number of releases in the scenario, the release times, the type of callback, and the buffer size. The passed parameters to

Table 1. Excerpt from the UPPAAL system configuration for SC2 instantiated system

```
H = WallTimeCallback(0, 5, 3, releasesH, SUBSCRIBER,10);
T0 = PeriodicCallback(0, 5, 13, TIMER, 0, 1);
ExecV1 = ExecutorV1(StopTime);
system ExecV1 < H, M, L, SH, SM, SL, T0;
```

the periodic timer `T0` are the ID, the execution time (5 for 500 ms), the period (13 for 1.3 s), the type, the initial release (0 for not released at initialization), and a constant one as the buffer size.

System Simulation in UPPAAL. The symbolic simulator in UPPAAL generates random traces of the model. An excerpt from such a trace can be found in Fig. 9, where timer `T0` is executed. The simulated traces are compared to the traces of the actual execution, out of which one crucial finding emerges. In the execution of ExV1 in SC2, there can be a deviation between the simulation and the trace of the actual execution. In some cases, the order of execution of one instance of callback `SH` and `T0` changes compared to the actual execution.

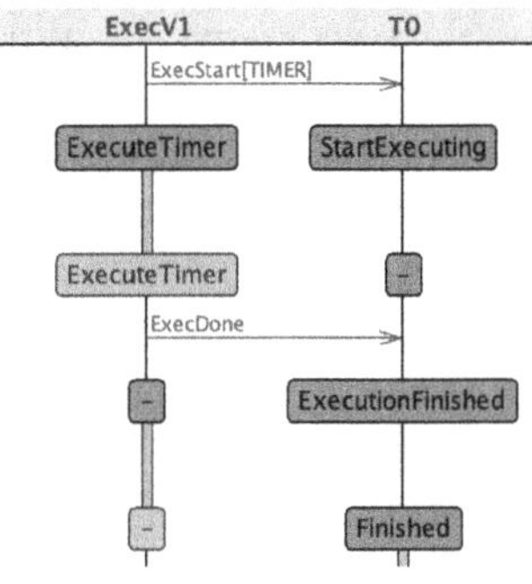

Fig. 9. A part of the UPPAAL simulation trace of ExecV1 and T0

This is because some transitions, such as releases, which occur independently from the scheduling of callbacks in ROS 2, may be running in parallel with the execution of other callbacks and influence the execution order nondeterministically. Therefore, the scheduling outcome differs depending on the action that the model takes first. As the experiments using the actual execution are not exhaustive, only one of all possible paths is obtained is this case. The difference between the simulation and the actual execution result shows the model's usefulness in determining worst-case scenarios. During verification, all possible paths are considered in the model. Nevertheless, it is possible to fix the execution order at the model level, by prioritizing the UTA of `T0` over the other callback UTAs in UPPAAL. This impacts the execution order in the model so that `T0` always executes before `SH`. Hence, prioritizing T0 can make the UTA model only reflect the observed real execution.

Verification of Buffer Sizes. In order to verify buffer sizes for detecting buffer overflow, the model contains a Boolean variable for each callback, which turns true when a buffer overflow occurs. Now, we define CTL queries in UPPAAL for verification. Examples of the queries and results in UPPAAL can be found in Fig. 10. It can be seen that a buffer overflow is detected in timer `T0` (i.e., the first query is unsatisfied). In general, all verification results correspond to the actual execution. To refine and verify specific buffer sizes that are smaller than the configured buffer size in the model, we design queries containing specific numbers of buffer sizes. For example, the last two queries in Fig. 10 check whether the buffer of callback H always contains less than two, and less than one element, respectively.

Overview

```
A[] T0.NoOverflow
A[] H.NoOverflow

A[] H.releases < 2
A[] H.releases < 1
```

Fig. 10. Example of queries verifying buffer overflow and utilization

Verification of Latencies. In order to find out the latency of a callback, the created array with the release times of each instance of a callback is utilized, and a query that searches for the highest possible value of the time elapsed from release time to the end of the execution for each callback is generated. It is essential to notice that the model disregards instances missed due to a buffer overflow, only showing the latency for executed callbacks. Therefore, it is always essential to check for buffer overflow as well. Furthermore, for periodic callbacks, buffer overflow is also determinable by the latency being higher than one period plus the execution time. During this evaluation, we calculate the latency of each callback using the model and compare the results to the extracted latencies from the actual execution (Fig. 7 and Fig. 8). The results from the model and the actual execution can be found in Tab. 2. The table shows that for all callbacks, the latency is the same as in the actual execution, except in ExV1 for T0 (marked in red). This is related to the possibility of one timer instance executing after the SH callback, and UPPAAL calculating the latencies of all possible executions.

Table 2. Comparison of determined latencies

	SCENARIO 1				SCENARIO 2			
	ExV1		ExV2		ExV1		ExV2	
Callback	Uppaal	Real	Uppaal	Real	Uppaal	Real	Uppaal	Real
SL	7.5	7.5	7.5	7.5	4.0	4.0	3.0	3.0
SM	7.0	7.0	7.0	7.0	3.5	3.5	2.5	2.5
SH	6.5	6.5	6.5	6.5	3.0	3.0	2.0	2.0
L	6.0	6.0	6.0	6.0	3.3	3.3	1.8	1.8
M	5.5	5.5	5.5	5.5	2.3	2.3	1.3	1.3
H	6.5	6.5	6.5	6.5	2.7	2.7	1.2	1.2
T0	0.8	0.8	2.8	2.8	1.0	0.9	2.2	2.2
T1	1.3	1.3	3.3	3.3	–	–	–	–
T2	0.7	0.7	1.7	1.7	–	–	–	–
T3	1.2	1.2	2.2	2.2	–	–	–	–

Answer to the Research Questions. Based on the experimental evaluation of our method, we answer the research questions as follows:

RQ1: Given the two behavioral semantics of single-threaded executors in ROS 2, how to ensure the correctness of a design of ROS 2-based systems with respect to the behaviour of timer callbacks, callback latency, and the sizes of input buffers of callbacks?

Answer: In this work, we apply formal modeling and model checking to verify callback latency and input buffer sizes. Utilizing pattern-based verification, we simplify the modeling process by creating templates for callbacks and executors that can be used to model any ROS 2 node.

RQ2: What are the patterns for modeling ROS 2 systems, which can be reused in verification?

Answer: A selection of essential features matching the verification goal is chosen during the creation of the formal models. The communication and execution of other nodes in the processing chain can be abstracted away and represented through release times of callbacks. Generally, any callback can be modeled as a periodic or a sporadic callback with defined releases. Other parameters, such as the type of callback, execution time, and priority, are parameters passed to the template. Callback input buffers can be represented as counters, where buffer size can be configured for callbacks triggered by communication, and set to one for timer callbacks. The data sent in the communication is irrelevant to the verification outcome. Two executor templates can be used to model ExV1 and ExV2, as both can execute the callback templates. The validity of the patterns is shown by comparing the simulation traces of the model and actual system execution.

RQ3: Can model checking find the errors of ROS 2 systems, which are shown in experiments, but also reveal potential errors that are not discovered via experimental evaluation?

Answer: Via a comparison between model-based calculated latencies and experimental results on a real system, we conclude that the model-based verification delivers the same results as the experiments. Furthermore, UPPAAL explores all possible execution scenarios. Therefore, model checking can find potential errors in ROS 2 systems that are not discovered in experiments.

5 Related Work

The response time analysis for callbacks in a node using the single-threaded executor and reservation-based scheduling has been proposed by Blass et al. [5], who assume the executor model that includes timers as part of the ready set; next, Tang et al. [15] look into the same problem yet using the executor model with timers being excluded from the ready set. Both works are significant for the research that we present in this paper, and the experiments conducted repeatedly show the differences in the revised executor model.

Formal verification of the communication and computation aspects of ROS 2 has gained significant attention in recent years. Halder et al. [8] propose an approach to model and verify the ROS 2 communication between nodes, using UPPAAL. Similar to our approach, the authors consider low-level parameters, such as queue sizes and timeouts, in their TA models, to verify queue overflow, yet they do not consider callback latency verification and do not take into account the two models of ROS 2 single-threaded executors. Moreover, the work does not validate the formal models as we do in our work by using the results of simulation experiments.

Carvalho et al. [6] present a model-checking technique to verify message-passing system-wide safety properties, based on a formalization of ROS launch configurations and loosely specified behaviour of individual nodes, by employing an Alloy extension called Electrum and its Analyzer. The Electrum models are automatically created from configurations extracted in continuous integration and specifications provided by the domain experts. The approach focuses on a high-level architectural-level verification of message passing, whereas our work focuses on a lower-level model checking of the scheduling of single-threaded executors assuming two kinds of timer semantics as found in different distributions of ROS 2. Webster et al. [17] propose a formal verification approach of industrial robotic programs using the SPIN model checker, focusing on behavioral refinement and verification of selected robot requirements. The solution is applied to an existing personal robotic system, it is not ROS-specific, and focuses only on the verification of high-level decision-making rules.

Anand and Knepper [3] present ROSCoq, a Coq framework for developing certified systems in ROS, which involves the use of CoRN's theory of constructive real analysis to reason about computations with real numbers. This work adopts a "correct-by-construction" approach, a different yet complementary approach to ours. However, we verify various timers scheduling mechanisms found in ROS 2 distributions, which is not within the scope of the mentioned work.

6 Conclusions and Future Work

In this paper, we introduce and demonstrate the application of pattern-based verification in the context of distributed robotic systems. We create UTA templates for modeling ROS 2 callback execution, allowing pattern-based verification of latencies, buffer overflow, and buffer utilization. Our UTA templates cover two kinds of callbacks and all existing versions of the single-threaded executor in ROS 2. All callbacks in ROS 2 systems using the single-threaded executors can be modeled by those templates. Finally, we show how verification of latencies and input buffer overflow can be performed in two scenarios and compare the verification results with the experimental results of actual system execution. The comparison shows that model checking is able to find potential system errors that might be overlooked by experiments. The verification produces counterexamples, which are infeasible configurations of the system. The models only include the scheduling of ROS 2, assuming 100 percent availability of a system thread in the underlying operating system for the executor module. Detected infeasible configurations remain when fewer resources are available in the underlying OS. Nevertheless, feasible designs in the model may not be feasible in a real system when limited system resources are available to the ROS 2 thread.

The model allows future refinements and improvements, including more system parameters, such as offsets for periodic callbacks, communication latencies, and jitter. In ROS 2, even multi-threaded executors exist for the callbacks, which are not considered in this paper and might become the object of future modeling. In general, the modeling proposed in this paper can be considered a first step towards pattern-based verification in the context of distributed robotic systems using ROS 2.

Acknowledgments. We acknowledge the support of the Swedish Knowledge Foundation via the profile DPAC - Dependable Platform for Autonomous Systems and

Control, grant nr: 20150022, the synergy ACICS - Assured Cloud Platforms for Industrial Cyber-Physical Systems, grant nr. 20190038, and HERO - Heterogeneous systems – software-hardware integration, grant nr: 20180039.

References

1. Albonico, M., Dordevic, M., Hamer, E., Malavolta, I.: Software engineering research on the robot operating system: a systematic mapping study. J. Syst. Softw. **197**(C) (2023). https://doi.org/10.1016/j.jss.2022.111574
2. Alur, R., Dill, D.L.: A theory of timed automata. Theoret. Comput. Sci. **126**, 183–235 (1994)
3. Anand, A., Knepper, R.: ROSCoq: robots powered by constructive reals. In: Urban, C., Zhang, X. (eds.) ITP 2015. LNCS, vol. 9236, pp. 34–50. Springer, Cham (2015). https://doi.org/10.1007/978-3-319-22102-1_3
4. Baheti, R., Gill, H.: Cyber-physical systems. Impact Control Technol. **12**(1), 161–166 (2011)
5. Blaß, T., Casini, D., Bozhko, S., Brandenburg, B.B.: A ros 2 response-time analysis exploiting starvation freedom and execution-time variance. In: IEEE Real-Time Systems Symposium, pp. 41–53. IEEE (2021)
6. Carvalho, R., Cunha, A., Macedo, N., Santos, A.: Verification of system-wide safety properties of ROS applications. In: 2020 IEEE/RSJ International Conference on Intelligent Robots and Systems (IROS) (2020)
7. Casini, D., Blaß, T., Lütkebohle, I., Brandenburg, B.: Response-time analysis of ros 2 processing chains under reservation-based scheduling. In: 31st Euromicro Conference on Real-Time Systems, pp. 1–23 (2019)
8. Halder, R., Proença, J., Macedo, N., Santos, A.: Formal verification of ROS-based robotic applications using timed-automata. In: 2017 IEEE/ACM 5th International FME Workshop on Formal Methods in Software Engineering (FormaliSE), pp. 44–50 (2017)
9. Hendriks, M., et al.: Uppaal 4.0. In: Third International Conference on the Quantitative Evaluation of Systems - (QEST 2006) (2006)
10. OpenRobotics: Ros : Distributions (2023). http://wiki.ros.org/Distributions
11. OpenRobotics: Ros 2: Distributions (2023). https://docs.ros.org/en/humble/Releases
12. OpenRobotics: Ros 2: Documentation (2023). https://docs.ros.org/en/humble
13. Quigley, M., et al.: Ros: an open-source robot operating system. In: ICRA Workshop on Open Source Software, vol. 3, p. 5. Kobe, Japan (2009)
14. Rajkumar, R., Lee, I., Sha, L., Stankovic, J.: Cyber-physical systems: the next computing revolution. In: Proceedings of the 47th Design Automation Conference, pp. 731–736 (2010)
15. Tang, Y., et al.: Response time analysis and priority assignment of processing chains on ros2 executors. In: IEEE Real-Time Systems Symposium, pp. 231–243 (2020)
16. Teper, H., Günzel, M., Ueter, N., von der Brüggen, G., Chen, J.J.: End-to-end timing analysis in ros2. In: 2022 IEEE Real-Time Systems Symposium (RTSS), pp. 53–65 (2022)
17. Webster, M., et al.: Toward reliable autonomous robotic assistants through formal verification: a case study. IEEE Trans. Hum.-Mach. Syst. **46**(2), 186–196 (2016)

Configurable Model-Based Test Generation for Distributed Controllers Using Declarative Model Queries and Model Checkers

Bence Graics(✉), Vince Molnár, and István Majzik

Department of Measurement and Information Systems, Budapest University of Technology and Economics, Műegyetem rkp. 3., Budapest 1111, Hungary
{graics,molnarv,majzik}@mit.bme.hu

Abstract. Distributed programmable controllers are getting prevalence in critical infrastructure, among others, in railway interlocking systems (RIS). Generally, such systems are integrated using various reactive components and must carry out critical tasks. Accordingly, their systematic testing is vital, which can be hindered by their complexity and distributed nature. This paper presents a model-based test generation approach using hidden formal methods. It is based on the collaborating statechart models of the system components and parametric test coverage criteria configurable by declarative model queries. Statecharts can be integrated using various composition modes (e.g., synchronous and asynchronous) and then automatically mapped into the inputs of model checker back-ends, namely UPPAAL, Theta and Spin. The model checkers generate tests by traversing the emergent analysis models to cover the elements of the test model as specified by pattern-based model queries. The returned diagnostic traces are then concretized to different execution environments. The approach is implemented in our open source Gamma Statechart Composition Framework and evaluated on a distributed RIS subsystem under development.

Keywords: Model-based testing · Collaborating statecharts · Configurable parametric coverage criteria · Hidden formal methods · Tool suite

1 Introduction

Programmable controllers are becoming widespread in critical infrastructure, e.g., in railway interlocking systems (RIS), whose development has lately been shifting from relay-based solutions to electronic-based ones [32,40]. In general, such systems are integrated using various components that may communicate in different ways at different hierarchy levels (e.g., synchronously and asynchronously) while being deployed to multiple communicating computation nodes, creating a distributed architecture. In addition, these systems are generally tightly embedded into their dynamic environments and have to coordinate

A. Cimatti and L. Titolo (Eds.): FMICS 2023, LNCS 14290, pp. 76–95, 2023.
https://doi.org/10.1007/978-3-031-43681-9_5

their components extensively to carry out critical tasks in response to external commands or internal events; therefore, they are considered *reactive systems*.

The development of these systems is encumbered by their distributed and heterogeneous architecture. Thus, sound methods are required to describe both the functional behavior of standalone system components and their integration, including their execution (e.g., sequential or parallel) and communication modes (e.g., signal- or message-based using message queues with different features), while considering the selected deployment solutions. Furthermore, as these systems conduct critical tasks, the systematic testing of their implementation is essential in the development process. However, the automated testing of component interactions is typically hindered by the informal handling of their execution and communication modes, and the large size (state space) of the system, resulting in prolonged test generation time and the proliferation of test cases.

In order to alleviate these challenges, model-based and component-based systems engineering (MBSE and CBSE) [2,3,13,30,35,55] approaches promote the employment of reusable models and components defined in high-level modeling languages, such as UML or SysML. Such languages can support defining the functional behavior of system components in a platform-independent way, such as statecharts [28] to capture reactive behavior, and system structure, e.g., block diagrams to define the (potentially hierarchical) interconnection of components. Model-based testing (MBT) [58] solutions can rely on these models to derive test cases for the system implementation.

However, many MBT approaches i) are based on low-level formalisms that are difficult to use in engineering practice, ii) do not provide configuration options for the systematic specification of test targets, or iii) cannot handle industrial-scale models [38]. These deficiencies may stem from informal or unsupported model descriptions, and the lack of sound and efficient test generation techniques, e.g., due to scalability issues in the underlying algorithms and the lack of traceability and integration between the design models and test generation back-ends [19,39].

Thus, MBSE and CBSE approaches for the development and testing of distributed control systems should support i) *high-level modeling languages* with *precise semantics* to capture standalone component behavior, and *component integration* (composition) using different execution and communication modes to support necessary deployment modes, ii) *automated methods* for *systematic test generation* based on the created models, supporting various *coverage criteria* for interaction testing (e.g., model element and dataflow-based) and preferably *customization options* for focused testing, e.g., to cover special states or situations, and iii) *efficient test generation* algorithms for large-scale systems in terms of generation time and test set size – all seamlessly integrated in a single tool.

As a solution, we propose an MBT approach in our open source Gamma Statechart Composition Framework[1] [43]. It relies on a high-level *statechart language* (GSL) [23] and a *composition language* (GCL) [27] with formal semantics to capture the functional behavior of standalone system components and their interconnections using various *composition modes*. Automated model transformations

[1] More information about the framework (e.g., preprints) and the source code can be found at http://gamma.inf.mit.bme.hu/ and https://github.com/ftsrg/gamma/.

map the emergent models into input formalisms of different *model checker* back-ends, namely, UPPAAL [4], Theta [56] and Spin [31]. The mappings feature *model reduction* and *slicing* algorithms to support industrial-scale systems. The verification results are automatically back-annotated to a high-level *trace language* (GTL) [27]. Using the formal verification and back-annotation functionalities [20], the approach supports the *automated generation* of *integration tests* based on customizable *coverage criteria*. As a key feature, the approach also supports the *custom specification* of *test targets* in the form of declarative model queries in the Gamma Parametric Property Language (GPPL). Test cases are *optimized* and *concretized* to different execution environments to detect faults in component implementations (e.g., missing implementation of transitions), interactions of components, and improper variable definitions and uses.

We applied our MBT approach in the development of an electronic RIS subsystem. The specific task required two extensions to our Gamma framework: i) the *modeling* and semantic-preserving mapping of the different *deployment modes* (using global and local message queues) into the formal languages used by model checkers, and ii) the specification of *custom test targets* that capture special situations in the functional models (e.g., the combination of trap states and timeout transitions) besides general coverage criteria based testing [24,26]. Extension i) was necessary to support the modeling style and semantic choices of the industrial partner, and it leverages the flexibility of our framework in defining semantic and syntactic flavors for different input models. Extension ii) was needed to provide a similar level of flexibility in the specification of test targets.

Accordingly, the novel contributions of the paper are as follows:

1. the extension of GCL to support the flexible configuration of *message queues* among communicating components, including local, as well as shared message queues with message *demultiplexing*;
2. the extension of GPPL to support the flexible specification of *test targets* as *declarative model queries*; and
3. the *evaluation* of the extended MBT approach on a distributed RIS[2] [22] subsystem received from our industrial partner.

The rest of the paper is structured as follows. Section 2 presents background needed to understand the rest of the work. Section 3 introduces message demultiplexing to message queues for various component interactions. Section 4 extends GPPL to specify test targets using declarative model queries. Section 5 evaluates our extended MBT approach. Finally, Sects. 6 and 7 present related work and close the paper with concluding remarks and directions for future work.

2 Preliminaries

First, Sect. 2.1 presents the railway interlocking system (RIS) that motivates our work and gives a context for our presented contributions. Next, Sect. 2.2 outlines

[2] https://www.prolan.hu/en/products/PRORIS.

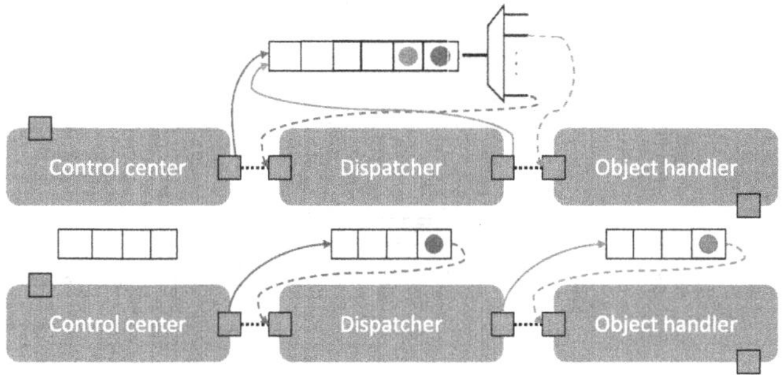

Fig. 1. Two deployment modes of the OM with a *global* and *local message* queues.

our MBT approach in the Gamma framework which we extend in this work. Finally, Sect. 2.3 overviews the query language of VIATRA that we integrate into our framework for the declarative specification of test targets.

2.1 Railway Interlocking System and its Object Manager Subsystem

The presented RIS [22] is an electronic control system, featuring a distributed component-based architecture. As a special characteristic, the communication modes of its components vary depending on their functionality and selected deployment options and thus may rely on synchronous, *signal-based* (e.g., hardware-related components deployed to the same computation node), and asynchronous, *message queue based* interactions (components deployed to different computation nodes). Accordingly, it has been developed based on *models* in accordance with the MBSE and CBSE paradigms. As the RIS conducts critical tasks, it must have a deterministic behavior to allow for verifiability. Regarding the testing of the integration of components, the safety standards (cf. EN 50128 [6]) require i) *coverage criteria based* and *integration testing* in addition to ii) the *focused testing* of safety mechanisms (e.g., handling of detected errors, communication timeouts) in the development process; all of which can be supported by our MBT approach.

This paper focuses on a critical subsystem of the RIS, called *object manager* (OM), which realizes a proprietary communication protocol (called Rigel) between the *human-computer interface* and *physical railway objects* tailored to the characteristics of the RIS. The OM model comprises three components (see Fig. 1) defined in the proprietary XSML statechart language integrated to Gamma [24], namely *control center*, *dispatcher* and *object handler*. The *control center* is responsible for the human-computer interface (receiving commands and returning status messages), the *dispatcher* handles message transmission between the other components and the *object handler* handles physical railway objects. The model's deterministic behavior is ensured by the semantics of XSML at the component level, and the specified execution and communication mode at the

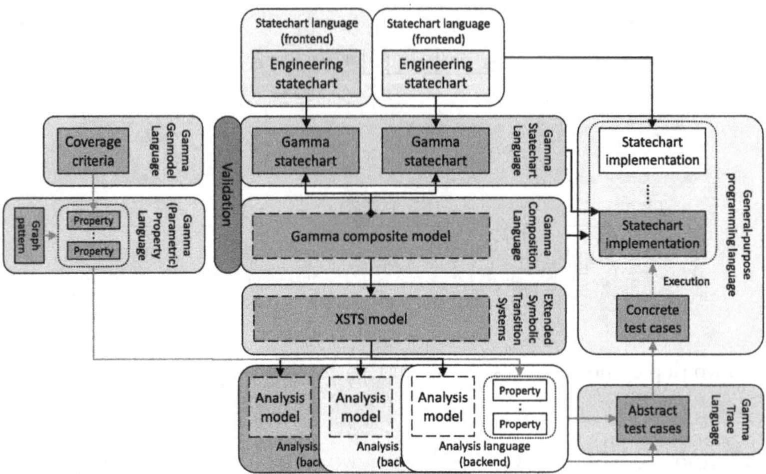

Fig. 2. Model transformation chains and modeling languages of our MBT approach in the Gamma framework.

integration level: components are executed *sequentially*, and communicate with *messages* stored in message queues; according to the topology, the *control center* and *object handler* can communicate only via the *dispatcher*. The number and application of the message queues depend on the deployment modes of the OM: in case all three components are deployed to the same computation node, they will use a *single shared* (global) message queue with some demultiplexing logic; in case a component (or all of them) is deployed to a separate node, it will use its own *local* message queue.

2.2 Component Integration and Test Generation Approach

This section first overviews the underlying *modeling languages*, which is followed by the *steps* (user activities and internal model transformations) that constitute the design and test generation phases of our MBT approach in Gamma.

- The **Gamma Statechart Language (GSL)** is a UML/SysML-based *configurable* formal statechart [28] language supporting different semantic variants of statecharts, e.g., different conflict resolution methods for enabled transitions (nondeterministic choices or priorities for transitions leaving the same state, and transitions of regions at higher/lower hierarchy level) and execution of orthogonal regions (sequential, unordered or parallel) [23].
- The **Gamma Composition Language (GCL)** is a composition language for the formal hierarchical composition of GSL components based on the *binding* of communication ports (for standardized event transmission) and their connection with *channels* [27] according to multiple *execution* and *communication* (composition) modes. GCL supports i) synchronous systems where components communicate with *sampled signals* (synchronous events) and

are executed *concurrently* (*synchronous-reactive*) or *sequentially* (*cascade*), and ii) asynchronous systems where components communicate with *queued messages* (asynchronous events) and are executed *sequentially* (*scheduled asynchronous-reactive*) [24] or *in parallel* (*asynchronous-reactive*).
- The **Gamma Genmodel Language (GGL)** is a configuration language for configuring model transformations, e.g., to select the model checker for verification or the coverage criteria for test generation.
- The **Gamma Property Language (GPL)** is a property language for the definition of CTL* [17] properties (combination of `E` and `A` quantifiers, as well as `F`, `G`, `X` and `U` temporal operators) and thus, the formal specification of requirements (e.g., state reachability) regarding component or composite component behavior. The **Gamma Parametric Property Language (GPPL)** extends GPL with *parameter declarations* in properties that can be bound to model elements based on declarative *model queries* (see Sect. 4).
- The **Gamma Trace Language (GTL)** is a high-level trace language for reactive systems to describe execution traces, i.e., reached state configurations, variable values and output events in response to input events, time lapse and scheduling from the environment organized into subsequent steps. Such execution traces are also interpretable as *abstract tests* as the language supports the specification of general assertions targeting variables.

Figure 2 depicts the modeling languages, modeling artifacts and the internal model transformations of our MBT approach in the Gamma framework. In the following, we overview the steps of the workflow's three phases, i.e., *model design*, potential *formal verification* and *test generation*; for more details regarding the formalization of the *test coverage criteria*, as well as *model reduction* and *model slicing* algorithms, we direct the reader to [26] and [24].

Model Design. The model design phase consists of three steps. As an optional step, *external component models*, i.e., statecharts created in integrated modeling tools (front-ends like Yakindu [25], MagicDraw and SCXML [46]), are *imported* to Gamma by executing model transformations that map these models into GSL statecharts. Alternatively, statecharts can be defined directly in GSL. Next, the GSL models can be *hierarchically integrated* in GCL according to different (and potentially mixed) composition modes [27].

Formal Verification. Optionally, the integrated GCL model can be *formally verified* using a sequence of *model transformations* that automatically map the model and verifiable properties (specified in GPL or GPPL) into the inputs of *model checker* back-ends, i.e., UPPAAL, Theta or Spin. The mappings are configured using GGL to select back-ends, add optional constraints (e.g., scheduling) and set model reduction and slicing algorithms [26]. The selected model checker *exhaustively explores* the state space of the model with respect to the given property and potentially returns a diagnostic trace that is *back-annotated* to the GCL model, creating a representation in GTL.

Test Generation. Implementation from the design models can be derived using the code generators of the front-ends or Gamma. *Integration tests* for the

```
pattern transitions(transition : Transition,
  source : StateNode, target : StateNode) {
 Transition.source(transition, source);
 Transition.target(transition, target);
}
pattern errorStates(state : State) {
 State.name(_state, name);
 check(name.matches(".*Error")); // Regex
}
```

```
pattern loopTransitions(loop : Transition,
  source : StateNode) {
 find transitions(loop, source, target);
 source == target; // Loop property
}
pattern trapStates(trapState : State) {
 neg find transitions(_, trapState, target);
 trapState != target;
}
```

Fig. 3. Example VIATRA (VQL) patterns for GSL models.

implementation can be *generated* based on the GCL model, utilizing the aforementioned verification facilities [20]. Test generation is driven by customizable dataflow-based, structural (model element-based) and behavior-based (interactional) *coverage criteria*, which are *formalized* as reachability properties in GPL representing *test targets*, and control the model checkers to compute *test target (criterion) covering paths* during model traversal. These paths, i.e., returned witnesses for satisfying the reachability properties, are represented as GTL execution traces and, in a testing context, are regarded as *abstract test cases* for the property based on which they are generated. *Optimization algorithms* are used to discard unnecessary tests that do not contribute to the coverage of the specified criteria [26]. The abstract tests can be concretized to execution environments (e.g., JUnit), considering the characteristics of the targeted test environment and that of the concrete implementation (i.e., signatures) of system interfaces. The test cases generate concrete calls in the environment to provide test inputs, time delay and schedule system execution, and then retrieve and evaluate outputs, this way, checking the *conformance* of the system model and implementation for these particular execution traces.

2.3 VIATRA Query Language

Our MBT approach relies on model queries for the declarative specification of test targets (based on formal properties) and their automatic exploration in GSL and GCL models. These facilities are provided by the VIATRA Query Language[3] (VQL) [59]. The language supports the high-level, declarative description of complex interrelations between model elements as graph patterns. These graph patterns are evaluated on concrete models using the query engine of VIATRA to return model elements that conform to the specified interrelations. Fig. 3 describes example patterns specifying *transitions*, *error states*, *loop transitions* and *trap states*, whose interpretation is as follows.

Model elements expected to be returned by model queries i.e., the *matches* of a pattern, are defined in the parameter list of the graph pattern. The body of a graph pattern specifies interrelations between model elements (nodes) via references (edges) based on the elements of an EMF [54] metamodel, e.g., that of GSL or GCL. In a single block, the specifications are *conjunctive*, i.e., each

[3] https://eclipse.org/viatra/.

```
adapter omGlobalQueue of component om : OM { // Wrapped component
 // Single control specification: execute once upon any incoming message
 when any / run
 // Shared global queue
 queue globalQueue(priority = 1, capacity = 6, discard = incoming) {
  controlCenterOut.rigel -> dispatcherIn.rigel, // Demultiplexing a single message
  dispatcherOut.any -> objectHandler.any, // Demultiplexing all messages of a port
  ... }
}
// Cascade composite component (CCC)
cascade OM [
 // Internal ports of the CCC
 port controlCenterIn : requires Rigel
 port controlCenterOut : provides Rigel
 ... // Additional in and out ports of other components
] {
 // Statechart components of the OM model
 component controlCenter : ControlCenter
 component dispatcher : Dispatcher
 component objectHandler : ObjectHandler
 // Binding component ports to the ports of the CCC
 bind controlCenterIn -> controlCenter.In
 bind controlCenterOut -> controlCenter.Out
 ... // Note the lack of channels
}
```

Fig. 4. OM model variant excerpt with a *shared global queue* that utilizes *message demultiplexing* (corresponding to the upper topology of Fig. 1).

specification must hold in the result set. In addition, VQL supports *disjunctive blocks* (*or* keyword), i.e., the result set of the query will be the union of the result sets of these blocks. The language also supports pattern reuse (*find* keyword) potentially in a restrictive way (*neg* keyword), i.e., the pattern cannot match, or even for computing transitive closures ($*$ and $+$ operators). Matches of reused patterns can also be counted (*count* keyword), and arbitrary boolean expressions required to hold for pattern matching can be defined using the *check* keyword.

3 Configuring Message Queues for Component Interactions

As presented in Sect. 2.2, GCL supports the formal mixed-semantic composition of reactive systems by hierarchically integrating GSL atomic statechart components. In GCL, synchronous components are the basic building blocks of composite systems. Asynchronous components are created from simple or composite synchronous ones by wrapping them using a so-called *asynchronous adapter* [27]: an adapter maps *signals* used in the synchronous domain into *messages* and related message queues in the asynchronous domain.

Message queues of asynchronous adapters have the following attributes: *priority*, *capacity* and *message discard strategy* in case the queue is full, i.e., *oldest* message in the queue or *incoming* one is discarded. During execution, messages are retrieved from the queues *one by one*; a message is always popped from the highest priority non-empty queue. The processing of a message comprises its conversion into a signal that is transmitted to the wrapped synchronous component; the synchronous component is then executed according to the control specifications, i.e., it is i) reset, ii) executed once or iii) multiple times while the internal components generate internal signals that can be processed [27].

As a limiting factor however, there has been no support for configurable message processing in message queues to facilitate their application in different contexts, e.g., for local or shared (global) queues. In the following, we give and compare two solutions supporting global and local message queue based variants for the OM model depicted in Fig. 1.

Message Demultiplexing. In order to support shared message queues in GCL, we extend them with *message demultiplexing*, i.e., the separation and transmission of incoming messages to different ports according to an internal logic. In the context of asynchronous adapters, message demultiplexing allows for defining what signals a message is converted into during message processing.

The *omGlobalQueue* component in Fig. 4 shows an excerpt of the asynchronous adapter that wraps the OM component, and executes it once for every incoming message based on demultiplexed messages in the *globalQueue*, e.g., from the *Out* port of the *control center* to the *In* port of the *dispatcher*. Demultiplexing is defined using the -> operator in the body of a queue definition: its left hand side specifies a message type (asynchronous event received via an adapter port) the message queue stores, whereas the right hand side defines a set of signals (synchronous events via the wrapped component's port) that the message is converted into during its processing; multiple signals can be specified using & symbols. Note that the events of the left and right hand side must have parameter declarations with the same type. As syntactic sugar, GCL supports the *any* keyword to reference each event of a port. Also, the -> operator and its right hand side can be omitted if the two sides are equal.

Message demultiplexing provides configurability options for component integration and allows for capturing structure-related aspects (port connections). For example, the feature can be utilized to define a *shared* global message queue for a composite component that stores messages sent among contained components (as depicted in Fig. 4). Such a solution can be modeled featuring message demultiplexing in GCL as follows:

1. a single cascade composite component (CCC) is defined that contains every necessary component while also specifying their execution order (channels between the components are not defined);
2. the CCC declares *internal* ports for each component, i.e., ports that transform raised events into received events for inter-component communication;
3. the CCC is wrapped by an asynchronous adapter that defines a single message queue with the required attributes and message demultiplexing for the internal ports: the left hand side will contain the sender port, whereas the receivers will be on the right hand side.

Messages in Local Queues. In this case, a scheduled asynchronous-reactive composite (SARCC) model variant [24] of OM can be created that integrates separate asynchronous adapters of the corresponding component models with local message queues. As a key feature, SARCC models enable the sequential execution of contained components. Note that the main differences between the two model variants are i) the used component types (one SARCC and three asynchronous adapters in contrast to one adapter and one CCC), ii) the number of message queue definitions (one global contrasted to three local queues in the adapter models), and iii) the way port connections are defined (message demultiplexing in the global queue contrasted to channels between the ports of adapters). Naturally, the two model variants display different behaviors, stemming from the different storage and thus, processing order of the messages; even though, both OM model variants have the same number of statechart-related elements as the statechart models are not affected by the different integration solutions.

Regarding applicability, the above solutions enable the description of all deployment options relevant in GCL model compositions (thus, also in the context of the RIS presented in Sect. 2.1), in terms of the combination of components and message queues.

4 Property Specification Using Model Queries

With the primary goal of increasing the flexibility and expressive power of test target specifications, we use a declarative language, called **Gamma Parametric Property Language (GPPL)**. Instead of listing concrete model elements (with their temporal reachability), this language facilitates the identification of target model elements by specifying *model patterns* that shall be matched.

Specification of test targets using GPPL comprises the following parts:

1. the *model* (GSL statechart component or GCL composite model on the basis of which the tests are to be generated);
2. a *model query* specified by a VQL graph pattern that returns the set(s) of matching concrete model elements for the parameter(s) of the pattern;
3. a *temporal property* (in CTL*) referring to the parameter(s) of the pattern, this way, each concretization of the parameter(s) – as returned by the query in the model – will also result in a concrete temporal property that is considered as a separate test target.

For example, in the left snippet of Fig. 5, the model is the GCL model OM; the model query is specified by pattern *loopTransitions* (with parameters *loop* and *source* as shown in Fig. 3), which returns the set of loop transitions and their sources in OM; and the temporal property is `E F loop` (sharing the parameter *loop* with the graph pattern) that will result in a separate `E F <loopInstance>` test target for each loop transition instance in OM returned by the model query.

Thus, GPPL test targets do not refer directly to concrete model elements, i.e., do not list their identifiers, but enable using generic model queries (constructed based on the GSL and GCL metamodels) and parametric temporal specifications.

In the following, we overview the previous version of GPPL [26], as well as its extension, and demonstrate the extended GPPL in the context of reachability properties for error states, trap states and loop transitions in the OM model.

```
component omGlobalQueue  // Concrete model
@("$hu.bme.mit.gamma.gppl.loopTransitions")
E F parameter loop // Reachability prop.
```

```
component omGlobalQueue
@("$hu.bme.mit.gamma.gppl.trapStates")
E F parameter trapState
```

Fig. 5. GPPL reachability properties (test targets) for *loop transitions* and *trap states.*

Previous Version of GPPL. The previous version of GPPL [26] supported only the specification of interconnections between states and transitions. For state parameters, the name could be matched against regular expressions. For transition parameters, source and target references were supported; such references could be compared using equality and inequality operators. The language did not support references to variable or event declarations, disjunctive constraints, pattern reuse (potentially in a negative way) or transitive closure specification; thus, it could not be used to express e.g., trap states.

Extended GPPL. As a novelty compared to [26], we have introduced VIATRA and its query language VQL to support pattern-based model queries in GPPL. As a result, i) pattern specifications are defined independently, i.e., in separate files (supporting reusability) and are *bound* via textual pattern references, and ii) all features of VQL (see Sect. 2.3) are now available in GPPL. Regarding the syntax of GPPL specifications (see Fig. 5), the bound VQL pattern (see Fig. 3) can be given in a comment (see @ symbol) starting with a $ symbol (its package name also has to be included); the pattern must have a parameter declaration with the *same name* (identifier) for each parameter in the temporal property (see, e.g., the *loop* parameter in the GPPL property in Fig. 5 and in the *loopTransitions* VQL pattern in Fig. 3). During property concretization, the patterns are evaluated using the query engine of VIATRA and the temporal property's parameters are replaced by references to the returned model elements in the matches (set of tuples in general), creating unique GPL properties (duplications are filtered); see Fig. 6 for the concretized GPL properties specifying the reachability of trap states and loop transitions in OM's *control center* component.

As an added value of this solution, the reusability and expressive power of specifying the interrelations of model elements have increased in GPPL due to the separation of pattern descriptions and the introduction of VQL, respectively. The expressive power of VQL has been proven by its decade-long successful use in model processing and transformation applications. Model queries, based on these patterns, can find instances of the specified interrelations in a given model. VIATRA also increases the efficiency of model queries based on its incremental engine. As the property specifications (patterns and temporal expressions) are independent of any concrete model, the solution allows for the definition of generic property sets utilized in Gamma i) in various formal verification scenarios, e.g., defining *requirement templates* (different safety and liveness properties, potentially given using restricted natural language keywords like "must always," as well as "may eventually" or "leads to") that can be concretized into properties for different models, and ii) in *focused coverage-based testing* for the concise specification of test targets in our MBT approach.

This way, our open source Gamma framework offers for industrial MBT the use of *classic test targets* (state, transition, interaction and dataflow coverages), as well as unique configuration capabilities for *focused testing*: i) model structure related aspects of the test targets can be specified by means of expressive VQL patterns, while ii) behavior-related aspects of the test targets can be specified using natural language reachability templates or temporal logic operators in GPPL (as supported by the underlying model checkers).

5 Practical Evaluation

The design and verification of the RIS shall conform to safety standards, especially EN 50128, which requires (among others) thorough integration testing to check the system implementation. Thus, the need was to support testing activities by model-based test generation in an automated and efficient way, considering general coverage criteria, as well as special safety-related characteristics relevant in the context of the OM model (focused testing). Accordingly, the presented contributions are aligned with the following requirements (R) of our industrial partner:

R-1. we shall *capture* the OM in *formal models* to *verify* different deployment modes, featuring a global and local message queues (see Fig. 1); and
R-2. we shall conduct *coverage criteria based* and *integration testing*, as well as *focused testing* in regard to special (safety-related) situations.

R-1 is addressed by *message demultiplexing* in the queues of asynchronous adapters (see Sect. 3), which supports the application of shared message queues in GCL models. This new feature allows for the modeling of the OM with a single global message queue (see Fig. 4), whereas the SARCC composition mode enables the modeling of the OM with individual local queues of the components.

R-2 is addressed primarily by integrating the above features into the Gamma framework (i.e., they are supported by internal model transformations); thus, the created model variants can be used for test generation in our MBT approach. We showed the applicability of our approach on the OM model for generating integration tests based on general coverage criteria in [24], e.g., generating a test set covering all possible 387 interactions between the components in the OM model variant with local queues took nearly 90 min and resulted in 22 test cases comprising 240 steps. Test generation experiments on other models (but without the GPPL extension) were reported in [26]. For instance, test generation targeting transition and transition-pair coverage was successful for two synchronous variants of a RIS distributed railway path locking model with 110 model states, 407 transitions and 61 variables (before model reduction and slicing); in every case, test generation took less than half a minute.

Consequently, now we evaluate how our pattern-based property specification solution presented in Sect. 4 can be used for *focused testing* on both OM model variants. Note that the complete OM model consists of 22 (potentially orthogonal) regions, 38 states, 118 transitions, 10 variables and 13 clock variables.

```
component omGlobalQueue
// Loop transitions in control center
E F transition Connected_Reception_Loop_1
E F transition Connected_Reception_Loop_2
E F transition Connected_Transmission_Loop_1
```

```
component omGlobalQueue
// Trap states in control center
E F state Connecting.Connected_Reception
E F state Connecting.Connected_Transmission
```

Fig. 6. Concretized GPL properties (test targets) for *loop transitions* and *trap states.*

We consider the requirements to be satisfied if i) our solution can capture the test targets proposed by our partner using GPPL, and ii) our framework can carry out the automated test generation procedure (cover the specified model elements) using the integrated model checker back-ends in a reasonable time (less than a few hours); resulting in test cases executable on the OM implementation.

Focused Testing of OM. The test targets (TT) in the OM model specified by our partner – all of which shall be covered by test cases – and their rationale that drive focused testing are summarized as follows:

TT-1. The *dispatcher* component has *loop transitions* representing message transmission between the *central controller* and *object handler.*
TT-2. Each component has *trap states* representing the correct processing of a message sequence in the communication protocol.
TT-3. Each component has *transitions* that enter the initial states of their corresponding region representing *timeouts*, i.e., the absence of expected messages in a period in certain states.
TT-4. The *dispatcher* and *object handler* have orthogonal region pairs where one of them contains a *trap state*, and the other one contains a *timeout.*

The patterns and GPPL property specifications of TT-1 and TT-2 are defined in Figs. 3 and 5; those of TT-3 and TT-4 are defined in Figs. 7 and 8. For test generation, we used the UPPAAL back-end (see XU mapping in [26]) as it provided the shortest generation time for these models, and *every* supported model reduction, slicing and test optimization algorithm of the MBT approach [24,26]. Table 1 shows the test generation results in terms of the number of concretized test targets (#TT), i.e., generated GPL reachability properties capturing the

```
pattern initialStates(initState : State) {
 EntryState(entry);
 Transition.source(transition, entry);
 Transition.target(transition, initState); }
pattern timeouts(timeout : Transition,
  source : State) {
 find initialStates(initState);
 Transition.target(timeout, initState);
 Transition.source(timeout, source);
 Transition.trigger(timeout, trigger);
 TimeoutTrigger(trigger); }
```

```
component omGlobalQueue
@("$hu.bme.mit.gamma.gppl.timeouts")
E F parameter timeout
```

```
component omLocalQueues
@("$hu.bme.mit.gamma.gppl.timeouts")
E F parameter timeout
```

Fig. 7. VQL patterns and GPPL property specifications of *timeout transitions.*

```
pattern orthogonalChildStates(
  child1 : State, child2 : State) {
 State.regions(parent, region1);
 Region.stateNodes(region1, child1);
 region1 != region2;
 State.regions(parent, region2);
 Region.stateNodes(region2, child2); }
pattern childStates(parent : State,
  child : State) {
 State.regions(parent, region);
 Region.stateNodes(region, child); }
pattern orthogonalStates(state1 : State,
  state2 : State) {
 find orthogonalChildStates(child1, child2);
 find childStates*(child1, state1);
 find childStates*(child2, state2); }
```

```
pattern trapStateTimeouts(trapState : State,
  timeout : Transition) {
 find trapStates(trapState);
 find timeouts(timeout, source);
 find orthogonalStates(trapState, source); }
```

```
component omGlobalQueue
@("$hu.bme.mit.gamma.gppl.trapStateTimeouts")
E F parameter trapState and parameter timeout
```

```
component omLocalQueues
@("$hu.bme.mit.gamma.gppl.trapStateTimeouts")
E F parameter trapState and parameter timeout
```

Fig. 8. VQL patterns and GPPL property specifications of *trap state* and *timeout transition* pairs in orthogonal regions.

coverage of the targeted elements, and the generated test set size, including test cases (#TC) and the contained number of steps (ΣS) for both OM models.

The results show the efficiency of our approach, automatically identifying 13 and 7 test targets (transitions) for TT-1 and TT-3, 9 for TT-2 (states), and 13 for TT-4 (state-transition pairs). Every specified test target for TT-1, TT-2 and TT-3 – after fixing minor faults in the original OM model (see next paragraph) – was coverable, whereas in the case of TT-4, 2 were coverable; the differences in the TT and TC columns are due to the employed test optimization algorithm (a single test case could cover multiple test targets). Generating a test case for a single test target took a little less than 4 s on average due to the applied model reduction and slicing techniques. There were not large differences between the two OM variants; the generated test sets are slightly larger for the OM model with local queues due to the characteristics of that communication modes.

To conclude, the experiment was *successful* as i) we could capture the test targets proposed by our partner, and ii) our framework could carry out test generation in a reasonable time (naturally, additional testing shall be conducted with respect to EN 50128). The examination of tests generated for TT-2 helped to identify inconsistencies between the textual documentation of the OM and the created models: the latter lacked two transitions, preventing the reachability of a small set of states. As an impact on the current test methodology of our partner, hidden formal methods have been introduced as a basis of our MBT approach. This introduction reduces manual testing efforts via the automated generation of extensive test sets, targeting both typical coverage criteria, as well as focused testing of special safety conditions that can be specified by the engineers in a general way. These aspects were previously addressed either by manual testing, or by elementary and manually implemented model exploration techniques that did not support the complete set of elements in the applied modeling languages.

Table 1. Number of concretized *test targets* (TT), generated *test cases* (TC) and contained *steps* (S) for the OM model variants with a *global* and *local* message queues.

OM (*global* queue)	**#TT**	**#TC**	Σ **S**	OM (*local* queues)	**#TT**	**#TC**	Σ **S**
Loop transitions (TT-1)	13	8	69	*Loop transitions* (TT-1)	13	10	83
Trap states (TT-2)	9	7	15	*Trap states* (TT-2)	9	7	22
Timeouts (TT-3)	7	3	32	*Timeouts* (TT-3)	7	4	42
Trap states-timeouts (TT-4)	13	2	17	*Trap states-timeouts* (TT-4)	13	2	23

6 Related Work

The main features of our solution revolve around i) the declarative and pattern-based specification of behavioral properties, and ii) an integrated MBT approach for composite high-level state-based models using hidden formal methods. In the following, we present related work according to these aspects.

Pattern-Based Specification of Behavioral Properties. Specifying patterns defined in temporal logic is a well-established solution to facilitate behavioral property specification. Foundational work was established for finite-state verification in [16], which has since been refined and extended for events [12,45], abstract graph structures (graph grammars) [15], as well as standalone or compositional automata-based specifications [11,51]. Approaches featuring high-level UML design models as property specifications have also been proposed in [34,47].

Property specification patterns tailored to various aspects of systems engineering, such as safety [5] and security [52] have also been introduced. These approaches focus on a well-defined subset of the property specification problem and facilitate their adoption in certain fields. In addition, several solutions, independently of a field or domain, allow for generic (formalism-independent), tool-assisted methods [21,44,49] potentially with natural language support, and the graphical specification of properties [36,50,53].

Domain-Specific Languages (DSLs) have been used to facilitate behavioral property specification in complex control systems, e.g., autonomous vehicle missions [1,9,14,48]. These DSLs allow for the production and analysis of behavior descriptions, property verification, and planning. Nonetheless, their features are commonly tailored to the targeted domain and the experience of its engineers, e.g., they support only a predefined catalog of behavioral patterns [41].

Compared to these solutions, ours is unique in the sense that it supports the *specification* of *parametric* temporal properties using declarative *model queries* specified as *graph patterns*. These patterns can specify complex interrelations between model elements based on which model queries return the corresponding pattern matches from a concrete model to concretize the parameters.

Integrated Test Generation Approaches. The general idea of utilizing *hidden formal methods* to *generate tests* based on *integrated models* has been employed in several tool-based approaches. In [18], the CompleteTest tool is presented for verifying software written in the Function Block Diagram (FBD) language. The approach derives tests based on logical coverage criteria (e.g., MC/DC) while mapping FBD into the timed automata formalism of UPPAAL.

Smartesting CertifyIt [37] is an MBT tool suite that integrates editors to define requirements and traceability, test adapters and test models. Test models comprise UML class diagrams (for data description), state machines and object diagrams (initial states of executions) and BPMN notations. Test cases are generated using the CertifyIt Model Checker, which supports state, transition and transition-pair coverage criteria.

Authors in [42] introduce the AutoMOTGen tool suite that supports translating Simulink/Stateflow models into the SAL framework and model checking based test generation based on different logical coverage criteria.

AGEDIS [29] is also an MBT tool suite for component-based distributed systems, which integrates model and test suite editors, test simulation and debugging tools, test coverage and defect analysis tools and report generators. Test models are defined in UML class, state machine and object diagrams. Test generation uses the TGV engine [33] to support state and transition coverage.

The FormaSig project [8] supports the EULYNX initiative for European railways with verification facilities based on SysML internal block diagrams and state machine diagrams. FormaSig maps these SysML models into a formal process model defined in mCRL2 [7]. The mCRL2 toolset provides model checking facilities to verify the correctness of the model with respect to high-level requirements [10]. In addition, it also supports the automated model-based testing of implementations to the standard according to formal testing theory [57].

Our Gamma framework is special in the aspect that it supports multiple composition modes [27] (including support for both synchronous and asynchronous communication), and formally defined but also configurable test coverage criteria with model reduction, model slicing, and test optimization techniques [24,26].

7 Conclusion and Future Work

In this paper, we presented how we adapted our Gamma framework to support the development methodology of an industrial partner. We proposed an extended MBT approach based on the hierarchical integration of statechart components according to various composition semantics, which features test generation using model checkers to cover test criteria in the integrated models. Our approach was applied in a RIS subsystem under development, which required supporting i) the modeling style and semantic choices of the industrial partner, and ii) the flexible specification of test targets in a general way. Thus, the two extensions that we built on our existing tools and methodologies are i) the introduction of *message demultiplexing* facilities in the composition language of the framework to support shared (global) message queues among multiple components, and ii) the *declarative specification* of *test targets* based on parametric temporal properties and pattern-based model queries for their instantiation. These extensions demonstrated the flexibility of the Gamma framework and illustrated some of the challenges of applying formal methods in an industrial setting.

Subject to future work, we plan to integrate our approach with model-based mutation testing, i.e., inject mutations into the model and extend the test set by generating tests to detect and reject these mutations.

Acknowledgements. We would like to thank the anonymous reviewers for their thorough and constructive feedback. Project no. 2019-1.3.1-KK-2019-00004 has been implemented with the support provided from the National Research, Development and Innovation Fund of Hungary, financed under the 2019-1.3.1-KK funding scheme.

References

1. Adam, S., Larsen, M., Jensen, K., Schultz, U.P.: Rule-based dynamic safety monitoring for mobile robots. J. Softw. Eng. Robot. **7**(1), 120–141 (2016)
2. Amendola, A., et al.: A model-based approach to the design, verification and deployment of railway interlocking system. In: Margaria, T., Steffen, B. (eds.) ISoLA 2020. LNCS, vol. 12478, pp. 240–254. Springer, Cham (2020). https://doi.org/10.1007/978-3-030-61467-6_16
3. Basu, A., et al.: Rigorous component-based system design using the BIP framework. IEEE Softw. **28**(3), 41–48 (2011). https://doi.org/10.1109/MS.2011.27
4. Behrmann, G., et al.: UPPAAL 4.0. In: Proceedings of the 3rd International Conference on the Quantitative Evaluation of Systems, QEST 2006, pp. 125–126. IEEE Computer Society, USA (2006). https://doi.org/10.1109/QEST.2006.59
5. Bitsch, F.: Safety Patterns—the key to formal specification of safety requirements. In: Voges, U. (ed.) SAFECOMP 2001. LNCS, vol. 2187, pp. 176–189. Springer, Heidelberg (2001). https://doi.org/10.1007/3-540-45416-0_18
6. Boulanger, J.L.: CENELEC 50128 and IEC 62279 Standards. Wiley, Hoboken (2015)
7. Bouwman, M., Luttik, B., van der Wal, D.: A formalisation of SysML state machines in mCRL2. In: Peters, K., Willemse, T.A.C. (eds.) FORTE 2021. LNCS, vol. 12719, pp. 42–59. Springer, Cham (2021). https://doi.org/10.1007/978-3-030-78089-0_3
8. Bouwman, M., Luttik, S., Rensink, A., Stoelinga, M., van der Wal, D.: Formal methods in railway signalling infrastructure standardisation processes. In: Margaria, T., Steffen, B. (eds.) ISoLA 2021. Lecture Notes in Computer Science, vol. 13036, pp. 500–501. Springer, Cham (2021). https://doi.org/10.1007/978-3-030-89159-6
9. Bozhinoski, D., Di Ruscio, D., Malavolta, I., Pelliccione, P., Tivoli, M.: FLYAQ: enabling non-expert users to specify and generate missions of autonomous multicopters. In: 2015 30th IEEE/ACM International Conference on Automated Software Engineering (ASE), pp. 801–806. IEEE (2015)
10. Bunte, O., et al.: The mCRL2 toolset for analysing concurrent systems. In: Vojnar, T., Zhang, L. (eds.) TACAS 2019. LNCS, vol. 11428, pp. 21–39. Springer, Cham (2019). https://doi.org/10.1007/978-3-030-17465-1_2
11. Castillos, K.C., Dadeau, F., Julliand, J., Kanso, B., Taha, S.: A compositional automata-based semantics for property patterns. In: Johnsen, E.B., Petre, L. (eds.) IFM 2013. LNCS, vol. 7940, pp. 316–330. Springer, Heidelberg (2013). https://doi.org/10.1007/978-3-642-38613-8_22
12. Chechik, M., Păun, D.O.: Events in property patterns. In: Dams, D., Gerth, R., Leue, S., Massink, M. (eds.) SPIN 1999. LNCS, vol. 1680, pp. 154–167. Springer, Heidelberg (1999). https://doi.org/10.1007/3-540-48234-2_13
13. Childs, A., Greenwald, J., Jung, G., Hoosier, M., Hatcliff, J.: CALM and Cadena: metamodeling for component-based product-line development. IEEE Comput. **39**(2), 42–50 (2006). https://doi.org/10.1109/MC.2006.51

14. Ciccozzi, F., Di Ruscio, D., Malavolta, I., Pelliccione, P.: Adopting MDE for specifying and executing civilian missions of mobile multi-robot systems. IEEE Access **4**, 6451–6466 (2016)
15. da Costa Cavalheiro, S.A., Foss, L., Ribeiro, L.: Specification patterns for properties over reachable states of graph grammars. In: Gheyi, R., Naumann, D. (eds.) SBMF 2012. LNCS, vol. 7498, pp. 83–98. Springer, Heidelberg (2012). https://doi.org/10.1007/978-3-642-33296-8_8
16. Dwyer, M.B., Avrunin, G.S., Corbett, J.C.: Patterns in property specifications for finite-state verification. In: Proceedings of the 21st International Conference on Software Engineering, pp. 411–420 (1999)
17. Emerson, E.A., Halpern, J.Y.: "Sometimes" and "not never" revisited: on branching versus linear time temporal logic. J. ACM **33**(1), 151–178 (1986). https://doi.org/10.1145/4904.4999
18. Enoiu, E.P., Čaušević, A., Ostrand, T.J., Weyuker, E.J., Sundmark, D., Pettersson, P.: Automated test generation using model checking: an industrial evaluation. Int. J. Softw. Tools Technol. Transf. **18**(3), 335–353 (2016). https://doi.org/10.1007/s10009-014-0355-9
19. Ferrari, A., Mazzanti, F., Basile, D., ter Beek, M.H.: Systematic evaluation and usability analysis of formal methods tools for railway signaling system design. IEEE Trans. Software Eng. **48**(11), 4675–4691 (2022). https://doi.org/10.1109/TSE.2021.3124677
20. Fraser, G., Wotawa, F., Ammann, P.E.: Testing with model checkers: a survey. Softw. Test. Verif. Reliab. **19**(3), 215–261 (2009). https://doi.org/10.1002/stvr.402
21. Garcia, L.A.: Automatic generation and verification of complex pattern-based software specifications. The University of Texas at El Paso (2007)
22. Golarits, Z., Sinka, D., Jávor, A.: Proris—a new interlocking system for regional and moderate-traffic lines. SIGNAL+DRAHT - Signal. Datacommun. (114), 28–36 (2022)
23. Graics, B.: Documentation of the Gamma Statechart composition framework v0.9. Technical report, Budapest University of Technology and Economics, Department of Measurement and Information Systems (2016). https://tinyurl.com/yeywrkd6
24. Graics, B., Majzik, I.: Integration test generation and formal verification for distributed controllers. In: Renczes, B. (ed.) Proceedings of the 30th PhD Minisymposium. Budapest University of Technology and Economics, Department of Measurement and Information Systems (2023). https://doi.org/10.3311/minisy2023-001
25. Graics, B., Molnár, V.: Formal compositional semantics for Yakindu statecharts. In: Pataki, B. (ed.) Proceedings of the 24th PhD Mini-Symposium, Budapest, Hungary, pp. 22–25 (2017)
26. Graics, B., Molnár, V., Majzik, I.: Integration test generation for state-based components in the Gamma framework. Preprint (2022). https://tinyurl.com/4dhubca4
27. Graics, B., Molnár, V., Vörös, A., Majzik, I., Varró, D.: Mixed-semantics composition of statecharts for the component-based design of reactive systems. Softw. Syst. Model. **19**(6), 1483–1517 (2020). https://doi.org/10.1007/s10270-020-00806-5
28. Harel, D.: Statecharts: a visual formalism for complex systems. Sci. Comput. Program. **8**(3), 231–274 (1987). https://doi.org/10.1016/0167-6423(87)90035-9
29. Hartman, A., Nagin, K.: The AGEDIS tools for model based testing. ACM Sigsoft Softw. Eng. Notes **29**, 129–132 (2004). https://doi.org/10.1145/1007512.1007529

30. Heineman, G.T., Councill, W.T.: Component-Based Software Engineering. Putting the Pieces Together. Addison Wesley (2001). https://doi.org/10.5555/379381
31. Holzmann, G.: The SPIN Model Checker: Primer and Reference Manual, 1st edn. Addison-Wesley Professional (2011)
32. Huang, L.: The past, present and future of railway interlocking system. In: 2020 IEEE 5th International Conference on Intelligent Transportation Engineering (ICITE), pp. 170–174 (2020). https://doi.org/10.1109/ICITE50838.2020.9231438
33. Jéron, T., Morel, P.: Test generation derived from model-checking. In: Halbwachs, N., Peled, D. (eds.) CAV 1999. LNCS, vol. 1633, pp. 108–122. Springer, Heidelberg (1999). https://doi.org/10.1007/3-540-48683-6_12
34. Kaliappan, P.S., Kaliappan, V.K.: Deriving the behavioral properties from UML designs as LTL for model checking. In: 2015 IEEE International Conference on Signal Processing, Informatics, Communication and Energy Systems (SPICES), pp. 1–5 (2015). https://doi.org/10.1109/SPICES.2015.7091419
35. Ke, X., Sierszecki, K., Angelov, C.: COMDES-II: a component-based framework for generative development of distributed real-time control systems. In: 13th IEEE International Conference on Embedded and Real-Time Computing Systems and Applications (RTCSA), pp. 199–208 (2007). https://doi.org/10.1109/RTCSA.2007.29
36. Lee, I., Sokolsky, O.: A graphical property specification language. In: Proceedings 1997 High-Assurance Engineering Workshop, pp. 42–47. IEEE (1997)
37. Legeard, B., Bouzy, A.: Smartesting CertifyIt: model-based testing for enterprise IT. In: 2013 IEEE Sixth International Conference on Software Testing, Verification and Validation, pp. 391–397 (2013). https://doi.org/10.1109/ICST.2013.55
38. Li, W., Le Gall, F., Spaseski, N.: A survey on model-based testing tools for test case generation. In: Itsykson, V., Scedrov, A., Zakharov, V. (eds.) TMPA 2017. CCIS, vol. 779, pp. 77–89. Springer, Cham (2018). https://doi.org/10.1007/978-3-319-71734-0_7
39. Lukács, G., Bartha, T.: Formal modeling and verification of the functionality of electronic urban railway control systems through a case study. Urban Rail Transit **8**, 217–245 (2022). https://doi.org/10.1007/s40864-022-00177-8
40. Martinez, S., Pereira, D.I.D.A., Bon, P., Collart-Dutilleul, S., Perin, M.: Towards safe and secure computer based railway interlocking systems. Int. J. Transp. Dev. Integr. **4**(3), 218–229 (2020)
41. Menghi, C., Tsigkanos, C., Pelliccione, P., Ghezzi, C., Berger, T.: Specification patterns for robotic missions. IEEE Trans. Softw. Eng. **47**(10), 2208–2224 (2021). https://doi.org/10.1109/TSE.2019.2945329
42. Mohalik, S., Gadkari, A.A., Yeolekar, A., Shashidhar, K., Ramesh, S.: Automatic test case generation from simulink/stateflow models using model checking. Softw. Test. Verif. Reliab. **24**, 155–180 (2014). https://doi.org/10.1002/stvr.1489
43. Molnár, V., Graics, B., Vörös, A., Majzik, I., Varró, D.: The Gamma statechart composition framework. In: 40th International Conference on Software Engineering (ICSE), pp. 113–116. ACM, Gothenburg (2018). https://doi.org/10.1145/3183440.3183489
44. Mondragon, O.A., Gates, A.Q.: Supporting elicitation and specification of software properties through patterns and composite propositions. Int. J. Softw. Eng. Knowl. Eng. **14**(01), 21–41 (2004)
45. Paun, D.O., Chechik, M.: Events in linear-time properties. In: Proceedings IEEE International Symposium on Requirements Engineering (Cat. No. PR00188), pp. 123–132. IEEE (1999)

46. Radnai, B.: Integration of SCXML state machines to the Gamma framework. Technical report, Budapest University of Technology and Economics, Department of Measurement and Information Systems (2022). https://tinyurl.com/4mmtsw7v
47. Remenska, D., Willemse, T.A.C., Templon, J., Verstoep, K., Bal, H.: Property specification made easy: harnessing the power of model checking in UML designs. In: Ábrahám, E., Palamidessi, C. (eds.) FORTE 2014. LNCS, vol. 8461, pp. 17–32. Springer, Heidelberg (2014). https://doi.org/10.1007/978-3-662-43613-4_2
48. Ruscio, D.D., Malavolta, I., Pelliccione, P., Tivoli, M.: Automatic generation of detailed flight plans from high-level mission descriptions. In: Proceedings of the ACM/IEEE 19th International Conference on Model Driven Engineering Languages and Systems, pp. 45–55 (2016)
49. Salamah, S., Gates, A.Q., Kreinovich, V., Roach, S.: Verification of automatically generated pattern-based LTL specifications. In: 10th IEEE High Assurance Systems Engineering Symposium (HASE 2007), pp. 341–348 (2007). https://doi.org/10.1109/HASE.2007.37
50. Smith, M.H., Holzmann, G.J., Etessami, K.: Events and constraints: a graphical editor for capturing logic requirements of programs. In: Proceedings Fifth IEEE International Symposium on Requirements Engineering, pp. 14–22. IEEE (2001)
51. Smith, R.L., Avrunin, G.S., Clarke, L.A., Osterweil, L.J.: PROPEL: an approach supporting property elucidation. In: Proceedings of the 24th International Conference on Software Engineering, ICSE 2002, pp. 11–21. Association for Computing Machinery, New York (2002). https://doi.org/10.1145/581339.581345
52. Spanoudakis, G., Kloukinas, C., Androutsopoulos, K.: Towards security monitoring patterns. In: Proceedings of the 2007 ACM Symposium on Applied Computing, pp. 1518–1525 (2007)
53. Srinivas, S., Kermani, R., Kim, K., Kobayashi, Y., Fainekos, G.: A graphical language for LTL motion and mission planning. In: 2013 IEEE International Conference on Robotics and Biomimetics (ROBIO), pp. 704–709. IEEE (2013)
54. Steinberg, D., Budinsky, F., Merks, E., Paternostro, M.: EMF: Eclipse Modeling Framework. Pearson Education, London (2008)
55. Sztipanovits, J., Bapty, T., Neema, S., Howard, L., Jackson, E.: OpenMETA: a model- and component-based design tool chain for cyber-physical systems. In: Bensalem, S., Lakhneck, Y., Legay, A. (eds.) ETAPS 2014. LNCS, vol. 8415, pp. 235–248. Springer, Heidelberg (2014). https://doi.org/10.1007/978-3-642-54848-2_16
56. Tóth, T., Hajdu, A., Vörös, A., Micskei, Z., Majzik, I.: Theta: a framework for abstraction refinement-based model checking. In: Stewart, D., Weissenbacher, G. (eds.) Proceedings of the 17th Conference on Formal Methods in Computer-Aided Design, pp. 176–179 (2017). https://doi.org/10.23919/FMCAD.2017.8102257
57. Tretmans, J.: Model based testing with labelled transition systems. In: Hierons, R.M., Bowen, J.P., Harman, M. (eds.) Formal Methods and Testing. LNCS, vol. 4949, pp. 1–38. Springer, Heidelberg (2008). https://doi.org/10.1007/978-3-540-78917-8_1
58. Utting, M., Pretschner, A., Legeard, B.: A taxonomy of model-based testing approaches. Softw. Test. Verif. Reliab. **22**(5), 297–312 (2012). https://doi.org/10.1002/stvr.456
59. Varró, D., Bergmann, G., Hegedüs, Á., Horváth, Á., Ráth, I., Ujhelyi, Z.: Road to a reactive and incremental model transformation platform: three generations of the VIATRA framework. Softw. Syst. Model. **15**(3), 609–629 (2016). https://doi.org/10.1007/s10270-016-0530-4

Refinement of Systems with an Attacker Focus

Kim Guldstrand Larsen[1], Axel Legay[2], and Danny Bøgsted Poulsen[1](✉)

[1] Department of Computer Science, Aalborg University, Aalborg, Denmark
dannybpoulsen@cs.aau.dk
[2] UCLouvain, Louvain-La-Neuve, Belgium

Abstract. Tools and techniques for assessing the possibilities and impacts of attacks on IT systems are necessary to ensure the IT systems upon which society depends on continue to operate despite targeted attacks. This reality compels the development of intuitive brainstorming formalisms like attack-defense trees. With an attack-defense tree and a suitable system description, one can validate if a system succumbs to or withstands a described attack. Yet having established a secure system, it is still necessary to understand if and how system security may or may not be compromised or improved when the system requires modifications. Our research describes how we develop and implement a modeling methodology to resolve attacker-oriented *refinement* between systems.

1 Introduction

IT infrastructures are an integral aspect of efficiency in any modern organization. Many companies employ IT infrastructures to optimize the use of resources and raise profits, and governments deploy IT to ease public administration and reduce costs. Digital public administration improves information access for citizens and saves government officials and contractors money and time. As a result, today one or more IT systems directly or indirectly control many aspects of society. In fact, most individuals rely heavily on consistent, well-behaved IT. When bad faith actors interfere with essential IT infrastructures, the impact can be disastrous, even deadly; such interference results in, for example, leaks of private personal information at a massive scale (e.g., patient data), major transit issues and accidents (e.g., if a bad faith actor tampers with train location data), or an overload of critical systems at a pivotal moment (e.g., meddling in campaigning or voting systems during an election.) Attacks on IT infrastructure are an increasingly salient risk that can seriously damage any actor, including a country.

Distributed Denial of Service attacks have recently targeted European public administration and companies [1–3], leading to a widespread, overdue critique of institutions' cyber-attack preparedness. Of course, criticism of the security measures is easier post-attack. Ascertaining how such an attack might occur

Work partially supported by the Villum Investigator grant S4OS and the FNRS PDF - T013721 project.

A. Cimatti and L. Titolo (Eds.): FMICS 2023, LNCS 14290, pp. 96–112, 2023.
https://doi.org/10.1007/978-3-031-43681-9_6

and developing appropriate protections is more difficult; this requires exploring potential attack vectors and adapting or creating models that capture the significance of any attack. With this in mind, the security community has developed the *attack-defence tree* [11,14,23] model to aid security analysts.

An attack-defense tree is a graphical representation of feasible options by which a system might be attacked and potential different defensive countermeasures. A security analyst first brainstorms potential attack strategies and gradually refines an overall attacker objective into sub-goals. A refinement can include a conjunctive form (all sub-goals must be achieved) or a disjunctive form (one sub-goal must be achieved.) Countermeasures can be added in similar fashion. Attack-defense trees were originally envisioned as a static brainstorming tool that did not incorporate temporal behavior or quantitative aspects. This has changed with the development of various extensions [11–13] supported by tools that allow assessing the probability and impact of a successful attack.

Techniques and tools developed thus far focus on defining and describing one attack to assess if it can be successfully deployed. This one-shot process works well within a *waterfall*-based development practice. However, much software is developed iteratively. New features can compromise the system in unforeseen ways. The only way to guarantee that a new software version is secure is to redo the entire security analysis. In this paper, we develop a technique that can assess whether a new software version is at least as secure as its older version, i.e., attacks and their successful countermeasures perform for the new software version as they do for the original version of the same software. This is an unexplored area of attack modeling. Our major contributions include:

1. We develop a *modeling framework* that splits the modeling into a system model, an attacker model, and an attacker objective. The system model and attacker model are given as timed transition systems while the objective is given as an attack tree with objectives defined over propositions of the system model.
2. We define a refinement relation between system models. The refinement relation draws inspiration from refinement relations of *timed systems* [8], but is parameterized on the attacker model and the attacker objectives.
3. We present a simulation-based algorithm for refuting refinements rather than verifying refinements, and we describe how to build a UPPAAL model that when simulated effectively runs the algorithm.
4. Finally, we develop a tool component that semi-automatically builds the UPPAAL model, and we explore the use of this tool component in two cases pulled from existing literature.

2 Modelling Systems and Attacks

To formally analyze a system, analysts need a representation of the system to which formal methods can be applied. We use timed transition systems as our semantic basis. Definition 1 deviate slightly from the standard by partitioning

$$\frac{\mathtt{s}^{\mathtt{Sys}} \xrightarrow{\mathtt{d}} \mathtt{s}^{\mathtt{Sys}\prime} \qquad \mathtt{s}^{\dagger} \xrightarrow{\mathtt{d}} \mathtt{s}^{\dagger\prime}}{\langle \mathtt{s}^{\mathtt{Sys}}, \mathtt{s}^{\dagger} \rangle \xrightarrow{\mathtt{d}} \langle \mathtt{s}^{\mathtt{Sys}\prime}, \mathtt{s}^{\dagger\prime} \rangle} \qquad\qquad \frac{\mathtt{s}^{\mathtt{Sys}} \xrightarrow{\mathtt{a}^{\tau}} \mathtt{s}^{\mathtt{Sys}\prime}}{\langle \mathtt{s}^{\mathtt{Sys}}, \mathtt{s}^{\dagger} \rangle \xrightarrow{\mathtt{a}^{\tau}} \langle \mathtt{s}^{\mathtt{Sys}\prime}, \mathtt{s}^{\dagger} \rangle}$$

$$\frac{\mathtt{s}^{\mathtt{Sys}} \xrightarrow{\mathtt{a}^{\dagger}} \mathtt{s}^{\mathtt{Sys}\prime} \qquad \exists p \subseteq \mathtt{P}(\mathtt{s}^{\mathtt{Sys}}) \qquad \mathtt{s}^{\dagger} \xrightarrow{p,\mathtt{a}^{\dagger}} \mathtt{s}^{\dagger\prime}}{\langle \mathtt{s}^{\mathtt{Sys}}, \mathtt{s}^{\dagger} \rangle \xrightarrow{\mathtt{a}^{\dagger}} \langle \mathtt{s}^{\mathtt{Sys}\prime}, \mathtt{s}^{\dagger\prime} \rangle}$$

Fig. 1. Transitions rules for a system and an attacker.

actions into distinct categories: actions controlled by the attacker ($\Sigma^{\dagger}$) and internal actions controlled by the system (Σ^{τ}). This categorization clearly indicates what *interface* the attacker uses for the system.

Definition 1 (Timed Transition System). *A timed transition system is a tuple* $\mathcal{T} = (\mathtt{S}^{\mathtt{Sys}}, \mathtt{s}^{\mathtt{Sys}}{}_{\mathtt{I}}, \Sigma, \rightarrow_{\mathtt{Sys}}, \mathtt{AP}^{\mathtt{Sys}}, \mathtt{P})$ *where*

- $\mathtt{S}^{\mathtt{Sys}}$ *is a set of states the system can be in,*
- $\mathtt{s}^{\mathtt{Sys}}{}_{\mathtt{I}} \in \mathtt{S}^{\mathtt{Sys}}$ *is the initial state,*
- $\Sigma = \Sigma^{\tau} \cup \Sigma^{\dagger}$ *a finite set of actions divided into*
  - Σ^{τ} *being actions performed by the system itself and*
  - $\Sigma^{\dagger}$ *being externally (attacker) controlled actions*
- $\rightarrow_{\mathtt{Sys}} \subseteq \mathtt{S}^{\mathtt{Sys}} \times (\Sigma \cup \mathbb{R}) \times \mathtt{S}^{\mathtt{Sys}}$ *is the transition relation,*
- $\mathtt{AP}^{\mathtt{Sys}}$ *is a finite set of* observable *atomic propositions, and*
- $\mathtt{P} : \mathtt{S}^{\mathtt{Sys}} \rightarrow 2^{\mathtt{AP}^{\mathtt{Sys}}}$ *gives what propositions are true in each state.*

We let $\mathtt{d}$ range over elements from $\mathbb{R}$ and lower-case letters $\mathtt{a}, \mathtt{b}, \ldots$ range over elements from Σ. As a further convention we use the symbols $\dagger$ and τ to denote attacker-controlled actions or internally controlled actions i.e., $\mathtt{a}^{\tau}$ denotes an internally controlled action while $\mathtt{a}^{\dagger}$ denotes an action controlled by the attacker. We also let $\alpha_1, \alpha_2, \ldots$ range over $\Sigma \cup \mathbb{R}$. As a shorthand, we write $\mathtt{s}^{\mathtt{Sys}} \xrightarrow{\alpha} \mathtt{s}^{\mathtt{Sys}\prime}$ whenever $(\mathtt{s}^{\mathtt{Sys}}, \alpha, \mathtt{s}^{\mathtt{Sys}\prime}) \in \rightarrow_{\mathtt{Sys}}$, $\mathtt{s}^{\mathtt{Sys}} \not\xrightarrow{\alpha}$ whenever there does not exist $\mathtt{s}^{\mathtt{Sys}\prime}$ such that $(\mathtt{s}^{\mathtt{Sys}}, \alpha, \mathtt{s}^{\mathtt{Sys}\prime}) \in \rightarrow_{\mathtt{Sys}}$ and we write $\mathtt{s}^0 \xrightarrow{\alpha_0} \xrightarrow{\alpha_1} \ldots \xrightarrow{\alpha_{n-1}} \mathtt{s}^n$ if there exist states $\mathtt{s}^1, \mathtt{s}^2 \ldots \mathtt{s}^{n-1}$ such that for all $0 \leq i < n$. $(\mathtt{s}^i, \alpha_i, \mathtt{s}^{i+1}) \in \rightarrow_{\mathtt{Sys}}$.

Definition 2 (Attacker). *An attacker is a tuple* $\mathcal{A} = (\mathtt{S}^{\dagger}, \mathtt{s}^{\dagger}{}_{\mathtt{I}}, \Sigma^{\dagger}, \mathtt{AP}^{\mathtt{Sys}}, \rightarrow_{\dagger})$ *where*

- $\mathtt{S}^{\dagger}$ *is a set of attacker states,*
- $\mathtt{s}^{\dagger}{}_{\mathtt{I}} \in \mathtt{S}^{\dagger}$ *is the initial attacker state,*
- $\Sigma^{\dagger}$ *is a set of actions the attacker may perform,*
- $\mathtt{AP}^{\mathtt{Sys}}$ *is a set of propositions the attacker may guard its actions on,*
- $\rightarrow_{\dagger} \subseteq \mathtt{S}^{\dagger} \times ((2^{\mathtt{AP}^{\dagger}} \times \Sigma^{\dagger}) \cup \mathbb{R}) \times \mathtt{S}^{\dagger}$

A system $\mathcal{T} = (\mathtt{S}^{\mathtt{Sys}}, \mathtt{s}^{\mathtt{Sys}}{}_{\mathtt{I}}, \Sigma, \rightarrow_{\mathtt{Sys}}, \mathtt{AP}^{\mathtt{Sys}}, \mathtt{P})$ and attacker $\mathcal{A} = (\mathtt{S}^{\dagger}, \mathtt{s}^{\dagger}{}_{\mathtt{I}}, \Sigma^{\dagger}, \mathtt{AP}^{\mathtt{Sys}}, \rightarrow_{\dagger})$ run in parallel and form a joint transition system. They interact through the actions ($\Sigma^{\dagger}$) of the attacker and the attacker condition his/her/their actions on the observable state of the final system. We define the composition of $\mathcal{T}$ and $\mathcal{A}$ as the tuple $\mathcal{T} \| \mathcal{A} = (\mathtt{S}^{\mathcal{T}\|\mathcal{A}}, \mathtt{s}^{\mathcal{T}\|\mathcal{A}}{}_{\mathtt{I}}, \rightarrow)$ where

- $\mathtt{S}^{\mathcal{T}\|\mathcal{A}} = \mathtt{S}^{\mathtt{Sys}} \times \mathcal{S}^{\mathcal{A}}$ is the set of composed states,
- $\mathtt{s}^{\mathcal{T}\|\mathcal{A}}{}_{\mathtt{I}} = (\mathtt{s}^{\mathtt{Sys}}{}_{\mathtt{I}}, \mathtt{s}^{\mathcal{A}}{}_{\mathtt{I}})$ is the initial state of the composition,
- $\rightarrow \subseteq \mathtt{S}^{\mathcal{T}\|\mathcal{A}} \times \mathtt{S}^{\mathcal{T}\|\mathcal{A}}$ is the transition relation as defined in Fig. 1

An (infinite) run of a transition system $\mathcal{T} = (\mathtt{S}^{\mathtt{Sys}}, \Sigma, \rightarrow_{\mathtt{Sys}}, \mathtt{AP}^{\mathtt{Sys}}, \mathtt{P})$ and attacker $\mathcal{A} = (\mathtt{S}^{\dagger}, \mathtt{s}^{\dagger}{}_{\mathtt{I}}, \Sigma^{\dagger}, \mathtt{AP}^{\mathtt{Sys}}, \rightarrow_{\dagger})$ from state $\langle \mathtt{s}^{\mathtt{Sys}}{}_0, \mathtt{s}^{\dagger}{}_0 \rangle$ is an alternating sequence of states, reals and actions, $\rho = \langle \mathtt{s}^0, \mathtt{s}^{\dagger} \rangle, \mathtt{d}_0, \mathtt{a}_0 \langle \mathtt{s}^{\mathtt{Sys}}{}_1, \mathtt{s}^{\dagger}{}_1 \rangle \ldots$ such that for all $i \geq 0$ $\langle \mathtt{s}^{\mathtt{Sys}}{}_i, \mathtt{s}^{\dagger}{}_i \rangle \xrightarrow{\mathtt{d}_i} \xrightarrow{\mathtt{a}_i} \langle \mathtt{s}^{\mathtt{Sys}}{}_{i+1}, \mathtt{s}^{\dagger}{}_{i+1} \rangle$.

Example 1. In practice, the attacker and system are not expressed directly as timed transition systems. Instead, they are expressed by a higher-level formalism with semantics given as a timed transition system. We use the extended timed automata [4] formalism used by UPPAAL [18]. Consider this exemplary artificial case. For convenience, a house owner decides to install a smart lock on his/her/their front door so that the door can be locked and unlocked using a mobile phone. Unfortunately, the door lock's wireless connection can be jammed by an attacker. If the wireless connection is jammed, the lock/unlock signals from the owner will be ignored. In Fig. 2 the `House` starts in the location with double concentric circles. From there it awaits synchronization on the `lock`? channel (the ? indicates the house receives the synchronization). At the moment the `lock`? synchronization is received the `House` sets the variable `locked` to true thereby indicating that the door is locked. From the initial location, the `House` might also be `jam`?ed which makes it ignore all synchronizations—it will however return itself to the initial location. The `Resident` in Fig. 2 starts in the `Home` location and will after `8` time units decide to go `Away`. When the `Resident` goes away, the `Resident` signals to lock the door via synchronizations on `lock`!. After `16` time units, the `Resident` will come home and `unlock`! the door. If unlocking fails, then the resident becomes `Frustrated` and will retry after `1` time unit. We model an *opportunistic* attacker: this attacker will simply occasionally `Jam`! the door lock. Thereby the attacker ensures the door is not locked when the `Resident` leaves. After that, the attacker waits for the door to be unlocked and `enter`!. Entering is only possible (expressed as !`locked`) while the `Resident` is away. In UPPAAL this is expressed as `Resident.Away` which is true whenever the `Resident` automaton is in the location named `Away`.

3 Attacker Objectives

Before concluding if one system is more secure than another, it is useful to determine what constitutes success for an attacker. Attack-trees offer an abstract way to discuss attacks. Within an attack-tree, we can refine an attacker's overall objective to a disjunction of sub-objectives or a conjunction of sub-objectives. Then the sub-objectives are subdivided to reach elementary objectives (e.g., *Camera is off*). In our work, we express elementary objectives as true propositions in the attacked system. An attack-tree is thus "just" a propositional

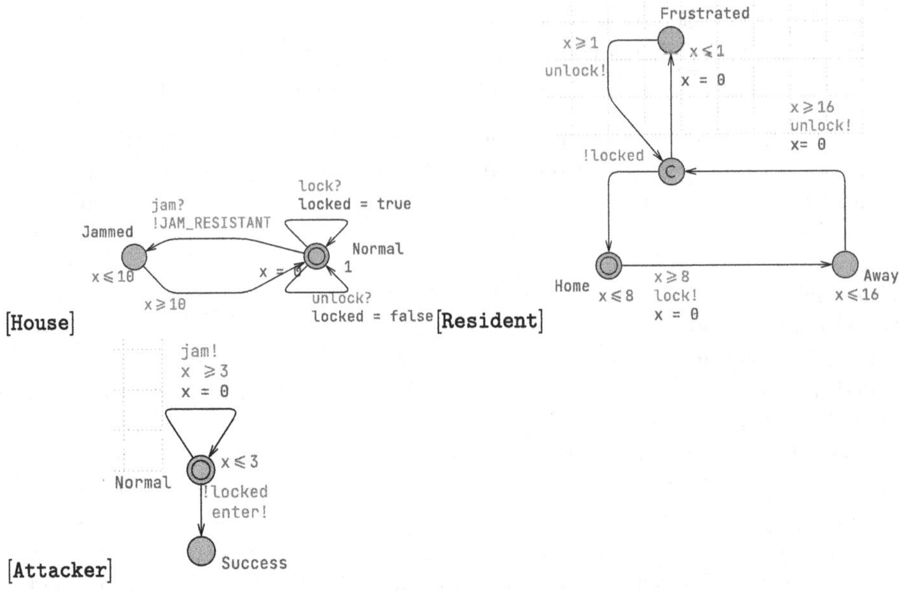

Fig. 2. UPPAAL templates for Example 1.

formula over the propositions of the system ($\texttt{AP}^{\texttt{Sys}}$). These propositions are, however, not necessarily observable to the attacker: in Example 1 it could be the case that the attacker can attempt to *Jam* the door but not know if s/t/he(y) were successful.

Definition 3. *Given a set of system propositions* $\texttt{AP}^{\texttt{Sys}}$ *all possible attack trees are generated by the EBNF*

$$\texttt{T} ::= p \mid \texttt{T} \wedge \texttt{T} \mid \texttt{T} \vee \texttt{T} \mid \neg\texttt{T}$$

where $p \in \texttt{AP}^{\texttt{Sys}}$.

For a subset of propositions $P \subseteq \texttt{AP}^{\texttt{Sys}}$ we define the satisfaction of a tree $\texttt{T}$ by simply using a propositional semantics [17]. We denote that $\texttt{T}$ is satisfied by P by $P \models \texttt{T}$.

Example 2. In the case of our running example, an attack-tree describing an attacker's goal is $\texttt{Resident.Away} \wedge \neg\texttt{locked}$

Let $\rho \in \Omega(\mathcal{T}, \mathcal{A})$ be a run of an attacker $\mathcal{A}$ and system $\mathcal{T}$ and let for all i $\rho[i] = \langle \texttt{s}^{\texttt{Sys}}{}_i, \texttt{s}^{\dagger}_i \rangle$. If the attacker's objective is given by the attack tree $\texttt{T}$ then we say the attack is successful in j steps if $\texttt{P}(\texttt{s}^j) \models \texttt{T}$.

4 Refinement Checking

Software systems are developed iteratively. Features are added and removed throughout a system's service. We are interested in developing a methodology that allows us to assess whether the additions and removals of features *refines* the system relative to possible attacks, i.e., a refined system does not add attack vectors but can remove some. More formally, a system $\mathcal{T}_1$ refines $\mathcal{T}_2$ if all the attacks realisable in $\mathcal{T}_1$ can also be realised in $\mathcal{T}_2$.

Definition 4 (Refinement). *Let* $\mathcal{T}_1 = (\mathtt{S^{Sys}}_1, \mathtt{s^{Sys}}^1{}_{\mathtt{I}}, \Sigma, \rightarrow_1, \mathtt{AP^{Sys}}, \mathtt{P}_1)$ *and* $\mathcal{T}_2 = (\mathtt{S^{Sys}}_2, \mathtt{s^{Sys}}^2{}_{\mathtt{I}}, \Sigma, \rightarrow_2, \mathtt{AP^{Sys}}, \mathtt{P}_2)$ *be two systems,* $\mathcal{A}$ *be an attacker,* $\mathtt{T}$ *be an attack tree, and for* $i \in \{1,2\}$ *let* $\mathcal{T}_i \| \mathcal{A} = (\mathcal{S}^i, \int^i{}_{\mathtt{I}}, \rightarrow_i)$*. We define that* $\mathcal{T}_1$ *refines* $\mathcal{T}_2$ *with respect to* $\mathcal{A}$ *and* $\mathtt{T}$ *– denoted* $\mathcal{T}_1 \rhd^{\mathtt{T}}_{\mathcal{A}} \mathcal{T}_2$ *– iff there exists a relation* $\mathcal{R} \subseteq \mathcal{S}^1 \times \mathcal{S}^2$ *containing* $(\int^1{}_{\mathtt{I}}, \int^2{}_{\mathtt{I}})$ *such that for each pair* $(s,t) \in R$

- *whenever* $s \xrightarrow{d} s'$ *there exists a* t' *such that* $t \xrightarrow{d} t'$ *and* $(s',t') \in R$*,*
- *whenever* $s \xrightarrow{\mathtt{a}^{\dagger}} s'$ *there exists a* t' *such that* $t \xrightarrow{\mathtt{a}^{\dagger}} t'$ *and* $(s',t') \in R$*,*
- *whenever* $s \xrightarrow{\mathtt{a}^{\tau}} s'$ *then* $(s',t) \in R$*,*
- *whenever* $t \xrightarrow{\mathtt{a}^{\tau}} t'$ *then* $(s,t') \in R$*, and*
- *if* $\mathtt{P}_1(s) \models \mathtt{T}$ *then* $\mathtt{P}_2(t) \models \mathtt{T}$

Our refinement relation is similar to the refinement relation between timed transition systems [8]. However, we incorporate attack-tree satisfaction into the refinement relation and we eschew *input* transitions to focus solely on attacker actions. We also ensure system components can perform internal actions without affecting the refinement. A tool like UPPAAL ECDAR [9] can check the refinement of timed systems by comparing the state space of the two systems with the refinement relation. This comparison is conducted using symbolic data structures (DBMs [10]) that grant a finite symbolic representation of the otherwise infinite state space.Yet even an efficient tool like UPPAAL ECDAR [9] will eventually encounter the *state space explosion problem* that troubles verification techniques.

To combat the state space explosion, Kiviriga et al. [15] suggests disproving a refinement by finding a counter-example in the concrete semantics. Algorithm 1 does this search: First, we instantiate the initial state s_1 of $\mathcal{T}_1 \| \mathcal{A}$ and s_2 of $\mathcal{T}_2 \| \mathcal{A}$. Then we select a delay and action for s_1 and validate that s_2 can perform the same action and delay. If s_2 cannot repeat the delay/action of s_1, then the refinement has failed. If s_2 can mimic s_1, then they perform the delay and action to present a new pair of states. This process continues up to a user-defined time limit D expressed in model-time units. During this simulation, if a state is reached where $\mathtt{P}_1(s_1) \models \mathtt{T}$, then we check if $\mathtt{P}_2(s_2) \models \mathtt{T}$. If not, then we have a violation. Algorithm 1 considers only a single simulation; thus, the algorithm must run several times to search for refinement violations. Together these multiple runs effectively compare the state spaces of $\mathcal{T}_1 \| \mathcal{A}$ and $\mathcal{T}_2 \| \mathcal{A}$ and, after a sufficient number of simulations, these runs will reveal any differences.

Remark 1. We find Algorithm 1 is similar to classic refinement verification algorithms except that the verification version searches through all pairs of states without revisiting any pair. The verification algorithm concludes that the refinement holds provided that no reached states result in a violation. In the case of verification, we would need to abstract the infinite concrete state space into a finite symbolic state space using DBMs to represent the time progression.

Example 3. Consider two system instantiations ($\mathcal{T}_1$ and $\mathcal{T}_2$) of Fig. 2 in which $\mathcal{T}_2$ has *Jam-protection*—meaning that it is not possible to block the locking and unlocking mechanism of the House. $\mathcal{T}_2$ makes the Jammed location unreachable; $\mathcal{T}_1$ does not. We next illustrate that $\mathcal{T}_1$ does not refine $\mathcal{T}_2$ by demonstrating that a concrete sequence of transitions of $\mathcal{T}_1$ are not replicable in $\mathcal{T}_2$.

Consider a scenario in which the attacker jams door communication while the resident routinely leaves (attempts to lock the door) after eight-time units. The resident leaves. The door is jammed. The attacker can then enter! immediately. A possible run of this scenario[1] in $\mathcal{T}_1$: [basicstyle=]

$$
\begin{aligned}
&\langle \texttt{H.Normal}, \texttt{R}, \texttt{Home}, \texttt{A.Normal}, [\texttt{locked} \mapsto \texttt{false}, \texttt{H.x} \mapsto 0, \texttt{R.x} \mapsto 0, \texttt{A.x} \mapsto 0]\rangle \\
\xrightarrow{\texttt{jam!}}&\langle \texttt{H.Jammed}, \texttt{R}, \texttt{Home}, \texttt{A.Normal}, [\texttt{locked} \mapsto \texttt{false}, \texttt{H.x} \mapsto 0, \texttt{R.x} \mapsto 0, \texttt{A.x} \mapsto 0]\rangle \\
\xrightarrow{3}&\langle \texttt{H.Jammed}, \texttt{R}, \texttt{Home}, \texttt{A.Normal}, [\texttt{locked} \mapsto \texttt{false}, \texttt{H.x} \mapsto 3, \texttt{R.x} \mapsto 3, \texttt{A.x} \mapsto 3]\rangle \\
\xrightarrow{\texttt{jam!}}&\langle \texttt{H.Jammed}, \texttt{R}, \texttt{Home}, \texttt{A.Normal}, [\texttt{locked} \mapsto \texttt{false}, \texttt{H.x} \mapsto 3, \texttt{R.x} \mapsto 3, \texttt{A.x} \mapsto 0]\rangle \\
\xrightarrow{3}&\langle \texttt{H.Jammed}, \texttt{R}, \texttt{Home}, \texttt{A.Normal}, [\texttt{locked} \mapsto \texttt{false}, \texttt{H.x} \mapsto 6, \texttt{R.x} \mapsto 6, \texttt{A.x} \mapsto 3]\rangle \\
\xrightarrow{\texttt{jam!}}&\langle \texttt{H.Jammed}, \texttt{R}, \texttt{Home}, \texttt{A.Normal}, [\texttt{locked} \mapsto \texttt{false}, \texttt{H.x} \mapsto 6, \texttt{R.x} \mapsto 6, \texttt{A.x} \mapsto 0]\rangle \\
\xrightarrow{2}&\langle \texttt{H.Jammed}, \texttt{R}, \texttt{Home}, \texttt{A.Normal}, [\texttt{locked} \mapsto \texttt{false}, \texttt{H.x} \mapsto 8, \texttt{R.x} \mapsto 8, \texttt{A.x} \mapsto 2]\rangle \\
\xrightarrow{\texttt{lock!}}&\langle \texttt{H.Jammed}, \texttt{R.Away}, \texttt{A.Normal}, [\texttt{locked} \mapsto \texttt{false}, \texttt{H.x} \mapsto 8, \texttt{R.x} \mapsto 0, \texttt{A.x} \mapsto 0]\rangle \\
\xrightarrow{\texttt{enter!}}&\langle \texttt{H.Jammed}, \texttt{R.Away}, \texttt{A.Normal}, [\texttt{locked} \mapsto \texttt{false}, \texttt{H.x} \mapsto 8, \texttt{R.x} \mapsto 0, \texttt{A.x} \mapsto 0]\rangle
\end{aligned}
$$

Trying to replay this transition sequence in $\mathcal{T}_2$ reveals that most transitions are replayable except the very last one: [basicstyle=]

$$
\begin{aligned}
&\langle \texttt{H.Normal}, \texttt{R}, \texttt{Home}, \texttt{A.Normal}, [\texttt{locked} \mapsto \texttt{false}, \texttt{H.x} \mapsto 0, \texttt{R.x} \mapsto 0, \texttt{A.x} \mapsto 0]\rangle \\
\xrightarrow{\texttt{jam!}}&\langle \texttt{H.Normal}, \texttt{R}, \texttt{Home}, \texttt{A.Normal}, [\texttt{locked} \mapsto \texttt{false}, \texttt{H.x} \mapsto 0, \texttt{R.x} \mapsto 0, \texttt{A.x} \mapsto 0]\rangle \\
\xrightarrow{3}&\langle \texttt{H.Normal}, \texttt{R}, \texttt{Home}, \texttt{A.Normal}, [\texttt{locked} \mapsto \texttt{false}, \texttt{H.x} \mapsto 3, \texttt{R.x} \mapsto 3, \texttt{A.x} \mapsto 3]\rangle \\
\xrightarrow{\texttt{jam!}}&\langle \texttt{H.Normal}, \texttt{R}, \texttt{Home}, \texttt{A.Normal}, [\texttt{locked} \mapsto \texttt{false}, \texttt{H.x} \mapsto 3, \texttt{R.x} \mapsto 3, \texttt{A.x} \mapsto 0]\rangle \\
\xrightarrow{3}&\langle \texttt{H.Normal}, \texttt{R}, \texttt{Home}, \texttt{A.Normal}, [\texttt{locked} \mapsto \texttt{false}, \texttt{H.x} \mapsto 6, \texttt{R.x} \mapsto 6, \texttt{A.x} \mapsto 3]\rangle \\
\xrightarrow{\texttt{jam!}}&\langle \texttt{H.Normal}, \texttt{R}, \texttt{Home}, \texttt{A.Normal}, [\texttt{locked} \mapsto \texttt{false}, \texttt{H.x} \mapsto 6, \texttt{R.x} \mapsto 6, \texttt{A.x} \mapsto 0]\rangle \\
\xrightarrow{2}&\langle \texttt{H.Normal}, \texttt{R}, \texttt{Home}, \texttt{A.Normal}, [\texttt{locked} \mapsto \texttt{false}, \texttt{H.x} \mapsto 8, \texttt{R.x} \mapsto 8, \texttt{A.x} \mapsto 2]\rangle \\
\xrightarrow{\texttt{lock!}}&\langle \texttt{H.Normal}, \texttt{R.Away}, \texttt{A.Normal}, [\texttt{locked} \mapsto \texttt{true}, \texttt{H.x} \mapsto 8, \texttt{R.x} \mapsto 0, \texttt{A.x} \mapsto 0]\rangle \\
\not\xrightarrow{\texttt{enter!}}&
\end{aligned}
$$

The door does not jam: thus, the difference. The resident can lock the door and block the attacker from entering the house

5 Implementation

Both system and attacker behaviors are given as UPPAAL timed automata. To check if $\mathcal{T}_1 \rhd_{\mathcal{A}}^{\mathtt{T}} \mathcal{T}_2$ holds, we will need Algorithm 1 integrated into UPPAAL. Algo-

[1] Resident abbreviated to R, House abbreviated to H and Attacker abbreviated to A.

rithm 1 checks refinement under attack by comparing the state space of components $\mathcal{T}_1$ and $\mathcal{T}_2$, generating and comparing executions of these two systems. We need to keep the distinction between these independent executions. The most direct way to achieve this is to integrate Algorithm 1 into UPPAAL as a separate simulation engine. But this idea has some flaws:

- UPPAAL has a feature-rich language. Building a new fully functional simulation engine with support for all features is time-consuming with a high risk of getting semantics slightly different from normal UPPAAL.
- If we are successful in building a fully functional simulation engine, then we will most likely have code duplication in the source code which complicates the maintenance of the UPPAAL ecosystem.
- Algorithm 1 is simulation strategy agnostic, but a dedicated implementation would not benefit from the several state space exploration strategies already implemented in UPPAAL.
- Implementation inside UPPAAL would be closed source and thus unavailable to outsiders. This lowers the transparency of our work.

Instead of implementing the algorithm inside the UPPAAL core, we opt for an implementation strategy in which we encode Algorithm 1 as an UPPAAL model.

Data: Transition Systems $\mathcal{T}_1$ $\mathcal{T}_2$, attacker $\mathcal{A}$ and attack tree $\mathtt{T}$, time limit D
Result: $\bot$ if $\mathcal{T}_1 \not\succcurlyeq^{\mathtt{T}}_{\mathcal{A}} \mathcal{T}_2$, $\top$ otherwise

Let s_1 be initial state of $\mathcal{T}_1 || \mathcal{A}$;
Let s_2 be initial state of $\mathcal{T}_2 || \mathcal{A}$;
$\delta \leftarrow 0$;
while $\delta < D$ **do**
  if $\mathtt{P}_1(s_1) \models \mathtt{T} \wedge \mathtt{P}_2(s_2) \not\models \mathtt{T}$ **then**
    return $\bot$
  end
  Let $(d, \mathtt{a}^\dagger) \in \{(d, \mathtt{a}^\dagger) | s_1 \xrightarrow{d} \xrightarrow{\mathtt{a}^\tau}{}^{*} \xrightarrow{\mathtt{a}^\dagger}\}$;
  if $s_2 \xrightarrow{d} \xrightarrow{\mathtt{a}^\tau}{}^{*} \xrightarrow{\mathtt{a}^\dagger}$ **then**
    $\delta \leftarrow \delta + d$;
    Let $s_1 \xrightarrow{d} \xrightarrow{\mathtt{a}^\tau}{}^{*} \xrightarrow{\mathtt{a}^\dagger} s_1'$;
    Let $s_2 \xrightarrow{d} \xrightarrow{\mathtt{a}^\tau}{}^{*} \xrightarrow{\mathtt{a}^\dagger} s_2'$;
    $s_1 \leftarrow s_1'$;
    $s_2 \leftarrow s_2'$;
  end
  else
    return $\bot$
  end
end
return $\top$

Algorithm 1: Refinement Refutation Algorithm. In this algorithm we use $\xrightarrow{\mathtt{a}^\tau}{}^{*}$ to mean a sequence of zero or more internal actions.

A simulation of this model corresponds to one execution of Algorithm 1. We look for refinement violations by checking if a certain condition is reached in the simulation. This strategy avoids reimplementing a simulation engine for the feature-rich language of UPPAAL, avoids code duplication, and provides access to all the various simulation engines of UPPAAL while ensuring our work benefits from future updates to UPPAAL (important to long-term maintenance.)

The Encoding

For encoding the check of $\mathcal{T}_1 \rhd^{\mathtt{T}}_{\mathcal{A}} \mathcal{T}_2$ we create a joint model, $\mathcal{T}_{\mathcal{J}}$, incorporating $\mathcal{T}_1, \mathcal{T}_2$, two versions of the attacker, $\mathcal{A}^1$ and $\mathcal{A}^2$, and T in such a way that a simulation in $\mathcal{T}_{\mathcal{J}}$ will reach a location $\mathcal{A}^2$.`RefineFail` if there exists a run of Algorithm 1 that returns $\perp$. The purpose behind the encoding is to let $\mathcal{A}^1$ select possible actions to perform and synchronize with $\mathcal{T}_1$ over these actions. We set up the model such that whenever $\mathcal{A}^1$ performs an action $\mathtt{a}^\dagger$ then $\mathcal{A}^2$ will also perform $\mathtt{a}^\dagger$, but only if that is allowed by the composition of $\mathcal{T}_2$. If it is not allowed, then $\mathcal{A}^2$ enters a dedicated `RefineFail` location, which corresponds to the check on line 9 in Algorithm 1. Otherwise, $\mathcal{A}^2$ synchronizes with $\mathcal{T}_2$ and the simulation continues.

The process for encoding a check of $\mathcal{T}_1 \rhd^{\mathtt{T}}_{\mathcal{A}} \mathcal{T}_2$ is a syntactic operation:

- For each non-attacker UPPAAL-channel `chan`, we create channels $\mathtt{chan}_{\mathcal{T}_1}$ and $\mathtt{chan}_{\mathcal{T}_2}$,
- For each attacker UPPAAL channel `chan` we create a channel $\mathtt{chan}_{\mathtt{T}}$,
- For each non-attacker UPPAAL template `Temp` we create templates $\mathtt{Temp}_{\mathcal{T}_1}$ and $\mathtt{Temp}_{\mathcal{T}_2}$. These are structurally equivalent to `Temp` except that they replace a channel-synchronizations on `chan` with a synchronization on their respective copy ($\mathtt{chan}_{\mathcal{T}_1}/\mathtt{chan}_{\mathcal{T}_2}$),
- For each attacker UPPAAL-template `Att` we create two templates $\mathtt{Att}_{\mathcal{A}^1}$ and $\mathtt{Att}_{\mathcal{A}^2}$:
  - $\mathtt{Att}_{\mathcal{A}^1}$ is copied exactly as the non-attacking templates,
  - $\mathtt{Att}_{\mathcal{A}^2}$ is first created as $\mathtt{Att}_{\mathcal{A}^1}$. Then all attacker-controlled synchronizations are changed from output to input. Finally, for each edge $\mathtt{L} \xrightarrow{g,\mathtt{a?},r} \mathtt{L}'$, we add an edge $\mathtt{L} \xrightarrow{\neg g,\mathtt{a?},r}$ `RefineFail` where `RefineFail` is a fresh location that indicates refinement failure.

We thus create a system in which $\mathtt{Att}_{\mathcal{A}^1}$ selects actions and $\mathtt{Att}_{\mathcal{A}^2}$ tries to replicate those actions. If this fails (i.e., a guard is false), then by definition we have a refinement failure, and we can see this in our encoding by reaching `RefineFail`. With this model, we can now use UPPAAL SMC to search for refinement violations by posing the query

$$\mathtt{Pr}[<= \tau](<> (\mathtt{Att}_{\mathcal{T}_2}.\mathtt{RefineFail}) || ([\mathtt{T}_{\mathcal{T}_1}] \&\& [!\mathtt{T}_{\mathcal{T}_2}])),$$

where τ is some time unit in model time units, as in Algorithm 1, and $[\mathtt{T}_{\mathcal{T}_i}]$ is encoding the attack T into UPPAAL syntax using the propositions from $\mathcal{T}_i$.

We developed a semi-automatic tool [21] to help create this joint model. It takes as input a single UPPAAL model that includes the attacker and the system. It will also need as input what template represents the attacker and which channels represent attacker-controlled actions.

Remark 2. We use the statistical model checking (SMC) engine of UPPAAL to generate simulations of the "refutation system." We are not interested in the probabilities UPPAAL calculates as a result of running the query. As we are not concerned with probabilities, we could also use the *random exploration engine* added to UPPAAL by Kiviriga et al. [15]. This engine is similar to the SMC engine in that it performs a random walk in the concrete semantics of the timed transition system; however, rather than guiding its search according to probabilistic semantics, the *random exploration engine* tries to calculate actions and delays that are interesting. Here we ultimately do not use this engine because it disallows certain UPPAAL features that our case models use.

6 Case Study

We next apply our toolchain to two different case studies. A reproduction package is available [22].

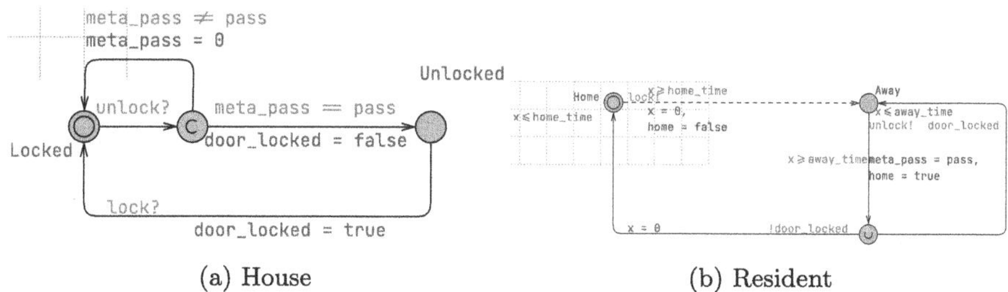

(a) House

(b) Resident

Fig. 3. Amazon Case Study Model

6.1 Amazon Delivery

As an example application of our refinement framework, we use a variation of the Amazon Key case study considered by Beaulaton et al. [6]. This is an Amazon delivery system deployed when a customer is not at home. To deliver an order, Amazon installs a digital lock on the customer's door and a video camera in the home. The homeowner has his/her/their digital key for the home and may enter whenever s/t/he(y) wishes. For a delivery person to enter the house, however, the delivery person must first pick up the parcel to receive a one-time key to enter the recipient's home. To make homeowners feel safer, the system starts the video camera the moment a delivery key is used to open the door.

In Fig. 3a we show the house component of the system. The house starts in the location with double concentric circles: from here someone may attempt to `unlock` the door with a password (transferred to the variable `meta_pass`). If the password matches, the door is `unlocked` and the door waits for a `lock` synchronization. The `Resident` (Fig. 3b) starts in the `Home` location and after some time leaves. As the resident leaves s/t/he(y) `locks` the door. After having been `Away`, the resident returns home and attempts to `unlock` the door. The door communicates if the `unlock` action succeeded via the variable `door_locked`.

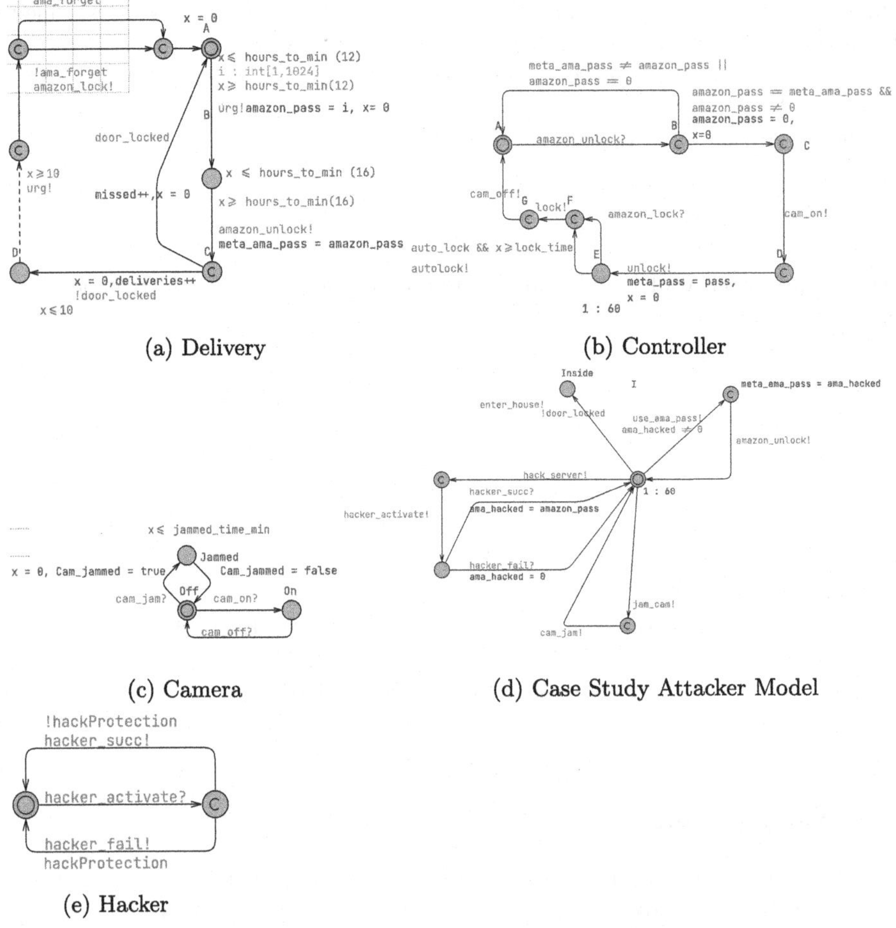

(a) Delivery

(b) Controller

(c) Camera

(d) Case Study Attacker Model

(e) Hacker

Fig. 4. Amazon Case Study Model

To model the *delivery* aspect of the system we have three automata (Fig. 4a, Fig. 4b and, Fig. 4c). Figure 4a models a delivery courier. The courier starts in `A` before receiving a package to deliver. With the package, the courier receives a password used to `amazon_unlock` the door. If the unlock action is successful (!`door_locked`) the courier delivers the package. Hopefully, the courier `amazon_lock`s the door when leaving, but we can configure the model to account for a courier who does not.

Unlocking the door is handled by the controller, (Fig. 4b) which simply waits for `amazon_unlock` requests. When the provided key matches an unlock key, then the camera starts (`cam_on`), and the door unlocks. After the door is unlocked, the controller waits for `amazon_lock` request to proceed to the door and turn off the camera. Here we see the difference between the auto-lock system and the non-auto-lock system; systems with `auto_lock` enabled will lock the door after `lock_time` has passed.

	$\mathcal{T}1$	$\mathcal{T}2$
Hack Protection	✔	
Auto Lock	✔	✔

Fig. 5. System Configurations

The `Camera` of the system is modeled in Fig. 4c where it begins as `Off` and is turned on by a synchronization on `cam_on`. As long as the camera is `On`, it can only be turned `Off`. When the camera is `Off`, an attacker can *jam* communication to the camera so that it will ignore `cam_on` requests.

Attacker Model. The attacker model can be seen in Fig. 4d. It is a *non-deterministic* attacker that randomly tries actions. Possible actions include:

- The attacker may try to `enter_house`!. This requires that the door is not locked (expressed as !`door_locked`).
- The attacker may try to `hack_server`!. This may or may not be successful. The attack success is determined by Fig. 4e which expresses whether the system is hacker resistant or not.
- The attacker may try to `jam_cam`!. The result of this action is not immediately visible to the attacker.
- The attacker may try to use the Amazon password (`use_ama_pass`!), but to do so the `hack_server` action must have succeeded (expressed as `ama_hacked` $\neq 0$).
- The attacker may attempt to `guess_password`. The attacker does not know if his guess is correct before he tries using the password.

The attacker's objective is to achieve entry when the Resident is absent and the camera is turned off. The attacker wishes to satisfy the attack tree.

$$\mathtt{T}_A = \mathtt{Attacker.Inside} \land \mathtt{Resident.Away} \land \mathtt{Camera.Off}.$$

Remark 3. This deceptively simple Amazon case study was an important experimental case study in the recent PhD-thesis of Beaulaton [7] and has previously been used to benchmark attack modeling formalisms. More importantly, this example has fairly complex interactions between individual system components that highlight attack scenarios showing how one system instantiation is more vulnerable than another.

Experiments. In the following, we examine refinement between two different variations of the systems. In Fig. 5, we provide an overview of the configurations. Since $\mathcal{T}1$ has more security features than $\mathcal{T}2$, it should be clear that $\mathcal{T}2 \not\preceq_{\mathcal{A}}^{\mathrm{TA}} \mathcal{T}1$. Running our toolchain, we are able to find proof that there is no refinement between the systems with respect to our defined attacker, and we can thus determine that we are more vulnerable if we roll out the system with fewer security features. A central benefit of the refinement checking performed by UPPAAL is that all the diagnostic features of UPPAAL are immediately available. In particular, UPPAAL can provide sequence charts: (Fig. 6) shows the sequence of actions performed in the refinement-refuting attack. If we follow the synchronizations between `SYS1Attacker` and `SYS2Attacker`, we notice that they are constantly in sync except at the very end where *SYS2Attacker* ends up in `RefineFail`. This indicates that *SYS2Attacker* was unable to match the action performed by *SYS1Attacker*. The difference is caused by the four transitions above it: a *hack* to retrieve the password is attempted and succeeds (`SYS1hacker_succ`) for `SYS1Attacker` but fails (`SYS2hacker_fail`) for `SYS2Attacker`.

6.2 Duqu Malware

The second use case that we examine is an encoding of how the Duqu malware works. We include this case study to show how our technique can compare large systems with respect to attacks. This is important because many methods focus on the analysis of a single attack on a single system but not on the difficult task of comparing systems with respect to attacks. The latter is necessary to evaluate, e.g., the effect of adding new defenses between two different implementations of the same system. Maynard et al. [20] describes this as an attack-tree with sequential gates; it includes some temporal behavior. We consider the attack-tree of Maynard et al. [20] as a system description and model it in UPPAAL using a similar encoding as Gadyatskaya et al. [11]. The construction is recursive on the parse-tree of the attack-tree such that each sub-formula is represented by one automaton, and sub-formulas report through channel-synchronization to parent formulas when they are satisfied. The attacker is a single automaton that non-deterministically selects which atomic proposition it wishes to set to true. Setting a proposition may fail or succeed depending on a defender's existing security configuration. Maynard et al. [20] has not included any definition of defenses. Thus we choose to let some of the atomic propositions of the attacker be countered by some security means. In Fig. 7d the counter of an attack step is indicated by setting `blocked` to true in the model configuration. The full UPPAAL model is too large to show in its entirety, but it consists of 112 automata and has 28 atomic attacker actions.

In our experimentation with this model, we run our tool on the model and set one of the blocking constants to true in one instantiation ($\mathcal{T}_1$) and false in another instantiation ($\mathcal{T}_2$). Running our tool reveals that $\mathcal{T}2 \not\preceq_{\mathcal{A}}^{\mathrm{TA}} \mathcal{T}1$.

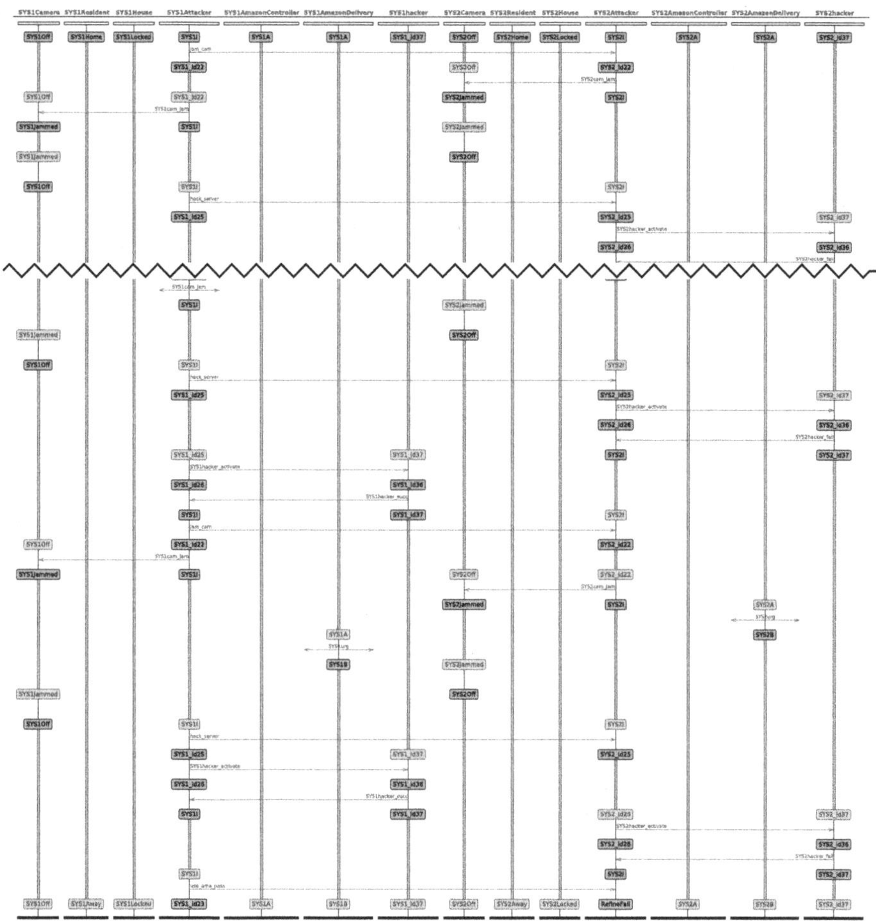

Fig. 6. Excerpt of Message Sequence Chart from UPPAAL showing the interaction among the automata in the system. In the case of our refinement checking procedure the major interest is the interaction between `SYS1Attacker` and `SYS2Attacker`.

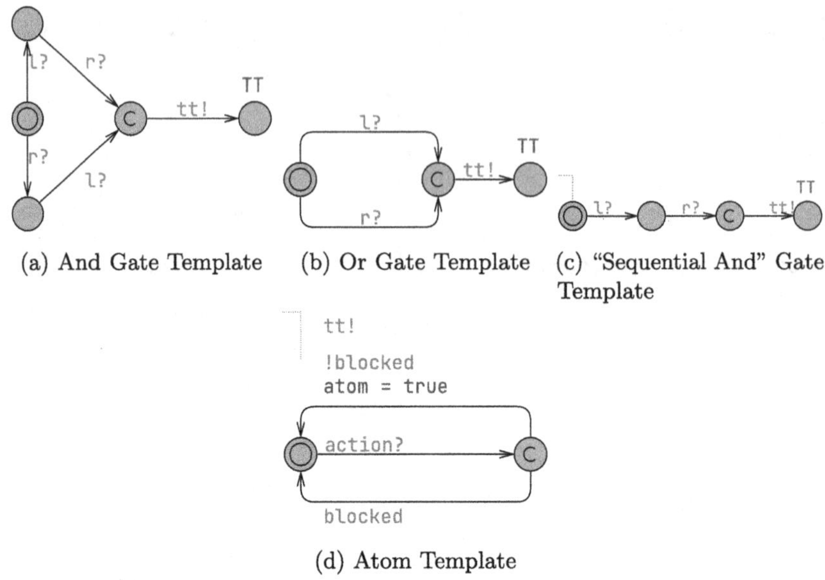

(a) And Gate Template (b) Or Gate Template (c) "Sequential And" Gate Template

(d) Atom Template

Fig. 7. Duqu Attack Tree Gates

7 Conclusion

We investigate how to compare two system models based on what attacks (enumerated with an attack-defence tree) are possible in the two systems. We set up a framework that models systems through a timed transition system with actions explicitly controlled by an attacker model. We also give the attacker model as a timed transition system, but we condition the attacker's actions to the system's state. We run both systems and the attacker in parallel to compare. The attacker tries to perform the same actions on both systems to determine if the attack tree becomes true or if the attacker cannot perform an action in one of the systems. This allows us to see if the two systems allow the same attacks. Along with this modeling framework, we develop the tools necessary for comparison.

Our comparison method is based on a Monte-Carlo search strategy utilizing the statistical model checking engine of UPPAAL. This is sufficient for the use cases in this paper, but it will not be sufficient for all systems. Luckily, our work is simulator-agnostic and can be used with any simulation technique. In the future, we plan to investigate further using the rare-event simulation technique importance splitting [19] to guide the search toward refinement violations. We also plan to extend our models to incorporate quantitative features (e.g., cost). This is a natural extension incorporated into many attack modeling formalisms [5,11,13,16]. Security mechanisms in systems do not always prevent attacks; they just make the attack extremely expensive for the attacker. We need to allow modelers to incorporate this into their models.

Acknowledgement. The authors would like to thank Linda Warnier for proofreading this paper.

References

1. Danish defence ministry says its websites hit by cyberattack, December 2022. https://www.reuters.com/world/europe/danish-defence-ministry-says-its-websites-hit-by-cyberattack-2022-12-08/
2. Airline SAS network hit by hackers, says app was compromised, February 2023. https://www.reuters.com/business/aerospace-defense/airline-sas-suffers-cyber-attack-customer-info-leaked-2023-02-14/
3. German airport websites hit by suspected cyber attack, February 2023. https://www.reuters.com/technology/websites-several-german-airports-down-focus-news-outlet-2023-02-16/
4. Alur, R., Dill, D.: Automata for modeling real-time systems. In: Paterson, M.S. (ed.) ICALP 1990. LNCS, vol. 443, pp. 322–335. Springer, Heidelberg (1990). https://doi.org/10.1007/BFb0032042
5. Aslanyan, Z., Nielson, F.: Pareto efficient solutions of attack-defence trees. In: Focardi, R., Myers, A. (eds.) POST 2015. LNCS, vol. 9036, pp. 95–114. Springer, Heidelberg (2015). https://doi.org/10.1007/978-3-662-46666-7_6
6. Beaulaton, D., Cristescu, I., Legay, A., Quilbeuf, J.: A modeling language for security threats of IoT systems. In: Howar, F., Barnat, J. (eds.) FMICS 2018. LNCS, vol. 11119, pp. 258–268. Springer, Cham (2018). https://doi.org/10.1007/978-3-030-00244-2_17
7. Beaulaton, D.: Security analysis of IoT systems using attack trees. Ph.D. thesis, UNIVERSITE DE VANNES UNIVERSITE BRETAGNE SUD (2019)
8. David, A., Larsen, K.G., Legay, A., Nyman, U., Wasowski, A.: Timed I/O automata: a complete specification theory for real-time systems. In: HSCC, pp. 91–100 (2010)
9. David, A., Larsen, K.G., Legay, A., Nyman, U., Wąsowski, A.: ECDAR: an environment for compositional design and analysis of real time systems. In: Bouajjani, A., Chin, W.-N. (eds.) ATVA 2010. LNCS, vol. 6252, pp. 365–370. Springer, Heidelberg (2010). https://doi.org/10.1007/978-3-642-15643-4_29
10. Dill, D.L.: Timing assumptions and verification of finite-state concurrent systems. In: Sifakis, J. (ed.) CAV 1989. LNCS, vol. 407, pp. 197–212. Springer, Heidelberg (1990). https://doi.org/10.1007/3-540-52148-8_17
11. Gadyatskaya, O., Hansen, R.R., Larsen, K.G., Legay, A., Olesen, M.C., Poulsen, D.B.: Modelling attack-defense trees using timed automata. In: Fränzle, M., Markey, N. (eds.) FORMATS 2016. LNCS, vol. 9884, pp. 35–50. Springer, Cham (2016). https://doi.org/10.1007/978-3-319-44878-7_3
12. Hansen, R.R., Jensen, P.G., Larsen, K.G., Legay, A., Poulsen, D.B.: Quantitative evaluation of attack defense trees using stochastic timed automata. In: Liu, P., Mauw, S., Stølen, K. (eds.) GraMSec 2017. LNCS, vol. 10744, pp. 75–90. Springer, Cham (2018). https://doi.org/10.1007/978-3-319-74860-3_5
13. Hermanns, H., Krämer, J., Krčál, J., Stoelinga, M.: The value of attack-defence diagrams. In: Piessens, F., Viganò, L. (eds.) POST 2016. LNCS, vol. 9635, pp. 163–185. Springer, Heidelberg (2016). https://doi.org/10.1007/978-3-662-49635-0_9
14. Jhawar, R., Kordy, B., Mauw, S., Radomirović, S., Trujillo-Rasua, R.: Attack trees with sequential conjunction. In: Federrath, H., Gollmann, D. (eds.) SEC 2015. IAICT, vol. 455, pp. 339–353. Springer, Cham (2015). https://doi.org/10.1007/978-3-319-18467-8_23
15. Kiviriga, A., Larsen, K.G., Nyman, U.: Randomized refinement checking of timed i/o automata. In: Pang, J., Zhang, L. (eds.) SETTA 2020. LNCS, vol. 12153, pp. 70–88. Springer, Cham (2020). https://doi.org/10.1007/978-3-030-62822-2_5

16. Kordy, B., Kordy, P., Mauw, S., Schweitzer, P.: ADTool: security analysis with attack–defense trees. In: Joshi, K., Siegle, M., Stoelinga, M., D'Argenio, P.R. (eds.) QEST 2013. LNCS, vol. 8054, pp. 173–176. Springer, Heidelberg (2013). https://doi.org/10.1007/978-3-642-40196-1_15
17. Kordy, B., Mauw, S., Radomirović, S., Schweitzer, P.: Attack-defense trees. J. Log. Comput. **24**(1), 55–87 (2014)
18. Guldstrand Larsen, K., Pettersson, P., Yi, W.: UPPAAL in a nutshell. STTT **1**(1–2), 134–152 (1997). https://doi.org/10.1007/s100090050010
19. Larsen, K.G., Legay, A., Mikucionis, M., Poulsen, D.B.: Importance splitting in UPPAAL. In: Margaria, T., Steffen, B. (eds.) ISoLA 2022. LNCS, vol. 13703, pp. 433–447. Springer, Cham (2022). https://doi.org/10.1007/978-3-031-19759-8_26
20. Maynard, P., McLaughlin, K., Sezer, S.: Modelling DUQU 2.0 malware using attack trees with sequential conjunction. In: ICISSPP, pp. 465–472. SciTePress (2016)
21. Poulsen, D.B.: dannybpoulsen/uppaalad: v0.1, July 2023. https://doi.org/10.5281/zenodo.8196631
22. Danny Bøgsted Poulsen. dannybpoulsen/uppaalad_rep_package: v0.1, July 2023. https://doi.org/10.5281/zenodo.8196634
23. Schneier, B.: Attack trees: modeling security threats. Dr. Dobb's J. (1999)

Modelling of Hot Water Buffer Tank and Mixing Loop for an Intelligent Heat Pump Control

Imran Riaz Hasrat(✉), Peter Gjøl Jensen, Kim Guldstrand Larsen, and Jiří Srba

Department of Computer Science, Aalborg University, Aalborg, Denmark
{imranh,pgj,kgl,srba}@cs.aau.dk

Abstract. The recent surge in electricity prices has increased the demand for cost-effective and sophisticated heat pump controllers. As domestic floor heating systems are becoming increasingly popular, there is an urgent need for more efficient control systems that include also heat buffer tanks to account for fluctuating energy prices. We propose a scalable thermal model of the hot water buffer tank together with a mixing loop and evaluate its operation and performance on an experimental Danish house from the OpSys project. We experimentally assess the buffer tank's quality by selecting the proper size and number of virtual layers using an industry-standard controller. Finally, we integrate the buffer tank and mixing loop into the heating system and create an intelligent STRATEGO controller to examine their performance. We analyze the tradeoff between cost and comfort for different buffer tank sizes to determine when a buffer tank or a mixing loop should be included in the system. By providing a detailed understanding of the buffer tank and mixing loop, our study enables the clients to make better decisions regarding the appropriate buffer tank size and when to install a mixing loop based on their specific heating needs.

Keywords: Intelligent heat pump control · Energy efficiency · Floor heating · Buffer tank modelling

1 Introduction

According to 2020 figures, Renewable Energy Sources (RESs) contribute up to 26% in domestic space heating [1]. The proportion of RES in Denmark's electricity market has increased from 44% in 2015 to 50% in 2020 with the ultimate objective of becoming carbon-free by 2050 [2].

There is a substantial potential for integrating RES into domestic heating systems to reduce energy consumption costs. Heat pumps enable the heating system to utilize flexible energy. Furthermore, a hot water buffer tank can enhance the heating system's energy flexibility. Integrating a hot water buffer tank can play a key role in improving energy efficiency. The tank model must accurately determine the water temperature inside the tank in order to better exploit the

A. Cimatti and L. Titolo (Eds.): FMICS 2023, LNCS 14290, pp. 113–130, 2023.
https://doi.org/10.1007/978-3-031-43681-9_7

buffer tank. In addition, in modern space heating a mixing loop can be introduced between the water tank and heaters to mix up the hot and cold water to improve efficiency and provide better regulation of water flow into the heaters. An intelligent heat pump controller is required to maximize the benefits of the buffer tank and the mixing loop.

When used in domestic heating control systems, Model Predictive Controllers (MPC) demonstrated the potential for energy and cost savings [3–5]. An estimated house model depicting the thermal dynamics of the house is required before developing an MPC. The thermodynamics model depicts the house's heat dynamics as well as the impacts of outdoor weather, residents' behaviour, and solar radiation on the room temperature. Given the thermodynamics model, an MPC is coupled with a control objective (e.g., reduce cost and optimize comfort) in a tight and periodic loop of "observe, solve, act." However, implementing an MPC has various challenges, such as the house dynamics needing to be discovered in advance and the behaviour and dynamics changing over time.

To tackle these issues, we use the control setup from our recent work [6], where we first identify the thermodynamics and heat transfer coefficient using CTSM-R (continuous time stochastic modelling in R) [7], and then design an intelligent UPPAAL STRATEGO [8] controller, which controls the heat pump for the floor heating using an online strategy synthesis approach. In this paper, we additionally propose and implement thermodynamic models of the hot water buffer tank and the mixing loop. We incorporate the models into the heating system and create intelligent STRATEGO controllers to operate it. Our main novel contributions are:

1. Development of a dynamic thermal model of the hot water buffer tank.
2. Quality assessment to examine the impact of virtual layers and tank sizes.
3. Integration of a mixing loop for mixing hot and cold water to achieve more flexibility and better control of forward water temperature.
4. Employment of the heat buffer tank and mixing loop models to design the STRATEGO MPC.
5. Extensive experimental evaluation.

Related Work: Recently, emerging studies on domestic heating systems yielded some particularly compelling findings. For instance, a study published in [9] optimized energy costs in an ultra-low temperature district heating system using an MPC for a 22-flat building in Copenhagen, demonstrating significant energy savings. Another study [4] suggested an online and compositional synthesis approach by employing STRATEGO controller for comfort optimization in a domestic floor heating problem. Similarly, [6] proposed a toolchain for controlling heat pump operation in a floor heating system, specifically for optimal cost and comfort optimizations. In this study, the authors identified the thermal dynamics of a target house using CTSM-R software and designed a STRATEGO controller to learn optimal control strategies. The results demonstrated that the intelligent controller saved energy costs while maintaining comfort, ultimately outperforming a traditional bang-bang controller. However, these studies [4,6,9] do not consider the buffer tank and mixing loop in the context of domestic heating. We extends these works, and in particular [6], by introducing these components.

Adding a hot water buffer tank to the heating system may improve the control and efficiency of the system. Several studies have examined the simulation and modeling of electric water heaters (EWHs). However, some of these studies, such as [10–20], have only considered a uniform water temperature in the tank and modelled it as a single mass of water using a first-order thermal model. This approach is not effective when there is a hot water out-flow and cold water in-flow in a relatively small buffer tank, as the temperature distribution in the tank tends to be uneven. Two and three-mass [21–23] models have been developed to overcome the limitations of one-mass models. These models assume a constant temperature profile within each water mass, resulting in improved accuracy in calculating the tank water temperature. However, there is still a need for more precise models to capture nonuniform temperatures in the tank effectively. The approaches proposed in [24,25] discuss how the water temperature in the buffer tank can be calculated with reasonable accuracy. The approaches propose dividing the tank water into several virtual layers to accommodate stratification created due to the temperature difference in different tank areas. Our buffer tank modelling approach is similar to [24,25], however, they use a simple boiler and we use a heat pump together with intelligent control to heat-up the water.

Furthermore, a mixing loop can be added to adjust the forward water temperature by mixing hot district heating water with cold returning domestic heating water, lowering energy costs [26]. Similarly, the mixing loop modelling methodologies proposed in [27–30] reduce energy costs in low-temperature district heating. Instead of district heating, we propose a mixing loop model together with its intelligent control for an individual house and extensively evaluate the interplay between the buffer tank and the mixing loop.

We believe that we are the first to study the impact of combined intelligent predictive control of both the heat-producing unit and the mixing loop in a buffer-tank-enabled heating system.

2 Case House and Problem Statement

To evaluate the performance of the buffer tank and mixing loop, we now present an overview of the house used in our experiments and the evaluation environment. Figure 1 extends the setup of a small family house modelled in [6] with two additional components: a hot water tank and a mixing loop. It is a $150m^2$ physical test house with four rooms, including a living room with a built-in kitchen (Room 1), two bedrooms (Rooms 2 and 4), and a bathroom (Room 3).

The heat pump system produces hot water and directs it to the buffer tank. This hot water is then distributed to the floor heaters through floor pipes to meet the heating demands of the house. With a buffer tank, the control of heat becomes more indirect. In order to provide better direct control, we integrate a mixing loop between the buffer tank and the floor heaters.

The system has three levels of control, i.e., heat pump, mixing loop, and room thermostat. We consider traditional bang-bang controller to control the room thermostats. Each thermostat operates independently of the heat pump

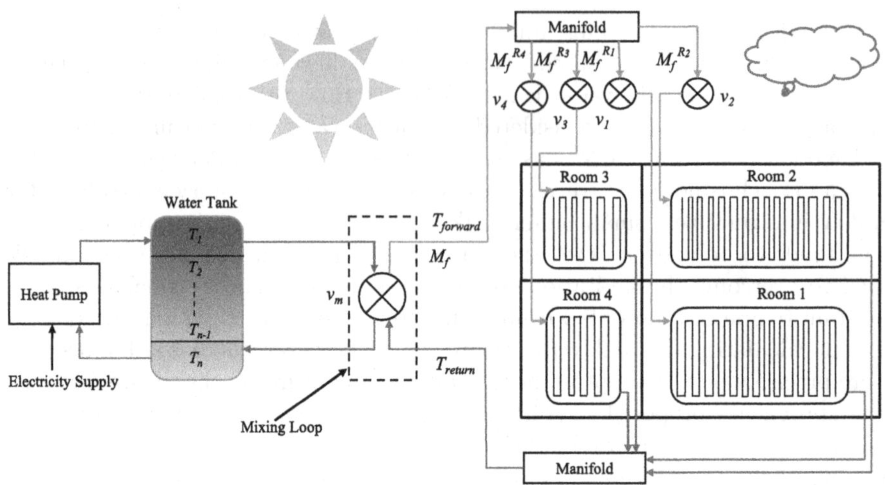

Fig. 1. The overview of the house and its heating system

and other thermostats; it is turned on if any room's temperature drops below the fixed set point (22 °C) and turned off if all the room temperatures exceed it. The incoming mass flow of water (M_f) has a fixed distribution key that distributes the hot water to the rooms via the manifold in fixed proportions denoted by ${M_f}^{R_i}$ where $i = 1, \ldots, k$ (k denotes the number of rooms). Individual room thermostats regulate binary valves v_i, with mass flow re-distributed proportionally to the remaining open valves if certain valves are shut. On the other hand, the heat pump and the mixing loop are controlled with a dedicated controller (e.g., UPPAAL STRATEGO [8] in our case). The control parameters for the heat pump and the mixing loop are the heat pump's operating intensity and level of mixing (through the valve v_m). The objective is to control the heat pump and the mixing loop to achieve optimal comfort and cost. The $T_{forward}$ and T_{return} represent forward and return water temperatures, respectively.

For the modelling purposes and the construction of a predictive controller of the heat pump and the mixing loop, we need to obtain the house's thermodynamic model. We extend the methodology proposed in [6] where the data recorded from the intended house (from OpSys Project [31]) modelled in DYMOLA [32] is used to determine the thermal model of the house, as well as related heat exchange coefficients.

3 Buffer Tank and Mixing Loop Thermodynamics

This section describes our proposed thermal dynamic models of the buffer tank and the mixing loop. In Fig. 2a, we present the schematic overview of the hot water buffer tank. We split the tank water into n virtual layers. The temperature of each layer is affected by the direction of the water pressure created either from

Table 1. List of variables and constants used in tank thermodynamic model

Variables	Description
$\tilde{T}_1 \cdots \tilde{T}_n$	temperatures of the n water layers in tank[°C]
T_{hp}	temperature of the water exiting the heat pump [°C]
T_{return}	temperature of the water returning from the room floors [°C]
$T_{outdoor}$	ambient temperature [°C]
F_{hp}	mass flow of water exiting the heat pump [litres/minute]
F_{fh}	mass flow of water exiting the floors to the tank [litres/minute]
$F_{(x,y)}$	mass flow of water from layer x to layer y [liters/minute]
Constants	
M	mass of water in each layer [litres]
A	area of each layer [m^2]
C_w	thermal capacitance in the water tank [J/kgC]
U_a	coefficient for heat conductivity to ambient
U_v	coefficient for heat conductivity in the tank water

top-to-bottom or bottom-to-top inside the tank, which is decided by the mass flows from the heat pump (F_{hp}) and to the floors (F_{fh}).

In Fig. 2b, we present thermal dynamics model of the buffer tank as a set of differential equations (Eqs. (1)–3)) representing the temperature of the top layer ($\tilde{T}_1$), finite number of intermediate layers ($\tilde{T}_\ell$), and the bottom layer ($\tilde{T}_n$). In these equations, the heat supply, thermal conductance of the water, and heat loss to the surrounding environment determine the heat balance. The related variables and constants are described in Table 1.

Equation (2) computes the water temperature ($\tilde{T}_\ell$) of any intermediate layer ℓ. The function $f(\ell)$ computes the heat effect (relative to mass flow $F_{(x,y)}$) to and from the layer $\ell - 1$ or $\ell + 1$ depending on the mass flows F_{hp} and F_{fh}. Whenever F_{hp} is greater than F_{fh}, water pressure is formed from the top to the bottom, causing direct heat gain from the adjacent upper layer $\ell - 1$ and heat loss to the adjacent lower layer $\ell + 1$. In contrast, when F_{fh} is greater than F_{hp}, the water creates pressure from the bottom to the top layer, resulting in a direct heat effect transferring from the adjacent lower layer $\ell + 1$ to ℓ, and from ℓ to $\ell - 1$. The second term calculates the heat loss incurred by the outside weather (related to the coefficient U_a). The fourth and fifth terms express the conductivity impact of the adjacent upper ($\ell - 1$) and lower layers' ($\ell + 1$) temperatures on the current layer (ℓ) (through the conductivity coefficient U_v). Equations (1) and (3) are specialized forms of Equation (2) and determine the temperatures $\tilde{T}_1$ and $\tilde{T}_n$. The hot water temperature (T_{hp}) entering the tank greatly influences the top layer. On the other hand, the direct heat influence on the bottom layer is caused by the return water temperature (T_{return}).

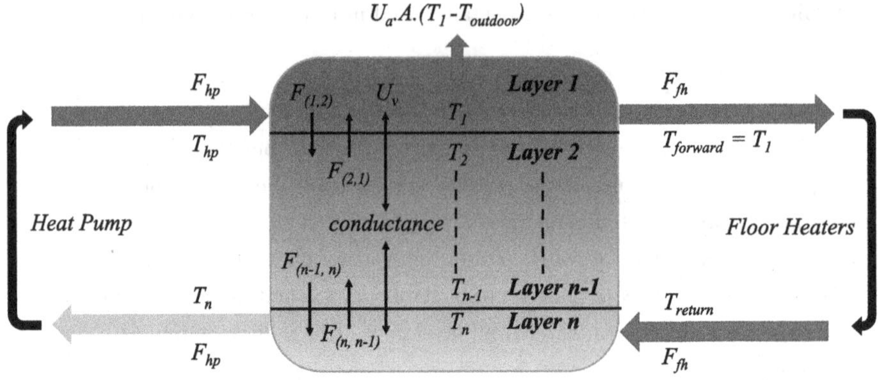

(a) Overview of the hot water buffer tank

$$\frac{d\tilde{T}_1}{dt} = ((F_{hp} \cdot C_w \cdot T_{hp}) - (F_{fh} \cdot C_w \cdot \tilde{T}_1) + f(1) - (U_a \cdot A \cdot (\tilde{T}_1 - T_{outdoor})) + (U_v \cdot (\tilde{T}_1 - \tilde{T}_2)))/(M \cdot C_w) \quad (1)$$

$$\textit{for every } \ell, \; 2 \leq \ell < n, \textit{we have the following equation}:$$

$$\frac{d\tilde{T}_\ell}{dt} = (f(\ell) - (U_a \cdot A \cdot (\tilde{T}_\ell - T_{outdoor})) - (U_v \cdot (\tilde{T}_{(\ell-1)} - \tilde{T}_\ell)) + (U_v \cdot (\tilde{T}_\ell - \tilde{T}_{(\ell-1)})))/(M \cdot C_w) \quad (2)$$

$$\frac{d\tilde{T}_n}{dt} = ((F_{fh} \cdot C_w \cdot T_{return}) - (F_{hp} \cdot C_w \cdot \tilde{T}_n) + f(n) - (U_a \cdot A \cdot (\tilde{T}_n - T_{outdoor})) - (U_v \cdot (\tilde{T}_{n-1} - T_n)))/(M \cdot C_w) \quad (3)$$

where

$$f(1) := \begin{cases} -(F_{(1,2)} \cdot C_w \cdot \tilde{T}_1) & \text{if } F_{hp} > F_{fh} \\ +(F_{(2,1)} \cdot C_w \cdot \tilde{T}_2) & \text{otherwise} \end{cases}$$

$$f(\ell) := \begin{cases} +(F_{(\ell-1,\ell)}) \cdot C_w \cdot \tilde{T}_{\ell-1}) - (F_{(\ell,\ell+1)} \cdot C_w \cdot \tilde{T}_\ell) & \text{if } F_{hp} > F_{fh} \\ +(F_{(\ell,\ell+1)}) \cdot C_w \cdot \tilde{T}_{\ell+1}) - (F_{(\ell,\ell-1)} \cdot C_w \cdot \tilde{T}_\ell) & \text{otherwise} \end{cases}$$

$$f(n) := \begin{cases} +(F_{(n-1,n)} \cdot C_w \cdot \tilde{T}_{n-1}) & \text{if } F_{hp} > F_{fh} \\ -(F_{(n,n-1)} \cdot C_w \cdot \tilde{T}_n) & \text{otherwise} \end{cases}$$

(b) Thermodynamics model of the hot water buffer tank

Fig. 2. Buffer tank schematic diagram and thermal equations for n layers

To evaluate the Eqs. (1)–(3), we let the buffer tank heat up (charging) and cool down (discharging) to see how the tank water temperatures evolve. To do so, we set the outdoor temperature ($T_{outdoor}$) and tank water's initial temperature to 10 °C and 30 °C, respectively. For simplicity, we limit the virtual layers to three (i.e., $\tilde{T}_1$, $\tilde{T}_2$, and $\tilde{T}_3$) and assume a 75-litre tank size. Figure 3a shows the

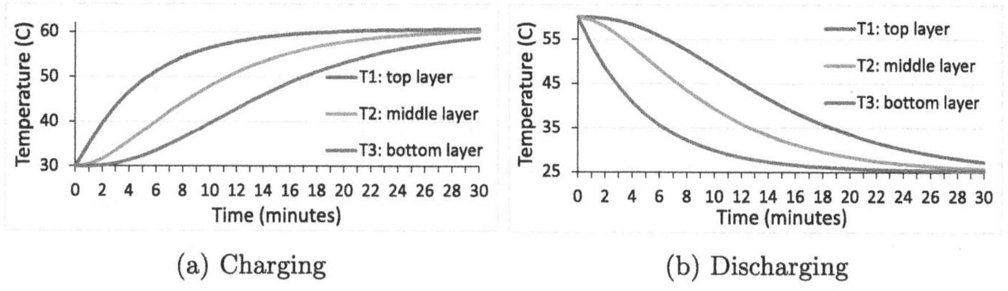

(a) Charging (b) Discharging

Fig. 3. Temperatures of buffer tank water during charging/discharging

temperature trends for all three layers during the charging period (30 min). The heat pump consumes 2.5 kWh of electricity and supplies hot water to the tank from the top layer at a rate of 5 litres per minute (F_{hp}). However, we restrict the hot water from flowing towards the floor heaters, i.e., $F_{fh} = 0$. The tank water temperatures keep rising, and the gap between them decreases as the heat pump keeps providing the hot water. After a while, the temperatures reach the same point, and no further heat exchange occurs.

During discharging phase (Fig. 3b), we keep the heat pump off, and the floor heaters get 5 litres per minute of hot water from the top layer. However, the cold water (T_{return} is 25 °C) returns to the tank via the bottom layer. Due to the continuous infusion of cold water, the layers' temperatures keep dropping and, after some time, become constant at 25 °C.

Finally, we present the thermal model of the mixing loop. The mixing is done with a mixing valve (v_m in Fig. 1). Assuming that the *control_choice* is the mixing option selected by the controller from the available mixing levels (*mixing_levels*), the percentage of cold water (*mixing_value*) to be mixed with the hot water can be calculated using Eq. (4). Equation (5) computes the temperature of the water to be forwarded ($T_{forward}$) towards the floor heaters using the relative share of cold (T_{return}) and hot water (T_1, top layer). The mass flow of cold water entering the buffer tank (F_{fh}) is calculated using Eq. (6).

$$mixing\_value = \frac{control\_choice}{mixing\_levels} \tag{4}$$

$$T_{forward} = T_{return} \cdot mixing\_value + T_1 \cdot (1 - mixing\_value) \tag{5}$$

$$F_{fh} = F_{fh} \cdot (1 - mixing\_value) \tag{6}$$

4 System Modelling in Uppaal Stratego

Given the thermal dynamics model of the buffer tank, we now create its model in Uppaal. We employ the tool Uppaal Stratego [8], which is a branch of the Uppaal tool suit [33–36]. In Stratego, systems are modelled as networks of finite-state automata equipped with discrete data types (e.g., bounded integers, arrays) and a finite number of clocks (continuous variables). Transitions in the automata are conditioned on the values of the discrete variables and clocks and when executed, both the discrete variables and clocks can be updated. The transitions can be controllable (represented by solid lines) or uncontrollable (represented by dashed lines) guarded with specific conditions. If two parallel processes reach a controllable and uncontrollable transition simultaneously; the environment has priority to take any transition or pass control over to the controller. The clocks facility in STRATEGO captures the timing aspects of the real systems and serves as continuous variables to represent differential equations. Moreover, STRATEGO enables communication with C libraries [37], making it possible to use a C library to write complex functions and interact with other libraries.

4.1 Buffer Tank Modelling in UPPAAL STRATEGO

Figure 4 depicts the complete system composition as a buffer tank in STRATEGO. In STRATEGO, the sub-parts of the model are named templates. The model comprises seven parameterized automata templates, namely *Room*, *Controller*, *FitnessFunction*, *DataReader*, *BufferTank*, *BufferLayer*, and *BufferUpdate*. The continuous variables $\tilde{T}_r^i$, $\tilde{T}_h^i$, and $\tilde{T}_e^i$ representing room, floor, and envelope temperature (for Room i) are expressed as real-time clocks in the *Room* template. *DataReader* brings historical *weather* and day-ahead *electricity* pricing information into the model. The *Fitness* function (see Eq. (7)) is implemented by the *FitnessFunction* template. The *Controller* template implements the controller's control mechanism, which allows the system to choose between different energy levels for the heat pump and different valve settings for the mixing loop. The current work focuses mainly on describing the modelling of the buffer tank, so we here explain only the buffer tank-related templates. The complete model with details of the remaining templates can be found on GitHub [38].

The buffer tank-related templates are grouped within the red dashed-line area (see Fig. 4a). The *BufferTank* template incorporates two continuous variables (called clocks) to represent the temperature of the top ($\tilde{T}_1$) and bottom ($\tilde{T}_n$) layers, which evolve with time. On the other hand, the *BufferLayer* template calculates the temperature of an arbitrary number of intermediate ($\tilde{T}_\ell$) water layers. The functions `calculate_top()`, `calculate_layer()`, and `calculate_bottom()` employ Equations (1), (2) and (3) to compute $\tilde{T}_1$, $\tilde{T}_\ell$, and $\tilde{T}_n$, respectively. In Fig. 4c, we show `calculate_top()` definition as an example to highlight the one-to-one mapping of these functions with buffer tank thermal equations (Equation (1) in this case). The invariant `t≤min` and guard `t≥min` in *BufferUpdate* template combinely force the system (every minute) to take the uncontrollable transition and update the functions `conductivity()`, `massflows_hp_fh()` and reset the local clock `t`. These functions are defined in Fig. 4d, while their declarations are presented in Fig. 4b. The number of layers, volume, and area of the tank is defined by external calls to the functions in external C libraries.

In Fig. 4d, the `conductivity()` function calculates the water mass flow ($\mathsf{F_{xy}}$) between any two consecutive layers by computing the difference of $\mathsf{F_{hp}}$ and $\mathsf{F_{fh}}$. The `massflows_hp_fh()` function is responsible for determining the $\mathsf{F_{hp}}$ and $\mathsf{F_{fh}}$ values. The `massflow[]` and `is_massflow_on[]` arrays used in the *for loop*

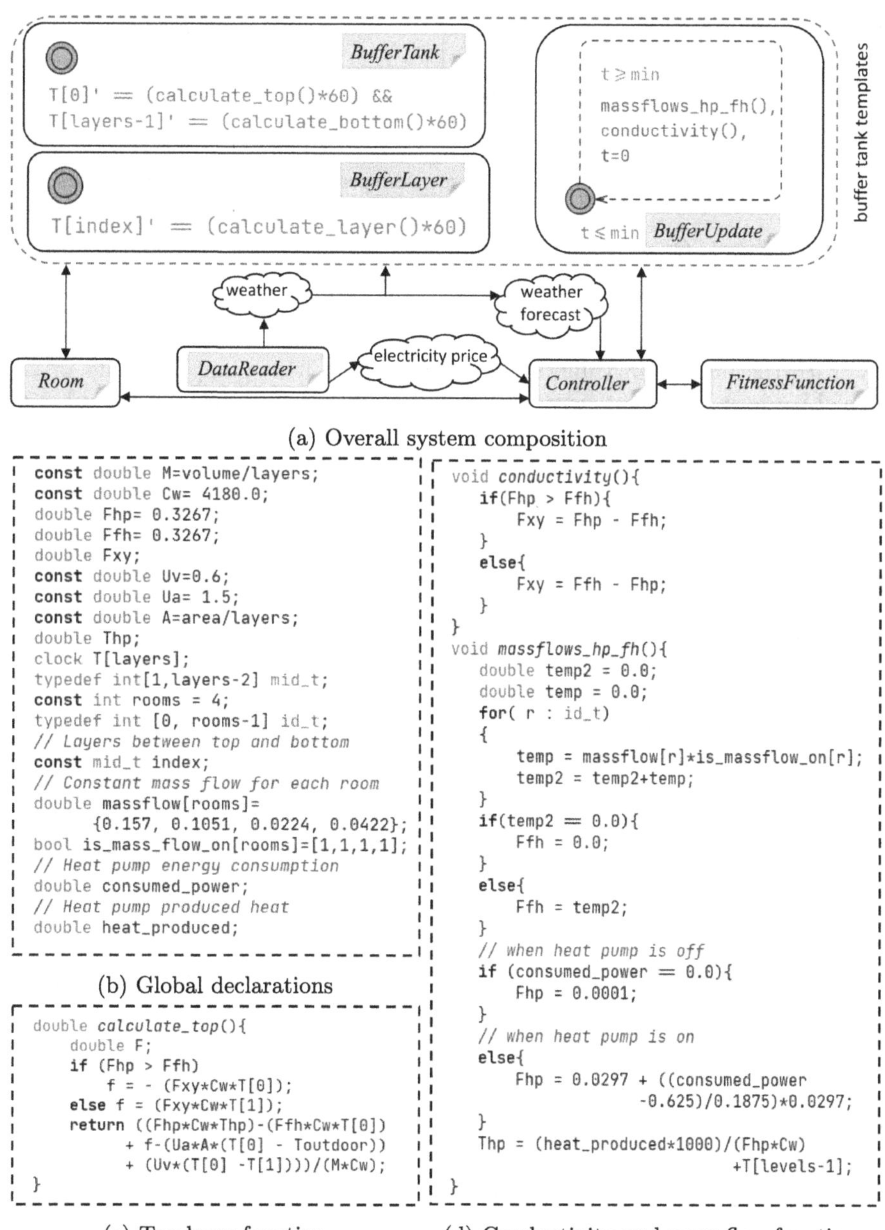

(a) Overall system composition

(b) Global declarations

(c) Top layer function

(d) Conductivity and mass-flow functions

Fig. 4. Composition of the complete system in STRATEGO

contain the constant mass flows for each room and Boolean values representing each room's thermostat's *opening/closing* status, respectively. The variable `temp2` adds the contribution of mass flow from each room to determine their

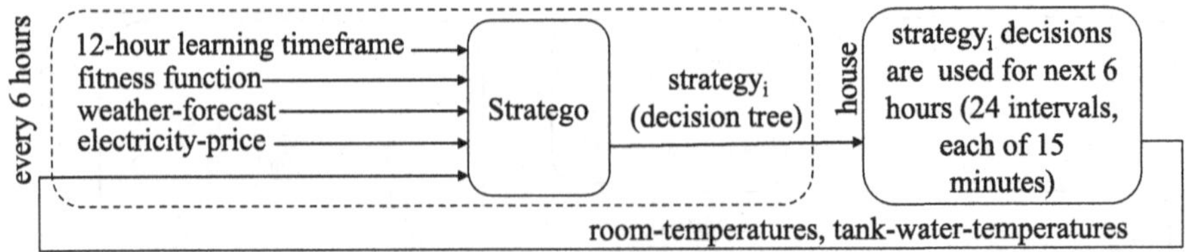

Fig. 5. Online synthesis approach shown on two days period

combined mass flow $\mathsf{F_{fh}}$ value. However, $\mathsf{F_{hp}}$ depends on the heat pump's intensity, with the maximum value being 0.3267 at full heat pump intensity of 2.5 kWh. Like heat-pump intensity, we split $\mathsf{F_{hp}}$ into equal levels with a value of 0.0297 on each level. The power consumption for the first intensity level is 0.625 kWh, adding 0.1875 kWh against each adjacent intensity level. The function also computes the temperature ($\mathsf{T_{hp}}$) of the water exiting the heat pump.

4.2 Online Synthesis

In Fig. 5, we depict an overview of online synthesis algorithm to give a better understanding. Looking further into the future, we see that 24 h in advance known electricity prices and weather forecasts have diminished predictive power. To address this issue, we propose an online strategy synthesis approach where the controller periodically observes the state of the room, buffer water temperature, electricity price, and weather forecast to learn appropriate control decisions by optimizing the fitness function that balances the comfort and cost. The decisions are generated as a decision tree (i.e., $strategy_i$ in Fig. 5 where i represents 6 h) for operating the heat pump and mixing loop accordingly. The controller uses quick recomputation to compensate for inaccuracies in the initial state. As a result, the volatile variables are monitored and communicated to the strategy $strategy_i$ every 15 min to get the control decisions that suit the current situation. A single strategy is used for the subsequent 24 intervals (6 h) to reduce the computational effort.

5 Experimental Evaluation

We begin by describing the experimental setup and then evaluate our approach by presenting a series of experiments as follows:

1. buffer tank quality assessment with an industry-standard controller,
2. buffer tank evaluations with intelligent STRATEGO controller,
3. buffer and mixing loop evaluations with intelligent STRATEGO controller.

5.1 Evaluation Setup

In our experiments, we control the heat pump from the STRATEGO model for February (week 6) and April (week 14) of 2018 while maintaining corresponding weather conditions. For all trials described in the following sections, we use the energy prices from the Danish day-ahead electricity market as of autumn 2022.

We optimize the control mechanism against the *objective/fitness* function (in Eq. 7, which is similar to one introduced in [6]). The fitness function (F) provides flexibility to handle the tradeoff between cost and comfort in a balanced way by adjusting the relative weights. Typically, a consumer wishes to manage the tradeoff between cost and comfort by adjusting the weight against each parameter. Therefore, we state the optimization criteria that allow the customer to perform such tuning with $0 \leq W_{comf} \leq 1$ weighting factor. This encourages us to express the fitness function for our controllers parameterized as W_{comf}. For each W_{comf} setting, W_{cost} is computed as $W_{cost} = 1 - W_{comf}$. To ensure proportional weighting between two units, cost (DKK), and squared degrees Celsius, we calculated a normalization factor, *norm*, based on the performance of the traditional bang-bang (BB) controller. The controller simply turns the heat pump on if the temperature in any room falls below 22°C and turns it off otherwise. We calculated the normalization factor by assessing the performance of the BB controller in terms of cost and comfort in the week preceding the experimental week using the formula $norm = \frac{comfort}{cost}$. The main purpose of the heat pump is to minimize the gap between the room temperatures $\tilde{T}_r^i$ and a given set point T_g with the heating cost. The heating cost $cost(\tau) = price_\tau \cdot w_\tau$ is a time-dependent function and product of the heat pump energy consumption w_τ (determined directly by the controller) and the hourly basis (known 24 h in advance) market electricity price ($price_\tau$). We apply the function over a period τ_0 to τ_n given that the heat-pump settings, energy prices, and room temperatures (denoted by $T_r^i(\tau)$) are known for k rooms:

$$F(\tau_0, \tau_n) = \int_{\tau_0}^{\tau_n} \left((W_{cost} \cdot norm \cdot cost(\tau)) + W_{comf} \cdot \sqrt{\sum_{i=1}^{k} (T_g - \tilde{T}_r^i(x))^2} \right) d\tau \tag{7}$$

where the first part represents the energy cost (linear impact on fitness), and the second part records the room temperature deviations (from the set point (T_g)) such that the large deviations are penalized substantially as compared to minor deviations due to its squared manner.

We limit the controller to 15-min control intervals, which is enough for systems with slow dynamics, such as floor heating. Each reported configuration is tested ten times, and the mean value and standard deviation intervals are displayed in bar charts. Throughout the study, W_{comf} values are changed in 0.1 increments.

5.2 Buffer Tank Quality Assessment

In this section, we analyze the buffer tank size and the number of virtual layers that are sufficient to calculate the water temperature within the tank with adequate accuracy. Selecting the buffer tank's proper size can save installation and operation costs. A too small buffer tank sometimes needs more storage capacity to fulfil the heating demand of the heating system. The limited capacity enforces the heat pump for frequent cycling and may reduce system efficiency. On the other hand, too large buffer tanks need higher installation costs and may cause significant heat losses. Another interesting aspect is the precision of the buffer tank, which is affected by the number of virtual layers.

To investigate these issues, we use a heat pump control strategy presented in the reference curve of an industry-standard product sheet[39]. The product sheet proposes regulating the forward water temperature according to outside weather for a heat pump with no buffer; however, regulating return water temperature instead ensures reasonable forward temperatures for a heat pump with a buffer tank. Therefore, we implement this strategy to operate the heat pump based on the return water temperature (T_{return}). The strategy turns on the heat pump if the return water temperature drops below 50 °C and turns it off if it exceeds 55 °C. We name this strategy as Return Water Control Strategy (RWCS-BT, where BT refers to buffer tank).

Now we consider February (week 6) to examine the influence of tank sizes and levels on the performance of a heat pump under the control of the RWCS-BT controller, equally focusing on cost and comfort. The investigation utilizes a simulation horizon of one week, with a target temperature of 22 °C. Figure 6 displays the experiment results. The vertical axis displays the absolute values of the fitness function, energy cost (in DKK) and discomfort, where discomfort records the room temperature deviations from the target temperature. Figures 6a, 6b, and 6c illustrate the impact of tank sizes concerning fitness, discomfort and cost using the test house from Sect. 2. Our findings suggest that increasing the tank size leads to a decrease in discomfort and a rise in cost, with the improvement in comfort being relatively less significant than the corresponding increase in energy cost. The increase in cost is attributed to the greater heat dissipation to the surrounding environment that arises when larger tanks are considered. Fitnesswise 150-litre option is better than the 75-litre; however, the 75-litre tank is the most cost-effective option, exhibiting an approximately similar level of discomfort compared to other tank sizes. The 75-litre tank size can also save the installation cost significantly compared to the 150-litre tank. As a result, we employ the 75-litre tank in subsequent experiments.

In Fig. 6d, we investigate the impact of virtual layers in a buffer tank. We observe that the fitness value increases up to 7 layers and becomes stable afterwards. Therefore, we conclude that the 7 virtual layers give sufficient precision for a 75-litre tank. As a result, we have decided to employ the 7 virtual layers in 75 litres tank in subsequent sections of this paper. We note that the precision of the buffer tank is dependent on many factors, e.g., the size of the buffer tank and operational circumstances (i.e., heat pump dimensionality and user patterns).

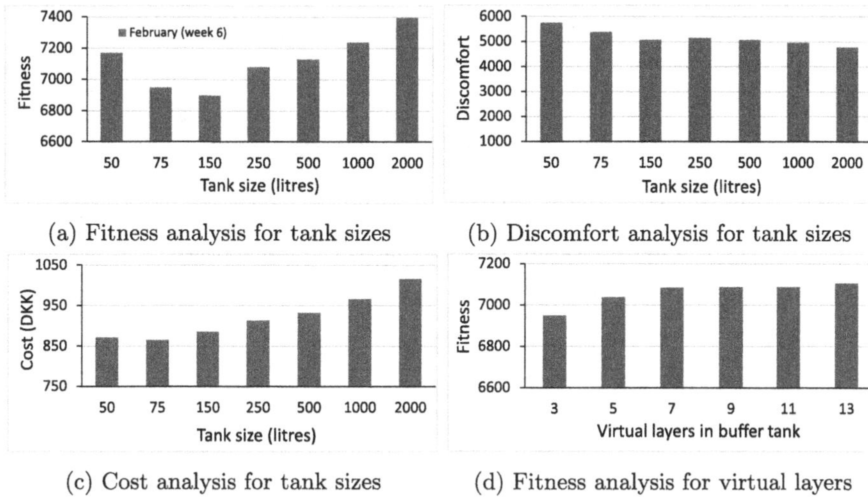

(a) Fitness analysis for tank sizes (b) Discomfort analysis for tank sizes

(c) Cost analysis for tank sizes (d) Fitness analysis for virtual layers

Fig. 6. The effect of tank sizes and virtual layers on the cost and comfort

5.3 Buffer Tank Evaluations with Intelligent Stratego Controller

In this section, we discuss the performance of various iterations of the online STRATEGO-based controller. We include random noise (upto 1 °C) in the historical weather data to account for discrepancies in weather information between the house and the controller as the house experiences actual weather and the controller relies on weather forecasts. We introduce several controllers to evaluate our approach:

- BB: It is a traditional bang-bang controller to control the heat pump without a buffer tank. This controller turns the heat pump on if the temperature in any room falls below 22 °C and turns it off otherwise,
- Stratego: A predictive controller that trains on the house model to learn good decisions to operate the heat pump. It controls the intensity of the heat pump between 11 levels. Like BB, it operates the heat pump without a buffer tank,
- RWCS-BT: As already described in Sect. 5.2, it is a controller from industry-standard that maintains the return water temperature between 50–55 °C. It operates the heat pump with a buffer tank.
- Stratego-BT: It is also a predictive controller. Like RWCS-BT, this it is designed to control the heat pump with a buffer tank (but no mixing loop).

We consider BB to be the baseline controller because its behaviour in the model is deterministic when repeated with historical weather. The experimental findings of the controllers for April (week 14) control are shown in Fig. 7. The fitness and cost measures on vertical axis represent the fitness function (F) and energy cost (in DKK). Discomfort measure, on the other hand, displays the recorded

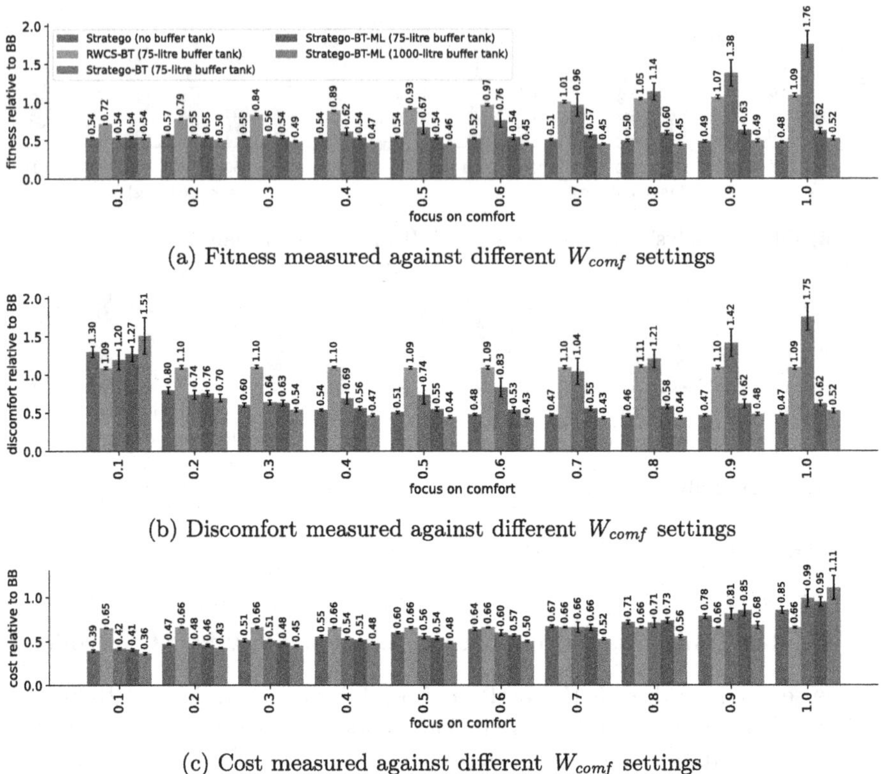

(a) Fitness measured against different W_{comf} settings

(b) Discomfort measured against different W_{comf} settings

(c) Cost measured against different W_{comf} settings

Fig. 7. Experimental results for April (week 14) control under STRATEGO-BT-ML (Color figure online)

deviations in room temperatures from the set point. Each measure on the vertical axis is calculated by computing its value from a specific controller and BB using the formula $measure = \frac{controller}{\text{BB}}$ which means a relative value below 1 implies that a controller outperforms BB and vice versa. The horizontal axis emphasizes comfort (with W_{comf} values). We avoid reporting a pure focus on cost (i.e., $W_{comf} = 0.0$) because it causes the controller to turn off all heat.

Figure 7 shows the comparison of STRATEGO, RWCS-BT, and STRATEGO-BT controllers (shown by the first three bar charts i.e., blue, yellow and green) relative to the BB controller. Here STRATEGO-BT is unexpectedly underperforming STRATEGO with respect to fitness, comfort, and cost (see Figs. 7a, 7b and 7c), especially with more focus on comfort. The higher cost is due to the heat loss from the buffer tank to the ambient. The loss in comfort is attributed to STRATEGO-BT controller's lack of control over room thermostats; they get activated whenever the temperature in corresponding rooms goes below 22 °C. With an increased focus on comfort, STRATEGO-BT anticipates heat demand and produces high-temperature hot water in the buffer tank. This water is released when a thermostat valve opens, causing discomfort (overheating). Hence the introduction of a buffer tank without a mixing loop is not benificial.

5.4 Mixing Loop Evaluations with Intelligent STRATEGO Controller

We integrate a mixing loop between the buffer tank and the floor heaters to improve the cost and comfort. We create controller STRATEGO-BT-ML, which controls the heat pump and water mixing proportions, and we experiment with several mixing level settings. Our finding is that 11 mixing levels give the controller enough flexibility to mix hot and cold water appropriately. It can be seen in Fig. 7 that STRATEGO-BT-ML (75-litre) outperforms STRATEGO-BT; however, with a higher focus on comfort, it still performs worse than STRATEGO indicating that 75-litre tank is insufficient for optimal mixing loop operation. Therefore, we include a 1000-litre tank that allows the heat pump to store heat when it is cheap and better handle the mixing loop. STRATEGO-BT-ML (1000 litres) consistently outperforms STRATEGO except for extreme cases where we ignore comfort or cost (i.e., W_{comf} at 0.1 or 1.0). For example, with equal focus on comfort and cost ($W_{comf} = 0.5$), it saves 12% energy costs with 7% better comfort than STRATEGO. We want to remark here, that these numbers are specific to our case house and may differ for houses with different thermodynamics.

6 Conclusion

We proposed scalable thermal models for the hot water buffer tank and the mixing loop, which we then incorporated into a 150 m^2 test house used in the toolchain from [6]. First, we examined the buffer tank's quality using an industry-standard controller (RWCS-BT). The results suggest that a 75-liter capacity with seven virtual layers is sufficient for adequate heat pump operation.

We compared the performance of RWCS-BT and three intelligent controllers having: no buffer tank (STRATEGO), a buffer tank (STRATEGO-BT), and a buffer tank and a mixing loop (STRATEGO-BT-ML). Our findings reveal that both RWCS-BT and STRATEGO-BT perform worst than STRATEGO in terms of cost and comfort due to the lack of the mixing loop. STRATEGO-BT-ML (75-litre) with a mixing loop mitigates the higher cost and comfort to some extent, but still, it underperforms STRATEGO. However, a 1000-litre tank with a mixing loop enables STRATEGO-BT-ML to outperform all other controllers, saving substantial energy costs while improving comfort. Larger tanks are expensive, but they can save energy by storing heat when it is cheap.

Our method gives a more in-depth understanding of buffer tanks and mixing loops, allowing customers to choose the optimal tank size for their heating requirements. Before purchasing a buffer tank, customers may conduct model-based simulations to explore a variety of different tank sizes under the local weather conditions in order to calculate the possible savings.

Acknowledgements. We would like to thank Per Printz Madsen and Hessam Golmohammadi for their extensive help in understanding the physics of the buffer tanks. This research is partly funded by the ERC Advanced Grant Lasso, the Villum Investigator Grant S4OS, and DIREC: Digital Research Centre Denmark.

References

1. Energy consumption in households, April 2023. https://ec.europa.eu/eurostat/statistics-explained/index.php?title=Energy_consumption_in_households
2. Daryabari, M.K., Keypour, R., Golmohamadi, H.: Stochastic energy management of responsive plug-in electric vehicles characterizing parking lot aggregators. Appl. Energy **279**, 115751 (2020)
3. Agesen, M.K., et al.: Toolchain for user-centered intelligent floor heating control. In: IECON 2016–42nd Annual Conference of the IEEE Industrial Electronics Society, pp. 5296–5301 (2016)
4. Larsen, K.G., Mikučionis, M., Muñiz, M., Srba, J., Taankvist, J.H.: Online and compositional learning of controllers with application to floor heating. In: Chechik, M., Raskin, J.-F. (eds.) TACAS 2016. LNCS, vol. 9636, pp. 244–259. Springer, Heidelberg (2016). https://doi.org/10.1007/978-3-662-49674-9_14
5. Vogler-Finck, P.J.C., Wisniewski, R., Popovski, P.: Reducing the carbon footprint of house heating through model predictive control - a simulation study in Danish conditions. Sustain. Cities Soc. **42**, 558–573 (2018)
6. Hasrat, I.R., Jensen, P.G., Larsen, K.G., Srba, J.: End-to-end heat-pump control using continuous time stochastic modelling and UPPAAL STRATEGO. In: Aït-Ameur, Y., Crăciun, F. (eds.) TASE 2022. LNCS, vol. 13299, pp. 363–380. Springer, Cham (2022). https://doi.org/10.1007/978-3-031-10363-6_24
7. Juhl, R., Møller, J.K., Madsen, H.: CTSMR - Continuous Time Stochastic Modeling in R. arXiv (2016)
8. David, A., Jensen, P.G., Larsen, K.G., Mikučionis, M., Taankvist, J.H.: UPPAAL STRATEGO. In: Baier, C., Tinelli, C. (eds.) TACAS 2015. LNCS, vol. 9035, pp. 206–211. Springer, Heidelberg (2015). https://doi.org/10.1007/978-3-662-46681-0_16
9. Hermansen, R., Smith, K., Thorsen, J.E., Wang, J., Zong, Y.: Model predictive control for a heat booster substation in ultra low temperature district heating systems. Energy **238**, 121631 (2022)
10. Sepulveda, A., Paull, L., Morsi, W.G., Li, H., Diduch, C.P., Chang, L.: A novel demand side management program using water heaters and particle swarm optimization. In: 2010 IEEE Electrical Power and Energy Conference, pp. 1–5. IEEE (2010)
11. Paull, L., MacKay, D., Li, H., Chang, L.: Awater heater model for increased power system efficiency. In: 2009 Canadian Conference on Electrical and Computer Engineering, pp. 731–734. IEEE (2009)
12. Lu, S., et al.: Centralized and decentralized control for demand response. In: ISGT 2011, pp. 1–8. IEEE (2011)
13. Nehrir, M.H., Jia, R., Pierre, D.A., Hammerstrom, D.J.: Power management of aggregate electric water heater loads by voltage control. In: 2007 IEEE Power Engineering Society General Meeting, pp. 1–6. IEEE (2007)
14. Hock, C., Goh, K., Apt, J.: Consumer strategies for controlling electric water heaters under dynamic pricing. In: Carnegie Mellon Electricity Industry Center Working Paper (2004)
15. Dolan, P.S., Nehrir, M.H., Gerez, V.: Development of a Monte Carlo based aggregate model for residential electric water heater loads. Electr. Power Syst. Res. **36**(1), 29–35 (1996)
16. Laurent, J.C., Malhame, R.P.: A physically-based computer model of aggregate electric water heating loads. IEEE Trans. Power Syst. **9**(3), 1209–1217 (1994)

17. Lane, I.E., Beute, N.: A model of the domestic hot water load. IEEE Trans. Power Syst. **11**(4), 1850–1855 (1996)
18. Jia, R., Nehrir, M.H., Pierre, D.A.: Voltage control of aggregate electric water heater load for distribution system peak load shaving using field data. In: 2007 39th North American Power Symposium, pp. 492–497 (2007)
19. Elgazzar, K., Li, H., Chang, L.: A centralized fuzzy controller for aggregated control of domestic water heaters. In: 2009 Canadian Conference on Electrical and Computer Engineering, pp. 1141–1146. IEEE (2009)
20. Paull, L., Li, H., Chang, L.: A novel domestic electric water heater model for a multi-objective demand side management program. Electr. Power Syst. Res. **80**(12), 1446–1451 (2010)
21. Kondoh, J., Lu, N., Hammerstrom, D.J.: An evaluation of the water heater load potential for providing regulation service. In: 2011 IEEE Power and Energy Society General Meeting, pp. 1–8. IEEE (2011)
22. Diao, R., Lu, S., Elizondo, M., Mayhorn, E., Zhang, Y., Samaan, N.: Electric water heater modeling and control strategies for demand response. In: 2012 IEEE Power and Energy Society General Meeting, pp. 1–8. IEEE (2012)
23. Yang, X., Svendsen, S.: Improving the district heating operation by innovative layout and control strategy of the hot water storage tank. Energy Build. **224**, 110273 (2020)
24. Farooq, A.A., Afram, A., Schulz, N., Janabi-Sharifi, F.: Grey-box modeling of a low pressure electric boiler for domestic hot water system. Appl. Thermal Eng. **84**, 257–267 (2015)
25. Furbo, S.: Heat storage for solar heating systems. Educational Note, BYG.DTU U-071, ISSN 1396-4046 (2005)
26. Hessam Golmohamadi and Kim Guldstrand Larsen: Economic heat control of mixing loop for residential buildings supplied by low-temperature district heating. J. Build. Eng. **46**, 103286 (2022)
27. Overgaard, A., Nielsen, B.K., Kallesøe, C.S., Bendtsen, J.D.: Reinforcement learning for mixing loop control with flow variable eligibility trace. In: 2019 IEEE Conference on Control Technology and Applications (CCTA), pp. 1043–1048 (2019)
28. Volkova, A., et al.: Energy cascade connection of a low-temperature district heating network to the return line of a high-temperature district heating network. Energy **198**, 117304 (2020)
29. Meesenburg, W., Ommen, T., Thorsen, J.E., Elmegaard, B.: Economic feasibility of ultra-low temperature district heating systems in newly built areas supplied by renewable energy. Energy **191**, 116496 (2020)
30. Rahmatmand, A., Vratonjic, M., Sullivan, P.E.: Energy and thermal comfort performance evaluation of thermostatic and electronic mixing valves used to provide domestic hot water of buildings. Energy Build. **212**, 109830 (2020)
31. Jensen, S.Ø.: OPSYS tools for investigating energy flexibility in houses with heat pumps (2018). https://www.annex67.org/media/1838/report-opsys-flexibilitet.pdf
32. Dayssault systems. dymola (dynamic modeling laboratory) systems engineering), October 2022. https://www.3ds.com/products-services/catia/products/dymola/
33. Larsen, K.G., Pettersson, P., Yi, W.: Uppaal in a nutshell. Int. J. Softw. Tools Technol. Transf. **1**(1-2), 134–152 (1997)
34. Behrmann, G., et al.: Uppaal 4.0. IEEE Computer Society (2006)
35. Bulychev, P., Legay, A., Wang, Z.: Uppaal-SMC: statistical model checking for priced timed automata. arXiv preprint arXiv:1207.1272 (2012)

36. Behrmann, G., Cougnard, A., David, A., Fleury, E., Larsen, K.G., Lime, D.: UPPAAL-Tiga: time for playing games! In: Damm, W., Hermanns, H. (eds.) CAV 2007. LNCS, vol. 4590, pp. 121–125. Springer, Heidelberg (2007). https://doi.org/10.1007/978-3-540-73368-3_14
37. Jensen, P.G., Larsen, K.G., Legay, A., Nyman, U.: Integrating tools: co-simulation in Uppaal using FMI-FMU. In: 2017 22nd International Conference on Engineering of Complex Computer Systems (ICECCS), pp. 11–19. IEEE (2017)
38. Hasrat, I.R., Jensen, P.G., Larsen, K.G., Srba, J.: Complete Uppaal Stratego model for "modelling of hot water buffer tank and mixing loop for an intelligent heat pump control", May 2023. https://github.com/ImranRiazAAU/BufferTankModelling.git
39. Control technology: weather compensated controls (Viessmann: climate of innovation) (2023). https://viessmanndirect.co.uk/files//8e57dbc7-8a10-4065-bcc6-a27700ee752a/weather_comp.pdf

Automated Property-Based Testing from AADL Component Contracts

John Hatcliff[1(✉)], Jason Belt[1], Robby[1], Jacob Legg[1], Danielle Stewart[2], and Todd Carpenter[2]

[1] Kansas State University, Manhattan, KS 66506, USA
hatcliff@ksu.edu
[2] Galois, Inc., Minneapolis, MN 55401, USA

Abstract. Effective and scalable quality assurance techniques are essential for realizing formal model-based development techniques for high-assurance systems. In this paper, we present the GUMBOX property-based testing framework for the SAE standard Architecture and Analysis Definition Language (AADL) integrated with HAMR AADL code generation tool chain. In GUMBOX, automated testing infrastructure for AADL component application code is automatically generated from AADL models and formal specifications written in the GUMBO contract language. This testing framework complements our previous work on using code-level symbolic execution to verify that component source code conforms to model-level GUMBO contracts, and it allows developers to switch between using testing and formal verification with specifications derived from a common contract language. We describe how the GUMBOX framework is incorporated in continuous integration infrastructure with parallel and distributed execution of tests in industrial workflows.

1 Introduction

The Architecture Analysis and Design Language (AADL) [18] is an SAE standard [7] supporting Model-Based Systems Engineering (MBSE) for real-time embedded systems. AADL has been used in many industrial projects in both Europe and the US to develop critical systems [4,5,11,19,35,45,46]. AADL is distinguished by its relatively strong semantic emphasis (compared to other modeling languages like UML and SysML) and by its ecosystem of analysis tools that leverage that semantics. Tools that generate code from AADL models such as Ocarina [35], RAMSES [8], and HAMR [25] are helping fulfill the AADL community's MBSE visions by supporting the deployment of critical systems derived directly from models.

Due to the strong semantics of AADL, researchers have developed formal model-based behavior specification and verification techniques. In particular, AADL component contract languages such as AGREE [12] and BLESS

This work is supported in part by the U.S. Army Combat Capabilities Development Command, Aviation and Missile Center under Contract No.W911W6-20-C-2020 and the U.S. Defense Advanced Research Projects Agency (DARPA).

A. Cimatti and L. Titolo (Eds.): FMICS 2023, LNCS 14290, pp. 131–150, 2023.
https://doi.org/10.1007/978-3-031-43681-9_8

[34] have illustrated how system requirements can be stated as system and component-level formal specifications based on propositional and first-order logic [27]. However, both AGREE and BLESS analyses apply to the *model-level* and only address thread behavior specifications based on rather abstract notations (Lustre-based notations for AGREE, and state transition notations for BLESS).

In an industry/academic research partnership, Kansas State University and Galois developed the GUMBO AADL contract language which: (a) unifies concepts from AGREE and BLESS, and (b) provides a stronger connection to AADL-aligned code generation. In particular, GUMBO integrates model-level contracts and code-level contracts. As demonstrated with the HAMR AADL code generation tool, model-level component contracts are compiled, translated, and woven into thread application code interfaces as part of the automated HAMR code generation process.

In previous work [28], we showed how: (a) code-level contracts can be generated for AADL GUMBO model contracts, and (b) developer-written thread application code could be automatically verified against contracts using an IDE-integrated verification environment based on symbolic execution. Since the code-level contracts are a refinement of the model-level contracts, the code-level contract verification implies that the thread application code conforms to the model-level contracts. Given that the AADL standard has a number of dimensions related to code generation including a code generation annex, descriptions of thread code organization (thread entry points), and descriptions of run-time services that implement foundational thread dispatching and communication steps, a stronger connection between model-level contract languages and code-level contract languages is a significant step forward in further developing the AADL MBSE vision.

In this paper, we extend the GUMBO framework to support automated and scalable property-based testing that interoperates seamlessly with the existing symbolic execution contract verification framework. We refer this extension as GUMBOX (i.e., GUMBO eXecutable contracts for testing).

- We describe a scheme for automatically translating GUMBO AADL contracts to code-level executable contracts that can be called by testing and run-time monitoring frameworks to determine if thread application code pre- and post-states satisfy the contracts.
- We present an automatically generated randomized property-based testing framework that can (in "push-button fashion") automatically test thread application code against the generated executable contracts.
- We implement the above framework in the HAMR AADL code generation tool chain.
- We further provide an automatically generated server-based architecture for running the property-based test suite in a parallel and distributed fashion on a collection of servers, e.g., as part of an industrial continuous integration framework, and we generate infrastructure for collecting coverage and other information needed to support assurance arguments.
- We demonstrate the property-based testing framework on industry-derived examples and illustrate how the testing framework works hand-in-hand with

the contract verification framework to provide complementary approaches to assurance as part of industry workflows.

The GUMBO contract framework and its associated verification and testing capabilities were developed in two US Department of Defense research projects: (1) the GUMBO project, funded by the US Army, aimed to unify previous AADL behavioral specification languages, and (2) the SIRFUR project, funded by the US Defense Advanced Research Projects Agency (DARPA) had the goal of providing a developer-friendly workflow-integrated verification environment for code-level reasoning. The implementation [23] and examples [22] discussed in this paper are publicly available under an open source license.

2 Background

AADL: SAE International standard AS5506C [7] defines the AADL core language for expressing the structure of embedded real-time systems via definitions of software and hardware components, their interfaces, and their communication. The AADL provides a precise, tool-independent, and standardized modeling vocabulary of common embedded software and hardware elements using a component-based approach [18,30]. The AADL standard also describes Run-Time Services (RTS) – a collection of run-time libraries that provide key aspects of threading and communication behavior. A major subset of the Run-Time Services has been formalized and a reference implementation has been developed [26], and we have designed our contract language and associated translation to code-level contracts with these definitions in mind.

HAMR: The High Assurance Modeling and Rapid engineering framework (HAMR) generates code from AADL models for multiple execution platforms [25]. This includes generating threading, port communication, and scheduling infrastructure code that conforms to AADL run-time semantics as well as application code skeletons that engineers fill in to complete the behavior of the system. For the JVM platform, HAMR generates code in Slang [43], a high-integrity subset of Scala, which can be integrated with support code written in Scala and Java. Mixed Slang/Scala-based HAMR systems can also be translated to JavaScript (e.g., for simulation and prototyping) and run in a web browser or on the NodeJS platform. HAMR generates C infrastructure and application skeletons when targeting Linux and the seL4 micro-kernel [44]. Slang can be transpiled to C, and HAMR factors its C code through a Slang-based "reference implementation" of the AADL run-time and application code skeletons. Using the Logika verification framework for Slang (described below), Slang code can be verified with a high-degree of automation. This provides a basis for developing high-assurance AADL-based systems using Slang directly or via translation of Slang to C. C code transpiled from Slang can be compiled using standard C compilers, as well as the CompCert Verified C compiler [37]. In the DARPA CASE program, HAMR was used by Collins Aerospace engineers to develop experimental versions of the mission control software for the Boeing's CH-47 Chinook military helicopter platform [11].

Logika: Logika is a highly automated program verifier for Slang [38]. Slang's integrated contract language enables developers to formally specify method pre- and post-conditions, data type invariants, and global invariants for global states. Verification of code conformance to contracts is performed compositionally and employs multiple back-end solvers in parallel, including Alt-Ergo [13], CVC4 [2], CVC5 [1], and Z3 [40]. Logika scalability is enhanced using incremental and parallel (distributable) verification algorithms. Verification results, developer-friendly feedback on verification results, and contract/proof editing are directly supported in the Sireum Integrated Verification Environment (IVE) – a customization of the popular IntelliJ IDE.

The Logika verification engine uses asynchronous communications between the Sireum IntelliJ plugin client and its corresponding server. This enables a seamless, on-the-fly integration similar to static type checking analysis usually offered by IDEs. That is, Logika's main usability features include an as-you-type well-formedness analysis and verification of Slang programs by sending the checking tasks to a background server process, and visualizations of various helpful feedback propagated from the server as responses of the verification requests.

3 Example

We illustrate the GUMBOX framework using the Isolette example from the US Federal Aviation Administration (FAA) Requirements Engineering Management Handbook (REMH) [36]. An Isolette is an infant incubator (medical device), and the REMH presentation focuses on a heat (infant warming) control subsystem and a safety monitoring subsystem. The REMH uses the example to illustrate best practices in requirements engineering for critical embedded systems, and presents detailed requirements at multiple levels of abstraction.

We constructed an AADL model from Isolette design information in the REMH, and used HAMR to develop Slang implementations of the two subsystems. The architecture (directed by the REMH description) emphasizes periodic threads and data ports. The control system and the safety monitoring system include three periodic threads each. An additional periodic thread is used to implement/simulate the operator interface. Slang extensions were used to simulate the temperature sensor and heater components. HAMR generates the JVM deployment of the system (Scala and Java are used to develop the simulated hardware elements and the GUI for the operator interface). There are 11 thread components, 49 component ports, and 27 connections between the ports, with 10612 non-comment/space source lines of Slang/Scala code (NCSLOC) in the infrastructure code and 184 NCSLOC in the application logic.

Figure 1 presents the AADL graphical view of the thread components in the Regulate (controller) and Monitor (safety) subsystems. We use the Manage Heat Source (MHS) thread to illustrate framework concepts.

```
thread Manage_Heat_Source
  features
    current_tempWstatus: in data port TempWstatus.impl;
```

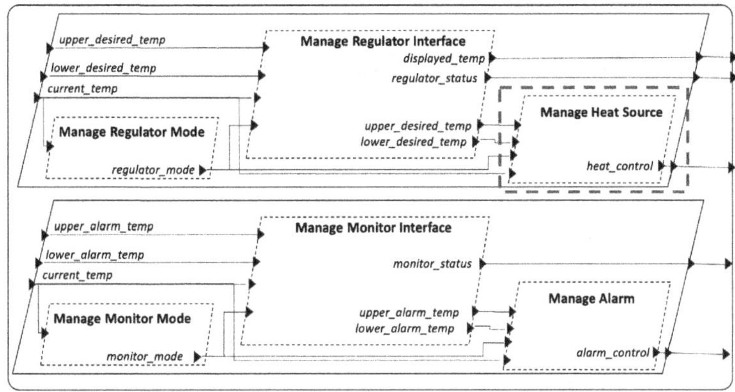

Fig. 1. Isolette - AADL Graphical View of Regulate and Monitor Subsystems

```
    lower_desired_temp: in data port Temp.impl;
    upper_desired_temp: in data port Temp.impl;
    regulator_mode: in data port Regulator_Mode;
    heat_control: out data port On_Off;
  properties
    Dispatch_Protocol => Periodic;
    Period => 1000ms;
  annex GUMBO {**
    state
      lastCmd: On_Off;

    initialize
      guarantee REQ_MHS_1 "If the Regulator Mode is
        |INIT, the Heat Control shall be set to Off":
        heat_control == On_Off.Off
         & lastCmd == heat_control;

    compute
      assume lower_is_less_than_upper_temp:
        lower_desired_temp.value < upper_desired_temp.value;
      guarantee lastCmd
        "Set lastCmd to value of output port":
        lastCmd == heat_control;

      cases
        case REQ_MHS_1
          "If the Regulator Mode is INIT, the Heat
            |Control shall be set to Off.":
          assume regulator_mode == Regulator_Mode.Init_Regulator_Mode;
          guarantee heat_control == On_Off.Off;
        case REQ_MHS_2
          "If the Regulator Mode is NORMAL and the
            |Current Temperature is less than the
            |Lower Desired Temperature, the Heat
            |Control shall be set to On.":
          assume regulator_mode == Regulator_Mode.Normal_Regulator_Mode
            & current_tempWstatus.value < lower_desired_temp.value;
          guarantee heat_control == On_Off.Onn;
        case REQ_MHS_3
```

```
43              "If the Regulator Mode is NORMAL and the
44                |Current Temperature is greater than
45                |the Upper Desired Temperature, the Heat
46                |Control shall be set to Off.":
47              assume regulator_mode == Regulator_Mode.Normal_Regulator_Mode
48                & current_tempWstatus.value > upper_desired_temp.value;
49              guarantee heat_control == On_Off.Off;
50            case REQ_MHS_4
51              "If the Regulator Mode is NORMAL and the
52                |Current Temperature is greater than or
53                |equal to the Lower Desired Temperature
54                |and less than or equal to the Upper
55                |Desired Temperature, the value of the
56                |Heat Control shall not be changed.":
57              assume regulator_mode == Regulator_Mode.Normal_Regulator_Mode
58                & current_tempWstatus.value >= lower_desired_temp.value
59                & current_tempWstatus.value <= upper_desired_temp.value;
60              guarantee heat_control == In(lastCmd);
61            case REQ_MHS_5
62              "If the Regulator Mode is FAILED, the Heat
63                |Control shall be set to Off.":
64              assume regulator_mode == Regulator_Mode.Failed_Regulator_Mode;
65              guarantee heat_control == On_Off.Off;
66    **};
67  end Manage_Heat_Source;
```

Listing 1.1. Manage Heat Source AADL

Listing 1.1 provides the AADL textual definition of the MHS thread interface, including component ports (lines 2–7) and thread properties (lines 8–10). Using AADL's annex mechanism, lines 11–66 provide the GUMBO behavioral contract for the component. Like other contract languages (e.g., the `state` declarations in SPARK Ada), GUMBO contracts include declarations of local state that are relevant to the contract-specified behavior (lines 12–13). The AADL standard dictates that thread code should be structured as "entry point" methods that will be invoked by the underlying scheduling framework. GUMBO provides dedicated contracts for each thread's: (a) *initialize* entry point that is executed once in the system's initialization phase, and (b) the *compute* entry point that is executed repeatedly (either event-triggered for sporadic components or time-triggered for periodic components) during system execution. Compute entry point contracts can take multiple forms. For sporadic components, contracts clauses can be organized in sections that specify component behavior on arrival of specific events. For periodic components (as in the MHS thread), lines 22–23 provide general pre-conditions (`assume` clauses) and post-conditions (`guarantee` clauses) which apply to every dispatch, and these can be extended with contract `cases` (e.g., as in JML [6]). A contract case applies when its `assume` clause is satisfied in the pre-state, and the associated `guarantee` clause must hold in the post-state.

```
def timeTriggered(api: Manage_Heat_Source_impl_Operational_Api): Unit = {
  // --------  Auto-generated contract (excerpts) -----------
  Contract(
    Requires(
      // BEGIN COMPUTE REQUIRES timeTriggered
        // assume lower_is_less_than_upper_temp
        api.lower_desired_temp.value < api.upper_desired_temp.value
```

```
8        // END COMPUTE REQUIRES timeTriggered ),
9      Modifies(api,lastCmd),
10     Ensures(
11       // BEGIN COMPUTE ENSURES timeTriggered
12         // guarantee lastCmd
13         //   Set lastCmd to value of output port
14         lastCmd == api.heat_control,
15         // (...other aspect elided...)
16         // case REQ_MHS_2
17         //   If the Regulator Mode is NORMAL and the
18         //   Current Temperature is less than the
19         //   Lower Desired Temperature, the Heat
20         //   Control shall be set to On.
21         (api.regulator_mode == Regulator_Mode.Normal_Regulator_Mode &
22            api.current_tempWstatus.value < api.lower_desired_temp.value)
23             -->: (api.heat_control == On_Off.Onn),
24         // (...other aspects elided)
25       // END COMPUTE ENSURES timeTriggered
26       ))
27   // -------- Developer-supplied application code -----------
28   val lower = api.get_lower_desired_temp().get
29   val upper = api.get_upper_desired_temp().get
30   val regulator_mode = api.get_regulator_mode().get
31   val currentTemp = api.get_current_tempWstatus().get
32
33   var currentCmd = lastCmd
34   regulator_mode match {
35     case Regulator_Mode.Init_Regulator_Mode =>
36       currentCmd = On_Off.Off
37     case Regulator_Mode.Normal_Regulator_Mode =>
38       if (currentTemp.value > upper.value) {
39         currentCmd = On_Off.Off
40       } else if (currentTemp.value < lower.value) {
41         currentCmd = On_Off.Onn }
42     case Regulator_Mode.Failed_Regulator_Mode =>
43       currentCmd = On_Off.Off }
44   api.put_heat_control(currentCmd)
45   lastCmd = currentCmd }
```

One of the significant design aspects of the framework involves the combining and arranging the many different forms of model-level contracts (including data invariants, integration constraints, entry point contracts, etc.) into code-level contracts appropriate for a code verification or testing tool. In the listing above, lines 3–26 show the HAMR auto-generated code-level contract for the Slang MHS thread compute entry point method (named `timeTriggered()`). The general **assume** clause in the GUMBO **compute** block (Listing 1.1, line 22) is translated to a pre-condition in the code-level `Requires(..)` clause (line 7), and the general **guarantee** clause (Listing 1.1, line 24) is translated to a post-condition in the code-level `Ensures(..)` clause (lines 14). Note that the translation provides traceability information by embedded GUMBO clause descriptions and identifiers in the code-level contracts. In addition, HAMR includes delimiters such as those at lines 11 and 25 to mark the beginning and ending of auto-generated contracts. If GUMBO contracts are updated in the AADL model, HAMR can regenerate updated contracts into the same position in the code (by parsing the file to locate the delimiters), and thus can keep the code-level contracts in sync with the model contracts without clobbering the developer's application code.

The developer implements the behavior code for the thread shown at lines 28–45. AADL's semantics for threading and port-manipulation ensure that thread implementations can be verified compositionally; abstractly, a thread's behavior is a function from its input port state and local variables to its output port state, with possibly updated local variables (see [26]). Logika can be applied interactively (with many features supporting industrial usability and explanation of verification results) or in batch mode as part of a server-based continuous integration process. Logika verifies absence of run-time exceptions and code conformance to contracts in around 25 s for the MHS thread initialize and compute entry points. Smart incremental verification, SMT-query caching, and other optimizations gives substantially faster performance to support on-the-fly re-checking during code editing. HAMR integrates the verified application code of Listing 3 with a Slang-based implementation of the AADL run-time to create a JVM-based system deployment. If desired, the code be transpiled to C to create a system deployment on Linux or seL4 (all artifacts available at [22]).

4 Property-Based Testing Framework Overview

The automated verification that Logika provides for HAMR components can be very effective. However, like any formal methods approach, in certain situations, decideability boundaries require developers to supply annotations including loop invariants, assert statements that include facts to help SMT-based reasoning (and sometimes explicit reasoning steps in Logika's manual proof language). Moreover, many certification regimes and industry quality assurance practices still emphasize testing to a great extent. Therefore, we aim to provide multiple ways for industrial developers to leverage GUMBO contracts. Even when contracts are lightly used or not used at all, developers can still benefit from HAMR automatically generating testing infrastructure to accompanying automatically generated infrastructure and application code skeletons.

An overarching objective is to provide a testing framework that is easy to use "out of the box". That is, when HAMR generates code and contract-based testing infrastructure, developers from the outset should be able to "push a button" to launch a test suite that exercises the code with randomized inputs and contract-derived oracles. Developers should be able to increase behavior coverage by simply running the test suite for longer periods of time (generating more tests) rather than having to add formal methods-based annotations, etc. The testing infrastructure should be incorporated in a continuous integration/DevOps style of development. Of course, to get high degrees of coverage, it is expected that developers may need to customize, e.g., the test vector generators, but the required actions and workflows should be based on testing concepts with which industrial developers are familiar.

Figure 2 presents the main elements of our HAMR-integrated GUMBOX framework, which we believe meets the objectives outlined above. First, from

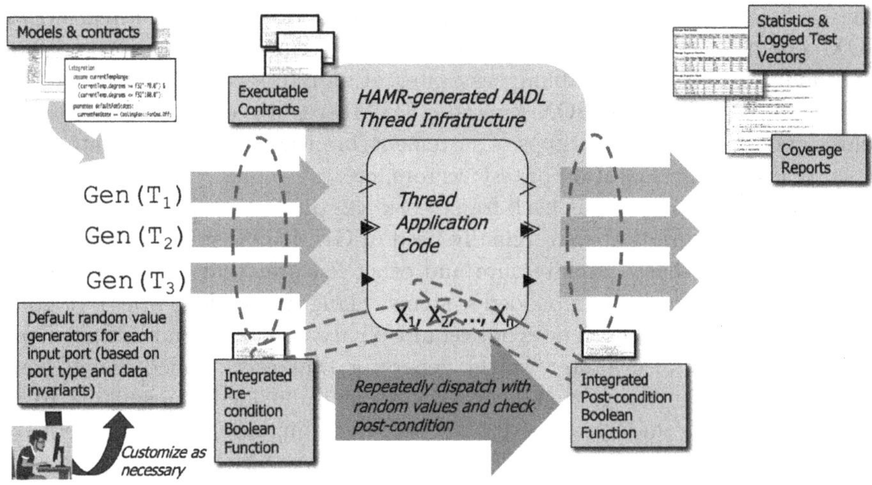

Fig. 2. GUMBO-X Property-Based Testing Architecture

AADL-based GUMBO contracts, GUMBOX generates executeable versions of each GUMBO contract clause represented as Slang side-effect free boolean function that takes as parameters thread port and local variable values. These contracts are emitted into a test infrastructure library separate from application code so they can be easily automatically re-generated without interferring with application code. Second, HAMR automatically generates random value generators for each input port and GUMBO-declared local state variable. Note that typical use of property-based testing frameworks in the QuickCheck [10] family (like ScalaCheck [42]) rely on the developer to design generators for user-defined types using framework libraries. In contrast, for each user type specified in AADL's Data Modeling annex, GUMBOX will automatically generate an initial random value generator based on the type's structure. The goal is to get a serviceable generator for initial testing that the user can subsequently easily adapt to achieve more effective value generation and increased coverage. Third, GUMBOX generates boolean-valued pre- and post- condition methods for thread entry points that integrate all relevant contract clauses from data invariants, integration constraints, and entry point contracts to form the checks of the thread dispatch pre- and post-states implied by the GUMBO contract language semantics. Fourth, GUMBOX generates test harnesses and unit tests that combine the above elements to: (a) generate vectors of random values for input ports and local variables, (b) discard test vectors that do not satisfy the generated pre-condition method and applicable invariants, (c) dispatch the thread application code, (d) retrieve output port and updated local variable values and then invoke the post condition method on (saved) input values and output values, and (e) provide a pass/fail result that is incorporated into the test reporting mechanism. The resulting test suite can be launched for a single thread or all threads in the system with a single button push in the IDE.[1] Fifth, GUMBOX generates deployment scripts for parallel/distributed execution on a family of multi-core servers, enabling easy integration into a continuous integration framework. Finally, GUMBOX generates HTML reports of coverage statistics, source-code color-coded markups of statement/branch coverage, with integrated links to JSON representation of test vectors, etc.

While the existing ScalaCheck framework [42] provides a nice library of generator infrastructure that we originally used in GUMBOX, it includes a higher-order combinator-based architecture and other features that lie outside of the Slang subset designed for embedded systems (Slang Embedded) where we guarantee that the C translation does not require a garbage collection runtime. Thus, we developed our own lighter weight generator framework called SlangCheck, written entirely in Slang, that generates Slang Embedded transpilable to C. Thus, the entire framework described above, including application and HAMR infrastructure code can be transpiled to C and used to test HAMR deployments for Linux or seL4. Moreover, for HAMR workflows in which developers write application logic directly in C instead of Slang, our framework allows GUMBO contracts to be leveraged for testing C code even when the architectural contracts cannot be utilized for formal code-level contract-based verification in Logika.

5 GUMBOX Illustrated

In this section, we illustrate each category of GUMBOX artifact from Fig. 2.

```
/** guarantees REQ_MHS_2
  *   If the Regulator Mode is NORMAL and the
  *   Current Temperature is less than the
  *   Lower Desired Temperature, the Heat
  *   Control shall be set to On.
  * @param api_current_tempWstatus incoming data port
  * @param api_lower_desired_temp incoming data port
  * @param api_regulator_mode incoming data port
  * @param api_heat_control outgoing data port
  */
@strictpure def compute_case_REQ_MHS_2(
    api_current_tempWstatus: TempWstatus_impl,
    api_lower_desired_temp: Temp_impl,
    api_regulator_mode: Regulator_Mode.Type,
    api_heat_control: On_Off.Type): B =
  (api_regulator_mode == Regulator_Mode.Normal_Regulator_Mode &
     api_current_tempWstatus.value < api_lower_desired_temp.value) -->:
    (api_heat_control == On_Off.Onn)
```

Listing 1.2. Slang executable representation of the MHS 2 requirement clause

To illustrate how each clause from the GUMBO AADL-level contracts are translated to Slang, Listing 1.2 above shows the pure boolean function representing the AADL MHS compute entry point contract clause in Listing 1.1 at line 34.

[1] As with any testing/code-level formal method, I/O and interactions with physical devices or stateful services may need to be supported by manually crafted stubs.

The assume/guarantee case structure is represented using implication. Auto-generated comments hold traceability information including the clause identifier REQ_MHS_2, description, and state elements mentioned by the contract.

```
/** CEP-T-Case: Top-Level case contracts for
  *   manage_heat_source's compute entrypoint  */
@strictpure def compute_CEP_T_Case (
    In_lastCmd: On_Off.Type,
    api_current_tempWstatus: TempWstatus_impl,
    api_lower_desired_temp: Temp_impl,
    api_regulator_mode: Regulator_Mode.Type,
    api_upper_desired_temp: Temp_impl,
    api_heat_control: On_Off.Type): B =
  compute_case_REQ_MHS_1(api_regulator_mode, api_heat_control) &
  compute_case_REQ_MHS_2(api_current_tempWstatus, api_lower_desired_temp,
      api_regulator_mode, api_heat_control) &
  compute_case_REQ_MHS_3(api_current_tempWstatus, api_regulator_mode,
      api_upper_desired_temp, api_heat_control) &
  compute_case_REQ_MHS_4(In_lastCmd, api_current_tempWstatus,
      api_lower_desired_temp, api_regulator_mode, api_upper_desired_temp,
      api_heat_control) &
  compute_case_REQ_MHS_5(api_regulator_mode, api_heat_control)
```

Listing 1.3. Slang executable representation of conjoined compute contract cases

Listing 1.3 above shows how the contract case clause functions (e.g., from Listing 1.2) are conjoined in a single function.

```
/** CEP-Post: Compute Entrypoint Post-Condition for manage_heat_source */
@strictpure def compute_CEP_Post (
    In_lastCmd: On_Off.Type,
    lastCmd: On_Off.Type,
    api_current_tempWstatus: TempWstatus_impl,
    api_lower_desired_temp: Temp_impl,
    api_regulator_mode: Regulator_Mode.Type,
    api_upper_desired_temp: Temp_impl,
    api_heat_control: On_Off.Type): B =
  (// CEP-Guar: guarantee clauses of manage_heat_source's compute entrypoint
   compute_CEP_T_Guar (lastCmd, api_heat_control) &
   // CEP-T-Case: case clauses of manage_heat_source's compute entrypoint
   compute_CEP_T_Case (In_lastCmd, api_current_tempWstatus,
      api_lower_desired_temp, api_regulator_mode, api_upper_desired_temp,
      api_heat_control))
```

Listing 1.4. Slang executable representation of MHS post-condition

Then, the complete post-condition method in Listing 1.4 references the function for the general guarantee clause at Listing 1.1 line 24 along with the composite function for the case clauses in Listing 1.3.

```
/** CEP-Pre: Compute Entrypoint Pre-Condition for manage_heat_source  */
@strictpure def compute_CEP_Pre (
    In_lastCmd: On_Off.Type,
    api_current_tempWstatus: TempWstatus_impl,
    api_lower_desired_temp: Temp_impl,
    api_regulator_mode: Regulator_Mode.Type,
    api_upper_desired_temp: Temp_impl): B =
  (// CEP-Assm: assume clauses of manage_heat_source's compute entrypoint
   compute_CEP_T_Assm (api_lower_desired_temp, api_upper_desired_temp))
```

Listing 1.5. Slang executable representation of MHS pre-condition

For the MHS contracts, the composite pre-condition in Listing 1.5 above is much simpler; it includes only the function for the general `assume` clause in Listing 1.1 line 22.

```
1  def next_TempWstatus_impl(): TempWstatus_impl = {
2    var value: F32 = next_F32()
3    var status: ValueStatus.Type =  next_ValueStatusType()
4
5     var v: TempWstatus_impl = TempWstatus_impl(value, status)
6
7     for(i <- 0 to 100) {
8       if(get_Config_TempWstatus_impl.filter(v)) {
9         return v }
10      println(s"Retrying for failing value: $v")
11      value = next_F32()
12      status = next_ValueStatusType()
13      v = TempWstatus_impl(value, status)
14    }
15    assert(F, "Requirements to strict to generate")
16      halt("Requirements to strict to generate")
17    }
```

Listing 1.6. SlangCheck value generator for AADL-declared TempWStatus type

Next, Listing 1.6 above shows the SlangCheck `next_` random value generator automatically generated for the user-defined `TempWstatus` type specified by the developer in the AADL model using AADL Data Modeling Annex. This is the generator used to generate values for the `current_tempWstatus` input port in Listing 1.1 line 3. The AADL type is a struct type with two fields: `value` (AADL `F32` base type) and `status` (with user-defined `Status` type), and the `TempWstatus` generator uses the `next_F32()` (line 2) and `next_ValueStatusType` (line 3) generators that are automatically generated for the types of those fields. Each auto-generated generator object includes a `filter` method which can be customized by the developer, but by default is used to hold an executable representation of any data invariants associated with the type. The `next_` method for each type uses a `for` loop to repeatedly built candidate values for the type that satisfy the configured filter. After a certain number of failed attempts to find a value that satisfies the filter, the `next_` method will halt (aborting any associated tests) – indicating to the developer that they may need to customize the method in some way to obtain a random value that will satisfy the filter with fewer retries (or the bound on retries can be increased).

```
def testComputeCB(
    api_current_tempWstatus: TempWstatus_impl,
    api_lower_desired_temp: Temp_impl,
    api_regulator_mode: Regulator_Mode.Type,
    api_upper_desired_temp: Temp_impl): GumboXResult.Type = {
  // Step 1 [SaveInLocal]: retrieve and save the current (input) values of
  //   GUMBO-declared local state vars as retrieved from the component state
  val In_lastCmd: On_Off.Type = isolette.Regulate.Manage_Heat_Source.lastCmd

  // Step 2 [CheckPre]: check/filter based on pre-condition.
  if (!isolette.Regulate.Manage_Heat_Source_GumboX.compute_CEP_Pre (
      In_lastCmd, api_current_tempWstatus, api_lower_desired_temp,
      api_regulator_mode, api_upper_desired_temp)) {
```

```
      return GumboXResult.Pre_Condition_Unsat
    }

    // Step 3 [PutInPorts]: put values on the input ports
    put_current_tempWstatus(api_current_tempWstatus)
    put_lower_desired_temp(api_lower_desired_temp)
    put_regulator_mode(api_regulator_mode)
    put_upper_desired_temp(api_upper_desired_temp)

    // Step 4 [InvokeEntryPoint]: invoke the entry point test method
    testCompute()

    // Step 5 [RetrieveOutState]: retrieve values of the output ports
    //         via get operations and GUMBO declared local state variables
    val api_heat_control: On_Off.Type = get_heat_control().get
    val lastCmd: On_Off.Type = isolette.Regulate.Manage_Heat_Source.lastCmd

    // Step 6 [CheckPost]: invoke the oracle function
    if (!isolette.Regulate.Manage_Heat_Source_GumboX.compute_CEP_Post(
        In_lastCmd, lastCmd, api_current_tempWstatus, api_lower_desired_temp,
        api_regulator_mode, api_upper_desired_temp, api_heat_control)) {
      return GumboXResult.Post_Condition_Fail
    }
    return GumboXResult.Post_Condition_Pass
  }
```

Listing 1.7. Test runner for MHS compute entry point

The elements from the previous listings are combined in an auto-generated test runner in Listing 1.7 for a property-based test testing the developer's MHS compute entry point implementation against the AADL specified contract, and then this runner is automatically called repeatedly from the testing infrastructure with random values created by `next_` methods to achieve the desired number of tests for the MHS thread. The method contains an `api_` parameter for each input port. In Step 1 (as indicated by the auto-generated comments), the current value for the GUMBO declarated thread local state variable `lastCmd` (Listing 1.1 line 13) is retrieved from the thread's local state. Step 2 checks to see if the constructed pre-state of random port values and current local state satisfy the executable pre-condition. On failure to satisfy, a special status value (distinct from a failing test) is returned, indicating that a new set of random inputs needs to be generated to achieve an effective test. Step 3 uses HAMR-generated `put_` methods to put randomized inputs into the input ports. Step 4 uses the HAMR infrastructure method `testCompute` to launch the compute entry point application code for the thread. Step 5 uses HAMR-generated `get_` methods to get the values on output ports. Step 6 passes both pre-state and post-state values to the executable post-condition, and then returns an appropriate pass/fail status value. As explained earlier, AADL's run-time semantics [26] for port communication and tasking enables the application code of each thread to be viewed as a function from port inputs and local variables to port outputs (and possibly updated port values), which is key to enabling us to design contracts and test behavior as explained above.

As one can imagine, generating random test objects that should satisfy complex properties may take a long time to find satisfying object structures. To address this issue, GUMBOX generates infrastructure for parallelizing random test objects leveraging modern multi/many-core hardware and distributing them across available networked computing nodes. Once satisfying objects are generated, they are serialized and sent to a common computing node that serves as a test objects accumulator. This common node can then deserialize the test objects, run tests using the objects as input, and generate test result reports, including code coverage information (e.g., branch/instruction coverage).

6 Experience Report

We describe our experience in applying the property-based testing infrastructure in end-to-end development (models+contracts to deployed systems). Logika symbolic execution verification has also been applied to the same artifacts.

We consider two additional examples beyond the Isolette example.

Temperature Control: This is a "hello world" example used in our HAMR tutorial that includes 4 thread components, 9 thread component ports, and 5 connections between thread ports, with 6410 non-comment/space source lines of Slang/Scala code (NCSLOC) in the infrastructure code and 97 NCSLOC in the application logic.

Nuclear Reactor Safety Subsystem: The HARDENS system artifacts [24] were originally developed on a Galois project that aimed to demonstrate end-to-end model-based development technologies and formal methods for the US Nuclear Regulatory Commission. The artifacts included requirements developed according to a rigorous methodology, SysMLv2 system models, application logic written in Galois' Cryptol domain-specific language, and executables derived from the Cryptol tooling (as well as many other artifacts such as assurance cases not relevant to this paper). From these artifacts, we considered the *actuation logic subsystem* (trip signal voting logic) and developed a corresponding AADL model (the Galois SysMLv2 modeling and our AADL model are structurally very similar), contracts in GUMBO, and component implementations in Slang. System deployments where developed for the JVM, Linux, and seL4 microkernel. In this subsystem, there are 15 thread components, 76 thread component ports, and 38 connections between thread ports, with 8847 non-comment/space source lines of Slang/Scala code (NCSLOC) in the infrastructure code and 156 NCSLOC in the application logic.

Experience: We are primarily interested in understanding if GUMBOX can automatically give quick feedback on code conformance to contracts with "reasonable" statement and branch code coverage without any formal-methods-oriented code annotations or verification tool configuration. We ran experiments on a simple server configuration of three 8-core Linux Xeon 3.2 GHz 32 GB memory used to generate test vectors and a 8-core M1 Mac Mini with 16 GB memory to execute tests. To determine effectiveness for different "developer wait times", we ran the automated testing infrastructure for each thread using timeouts of 1, 5, 30, and 360 s. Detailed reports (linked from the README files for each system in our examples repository [22]) are provided to the user in the form of passing/failing tests and code coverage. These reports also break down tests into those "candidate" test vectors generated (that satisfied any declared data invariants) and the subset of those vectors that were able to satisfy specified pre-conditions to achieve an "effective test".

For the MHS Isolette thread, in 1 s 78 candidate vectors and 45 effective tests were generated with 100% coverage; in 30 s 1149 effective tests were generated. The code base did not have any declared data invariants, and so random values were being generated across the entire F32 range. We conjecture that adding a simple framework option to set lower and upper bounds on base type generators would make the framework even more effective for "tire kicking" (e.g., increasing the percentage of effective tests). In general, this would require the developer to have some basic understanding of the ranges of computation in the code to get "decent" coverage. For 5 of the 6 Isolette threads, our existing capabilities were very effective out of the box. A Manage Alarm thread from the safety subsystem had a complex precondition with tolerance calculations in the application code, and even for the 360 s experiment there were a few statements not covered with 819 effective tests.

The temperature control example included data invariants on multiple F32 temperature values (values must always be greater than absolute zero) and a desired temperature range (must satisfy base temperature invariant and low bound must be less than high bound). One thread included some strong pre-conditions, and the framework was only able to achieve 72% coverage with 9 effective tests after 30 s. In this situation, the tool is randomly generating values across the entire F32 range and then discarding vectors that don't satisfy the data invariants or pre-conditions. When we use a developer customized generator which simply bounds all F32 temperature ranges to between −150 and +150° (which would be a reasonable environmental assumption for this system), we were about to generate 200 effective tests in 5 s with 100% coverage. Nevertheless, this indicates the potential benefit of using more sophisticated automated fuzzing and model finding techniques to generate initial test vectors with a given set of constraints.

Even though the HARDENS RTS example is the largest in terms of model elements, its state space is simpler because it only involves boolean values in the trip/voting logic. For example, in each of the 12 threads, we were able to generate around 420 effective tests in 5 s with 100% coverage.

Summary: Our overall approach includes two orthogonal technical facets: (1) the generation of the executable contracts, e.g., for thread entry points, and (2) the generation of test vector generators. The executable contracts can be used with manually written tests or with generators from other frameworks like ScalaCheck. They can also be used directly for run-time monitoring. For (2), our goal in this initial phase of the work was to build an auto-generated framework in Slang that also could be compiled to C. Now that this is in place, we will have an opportunity to enhance the techniques used in the test vector generation.

Our initial experience with this new framework confirms our expectations: for many situations, with no intervention of the developer, we are able to get effective debugging of code-to-contract conformance in 5 s or less. As expected, there are also situations where Logika verification is needed to get complete coverage, and of course, we want full verification if at all possible to address problematic code issues that can arise even when statement/branch coverage is achieved. Obviously, we would like to implement more effective test generation techniques. In the absence of more sophisticated techniques, we believe that giving the developer the ability to define set profiles for base type random value ranges can be highly effective.

7 Related Work

Early work on model-based testing with AADL used Markov Chains derived from AADL Error Model specifications to construct tests for very simple AADL systems whose behaviors are specified using automata [16]. Johnsen et al. [31] provide a sketch of how AADL data flow and control flow information can be used to derive system tests for reachability between modeling elements. Neither of these address executable code generated from AADL models or testing against strong behavioral specifications. Recent unpublished work describes an industrial framework called Automated Test and Re-Test (ATRT) [33] that enhances AADL modeling and code generation via Ocarina [35] to support system testing and run-time monitoring of system properties based on system events and state changes gathered through telemetry. This approach has a number of benefits in industrial development, but it is complementary to our work because it does not focus on contract-based reasoning nor integrated verification and testing of component code against rich contracts. In the next phase of our work, we plan to add similar system testing and monitoring capabilities.

There have been a number of efforts that integrate contract based verification and testing at the code level (e.g., [9,17,39]). A line of work that has been very influential for us is the *GNATTest/GNATProve* framework for SPARK2014 [29,32] that integrates contract-based testing and SMT-based verification in industrial workflows in support of certification (e.g., for DO-178C) [41]. In particular, we are aiming to follow their philosophy that assurance arguments should be able to able to freely combine verification and testing evidence that code for software units conforms to unit-level requirements captured as contracts. What primarily distinguishes our work from these other efforts is that we aim to integrate model and code-level contracts where the contracts and structure of the unit interfaces is conformant to the AADL computational model for real-time tasking and port-based communication, and we include infrastructure for automated test generation.

8 Conclusion

Our previous work on GUMBO [28] provided the first integrated model- and code-level contract verification framework for AADL. This paper, to the best of our knowledge, provides the first integrated automated contract-derived property-based testing framework for AADL. Moreover, the GUMBOX framework presented here is designed to enable a seamless integration of component testing and verification for properties uniformly captured by contracts. This is achieved by carefully designing the frameworks (informed by a formal semantics of the AADL run-time [26]) so that the same contract language can be applied to test/verify input/output behavior of components at the exact same "execution observation points" associated with thread dispatching and port enqueuing/dequeuing. Both the testing and verification support is incorporated in a widely-used IDE and an industrial-strength distributed continuous integration framework.

We are developing several additional capabilities. First, although our scalable distributed based testing infrastructure combined to developer customization of generators seems to provide sufficient numbers of random test vectors that pass component preconditions, we are working on integrating model-finding and fuzzing capabilities into the random value generators so that the generators will be much more likely to produce filter-satisfying values without retries. We're also considering how our Logika symbolic execution engine for Slang [43] can be enhanced with our previous symbolic-execution-based test generation techniques [3,14,15] as well as concolic execution and guided generation of test vectors based on path conditions [20,21]. Second, we are building an integrated system testing/verification driven by model-level system properties. GUMBOX executable pre/post-condition methods can be easily integrated into such a framework to support run-time verification of component contracts. Finally, work described in this paper focuses on testing of HAMR-generated Slang contracts and code. Utilizing the ability to transpile Slang to C, we plan to investigate how our infrastructure can be used directly to support C component implementations and system deployments on Linux and seL4.

References

1. Barbosa, H., et al.: cvc5: A versatile and industrial-strength SMT solver. In: TACAS 2022. LNCS, vol. 13243, pp. 415–442. Springer, Cham (2022). https://doi.org/10.1007/978-3-030-99524-9_24
2. Barrett, C., et al.: CVC4. In: Gopalakrishnan, G., Qadeer, S. (eds.) CAV 2011. LNCS, vol. 6806, pp. 171–177. Springer, Heidelberg (2011). https://doi.org/10.1007/978-3-642-22110-1_14
3. Belt, J., Hatcliff, J., Robby, Chalin, P., Hardin, D., Deng, X.: Bakar kiasan: flexible contract checking for critical systems using symbolic execution. In: Bobaru, M., Havelund, K., Holzmann, G.J., Joshi, R. (eds.) NFM 2011. LNCS, vol. 6617, pp. 58–72. Springer, Heidelberg (2011). https://doi.org/10.1007/978-3-642-20398-5_6
4. Belt, J., et al.: Model-driven development for the seL4 microkernel using the HAMR framework. J. Syst. Archit. (2022)
5. Borde, E., Rahmoun, S., Cadoret, F., Pautet, L., Singhoff, F., Dissaux, P.: Architecture models refinement for fine grain timing analysis of embedded systems. In: 2014 25nd IEEE International Symposium on Rapid System Prototyping, pp. 44–50 (2014)
6. Burdy, L., et al.: An overview of JML tools and applications. Int. J. Softw. Tools Technol. Transf. **7**(3), 212–232 (2005)
7. C, S.A.R.: Architecture analysis and design language (AADL) (2017)

8. Cadoret, F., Borde, E., Gardoll, S., Pautet, L.: Design patterns for rule-based refinement of safety critical embedded systems models. In: 2012 IEEE 17th International Conference on Engineering of Complex Computer Systems, pp. 67–76. IEEE (2012)
9. Cheon, Y., Leavens, G.T.: A simple and practical approach to unit testing: the JML and JUNIT way. In: ECOOP 2002 – Object-Oriented Programming, pp. 231–255 (2002)
10. Claessen, K., Hughes, J.: Quickcheck: a lightweight tool for random testing of Haskell programs. In: Proceedings of the Fifth ACM SIGPLAN International Conference on Functional Programming, pp. 268–279 (2000)
11. Cofer, D.D., et al.: Cyberassured systems engineering at scale. IEEE Secur. Priv. **20**(3), 52–64 (2022)
12. Cofer, D., Gacek, A., Miller, S., Whalen, M.W., LaValley, B., Sha, L.: Compositional verification of architectural models. In: Goodloe, A.E., Person, S. (eds.) NFM 2012. LNCS, vol. 7226, pp. 126–140. Springer, Heidelberg (2012). https://doi.org/10.1007/978-3-642-28891-3_13
13. Conchon, S., Coquereau, A., Iguernlala, M., Mebsout, A.: Alt-ergo 2.2. In: SMT Workshop: International Workshop on Satisfiability Modulo Theories (2018)
14. Deng, X., Robby, Hatcliff, J.: Kiasan: a verification and test-case generation framework for java based on symbolic execution. In: Leveraging Applications of Formal Methods, Second International Symposium, ISoLA 2006, Paphos, Cyprus, 15–19 November 2006, pp. 137 (2006)
15. Deng, X., Robby, Hatcliff, J.: Kiasan/kunit: automatic test case generation and analysis feedback for open object-oriented systems. In: Testing: Academic and Industrial Conference Practice and Research Techniques (TAICPART 2007) (2007)
16. Dong, Y.W., Wang, G., Zhao, H.B.: A model-based testing for AADL model of embedded software. In: 2009 Ninth International Conference on Quality Software, pp. 185–190 (2009)
17. Fähndrich, M.: Static verification for code contracts. In: Static Analysis, pp. 2–5 (2010)
18. Feiler, P.H., Gluch, D.P.: Model-Based Engineering with AADL: An Introduction to the SAE Architecture Analysis and Design Language. Addison-Wesley, Boston (2013)
19. Fisher, K., Launchbury, J., Richards, R.: The HACMS program: using formal methods to eliminate exploitable bugs. Philos. Trans. Roy. Soc. A Math. Phys. Eng. Sci. **375**(2104) (2017)
20. Godefroid, P.: Test generation using symbolic execution. In: Foundations of Software Technology and Theoretical Computer Science (2012)
21. Godefroid, P., Klarlund, N., Sen, K.: Dart: directed automated random testing. In: Proceedings of the 2005 ACM SIGPLAN Conference on Programming Language Design and Implementation, pp. 213–223 (2005)
22. GUMBOX property-based testing case studies (2023). https://github.com/santoslab/gumbox-case-studies
23. HAMR project website (2022). https://hamr.sireum.org
24. HARDENS: high assurance rigorous digital engineering for nuclear safety (artifacts repository). https://github.com/GaloisInc/HARDENS
25. Hatcliff, J., Belt, J., Robby, Carpenter, T.: HAMR: an AADL multi-platform code generation toolset. In: Margaria, T., Steffen, B. (eds.) ISoLA 2021. LNCS, vol. 13036, pp. 274–295. Springer, Cham (2021). https://doi.org/10.1007/978-3-030-89159-6_18

26. Hatcliff, J., Hugues, J., Stewart, D., Wrage, L.: Formalization of the AADL runtime services. In: Margaria, T., Steffen, B. (eds.) ISoLA 2022. LNCS, vol. 13702, pp. 105–134. Springer, Cham (2022). https://doi.org/10.1007/978-3-031-19756-7_7
27. Hatcliff, J., Leavens, G.T., Leino, K.R.M., Müller, P., Parkinson, M.: Behavioral interface specification languages. ACM Comput. Surv. **44**(3) (2012)
28. Hatcliff, J., Stewart, D., Belt, J., Robby, Schwerdfeger, A.: An AADL contract language supporting integrated model- and code-level verification. In: Proceedings of the 2022 ACM Workshop on High Integrity Language Technology. HILT '22 (2022)
29. Hoang, D., Moy, Y., Wallenburg, A., Chapman, R.: SPARK 2014 and GNATprove. Int. J. Softw. Tools Technol. Transf. **17**(6) (2015)
30. Hugues, J., Wrage, L., Hatcliff, J., Stewart, D.: Mechanization of a large DSML: an experiment with AADL and coq. In: 20th ACM-IEEE International Conference on Formal Methods and Models for System Design, MEMOCODE 2022, Shanghai, China, 13–14 October 2022, pp. 1–9. IEEE (2022)
31. Johnsen, A., Pettersson, P., Lundqvist, K.: An architecture-based verification technique for AADL specifications. In: Crnkovic, I., Gruhn, V., Book, M. (eds.) ECSA 2011. LNCS, vol. 6903, pp. 105–113. Springer, Heidelberg (2011). https://doi.org/10.1007/978-3-642-23798-0_11
32. Kanig, J.: Leading-edge ADA verification technologies: combining testing and verification with gnattest and gnatprove - the hi-lite project. In: Proceedings of the 2012 ACM Conference on High Integrity Language Technology, HILT '12, 2–6 December 2012, Boston, Massachusetts, USA, pp. 5–6. ACM (2012)
33. Kline, S., Hudak, J., O'Neill, A.: Automated test and re-test for AADL (SBIR project between Innovative Defense Technologies and the Software Engineering Institute) (2022). https://resources.sei.cmu.edu/library/asset-view.cfm?assetid=651952
34. Larson, B.R., Chalin, P., Hatcliff, J.: BLESS: formal specification and verification of behaviors for embedded systems with software. In: Brat, G., Rungta, N., Venet, A. (eds.) NFM 2013. LNCS, vol. 7871, pp. 276–290. Springer, Heidelberg (2013). https://doi.org/10.1007/978-3-642-38088-4_19
35. Lasnier, G., Zalila, B., Pautet, L., Hugues, J.: Ocarina: an environment for AADL models analysis and automatic code generation for high integrity applications. In: Kordon, F., Kermarrec, Y. (eds.) Ada-Europe 2009. LNCS, vol. 5570, pp. 237–250. Springer, Heidelberg (2009). https://doi.org/10.1007/978-3-642-01924-1_17
36. Lempia, D., Miller, S.: DOT/FAA/AR-08/32. Requirements Engineering Management Handbook, Federal Aviation Administration (2009)
37. Leroy, X., Blazy, S., Kästner, D., Schommer, B., Pister, M., Ferdinand, C.: CompCert-a formally verified optimizing compiler. In: ERTS 2016: Embedded Real Time Software and Systems, 8th European Congress (2016)
38. Sireum logika (2022). https://logika.sireum.org
39. Meyer, B.: Eiffel as a framework for verification. In: Meyer, B., Woodcock, J. (eds.) VSTTE 2005. LNCS, vol. 4171, pp. 301–307. Springer, Heidelberg (2008). https://doi.org/10.1007/978-3-540-69149-5_32
40. de Moura, L., Bjørner, N.: Z3: an efficient SMT solver. In: Ramakrishnan, C.R., Rehof, J. (eds.) TACAS 2008. LNCS, vol. 4963, pp. 337–340. Springer, Heidelberg (2008). https://doi.org/10.1007/978-3-540-78800-3_24
41. Moy, Y., Ledinot, E., Delseny, H., Wiels, V., Monate, B.: Testing or formal verification: DO-178C alternatives and industrial experience. IEEE Softw. **30**(3), 50–57 (2013)

42. Nilsson, R.: ScalaCheck: The Definitive Guide. Artima Press, Walnut Creek (2014)
43. Robby, Hatcliff, J.: Slang: the Sireum programming language. In: Margaria, T., Steffen, B. (eds.) Leveraging Applications of Formal Methods, Verification and Validation - ISoLA 2021. Lecture Notes in Computer Science, vol. 13036, pp. 253–273. Springer, Cham (2021). https://doi.org/10.1007/978-3-030-89159-6_17
44. sel4 microkernel (2015). sel4.systems/
45. Stewart, D., Liu, J.J., Cofer, D., Heimdahl, M., Whalen, M.W., Peterson, M.: AADL-based safety analysis using formal methods applied to aircraft digital systems. Reliab. Eng. Syst. Saf. **213**, 107649 (2021)
46. Ward, D.T., Helton, S.B.: Estimating return on investment for SAVI (a model-based virtual integration process. SAE International J. Aerosp. (2011)

Impossible Made Possible: Encoding Intractable Specifications via Implied Domain Constraints

Chris Johannsen(✉), Brian Kempa, Phillip H. Jones, Kristin Y. Rozier, and Tichakorn Wongpiromsarn

Iowa State University, Ames, USA
{cgjohann,bckempa,phjones,kyrozier,nok}@iastate.edu

Abstract. We take another look at intractable temporal logic specifications, where the intractability stems from self-reference, unboundedness, or the need for explicit counting. A classic example is the specification, "Every file that gets opened eventually gets closed." In all cases, we show that we can capitalize on realistic constraints implied by the operating environment to generate Mission-time Linear Temporal Logic (MLTL) encodings with reasonably-sized memory signatures. We derive a new set of rewriting rules for MLTL, accompanied by proofs of correctness for each rule, and memory optimizations. We utilize these in creating MLTL encodings for all three patterns of "intractability," proving correctness, time complexity, and space complexity for each type of specification encoding.

Keywords: Mission-time Linear Temporal Logic (MLTL) · MLTL Satisfiability · Temporal Logic Specification

1 Introduction

Since it was named specifically in 2014 [32] as a particularly popular subset of the logics MTL [29] and STL [26] for industrial practice, Mission-time Linear Temporal Logic (MLTL) has become increasingly utilized as a specification logic for industrial applications. For a couple of examples, MLTL was utilized in formal verification on-board Robonaut2 [18], and the NASA Lunar Gateway project is currently using this logic for requirements capture, design-time testing, and online runtime verification [7–9]. While we can use established algorithms for evaluating more expressive logics of which MLTL is a subset, previous work has shown that there are substantial advantages to working in MLTL directly, for example in satisfiability checking [24], model checking [19], and runtime verification [16]. We know from these studies that MLTL brings the advantages of being easier to validate and more efficient to evaluate than more expressive, higher-order Logics [23]. However, these advantages come with an expressability trade off; the value of MLTL is limited to the specifications we can accurately capture in it.

Work supported in part by NSF:CPS Award 2038903, NSF:CAREER Award 1664356, and NASA Cooperative Agreement Grant 80NSSC21M0121.

A. Cimatti and L. Titolo (Eds.): FMICS 2023, LNCS 14290, pp. 151–169, 2023.
https://doi.org/10.1007/978-3-031-43681-9_9

There are common specifications that industrial practitioners tend to naturally express using, e.g., first order (FO) logic, but doing so precludes using their established, efficient evaluation tools developed for lower-order temporal logics like MLTL and LTL; satisfiability of first-order logic is undecidable [3]. This has spurred many advances in more-efficiently evaluating more-expressive extensions of linear-time temporal logics that capture higher-order sentiments. Using Petri nets as an intermediate specification language, [14] defined a full FO-LTL for specifying liveness in concurrent systems. Quantified Propositional Temporal Logic (QPTL) [35] extends MLTL with limited quantification while only incurring non-elementary complexity [35]. Quantified Linear Temporal Logic (QLTL) [30] specifically defines complexity with respect to Markov processes as a function of number of alternating quantifiers, thus providing a middle-ground restriction on both expressiveness and complexity. Variable-LTL (VLTL) [38] studies which quantifier patterns do and do not forfeit decidability and restricts specifications to those. FO-LTL [22] looks for finite models of infinite domains, relying on the structure of FO fragments and quantifier ordering to bound complexity.

Capitalizing on realistic limits on the evaluation domain led to several tractable algorithms for linear-time logics with first-order-like extensions. First order LTL over Finite Time Structures $\text{FO-LTL}^{\text{fin}}$ defined a procedure for checking validity given a finite time horizon [5]. Finite domains enabled reducing first-order properties to a satisfiability check on the sequential circuit representation of a program for model checking [27]. Finite Quantified LTL (FQLTL) [6] extends LTL with quantifiers over finite domains, targeting infinite time evaluation by generating LTL formulas during execution rather than enforcing restrictions in preprocessing.

With this in mind, we take another look at common "first order" specifications like "every file that gets opened eventually gets closed." Depending on the logical encoding of this specification, its evaluation could involve unboundedness (e.g., unbounded number of files), self-reference (e.g., closing a file refers back to the specific file that was opened), or counting, all of which are provably outside the expressability of linear-time logics including MLTL and LTL [12,39]. We note that industrial domains, i.e., the domain where we will evaluate this specification in performing some verification task, naturally impose restrictions that we can use to encode this specification in lower-order logic without changing its meaning. For example, we are tempted to start the encoding with "for all files," yet the default open-file limit in Linux is 1024 [37], quite a small number in practice. This leads to an important realization: by parameterizing specification patterns over reasonable limits we can expect to be imposed by the evaluation domain, we can design a set of MLTL encodings of many common "intractable" specifications without changing their meaning, extending the logic, or precluding the use of efficient existing tools for MLTL evaluation.

Having an extensive set of categorized rewriting rules for LTL enables the current state-of-the-art encodings of that logic for a variety of evaluation algorithms; see, e.g., SPOT [10,11]. Therefore, we contribute such a set for MLTL in Sect. 3 including their proofs of correctness and scalability in terms of reducing the memory signature of the MLTL formula; these utilize the MLTL semantics included in our preliminaries Sect. 2. We contribute MLTL specification patterns covering common statements that involve self-reference in Sect. 4, unboundedness in Sect. 5 and counting in Sect. 6, including proofs of correctness, time complexity, and memory scalability for the last two. Section 7 contributes an illustrative example to show the effectiveness of pairing the presented techniques to reduce memory requirements for realistic industrial domain parameters. Section 8 concludes with impacts and future work.

2 Preliminaries: Mission-Time LTL and Formula-Wise Encoding

Mission-time Linear Temporal Logic (MLTL) [24] is a bounded variant of MTL [1] where each temporal operator has an associated closed natural number interval bound.

Definition 1 ***(MLTL Syntax).*** *The syntax of an MLTL formula φ over a set of atomic propositions $\mathcal{AP}$ is recursively defined as:*

$$\varphi ::= \mathsf{true} \mid \mathsf{false} \mid p \mid \neg\psi \mid \psi \wedge \xi \mid \psi \vee \xi \mid \Box_I \psi \mid \Diamond_I \psi \mid \psi\, \mathcal{U}_I\, \xi \mid \psi\, \mathcal{R}_I\, \xi$$

where $p \in \mathcal{AP}$, ψ and ξ are MLTL formulas, and I is an interval $[l, u]$ such that $l, u \in \mathbb{N}$ and $l \leqslant u$.

We evaluate MLTL formulas over finite traces. Let π be a finite trace where an element at timestamp $i \in \mathbb{N}_0$ is $\pi[i] \subseteq \mathcal{AP}$ such that $|\pi|$ is the length of π where $i < |\pi| < +\infty$ and π_i is the suffix of π starting at and including i.

Definition 2 ***(MLTL Semantics).*** *The satisfaction of an MLTL formula by a trace π is defined recursively as:*

- $\pi \models p$ *iff* $p \in \pi[0]$
- $\pi \models \neg\varphi$ *iff* $\pi \not\models \varphi$
- $\pi \models \varphi \wedge \psi$ *iff* $\pi \models \varphi$ *and* $\pi \models \psi$
- $\pi \models \varphi\, \mathcal{U}_{[l,u]}\, \psi$ *iff* $|\pi| \geqslant l$ *and there exists a* $j \in [l, u]$ *such that* $\pi_j \models \psi$ *and* $\pi_k \models \varphi$ *for all* $k \in [l, u]$ *such that* $k < j$.

We say two MLTL formulas φ, ψ are *semantically equivalent* (denoted as $\varphi \equiv \psi$) if and only if $\pi \models \varphi \Leftrightarrow \pi \models \psi$ for all traces π over $\mathcal{AP}$. To complete the MLTL semantics, we define $\mathsf{false} \equiv \neg\mathsf{true}$, $\varphi \vee \psi \equiv \neg(\neg\varphi \wedge \neg\psi)$, $\neg(\varphi\, \mathcal{U}_I\, \psi) \equiv (\neg\varphi\, \mathcal{R}_I\, \neg\psi)$ and $\neg\Diamond_I \varphi \equiv \Box_I \neg\varphi$. MLTL keeps the standard operator equivalences from LTL, including $\Diamond_I \varphi \equiv (\mathsf{true}\, \mathcal{U}_I\, \varphi)$, $\Box_I \varphi \equiv (\mathsf{false}\, \mathcal{R}_I\, \varphi)$. Notably, MLTL discards the next ($\mathcal{X}$) operator, since $\mathcal{X}\varphi \equiv \Box_{[1,1]}\varphi$.

2.1 MLTL Formula-Wise AST Encoding Structure

We focus on memory usage optimization techniques that use an Abstract Syntax Tree-based (AST) representation for MLTL formulas. Each node in the AST of an MLTL formula φ computes and stores a result-timestamp pair $T_\varphi = (v, t)$ for the corresponding sub-formula with respect to an input trace where $v \in \{\mathsf{true}, \mathsf{false}\}$ and $t \in \mathbb{N}_0$. We call result-timestamp pairs *verdicts*.

Propagation Delay. To compute the required memory for each node in an AST-encoded MLTL formula, we must first compute the earliest and latest timestamps when we may have sufficient information to evaluate the formula. We bound these timestamps using the upper and lower interval bounds of the temporal operators in a given formula.

Definition 3 ***(Propagation Delay)*** *[17]. The propagation delay of an MLTL formula φ is the time between when a set of propositions $\pi[i]$ arrives and when it is possible to know if $\pi_i \models \varphi$. A node's* worst-case propagation delay *(**wpd**) is its maximum propagation delay, and the minimum value is its* best-case propagation delay *(**bpd**).*

Definition 4 ***(Propagation Delay Semantics)*** *[17]. Let $\varphi, \psi, \psi_1, \psi_2$ be well-formed MLTL formulas where $\varphi.bpd$ and $\varphi.wpd$ are the best- and worst-case propagation delays of formula φ respectively:*

$$if\ \varphi \in \mathcal{AP} : \begin{cases} \varphi.wpd = 0 \\ \varphi.bpd = 0 \end{cases} \qquad if\ \varphi = \neg\psi : \begin{cases} \varphi.wpd = \psi.wpd \\ \varphi.bpd = \psi.bpd \end{cases}$$

$$if\ \varphi = \Box_{[l,u]}\psi\ or\ \varphi = \Diamond_{[l,u]}\psi : \begin{cases} \varphi.wpd = \psi.wpd + u \\ \varphi.bpd = \psi.bpd + l \end{cases}$$

$$if\ \varphi = \psi_1 \vee \psi_2\ or\ \varphi = \psi_1 \wedge \psi_2 : \begin{cases} \varphi.wpd = max(\psi_1.wpd, \psi_2.wpd) \\ \varphi.bpd = min(\psi_1.bpd, \psi_2.bpd) \end{cases}$$

$$if\ \varphi = \psi_1\ \mathcal{U}_{[l,u]}\ \psi_2\ or\ \varphi = \psi_1\ \mathcal{R}_{[l,u]}\ \psi_2 : \begin{cases} \varphi.wpd = max(\psi_1.wpd, \psi_2.wpd) + u \\ \varphi.bpd = min(\psi_1.bpd, \psi_2.bpd) + l \end{cases}$$

The values of $\varphi.wpd$ and $\varphi.bpd$ are based solely on the structure of the given formula φ and do not take into account interactions between sub-formulas. For example, the formula $\Box_{[0,5]}\varphi \vee \Box_{[0,10]}\varphi$ has a structural worst-case propagation delay of 10 but the relationship between the two $\Box_I$ operators always allows evaluation of the formula by time step 5. In other words, we can simplify this formula to $\Box_{[0,5]}\varphi$.

2.2 MLTL AST Encoding Memory Requirements [17]

Consider an AST node g and its set of sibling nodes $\mathcal{B}_g$ (not including g). The minimum required memory (with respect to the number of verdicts) for g is

$$mem_{node}(g) = max(max\{b.wpd \mid b \in \mathcal{B}_g\} - g.bpd, 0) + 1. \tag{1}$$

We can recursively compute the memory requirements of an AST rooted at g, where $\mathcal{C}_g$ is the set of child nodes of g, as follows:

$$mem_{AST}(g) = mem_{node}(g) + \sum\{mem_{AST}(c) \mid c \in \mathcal{C}_g\}. \tag{2}$$

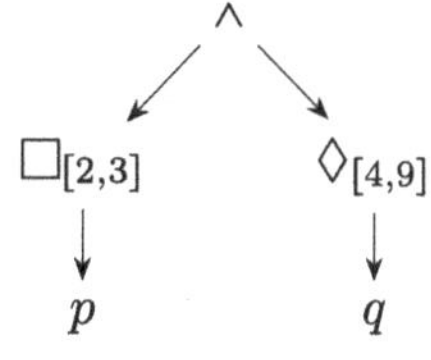

Fig. 1. AST for the MLTL formula $(\Box_{[2,3]}p) \wedge (\Diamond_{[4,9]}q)$ where $p, q \in \mathcal{AP}$.

Formula 1 accounts for the worst-case input with respect to evaluating the parent of g. Consider a trace π, time $0 \leqslant i < |\pi|$, and a node g such that g's value is known at index $i + g.bpd$ but the value of a sibling node b_{max} is known at index $i + b_{max}.wpd$ where $b_{max}.wpd = max\{b.wpd \mid b \in \mathcal{B}_g\}$. In order to evaluate g's parent at i, we must know the evaluations of both g and b_{max} at i and therefore buffer the values of g from indices $i + g.bpd$ to $i + b_{max}.wpd$. If $b_{max}.wpd - g.bpd \geqslant 0$, this requires a buffer of size $(i + b_{max}.wpd) - (i + g.bpd) = b_{max}.wpd - g.bpd$, otherwise we do not need to buffer values at node g.

As an example, consider the AST in Fig. 1. We see that $mem_{node}(\wedge) = 1$ since the node has no siblings. Now, for each temporal node we have

$$mem_{node}(\Box_{[2,3]}) = max(max\{\Diamond_{[4,9]}.wpd\} - \Box_{[2,3]}.bpd, 0) + 1 = 8,$$
$$mem_{node}(\Diamond_{[4,9]}) = max(max\{\Box_{[2,3]}.wpd\} - \Diamond_{[4,9]}.bpd, 0) + 1 = 1.$$

Finally, each $mem_{node}(p) = mem_{node}(q) = 1$. Putting this all together:

$$mem_{AST}(\wedge) = mem_{node}(\wedge) + mem_{node}(\Box_{[2,3]}) + mem_{node}(\Diamond_{[4,9]}) + mem_{node}(p) + mem_{node}(q) = 12.$$

3 MLTL Encoding Optimizations

We present rewriting rules for reducing the AST encoding size of MLTL formulas that can be applied automatically during MLTL formula encoding. This type of optimization is similar to SPOT's [11] optimizations for LTL, with the primary difference being SPOT minimizes the size of an LTL formula's automata representation.

Figure 2 contains the MLTL rewrite rules. We first prove that both sides of each rewrite rule are equivalent using trivially-derived equivalences from LTL and the semantic definitions of MLTL operators. We then show how each rewriting rule maintains or reduces the memory of a given MLTL formula. First, recall that MLTL does not include a Next-time operator ($\mathcal{X}$) as in LTL because it is equivalent to $\Box_{[1,1]}$. More generally, we can express $a \in \mathbb{N}_0$ nested $\mathcal{X}$ operations with a singleton interval such as in $\Box_{[a,a]}$. We therefore observe the following equivalences:

$$\square_{[l_1,u_1]}\square_{[l_2,u_2]}\varphi \mapsto \square_{[l_1+l_2,u_1+u_2]}\varphi \qquad \Diamond_{[l_1,u_1]}\Diamond_{[l_2,u_2]}\varphi \mapsto \Diamond_{[l_1+l_2,u_1+u_2]}\varphi \tag{R1}$$

$$\square_{[l_1,u_1]}\varphi \wedge \square_{[l_2,u_2]}\psi \mapsto \square_{[l_3,u_3]}(\square_{[l_1-l_3,u_1-u_3]}\varphi \wedge \square_{[l_2-l_3,u_2-u_3]}\psi)$$
$$\Diamond_{[l_1,u_1]}\varphi \vee \Diamond_{[l_2,u_2]}\psi \mapsto \Diamond_{[l_3,u_3]}(\Diamond_{[l_1-l_3,u_1-u_3]}\varphi \vee \Diamond_{[l_2-l_3,u_2-u_3]}\psi) \tag{R2}$$
$$\text{where } l_3 = min(l_1,l_2), u_3 = l_3 + min(u_1 - l_1, u_2 - l_2), l_3 < u_3$$

$$\square_{[a,a]}\Diamond_{[l,u]}\varphi \mapsto \Diamond_{[l+a,u+a]}\varphi \qquad \Diamond_{[l,u]}\square_{[a,a]}\varphi \mapsto \Diamond_{[l+a,u+a]}\varphi$$
$$\Diamond_{[a,a]}\square_{[l,u]}\varphi \mapsto \square_{[l+a,u+a]}\varphi \qquad \square_{[l,u]}\Diamond_{[a,a]}\varphi \mapsto \square_{[l+a,u+a]}\varphi \tag{R3}$$

$$\square_{[l_1,u_1]}\varphi \wedge \square_{[l_2,u_2]}\varphi \mapsto \square_{[l_1,u_3]}\varphi \qquad \Diamond_{[l_1,u_1]}\varphi \vee \Diamond_{[l_2,u_2]}\varphi \mapsto \Diamond_{[l_1,u_2]}\varphi$$
$$\text{where } l_1 \leqslant l_2 \leqslant u_1 + 1, u_3 = max(u_1,u_2) \tag{R4}$$

$$\square_{[l_1,u_1]}\varphi \vee \square_{[l_2,u_2]}\varphi \mapsto \square_{[l_2,u_2]}\varphi \qquad \Diamond_{[l_1,u_1]}\varphi \wedge \Diamond_{[l_2,u_2]}\varphi \mapsto \Diamond_{[l_2,u_2]}\varphi$$
$$\text{where } l_1 \leqslant l_2 \leqslant u_2 \leqslant u_1 \tag{R5}$$

$$\square_{[a,a]}(\varphi\,\mathcal{U}_{[l,u]}\,\psi) \mapsto \varphi\,\mathcal{U}_{[l+a,u+a]}\,\psi \qquad (\square_{[a,a]}\varphi)\,\mathcal{U}_{[l,u]}\,(\square_{[a,a]}\psi) \mapsto \varphi\,\mathcal{U}_{[l+a,u+a]}\,\psi \tag{R6}$$

$$(\varphi_1\,\mathcal{U}_{[l,u_1]}\,\varphi_2) \wedge (\varphi_3\,\mathcal{U}_{[l,u_2]}\,\varphi_2) \mapsto (\varphi_1 \wedge \varphi_3)\,\mathcal{U}_{[l,u_1]}\,\varphi_2$$
$$\text{where } l \leqslant u_1, l \leqslant u_2, u_1 \leqslant u_2 \tag{R7}$$

$$\varphi\,\mathcal{U}_{[l_1,u_1]}\,\square_{[0,u_2]}\varphi \mapsto \square_{[l_1,l_1+u_2]}\varphi \qquad \varphi\,\mathcal{U}_{[l_1,u_1]}\,\Diamond_{[0,u_2]}\varphi \mapsto \Diamond_{[l_1,l_1+u_2]}\varphi \tag{R8}$$

Fig. 2. Table of MLTL rewrite rules where $\varphi, \psi, \varphi_1, \varphi_2, \varphi_3$ are well-formed MLTL formulas and $a, l, u, l_1, u_2, l_2, u_2, l_3, u_3 \in \mathbb{N}_0$ such that $l \leqslant u, l_1 \leqslant u_1, l_2 \leqslant u_2, l_3 \leqslant u_3$. Each group of rules has identical constraints on their interval bounds.

$$\square_{[a,a]}\varphi \equiv \Diamond_{[a,a]}\varphi \equiv \psi\,\mathcal{U}_{[a,a]}\,\varphi. \tag{3}$$

The following directly follow from the semantics of $\mathcal{U}_I$:

$$\mathsf{false}\,\mathcal{U}_{[l,u]}\,\varphi \equiv \square_{[l,l]}\varphi \qquad \mathsf{true}\,\mathcal{U}_{[l,u]}\,\varphi \equiv \Diamond_{[l,u]}\varphi \qquad \varphi\,\mathcal{U}_{[l,u]}\,\varphi \equiv \square_{[l,l]}\varphi. \tag{4}$$

With these basic equivalences in hand, we can show that each rewrite rule preserves the MLTL semantics and thus is also an equivalence relation.

Theorem 1 (Equivalence of MLTL Rewrite Rules). *Let $\varphi, \psi, \varphi_1, \varphi_2, \varphi_3$ be well-formed MLTL formulas and a, l, u, l_1, u_2, l_2, u_2, l_3, $u_3 \in \mathbb{N}_0$ such that $l \leqslant u$, $l_1 \leqslant u_1$, $l_2 \leqslant u_2$, $l_3 \leqslant u_3$. Then each rewrite relation ($\mapsto$) in Fig. 2 is also an equivalence relation.*

Proof Sketch. [1] We case split over each rule and prove the left- and right-hand sides of each $\mapsto$ relation to be equivalent. Most rules follow directly from the semantics of MLTL (e.g., (R1)) and we present the more complicated proof for (R2) to illustrate:

(R1): Let π be a finite trace such that $\pi \models \square_{[l_1,u_1]}\square_{[l_2,u_2]}\varphi$. By the semantics of $\square_I$, we know that $\pi_i+ \models \square_{[l_2,u_2]}\varphi$ for each $i \in [l_1, u_1]$. Intuitively, this means that π

[1] The full proof for the entire set of rules can be found at https://temporallogic.org/research/FMICS2023/.

satisfies φ at timestamps $[l_2, u_2]$ *relative to* i i.e., $\pi_i \models \varphi$ starting at the timestamp $i + l_2$ and ending at $i + u_2$. So, applying the semantics of $\Box_I$ again, we have that $\pi_{i+j} \models \varphi$ for each $j \in [l_2, u_2]$. By the definition of trace suffixes, this means that $\pi_k \models \varphi$ for each $k \in [l_1 + l_2, u_1 + u_2]$. Therefore $\pi \models \Box_{[l_1+l_2,u_1+u_2]}\varphi$. The converse proof follows from a similar argument.

(R2): Using (R1), we see that

$$\Box_{[l_1,u_1]}\varphi \wedge \Box_{[l_2,u_2]}\psi \equiv \Box_{[l_3,l_3]}\Box_{[l_1-l_3,u_1-l_3]}\varphi \wedge \Box_{[l_3,l_3]}\Box_{[l_2-l_3,u_2-l_3]}\psi.$$

This follows if both intervals $[l_1 - l_3, u_1 - l_3]$, $[l_2 - l_3, u_2 - l_3]$ are valid i.e., (a) $l_1 - l_3 \geqslant 0$, (b) $l_2 - l_3 \geqslant 0$, and (c) $l_1 - l_3 \leqslant u_1 - l_3$, (d) $l_2 - l_3 \leqslant u_2 - l_3$.

(a) Recall that $l_3 = l_1$, then $l_3 \leqslant l_1$.
(b) Recall that $l_3 = l_1 \leqslant l_2$, then $l_2 - l_3 \geqslant 0 \Rightarrow l_2 \geqslant l_3 \Rightarrow l_3 \leqslant l_2$ holds.
(c) Since $l_1 \leqslant u_1$, we see that $l_1 - l_3 \leqslant u_1 - l_3 \Rightarrow l_1 \leqslant u_1$ holds.
(d) Since $l_2 \leqslant u_2$, we see that $l_2 - l_3 \leqslant u_2 - l_3 \Rightarrow l_2 \leqslant u_2$ holds.

Now, let $u_3 = l_3 + min(u_1 - l_1, u_2 - l_2)$. Applying (R1) once more, we have

$$\Box_{[l_3,l_3]}\Box_{[l_1-l_3,u_1-l_3]}\varphi \wedge \Box_{[l_3,l_3]}\Box_{[l_2-l_3,u_2-l_3]}\psi \equiv \Box_{[l_3,u_3]}\Box_{[l_1-l_3,u_1-u_3]}\varphi \wedge \Box_{[l_3,u_3]}\Box_{[l_2-l_3,u_2-u_3]}\psi.$$

Since this only affects the upper bounds of the inner $\Box$ operators, we show that (a) $l_1 - l_3 \leqslant u_1 - u_3$ and (b) $l_2 - l_3 \leqslant u_2 - u_3$.

(a) Consider the two cases of $u_1 - l_1 \leqslant u_2 - l_2$ and $u_2 - l_2 < u_1 - l_1$:
   (i) Assume $u_1 - l_1 \leqslant u_2 - l_2$, then $u_3 = u_1 - l_1 + l_3$. Replacing this in the target inequality, we have $l_1 - l_3 \leqslant u_1 - (u_1 - l_1 + l_3) \Rightarrow l_1 - l_3 \leqslant l_1 - l_3$.
   (ii) Otherwise, $u_2 - l_2 < u_1 - l_1$. Then $u_3 = u_2 - l_2 + l_3$, and replacing this in the target inequality, we have $l_1 - l_3 \leqslant u_1 - (u_2 - l_2 + l_3) \Rightarrow 0 \leqslant u_1 - l_3 - (u_2 - l_2) \Rightarrow u_2 - l_2 \leqslant u_1 - l_3$. Now, since $l_3 = l_1$, we have $u_2 - l_2 \leqslant u_1 - l_1$ which is true from our assumption.
(b) Consider the two cases of $u_1 - l_1 \leqslant u_2 - l_2$ and $u_2 - l_2 < u_1 - l_1$:
   (i) Assume $u_1 - l_1 \leqslant u_2 - l_2$, then $u_3 = u_1 - l_1 + l_3$. Replacing this in the target inequality, we have $l_2 - l_3 \leqslant u_2 - (u_1 - l_1 + l_3) \Rightarrow l_2 - l_3 \leqslant u_2 - u_1 + l_1 - l_3 \Rightarrow l_2 \leqslant u_2 - u_1 + l_1 \Rightarrow u_1 - l_1 \leqslant u_2 - l_2$, which is true from our assumption.
   (ii) Otherwise, $u_2 - l_2 < u_1 - l_1$, then $u_3 = u_2 - l_2 + l_3$. Replacing this in the target inequality, we have $l_2 - l_3 \leqslant u_2 - (u_2 - l_2 + l_3) \Rightarrow l_2 - l_3 \leqslant u_2 - u_2 + l_2 - l_3 \Rightarrow l_2 \leqslant u_2 - u_2 + l_2 \Rightarrow l_2 \leqslant l_2$.

Finally, we prove that

$$\Box_{[l_3,u_3]}\Box_{[l_1-l_3,u_1-l_3-u_3]}\varphi \wedge \Box_{[l_3,u_3]}\Box_{[l_2-l_3,u_2-l_3-u_3]}\psi \equiv \Box_{[l_3,u_3]}(\Box_{[l_1-l_3,u_1-l_3-u_3]}\varphi \wedge \Box_{[l_2-l_3,u_2-l_3-u_3]}\psi).$$

Let π be a finite trace such that

$$\pi \models (\Box_{[l_3,u_3]}\Box_{[l_1-l_3,u_1-l_3-u_3]}\varphi) \wedge (\Box_{[l_3,u_3]}\Box_{[l_2-l_3,u_2-l_3-u_3]}\psi).$$

We apply the semantic definitions of $\wedge$ and $\Box_I$ to see that $\pi_i \models \Box_{[l_1-l_3,u_1-l_3-u_3]}\varphi$ and $\pi_i \models \Box_{[l_2-l_3,u_2-l_3-u_3]}\psi$ for all $i \in [l_3, u_3]$. Combining these relations using the semantics of $\wedge$ once more, we see that

$$\pi_i \models \Box_{[l_1-l_3,u_1-l_3-u_3]}\varphi \wedge \Box_{[l_2-l_3,u_2-l_3-u_3]}\psi$$

for all $i \in [l_3, u_3]$. Using the semantics of $\Box_I$ again, we see that

$$\pi \models \Box_{[l_3,u_3]}(\Box_{[l_1-l_3,u_1-l_3-u_3]}\varphi \wedge \Box_{[l_2-l_3,u_2-l_3-u_3]}\psi).$$

The converse proof follows from a similar argument. $\Box$

Inapplicable LTL Equivalences. While the equivalences discussed so far have corresponding equivalence relations in LTL, there are some LTL equivalences without such a relation in MLTL. For instance, consider the LTL formula $\Diamond(\varphi\mathcal{U}\psi) \equiv \Diamond\psi$. Intuitively, so long as ψ holds at some timestamp i in a given trace, then it is trivially true that $\varphi\mathcal{U}\psi$ holds at i in that trace. However, once we add interval bounds to each temporal operator as in $\Diamond_{[l_1,u_1]}(\varphi\,\mathcal{U}_{[l_2,u_2]}\,\psi)$ there is now a constraint on when ψ can hold in a trace with respect to φ and still satisfy the formula. For example, if $\pi_{l_1+l_2} \not\models \psi$ for some trace π that models this MLTL formula, then necessarily $\pi_{l_1+l_2} \models \varphi$ i.e., the satisfaction of φ is still relevant for some satisfying traces.

Similarly, consider the LTL equivalence $\Diamond\Box\varphi \wedge \Diamond\Box\psi \equiv \Diamond\Box(\varphi \wedge \psi)$. Again, intuitively, the LTL operators $\Diamond$ and $\Box$ do not specify *when* their operands must hold, just that they both eventually always hold. When we add bounds to the left-hand side as in $\Diamond_{[l_1,u_1]}\Box_{[l_2,u_2]}\varphi \wedge \Diamond_{[l_3,u_3]}\Box_{[l_4,u_4]}\psi$, both φ and ψ have constraints on *when* they must hold in order for a trace to satisfy this formula, and when this is exactly may differ for either φ or ψ. Speaking generally, MLTL places more constraints on the set of traces that satisfy a given formula than LTL.

Memory Effects of Rewriting Rules on MLTL AST Encodings. Applying these rewriting rules strategically can reduce the overall memory requirements of the AST encoding of the MLTL formula. These rules reduce memory requirements in one of two ways: (1) by tightening propagation delays or (2) by reducing formula length.

From Eq. 2, an AST node g's required memory is the difference between that $g.bpd$, and the maximum wpd of its siblings. Therefore, reducing $max\{b.wpd \mid b \in \mathcal{B}_g\}$ for a set of sibling nodes $\mathcal{B}_g$ can reduce the memory requirements of all other sibling nodes in $\mathcal{B}_g$. Furthermore, reducing g's wpd can reduce its ancestors' wpd, which in turn could reduce the memory requirements for the ancestors' set of siblings in the same manner. In the following, we use $\varphi(\psi_1 \mapsto \psi_2)$ to denote an MLTL formula that is identical to a formula φ where a sub-formula ψ_1 of φ is replaced with ψ_2.

Lemma 1 ***(Memory Effect of Tighter BPD).*** *Let φ, ψ_1, ψ_2 be well-formed MLTL formulas where ψ_1 is a sub-formula of φ, ψ_2 is the sub-formula in $\varphi(\psi_1 \mapsto \psi_2)$, and $\psi_1.bpd \leqslant \psi_2.bpd$. Then*

$$mem_{node}(\psi_1) \geqslant mem_{node}(\psi_2).$$

Proof Sketch We first note that ψ_1, ψ_2 have the same set of siblings i.e., $\mathcal{B}_{\psi_1} = \mathcal{B}_{\psi_2} = \mathcal{B}$. Then from Eq. 1 we see that

$$\begin{aligned} mem_{node}(\psi_1) =& max(max\{b.wpd \mid \mathcal{B}\} - \psi_1.bpd, 0) + 1 \\ \geqslant& max(max\{b.wpd \mid \mathcal{B}\} - \psi_2.bpd, 0) + 1 \\ =& mem_{node}(\psi_2). \end{aligned}$$

□

Lemma 2 ***(Memory Effect of Tighter WPD).*** *Let φ, ψ_1, ψ_2 be well-formed MLTL formulas where ψ_1 is a sub-formula of φ, ψ_2 is the sub-formula in $\varphi(\psi_1 \mapsto \psi_2)$, and $\psi_2.wpd \leqslant \psi_1.wpd$. Then*

$$mem_{AST}(\varphi(\psi_1 \mapsto \psi_2)) - mem_{AST}(\psi_2) \leqslant mem_{AST}(\varphi) - mem_{AST}(\psi_1).$$

Proof Sketch. As in the proof for Lemma 1, ψ_1, ψ_2 have the same set of siblings i.e., $\mathcal{B}_{\psi_1} = \mathcal{B}_{\psi_2} = \mathcal{B}$. First, assume $\psi_1.wpd \leqslant max\{b_{\psi_1}.wpd \mid b_{\psi_1} \in \mathcal{B}_{\psi_1}\}$ i.e., ψ_1 does not have the maximum wpd of all of its sibling nodes. Then

$$max\{b_{\psi_1}.wpd \mid b_{\psi_1} \in \mathcal{B}_{\psi_1}\} = max\{b_{\psi_2}.wpd \mid b_{\psi_2} \in \mathcal{B}_{\psi_2}\}$$

since rewriting φ from ψ_1 to ψ_2 does not affect the sibling nodes for either ψ_1, ψ_2. Therefore $mem_{AST}(\varphi(\psi_1 \mapsto \psi_2)) - mem_{AST}(\psi_2) = mem_{AST}(\varphi) - mem_{AST}(\psi_1)$.

Otherwise, ψ_1 has the maximum wpd of all of its sibling nodes i.e.,

$$\psi_1.wpd > max\{b_{\psi_1}.wpd \mid b_{\psi_1} \in \mathcal{B}_{\psi_1}\}$$

Then the amount of memory required for each node $b_{\psi_1} \in \mathcal{B}_{\psi_1}$ is $mem_{node}(b_{\psi_1}) = max(\psi_1.wpd - b_{\psi_1}.bpd, 0)$. Importantly, each node $b_{\psi_1} \in \mathcal{B}_{\psi_1}$ has a structurally identical counterpart in $\mathcal{B}_{\psi_2}$ since we defined φ as identical to $\varphi(\psi_1 \mapsto \psi_2)$, except where ψ_1 is replaced with ψ_2. We define a mapping $Sib : \mathcal{B}_{\psi_1} \rightarrow \mathcal{B}_{\psi_2}$ such that $Sib(b_{\psi_1}) = b_{\psi_2}$. This implies that $b_{\psi_1}.bpd = Sib(b_{\psi_1}).bpd$ for each $b \in \mathcal{B}_{\psi_1}$. Therefore, we see that each sibling node of ψ_2 has a lower memory requirement than the corresponding sibling node of ψ_1 for all $b \in \mathcal{B}_{\psi_1}$:

$$mem_{node}(b_{\psi_1}) = max(\psi_1.wpd - b_{\psi_1}.bpd, 0) \leqslant max(\psi_2.wpd - Sib(b_{\psi_1}).bpd, 0).$$

Further, the propagation delay semantics (Definition 4) dictate that the wpd of a node is greater than or equal to the maximum wpd of all its children. Since we assumed that ψ_1 has the maximum wpd of its parent's children (i.e., ψ_1's siblings) and $\psi_2.wpd \leqslant \psi_1.wpd$, it follows that the ψ_2's parent would have a lower wpd than ψ_1's parent. We can apply this argument recursively to each ancestor of ψ_2 such that every ancestor of ψ_2 will have a lower or equal wpd than the corresponding ancestor of ψ_1, where the preceding relation holds if the wpd is lowered and the first assumption of the proof holds otherwise.

Then the sibling nodes of each ancestor of ψ_2 will have a lower or equal memory requirement than the sibling nodes of each ancestor of ψ_1. Therefore $mem_{AST}(\varphi(\psi_1 \mapsto \psi_2)) - mem_{AST}(\psi_2) \leqslant mem_{AST}(\varphi) - mem_{AST}(\psi_1)$. □

Intuitively, Lemmas 1 and 2 express the notion that a semantically equivalent formula with a tighter propagation delay results in reduced required memory. A tighter propagation delay provides more information as to *when* the formula will be evaluated in the best and worst cases, requiring less memory for storing intermediate results.

Theorem 2 (Memory Reduction of Rewriting Rules). *Let φ, ψ_1, ψ_2 be well-formed MLTL formulas where ψ_1 is a sub-formula of φ. Then applying a valid rewrite rule in Fig. 2 to ψ_1 will result in a new formula $\varphi(\psi_1 \mapsto \psi_2)$ such that $\varphi \equiv \varphi(\psi_1 \mapsto \psi_2)$ and*

$$mem_{AST}(\varphi(\psi_1 \mapsto \psi_2)) \leqslant mem_{AST}(\varphi).$$

Proof Sketch. [2] The proof case splits over each rewrite rule and applies Lemma 1 and Lemma 2 to show that each rule causes a memory reduction, where we know from Theorem 1 that each rule maintains semantics. We show the proof for (R2) to illustrate, since the rule increases the resulting formula size by 1 and does not tighten the propagation delays of the top-level node:

First, let $\psi_1 = \Box_{[l_1,u_1]}\varphi_1 \wedge \Box_{[l_2,u_2]}\varphi_2$ and $\psi_2 = \Box_{[l_3,u_3]}(\Box_{[l_1-l_3,u_1-u_3]}\varphi_1 \wedge \Box_{[l_2-l_3,u_2-u_3]}\varphi_2)$ where $l_1 \leqslant u_1$, $l_2 \leqslant u_2$, $l_3 = min(l_1, l_2)$, $u_3 = l_3 + min(u_1 - l_1, u_2 - l_2)$, and $l_3 < u_3$. We show that

$$\begin{aligned}
\psi_1.wpd =& max(\varphi_1.wpd + u_1, \varphi_2.wpd + u_2)\\
=& max(\varphi_1.wpd + u_1 + (u_3 - u_3), \varphi_2.wpd + u_2 + (u_3 - u_3))\\
=& max(\varphi_1.wpd + u_3 + (u_1 - u_3), \varphi_2.wpd + u_3 + (u_2 - u_3))\\
=& u_3 + max(\varphi_1.wpd + (u_1 - u_3), \varphi_2.wpd + (u_2 - u_3))\\
=& \psi_2.wpd.
\end{aligned}$$

Therefore we have $mem_{AST}(\varphi(\psi_1 \mapsto \psi_2)) - mem_{AST}(\psi_2) \leqslant mem_{AST}(\varphi) - mem_{AST}(\psi_1)$ by Lemma 2. A similar derivation is used to show that $\psi_1.bpd = \psi_2.bpd$, so $mem_{node}(\wedge_1) \geqslant mem_{node}(\Box_{[l_3,u_3]})$ by Lemma 1 where $\wedge_1, \wedge_2$ denote the $\wedge$-nodes in ψ_1, ψ_2 respectively.

Next we show that $mem_{AST}(\psi_1) \geqslant mem_{AST}(\psi_2)$. First, we see that because $l_3 < u_3$:

$$\begin{aligned}
mem_{node}(\Box_{[l_1,u_1]}) =& ((\varphi_2.wpd + u_2) - (\varphi_1.bpd + l_1) + 1)\\
>& ((\varphi_2.wpd + (u_2 - u_3)) - (\varphi_1.bpd + l_1 - l_3) + 1)\\
=& ((\varphi_2.wpd + u_2) - (\varphi_1.bpd + l_1) + 1) + (l_3 - u_3)\\
=& mem_{node}(\Box_{[l_1-l_3,u_1-u_3]}).
\end{aligned}$$

[2] The full proof can be found at https://temporallogic.org/research/FMICS2023/.

Similarly, $mem_{node}(\Box_{[l_2,u_2]}) \geqslant mem_{node}(\Box_{[l_1-l_3,u_1-u_3]})$. Then

$$\begin{aligned}
mem_{AST}(\psi_1) =& mem_{node}(\wedge_1) + mem_{node}(\Box_{[l_1,u_1]}) + mem_{node}(\Box_{[l_2,u_2]}) \\
& mem_{AST}(\varphi_1) + mem_{AST}(\varphi_2) \\
\geqslant & mem_{node}(\Box_{[l_3,u_3]}) + mem_{node}(\Box_{[l_1,u_1]}) + mem_{node}(\Box_{[l_2,u_2]}) \\
& mem_{AST}(\varphi_1) + mem_{AST}(\varphi_2) \\
\geqslant & mem_{node}(\Box_{[l_3,u_3]}) + mem_{node}(\Box_{[l_1-l_3,u_1-u_3]}) + 1 + \\
& mem_{node}(\Box_{[l_2-l_3,u_2-u_3]}) + mem_{AST}(\varphi_1) + mem_{AST}(\varphi_2) \\
=& mem_{node}(\Box_{[l_3,u_3]}) + mem_{node}(\Box_{[l_1-l_3,u_1-u_3]}) + mem_{node}(\wedge_2) \\
& mem_{node}(\Box_{[l_2-l_3,u_2-u_3]}) + mem_{AST}(\varphi_1) + mem_{AST}(\varphi_2) \\
=& mem_{AST}(\psi_2).
\end{aligned}$$

Combining Lemma 2 and the previous result, we have that $mem_{AST}(\varphi(\psi_1 \mapsto \psi_2)) \leqslant mem_{AST}(\varphi)$ for (R2). The rest of the rules rely on either tightening the propagation delay or reducing the number of nodes in the rewritten AST in order to reduce memory requirements. □

4 Realizing Self-Reference via Slot-Based MLTL Encoding

When monitoring formulas over sets, one area of concern deals with self-reference within a formula. The requirement "Every file that gets opened eventually gets closed" is a simple classical example that illustrates this concern [20].

One formalization of this requirement using First-order Logic is

$$\forall f.open(f) \rightarrow \Diamond close(f)$$

where the predicate $close(f)$ refers to an object that is referenced earlier in the specification (i.e., f in the predicate $open(f)$). While some have attempted to resolve this issue in runtime monitoring, wherein reference variables are dynamically instantiated during system execution [13], there is no way to ensure that these predicates refer to the same f in general without infinite space to accommodate an unbounded number of dynamically instantiated monitors. We present slot-based monitoring as an alterative technique to ensure consistency of an object's identity over the course of a formula evaluation within finite space.

To this end, we shift from reasoning about objects themselves to reasoning about an underlying data structure and introduce the notion of a "slot" that tracks the data necessary for evaluation of an MLTL formula.

Definition 5 ***(Slot).*** *A* slot S_m *is a set of atomic proposition symbols, has a slot ID* $m \in \mathbb{N}$*, has an object ID* $id(S_m) \in \mathbb{N} \cup \bot$*, and has a "no change" proposition* nc_m *that is true at time* i *if and only if* $id(S_m)$ *has not changed between time* $i-1$ *and* i.

We include the object ID number to track the identity of the contents in the slot as most real-world objects will have some identifier that can be encoded as a natural number. For a finite set of slots $\mathcal{S}$ and $m \in [1, |\mathcal{S}|]$, we rename each proposition $p \in S_m$ to

p_m and add it to $\mathcal{AP}$. If S_m is empty at time i, then $id(S_m) = \bot$ and none of its propositions p_m are in $\pi[i]$ for any trace π.

As an example, consider a slot $S_1 = \{open_1, close_1, nc_1\}$ and formula $open_1 \rightarrow \Diamond_{[0,t]} close_1$. Intuitively, this formula should evaluate to true at time step j if S_1 is empty, $open$ is not true for the object in S_1 at time j, or $open$ is true for the object in S_1 at time j and $close$ is true for the object S_1 for some time in $[j, j+t]$.

To formalize this notion of enforcing the consistency of an object in a slot S, we define a function h that adds this constraint to a "self-referential" MLTL formula using the available proposition nc_m. Let $l, u \in \mathbb{N}_0$ such that $l \leqslant u$ and $0 < u$ and φ be an MLTL formula. Then h is defined recursively by:

- $h(m, p) = p$
- $h(m, \neg\varphi) = \neg h(m, \varphi)$
- $h(m, \psi \vee \xi) = h(m, \psi) \vee h(m, \xi)$
- $h(m, \Box_{[l,u]}\varphi) = \Box_{[1,u]} nc_m \wedge \Box_{[l,u]} h(m, \varphi)$
- $h(m, \Diamond_{[l,u]}\varphi) = \Box_{[1,l-1]} nc_m \wedge nc_m\, \mathcal{U}_{[l,u]}\, (nc_m \wedge h(m, \varphi))$ if $l \geqslant 2$,
- $h(m, \Diamond_{[l,u]}\varphi) = nc_m\, \mathcal{U}_{[l,u]}\, (nc_m \wedge h(m, \varphi))$ otherwise
- $h(m, \psi\, \mathcal{U}_{[l,u]}\, \xi) = \Box_{[1,l-1]} nc_m \wedge ((nc_m \wedge h(m, \psi))\, \mathcal{U}_{[l,u]}\, (nc_m \wedge h(m, \xi)))$ if $l \geqslant 2$,
- $h(m, \psi\, \mathcal{U}_{[l,u]}\, \xi) = (nc_m \wedge h(m, \psi))\, \mathcal{U}_{[l,u]}\, (nc_m \wedge h(m, \xi))$ otherwise

Theorem 3 ***(Slot-based MLTL Encoding Correctness).*** *Let S_m be a slot, φ be an MLTL formula, and π be a finite trace. Then $\pi \models h(m, \varphi)$ if and only if $\pi \models \varphi$ and the object ID of slot S_m does not change while φ is evaluated.*

Proof Sketch We prove via induction on the form of φ that each sub-formula of $h(m, \varphi)$ maintains the semantics of φ and enforces that the object in S_m does not change until φ is evaluated. For a finite trace π:

- If $\varphi = p$, $\varphi = \neg\psi$ or $\varphi = \varphi_1 \vee \varphi_2$, then $h(m, \varphi)$ does not alter the φ's semantics.
- If $\varphi = \Box_{[l,u]}\psi$, then $h(m, \varphi)$ evaluates whether both $\pi \models \Box_{[l,u]}\psi$ and the object ID in S_m does not change between the current timestamp and u.
- If $\varphi = \Diamond_{[l,u]}\psi$, then $h(m, \varphi)$ evaluates whether both $\pi \models \Diamond_{[l,u]}\psi$ (implied by the semantics of $\mathcal{U}_I$) and the object ID in S_m does not change between the current timestamp and $l-1$ as well as until either $\pi \models \psi$ or $\pi \not\models \Diamond_{[l,u]}\psi$.
- If $\varphi = \psi\, \mathcal{U}_{[l,u]}\, \xi$, then $h(m, \varphi)$ evaluates whether both $\pi \models \psi\, \mathcal{U}_{[l,u]}\, \xi$ and the object ID in S_m does not change between the current timestamp and $l-1$ as well as until either $\pi \models \psi$ or $\pi \not\models \Diamond_{[l,u]}\xi$.

Note the constraints h places on l and u, where we can remove any temporal operator with an upper bound of 0. Further, we only reason about nc_m starting at time 1 since nc_m tracks whether the object has changed since the *previous* time step, so it is valid for the object to have changed before we start monitoring φ. □

5 Realizing Unboundedness via Dynamic Set Specification Unrolling

Another area of concern for set-based reasoning is unboundedness. For the file requirement mentioned in Sect. 4, the set of files being monitored is, as currently stated, unbounded. We argue that this set is never truly unbounded on a real-world system – every system has a bound on the number of files that can be open at one time, for instance, and in most cases these bounds are reasonable. To leverage these bounds, we formalize the notion of a set that changes during system execution then encode MLTL specifications over such "dynamic" sets.

Definition 6 ***(Domain-bounded Dynamic Sets).*** *A* domain-bounded dynamic set *(DBDS) is a set whose membership may change over time and has a maximum size $n \in \mathbb{N}_0$, for which n is derived from the application-domain in which the dynamic set is being used.*

In the context of our illustrative file system example, this definition captures both that the set of files open on a system may change over time as well as that there exists a bound on the maximum number of files that can be open at once (either because the bound exists in the system or the system runs out of memory, where the latter of which likely points to a design flaw). We can then leverage this construct to efficiently encode properties of DBDSs in MLTL.

Definition 7 ***(DBDS Specifications).*** *A* DBDS Specification *is an MLTL formula φ applied to a DBDS where π models the specification if and only if $\pi \models \varphi$ for each object in the DBDS and each each object in the DBDS does not leave the DBDS until after φ is evaluated for that object for a trace π and time i.*

Naturally, for a DBDS D with max size n, we introduce n slots to track the objects in D over time. This allows us to express MLTL formulas over the set of all objects in D at a given time.

Definition 8 ***(MLTL Encoding of DBDS Specifications).*** *Let D be a DBDS with maximum size n, $\mathcal{S} = \{S_1, \cdots, S_n\}$ be a set of n slots such that $id(d) = id(S_m)$ for each $d \in D$ and some $m \in [1, n]$, and φ be an MLTL formula. The* MLTL Encoding *of φ applied to D is defined as:*

$$\bigwedge_{i \in [1,n]} h(i, \varphi).$$

To continue the file system example, if we assume that there can only be a maximum of n files open at once and the underlying system arbitrarily places files into empty slots as files open and removes them once they close, then we can encode the requirement that an open file must close within t time steps as:

$$\bigwedge_{i \in [1,n]} (h(i, open \rightarrow \Diamond_{[0,t]} close)) = \bigwedge_{i \in [1,n]} (open_i \rightarrow (nc_i\, \mathcal{U}_{[0,t]}\, close_i)).$$

Theorem 4 ***(DBDS Specification Correctness).*** *Let D be a DBDS with maximum size n, $\mathcal{S} = \{S_1, \cdots, S_n\}$ be a set of n slots such that $id(d) = id(S_m)$ for each $d \in D$ and some $m \in [1, n]$, and φ be an MLTL formula, and π be a finite trace. Then π models φ applied to D (Definition 7) if and only if $\pi \models \bigwedge_{i \in [1,n]} h(i, \varphi)$ (Definition 8).*

Proof Sketch We apply Theorem 3 over each $S_m \in \mathcal{S}$ to show that $h(m, \varphi)$ accurately monitors φ and ensures a consistent object across timestamps during evaluation of φ.

Because we assume the objects in D are correctly reflected in the set of slots $\mathcal{S}$, π models the conjunction of each $h(m, \varphi)$ over $m \in [1, n]$ if and only if each object $d \in D$ satisfies φ at time i and d does not leave D until φ is evaluated. □

Theorem 5 ***(DBDS Specification Time Complexity).*** *The evaluation of the MLTL encoding of a DBDS specification φ has a time complexity of $\mathcal{O}(\log_2 \log_2 max(p, t) \cdot d \cdot n)$ where p is the maximum worst-case propagation delay of all nodes in $AST(\varphi)$, d is the depth of $AST(\varphi)$, $t \in \mathbb{N}_0$ is the timestamp φ is evaluated for (i.e., the trace π_t), and n is the maximum size of the set.*

Proof. We know that the time complexity for evaluating a given MLTL formula is $\mathcal{O}(\log_2 \log_2 max(p, t) \cdot d)$ [32]. Therefore, since the encoding has n conjunctive/disjunctive clauses and each clause has a time complexity of $\mathcal{O}(\log_2 \log_2 max(p, t) \cdot d)$, the proof follows. □

Theorem 6 ***(DBDS Specification Space Complexity).*** *The MLTL encoding of a dynamic set specification φ has a space complexity of $\mathcal{O}((2 + \lceil \log_2(t) \rceil) \cdot (2 \cdot m \cdot p) \cdot n)$ where p is the maximum worst-case propagation delay of all nodes in $AST(\varphi)$, m is the number of binary operations in the AST, $t \in \mathbb{N}_0$ is the timestamp φ is evaluated for (i.e., the trace π_t), and n is the maximum size of the set.*

Proof. We know that the space complexity for encoding an MLTL formula is $\mathcal{O}((2 + \lceil \log_2(t) \rceil) \cdot (2 \cdot m \cdot p))$ [32]. Therefore, since the encoding has n conjunctive/disjunctive clauses and each clause has a space complexity of $\mathcal{O}((2 + \lceil \log_2(t) \rceil) \cdot (2 \cdot m \cdot p))$, the proof follows. □

6 Realizing Counting via Domain-Bounded Dynamic Sets

LTL cannot express "counting" properties [40] e.g., that an event must occur every n time steps and may or may not occur during any other time step. Counting in temporal logics allow specifications to reason over buffers, queues, and FIFOs [36] as well as perform multi-agent planning [34]. Variants of LTL with counting that sacrifice decidability exist [31], but Metric Temporal Logic on finite words is elementarily decidable with counting and interval bounds on Until [21]. By leveraging system constraints and DBDSs, we can tractably encode specifications such as "No more than k tasks are active in the scheduler at once" in MLTL.

Definition 9 ***(Counting DBDS Specifications).*** *A* Counting DBDS Specification *with parameter k is an MLTL formula φ applied to a DBDS where π models the specification if and only if $\pi \models \varphi$ for exactly k objects in the DBDS and each object in the DBDS does not leave the DBDS until after φ is evaluated for that object in π.*

The MLTL encoding of these specifications is defined by enumerating all $\binom{n}{k}$ possible ways in which k φ-clauses hold at one time (called an *enumeration clause*).

Definition 10 ***(MLTL Encoding of Counting DBDS Specifications).*** *Let D be a DBDS with maximum size n, $\mathcal{S} = \{S_1, \cdots, S_n\}$ be a set of n slots such that $id(d) = id(S_m)$ for each $d \in D$ and some $m \in [1, n]$, φ be an MLTL formula, and*

$\mathcal{P}_k(X)$ be the subset of the powerset of X such that $|P| = k$ for each $P \in \mathcal{P}_k(X)$. The MLTL Encoding *of "exactly k" φ applied to D is defined as:*

$$\bigvee_{X \in \mathcal{P}_k([1,n])} \left(\bigwedge_{i \in X} h(i,\varphi) \wedge \bigwedge_{i \in [1,n] \setminus X} \neg h(i,\varphi) \right).$$

Theorem 7 ***(Counting Specification Correctness).*** *Let D be a DBDS with maximum size n, $\mathcal{S} = \{S_1, \cdots, S_n\}$ be a set of n slots such that $id(d) = id(S_m)$ for each $d \in D$ and some $m \in [1, n]$, φ be an MLTL formula, π be a finite trace, and $\mathcal{P}_k(X)$ be the subset of the powerset of X such that $|P| = k$ for each $P \in \mathcal{P}_k(X)$. Then π models φ applied to D with parameter k (Definition 9) if and only if*

$$\pi \models \bigvee_{X \in \mathcal{P}_k([1,n])} \left(\bigwedge_{i \in X} h(i,\varphi) \wedge \bigwedge_{i \in [1,n] \setminus X} \neg h(i,\varphi) \right) \text{ (Def. 10).}$$

Proof Sketch. The proof sketch follows a similar structure to the proof for Theorem 4: we apply Theorem 3 over each $S_m \in \mathcal{S}$ to show that $h(m, \varphi)$ accurately monitors φ and ensures a consistent object across timestamps during evaluation of φ. Because we assume the objects in D are correctly reflected in the set of slots $\mathcal{S}$, π models the disjunction of enumeration clauses $\bigwedge_{i \in X} h(i, \varphi) \wedge \bigwedge_{i \in [1,n] \setminus X} \neg h(i, \varphi)$ over $X \in \mathcal{P}_k([1, n])$ if and only if exactly k objects in D satisfy φ and each object does not leave D until φ is evaluated. □

We can then further encode counting specifications of the form "at least k of the elements in D satisfy φ" by:

$$\bigvee_{X \in \mathcal{P}_k([1,n]) \cup \mathcal{P}_{k+1}([1,n]) \cup \cdots \cup \mathcal{P}_n([1,n])} \left(\bigwedge_{i \in X} h(i,\varphi) \wedge \bigwedge_{i \in [1,n] \setminus X} \neg h(i,\varphi) \right)$$

where we enumerate all possible ways in which at least k enumeration-clauses are true at one time. While these encodings cause a factorial blowup in the number of terms in the MLTL formula (i.e., $\binom{n}{k}$ enumeration clauses for "exactly k" specifications), the value of $\binom{n}{k}$ is tractable in practice for previously published collections of real-world MLTL specifications [2,4,7,8,15,16,25].

Theorem 8 ***(Counting Specification Time Complexity).*** *The MLTL encoding of a counting specification φ has a space complexity of $\mathcal{O}\left((2 + \lceil \log_2(t) \rceil) \cdot (2 \cdot m \cdot p) \cdot \binom{n}{k}\right)$ where p is the maximum worst-case propagation delay of all nodes in $AST(\varphi)$, m is the number of binary operations in the AST, $t \in \mathbb{N}_0$ is the timestamp φ is evaluated for (i.e., the trace π_t), n is the maximum size of the set, and k is number of objects counted in φ.*

Proof. We know that the time complexity for evaluating a given MLTL formula is $\mathcal{O}(\log_2 \log_2 max(p,t) \cdot d)$ [32]. Therefore, since the encoding has $\binom{n}{k}$ clauses and each clause has a time complexity of $\mathcal{O}\left(\log_2 \log_2 max(p,t) \cdot d\right)$, the proof follows. □

Theorem 9 ***(Counting Specification Space Complexity).*** *The MLTL encoding of a counting specification* φ *has a space complexity of* $\mathcal{O}\left((2 + \lceil \log_2(t) \rceil) \cdot (2 \cdot m \cdot p) \cdot \binom{n}{k}\right)$ *where* p *is the maximum worst-case propagation delay of all nodes in* $AST(\varphi)$*,* m *is the number of binary operations in the AST,* $t \in \mathbb{N}_0$ *is the timestamp* φ *is evaluated for (i.e., the trace* π_t*),* n *is the maximum size of the set, and* k *is number of objects counted in* φ*.*

Proof. We know that the space complexity for encoding an MLTL formula is $\mathcal{O}((2 + \lceil \log_2(t) \rceil) \cdot (2 \cdot m \cdot p))$ [32]. Therefore, since the encoding has $\binom{n}{k}$ conjunctive/disjunctive clauses and each clause has a space complexity of $\mathcal{O}\left((2 + \lceil \log_2(t) \rceil) \cdot (2 \cdot m \cdot p)\right)$, the proof follows. □

Count Operator Encoding. The addition of a *count* operator allows for more efficient encodings of these specifications. We define

$$count(\varphi_1, \cdots, \varphi_n, k)$$

to take n MLTL formulas and a natural k such that *count* is true if and only if exactly k of the φ_i formulas for $i \in [1, n]$ are true. Then, we can encode counting specifications in MLTL as: $count(h(1, \varphi), \cdots, h(n, \varphi), k)$. This encoding is similar to *dynamic set specifications* in that it grows linearly with the maximum size of the dynamic set, though is not pure MLTL.

7 Applying MLTL Rewrite Rules to DBDS Specifications

Memory encoding size is a important metric for monitoring MLTL formulas. This is especially true for real-time, resource-constrained systems, which are natural targets for MLTL monitoring [17]. The techniques presented in Sect. 5,6 place a hard bound on the memory requirements for specifications over sets, and the rules in Sect. 3 reduce the overall memory signature of an encoded MLTL formula. These approaches are especially powerful when used in tandem, rewriting MLTL-encoded DBDS specifications.

To illustrate, consider a request arbiter that receives requests and either grants, rejects, or delays them and assume that the arbiter can only ever handle a maximum of 100 requests at once. Then say we want to monitor the requirement that for each active request R, R shall be either granted (g) or rejected (r) within 20 s otherwise R will be delayed (d) within 10 s and be granted or rejected within 20 s of being delayed. We formalize this in MLTL by introducing slots $S_1, \cdots, S_{100}$ such that active requests are arbitrarily assigned an empty slot during system execution:

$$\bigwedge_{i \in [1,100]} h(i, \Diamond_{[0,20]}(g \vee r) \vee \Diamond_{[0,10]}(d \wedge \Diamond_{[0,20]}(g \vee r))). \tag{5}$$

According to Eq. 2, encoding the MLTL formula given as an argument to h as a monitor requires space for at least 82 verdicts. We can apply (R2) to rewrite this MLTL formula:

$$\bigwedge_{i \in [1,100]} h(i, \Diamond_{[0,10]}(\Diamond_{[0,10]}(g \vee r) \vee (d \wedge \Diamond_{[0,20]}(g \vee r)))). \tag{6}$$

Evaluating this formula requires space for only 62 verdicts. If we assume a verdict size of 33 bits (32 for the timestamp, 1 for the result), Eq. 5 requires memory on the order of $(1 + 32) \times 100 \times 82 = 270,600$ bits (33.825 KB). Automatically applying (R2) therefore saves memory on the order of $(1+32) \times 100 \times (82-62) = 66,000$ bits (8.25 KB). This is a meaningful improvement for some resource-constrained systems, which only have on the order of KBs to dedicate towards runtime monitoring [28].

As specification is the biggest bottleneck in formal verification [33], a specification author is unlikely to recognize that Eq. 5 is more memory-intensive to monitor than Eq. 6. Automating the application of rewrite rules therefore aids in finding such optimizations. Additionally, applying rewrite rules to DBDS specifications saves n-times the memory as compared to applying the rules to a single MLTL formula, showing the power of pairing these two techniques in practice.

8 Impacts and Future Work

We argue that a large class of "intractable" specifications have corresponding temporal logic patterns based off of our novel constructions. By leveraging MLTL rewriting rules and encodings for dynamic set specifications, we enable the expression and memory optimization of "intractable" specification patterns. Systems that feature domain constraints (e.g., real-time systems) can leverage these encodings to express specifications that otherwise may have required higher-order logics.

Further investigation into optimizations for MLTL encodings is warranted, for instance, by deriving tighter bounds for the propagation delays of AST nodes. While we presented an instance of removing vacuous sub-formulas that can tighten these bounds (R5), generalized techniques for detecting vacuity may help tighten these bounds further. Similarly, an algorithm for detecting the optimal ordering of rewrite rules may reduce memory requirements further.

References

1. Alur, R., Henzinger, T.A.: Real-time logics: complexity and expressiveness. Inf. Comput. **104**(1), 35–77 (1993)
2. Aurandt, A., Jones, P., Rozier, K.Y.: Runtime verification triggers real-time, autonomous fault recovery on the CySat-I. In: Deshmukh, J.V., Havelund, K., Perez, I. (eds.) NASA Formal Methods. NFM 2022. LNCS, vol. 13260. Springer, Cham (2022). https://doi.org/10.1007/978-3-031-06773-0_45
3. Bartocci, E., Falcone, Y., Francalanza, A., Reger, G.: Introduction to runtime verification. In: Bartocci, E., Falcone, Y. (eds.) Lectures on Runtime Verification. LNCS, vol. 10457, pp. 1–33. Springer, Cham (2018). https://doi.org/10.1007/978-3-319-75632-5_1
4. Cauwels, M., Hammer, A., Hertz, B., Jones, P.H., Rozier, K.Y.: Integrating runtime verification into an automated UAS traffic management system. In: Muccini, H., et al. (eds.) ECSA 2020. CCIS, vol. 1269, pp. 340–357. Springer, Cham (2020). https://doi.org/10.1007/978-3-030-59155-7_26
5. Cerrito, S., Mayer, M.C., Praud, S.: First order linear temporal logic over finite time structures. In: Ganzinger, H., McAllester, D., Voronkov, A. (eds.) LPAR 1999. LNCS (LNAI), vol. 1705, pp. 62–76. Springer, Heidelberg (1999). https://doi.org/10.1007/3-540-48242-3_5

6. Chen, Y., Zhang, X., Li, J.: Finite quantified linear temporal logic and its satisfiability checking. In: Chen, Y., Zhang, S. (eds.) Artificial Intelligence Logic and Applications. AILA 2022 2022. Communications in Computer and Information Science, vol. 1657. Springer, Singapore (2022). https://doi.org/10.1007/978-981-19-7510-3_1
7. Dabney, J.B., Badger, J.M., Rajagopal, P.: Adding a verification view for an autonomous realtime system architecture. In: Proceedings of SciTech Forum, pp. 2021–0566. AIAA (2021). https://doi.org/10.2514/6.2021-0566
8. Dabney, J.B.: Using assume-guarantee contracts in autonomous spacecraft. Flight Software Workshop (FSW) (2021). https://www.youtube.com/watch?v=zrtyiyNf674
9. Dabney, J.B., Rajagopal, P., Badger, J.M.: Using assume-guarantee contracts for developmental verification of autonomous spacecraft. Flight Software Workshop (FSW) (2022). https://www.youtube.com/watch?v=HFnn6TzblPg
10. Duret-Lutz, A.: Manipulating LTL formulas using spot 1.0. In: Van Hung, D., Ogawa, M. (eds.) ATVA 2013. LNCS, vol. 8172, pp. 442–445. Springer, Cham (2013). https://doi.org/10.1007/978-3-319-02444-8_31
11. Duret-Lutz, et al.: From spot 2.0 to spot 2.10: What's new? In: Shoham, S., Vizel, Y. (eds.) Computer Aided Verification. CAV 2022. LNCS, vol. 13372. Springer, Cham (2022). https://doi.org/10.1007/978-3-031-13188-2_9
12. Havelund, K., Reger, G.: Runtime verification logics a language design perspective. Models, Algorithms, Logics and Tools: Essays Dedicated to Kim Guldstrand Larsen on the Occasion of His 60th Birthday, pp. 310–338 (2017)
13. Havelund, K., Reger, G., Thoma, D., Zălinescu, E.: Monitoring events that carry data. In: Bartocci, E., Falcone, Y. (eds.) Lectures on Runtime Verification. LNCS, vol. 10457, pp. 61–102. Springer, Cham (2018). https://doi.org/10.1007/978-3-319-75632-5_3
14. He, X., Lee, J.A.N.: Integrating predicate transition nets with first order temporal logic in the specification and verification of concurrent systems. Form. Asp. Comput. **2**(1), 226–246 (1990). https://doi.org/10.1007/BF01888226
15. Hertz, B., Luppen, Z., Rozier, K.Y.: Integrating runtime verification into a sounding rocket control system. In: Proceedings of the 13th NASA Formal Methods Symposium (NFM 2021) (2021). https://temporallogic.org/research/NFM21/
16. Kempa, B., Johannsen, C., Rozier, K.Y.: Improving usability and trust in real-time verification of a large-scale complex safety-critical system. Ada User J. **43** (2022)
17. Kempa, B., Zhang, P., Jones, P.H., Zambreno, J., Rozier, K.Y.: Embedding online runtime verification for fault disambiguation on robonaut2. In: Bertrand, N., Jansen, N. (eds.) FORMATS 2020. LNCS, vol. 12288, pp. 196–214. Springer, Cham (2020). https://doi.org/10.1007/978-3-030-57628-8_12
18. Kempa, B., Zhang, P., Jones, P.H., Zambreno, J., Rozier, K.Y.: Embedding online runtime verification for fault disambiguation on robonaut2. In: Under Submission. TBD (2021)
19. Kessler, F.B.: nuXmv 1.1.0 (2016–05-10) Release Notes. https://es-static.fbk.eu/tools/nuxmv/downloads/NEWS.txt (2016)
20. Khoury, R., Halle, S.: Tally keeping-LTL: An LTL semantics for quantitative evaluation of LTL specifications. In: 2018 IEEE International Conference on Information Reuse and Integration (IRI), pp. 495–502. IEEE Computer Society, Los Alamitos, CA, USA (2018). https://doi.org/10.1109/IRI.2018.00079. https://doi.ieeecomputersociety.org/10.1109/IRI.2018.00079
21. Krishna, S.N., Madnani, K., Pandya, P.K.: Metric temporal logic with counting. In: Jacobs, B., Löding, C. (eds.) FoSSaCS 2016. LNCS, vol. 9634, pp. 335–352. Springer, Heidelberg (2016). https://doi.org/10.1007/978-3-662-49630-5_20
22. Kuperberg, D., Brunel, J., Chemouil, D.: On finite domains in first-order linear temporal logic. In: Artho, C., Legay, A., Peled, D. (eds.) ATVA 2016. LNCS, vol. 9938, pp. 211–226. Springer, Cham (2016). https://doi.org/10.1007/978-3-319-46520-3_14

23. Li, J., Vardi, M.Y., Rozier, K.Y.: Satisfiability checking for mission-time LTL. In: Dillig, I., Tasiran, S. (eds.) CAV 2019. LNCS, vol. 11562, pp. 3–22. Springer, Cham (2019). https://doi.org/10.1007/978-3-030-25543-5_1
24. Li, J., Vardi, M.Y., Rozier, K.Y.: Satisfiability checking for mission-time LTL (MLTL). Inf. Comput. **289**, 104923 (2022)
25. Luppen, Z., et al.: Elucidation and analysis of specification patterns in aerospace system telemetry. In: Deshmukh, J.V., Havelund, K., Perez, I. (eds.) NASA Formal Methods. NFM 2022. LNCS, vol. 13260. Springer, Cham (2022). https://doi.org/10.1007/978-3-031-06773-0_28
26. Maler, O., Nickovic, D.: Monitoring temporal properties of continuous signals. In: Lakhnech, Y., Yovine, S. (eds.) FORMATS/FTRTFT -2004. LNCS, vol. 3253, pp. 152–166. Springer, Heidelberg (2004). https://doi.org/10.1007/978-3-540-30206-3_12
27. Noureddine, M.A., Zaraket, F.A.: Model checking software with first order logic specifications using AIG solvers. IEEE Trans. Software Eng. **42**(8), 741–763 (2016). https://doi.org/10.1109/TSE.2016.2520468
28. Okubo, N.: Using R2U2 in JAXA program. Electronic correspondence (November-December 2020). Series of emails and zoom call from JAXA to PI with technical questions about embedding R2U2 into an autonomous satellite mission with a provable memory bound of 200 KB
29. Ouaknine, J., Worrell, J.: Some recent results in metric temporal logic. In: Cassez, F., Jard, C. (eds.) FORMATS 2008. LNCS, vol. 5215, pp. 1–13. Springer, Heidelberg (2008). https://doi.org/10.1007/978-3-540-85778-5_1
30. Piribauer, J., Baier, C., Bertrand, N., Sankur, O.: Quantified linear temporal logic over probabilistic systems with an application to vacuity checking. In: CONCUR 2021–32nd International Conference on Concurrency Theory, pp. 1–18 (2021)
31. Regis, G., Degiovanni, R., D'Ippolito, N., Aguirre, N.: Specifying event-based systems with a counting fluent temporal logic. In: 2015 IEEE/ACM 37th IEEE International Conference on Software Engineering, vol. 1, pp. 733–743 (2015). https://doi.org/10.1109/ICSE.2015.86
32. Reinbacher, T., Rozier, K.Y., Schumann, J.: Temporal-logic based runtime observer pairs for system health management of real-time systems. In: Ábrahám, E., Havelund, K. (eds.) TACAS 2014. LNCS, vol. 8413, pp. 357–372. Springer, Heidelberg (2014). https://doi.org/10.1007/978-3-642-54862-8_24
33. Rozier, K.Y.: Specification: The Biggest Bottleneck in Formal Methods and Autonomy. In: Blazy, S., Chechik, M. (eds.) VSTTE 2016. LNCS, vol. 9971, pp. 8–26. Springer, Cham (2016). https://doi.org/10.1007/978-3-319-48869-1_2
34. Sahin, Y.E., Nilsson, P., Ozay, N.: Multirobot coordination with counting temporal logics. IEEE Trans. Rob. **36**(4), 1189–1206 (2020). https://doi.org/10.1109/TRO.2019.2957669
35. Sistla, A.P., Vardi, M.Y., Wolper, P.: The complementation problem for büchi automata with applications to temporal logic. Theoret. Comput. Sci. **49**(2–3), 217–237 (1987)
36. Sistla, A., Clarke, E., Francez, N., Meyer, A.: Can message buffers be axiomatized in linear temporal logic? Inf. Control **63**(1), 88–112 (1984). https://doi.org/10.1016/S0019-9958(84)80043-1. https://www.sciencedirect.com/science/article/pii/S0019995884800431
37. Software, F.: Setting the Open File Limit (Linux/Unix). https://docs.revenera.com/fnci6133/Content/helplibrary/Setting_the_Open_File_Limit__Linux_Unix_.html (2019)
38. Song, F., Wu, Z.: Extending temporal logics with data variable quantifications. In: 34th International Conference on Foundation of Software Technology and Theoretical Computer Science (FSTTCS 2014). Schloss Dagstuhl-Leibniz-Zentrum fuer Informatik (2014)
39. Vardi, M.Y.: Branching vs. linear time: final showdown. In: Margaria, T., Yi, W. (eds.) TACAS 2001. LNCS, vol. 2031, pp. 1–22. Springer, Heidelberg (2001). https://doi.org/10.1007/3-540-45319-9_1
40. Wolper, P.: Temporal logic can be more expressive. Inf. Control **56**(1–2), 72–99 (1983)

Robustness Verification of Deep Neural Networks Using Star-Based Reachability Analysis with Variable-Length Time Series Input

Neelanjana Pal(✉), Diego Manzanas Lopez, and Taylor T Johnson

Institute for Software Integrated Systems,
Vanderbilt University, Nashville, TN 37212, USA
{neelanjana.pal,diego.manzanas.lopez,taylor.johnson}@vanderbilt.edu

Abstract. Data-driven, neural network (NN) based anomaly detection and predictive maintenance are emerging as important research areas. NN-based analytics of time-series data provide valuable insights and statistical evidence for diagnosing past behaviors and predicting critical parameters like equipment's remaining useful life (RUL), state-of-charge (SOC) of batteries, etc. Unfortunately, input time series data can be exposed to intentional or unintentional noise when passing through sensors, making robust validation and verification of these NNs a crucial task. Using set-based reachability analysis, this paper presents a case study of the formal robustness verification approach for time series regression NNs (TSRegNN). It utilizes variable-length input data to streamline input manipulation and enhance network architecture generalizability. The method is applied to two data sets in the Prognostics and Health Management (PHM) application areas: (1) SOC estimation of a Lithium-ion battery and (2) RUL estimation of a turbine engine. Finally, the paper introduces several performance measures to evaluate the effect of bounded perturbations in the input on network outputs, i.e., future outcomes. Overall, the paper offers a comprehensive case study for validating and verifying NN-based analytics of time-series data in real-world applications, emphasizing the importance of robustness testing for accurate and reliable predictions, especially considering the impact of noise on future outcomes.

Keywords: Predictive Maintenance · Time Series Data · Neural Network Verification · Star-set · Reachability Analysis · Noise · Robustness Verification · Prognostics and Health Management

1 Introduction

Over time, Deep Neural Networks (DNNs) have shown tremendous potential in solving complex tasks, such as image classification, object detection, speech recognition, natural language processing, document analysis, etc., sometimes

A. Cimatti and L. Titolo (Eds.): FMICS 2023, LNCS 14290, pp. 170–188, 2023.
https://doi.org/10.1007/978-3-031-43681-9_10

even outperforming humans [15–17]. This has motivated a spurt in investigating the applicability of DNNs in numerous real-world applications, such as biometrics authentication, face authentication for mobile locking systems, malware detection, etc. In dealing with such susceptible information in these critical areas, safety, security, and verification thereof have become essential design considerations.

Unfortunately, it has been demonstrated that minimal perturbations in the input can easily deceive state-of-the-art well-trained networks, leading to erroneous predictions [11,23,36]. The most researched domain for verification of such networks involves image inputs, particularly safety and robustness checking of various classification neural networks [4,7,12,22,38,41]. Previous research has analyzed feed-forward neural networks (FFNN [39]), convolutional neural networks (CNN [38]), and semantic segmentation networks (SSN [41]) using different set-based reachability tools, such as Neural Network Verification (NNV [19,42]) and JuliaReach [5], among others.

However, input perturbations are not only confined to image-based networks but also have been extended to other input types, including time series data or input signals with different noises in predictive maintenance applications [8,43]. One such use case is in the manufacturing industry, where data from process systems, such as IoT sensors and industrial machines, are stored for future analysis [10,31]. Data analytics in this context provide insights and statistical information and can be used to diagnose past behavior [20,46], and predicts future behavior [6,18,35], maximizing industry production. This application is not only limited to manufacturing, but is also relevant in fields like healthcare digitalization [37,45] and smart cities [33,34]. Noisy input data, here, refers to data containing errors, uncertainties, or disturbances, caused by factors like sensor measurement errors, environmental variations, or other noise sources.

While NN applications with image data have received significant attention, little work has been done in the domain of regression-type model verification, particularly with time series data in predictive maintenance applications. Regression-based models with noisy data are crucial for learning data representations and predicting future values, enabling fault prediction and anomaly detection in high-confidence, safety-critical systems [13,29]. This motivated us to use verification techniques to validate the output of regression networks and ensure that the output(s) fall within a specific safe and acceptable range.

Contributions.

1. In this paper, we primarily focus on exploring a new case study, specifically examining time-series-based neural networks in two distinct industrial predictive maintenance application domains. We utilize the established concept of star-set-based reachability methods to analyze whether the upper and lower bounds of the output set adhere to industrial guidelines' permissible bounds. We develop our work[1] as an extension of the NNV tool to formally analyze

[1] The code is available at: https://github.com/verivital/nnv/tree/master/code/nnv/examples/Submission/FMICS2023.

and explore regression-based NN verification for time series data using sound and deterministic reachability methods and experiment on different discrete time signals to check if the output lies within pre-defined safe bounds.
2. Another significant contribution of our work is the flexibility of variable-length inputs in neural networks. This approach simplifies input manipulation and enhances the generalizability of network architectures. Unlike published literature that relied on fixed-sized windows [9,24], which necessitated preprocessing and experimenting with window sizes, our method allows for flexibility in utilizing any sequence length. This flexibility improves the generalizability of reachability analysis.
3. We run an extensive evaluation on two different network architectures in two different predictive maintenance use cases. In this paper, we have introduced a novel robustness measure called Percentage Overlap Robustness (POR). Unlike the existing Percentage Sample Robustness (PR/PSR) [41], which considers only instances where reachable bounds remain entirely within permissible bounds, the proposed POR accounts for all instances with any possible overlap.
4. Finally, we develop insights on evaluating the reachability analysis on those networks and possible future direction.

Outline. The paper is organized as follows: Sect. 2 provides the necessary context for the background; Sect. 3 details the adversarial noises considered; Sect. 4 defines the verification properties; Sect. 6 explains the reachability calculations for layers to accommodate variable-length input; Sect. 5 defines the research problem, and Sect. 7 describes the methodology, including dataset, network models, and input attacks. Section 8 presents the experimental results, evaluation metrics, and their implications. Finally, Sect. 9 summarizes the main findings and suggests future research directions.

2 Preliminaries

This section introduces some basic definitions and descriptions necessary to understand the progression of this paper and the necessary evaluations on time series data.

2.1 Neural Network Verification Tool and Star Sets

The Neural Network Verification (NNV) tool is a framework for verifying the safety and robustness of neural networks [19,42]. It analyzes neural network behavior under various input conditions, ensuring safe and correct operation in all cases. NNV supports reachability algorithms like the over-approximate star set approach [38,40], calculating reachable sets for each network layer. These sets represent all possible network states for a given input, enabling the verification of specific safety properties. NNV is particularly valuable for safety-critical applications, such as autonomous vehicles and medical devices, ensuring neural networks are trustworthy and reliable under all conditions, and maintaining public confidence. For this paper, we have implemented the work as an extension of NNV tool and used the star [Def. 1] based reachability analysis to get the reachable sets of the neural networks at the outputs.

Definition 1. A generalized star set *(or simply star)* Θ *is a tuple* $\langle c, V, P \rangle$ *where* $c \in \mathbb{R}^n$ *is the center,* $V = \{v_1, v_2, \cdots, v_m\}$ *is a set of* m *vectors in* $\mathbb{R}^n$ *called basis vectors, and* $P : \mathbb{R}^m \to \{\top, \bot\}$ *is a predicate. The basis vectors are arranged to form the star's* $n \times m$ *basis matrix. The set of states represented by the star is given as:*

$$[\![\Theta]\!] = \{x \mid x = c + \Sigma_{i=1}^{m}(\alpha_i v_i) \text{ and } P(\alpha_1, \cdots, \alpha_m) = \top\}. \tag{1}$$

In this work, we restrict the predicates to be a conjunction of linear constraints, $P(\alpha) \triangleq C\alpha \leq d$ *where, for* p *linear constraints,* $C \in \mathbb{R}^{p \times m}$, α *is the vector of* m*-variables, i.e.,* $\alpha = [\alpha_1, \cdots, \alpha_m]^T$, *and* $d \in \mathbb{R}^{p \times 1}$.

$$\Theta = c + \alpha v = \underbrace{\begin{bmatrix} 0 & 4 & 1 & 2 \\ 2 & 3 & 2 & 3 \\ 1 & 3 & 1 & 2 \\ 2 & 1 & 3 & 2 \end{bmatrix}}_{c \in R^{4x4}} + \alpha \underbrace{\begin{bmatrix} 0 & 1 & 0 & 0 \\ 0 & 0 & 0 & 0 \\ 0 & 0 & 0 & 0 \\ 0 & 0 & 0 & 0 \end{bmatrix}}_{v \in R^{4x4}}, P \equiv \begin{pmatrix} 1 \\ -1 \end{pmatrix} \alpha \leq \begin{pmatrix} 2 \\ 2 \end{pmatrix}$$

Fig. 1. Star for Time-series Data with four Feature Values (rows) with four time-steps (columns)

A 4×4 time series data with a bounded disturbance $b \in [-2, 2]$ applied on the time instance 2 of feature 1, i.e., position (1, 2) can be described as a Star depicted in Fig. 1.

2.2 Time Series and Regression Neural Network

Signal. The definition of a 'signal' varies depending on the applicable fields. In the area of signal processing, a ***signal*** S can be defined as some physical quantity that varies with respect to (w.r.t.) some independent dimension (e.g., space or time) [27]. In other words, a signal can also be thought of as a function that carries information about the behavior of a system or properties of some physical process [28].

$$S = g(q) \tag{2}$$

where q is space, time, etc. Depending on the nature of the spaces signals are defined over, they can be categorized as discrete or continuous. Discrete-time signals are also known as time series data.

We next define the specific class of signals considered in this paper, namely time series.

Definition 2. *A* ***time series signal*** S_T *is defined as an ordered sequence of values of a variable (or variables) at different time steps. In other words, a time series signal is an ordered sequence of discrete-time data of one or multiple features*[2].

$$\begin{aligned} S_T &= s_{t_1}, s_{t_2}, s_{t_3}, ... \\ T &= t_1, t_2, t_3, ... \end{aligned} \tag{3}$$

where, $t_1, t_2, t_3, \ldots$ *is an ordered sequence of instances in time* T *and* $S_T = s_{t_1}, s_{t_2}, s_{t_3}, \ldots$ *are the signal values at those time instances for each* $t = t_i$.

Here, sometimes we have used 'signal' to refer to the 'time series signal.'

Next, we define the specific types of neural networks considered in this paper, namely regression neural networks (specifically time series regression neural networks).

Definition 3. *A* ***time series regression neural network (TSRegNN)*** f *is a nonlinear/partially-linear function that maps each time-stamped value* $x(i,j)$ *(for* i^{th} *feature and* j^{th} *timestamp) of a single or multifeatured time series input* $\boldsymbol{x}$ *to the output* $\boldsymbol{y}$.

$$f: \ \boldsymbol{x} \in \mathbb{R}^{n_f \times t_s} \rightarrow \boldsymbol{y} \in \mathbb{R}^{p \times q} \tag{4}$$

where t_s, n_f *are the time-sequence length and the number of features of the input data, respectively,* $(j,i) \in \{1, \ldots, t_s\} \times \{1, \ldots, n_f\}$ *are the time steps and corresponding feature indices, respectively, and* p *is the number of values present in the output, while* q *is the length of each of the output values; it can either be equal to* t_s *or not, depending on the network design.*

Here, each row of $\boldsymbol{x}$ *represents a timestamped feature variable.*

2.3 Reachability of a Time Series Regression Network

In this section, we provide a description of how the reachability of a NN layer and the NN as a whole is computed for this study.

Here, we employ an alternative approach to define a Star set for time series data. It involves using the upper and lower bounds of the noisy input, centering the actual input. These bounds on each input parameter, along with the predicates, create the complete set of constraints the optimizer will solve to generate the initial set of states.

Definition 4. *A* ***layer*** L *of a TSRegNN is a function* $h: \ u \in \mathbb{R}^j \rightarrow v \in \mathbb{R}^p$, *with input* $u \in R^j$ *and output* $v \in R^p$ *defined as follows*

$$v = h(u) \tag{5}$$

where the function h *is determined by parameters* θ, *typically defined as a tuple* $\theta = \langle \sigma, W, b \rangle$ *for fully-connected layers, where* $W \in R^{j \times p}, b \in R^p$, *and activation function* $\sigma : R^j \rightarrow R^p$. *Thus, the fully connected NN layer is described as*

$$v = h(u) = \sigma(\boldsymbol{W} \times u + \boldsymbol{b}) \tag{6}$$

[2] Each **feature** is a measurable piece of data that is used for analysis.

For convolutional NN-Layers, θ may include parameters like the filter size, padding, or dilation factor, and the function in Eq. 6 may need alterations.

Definition 5. *Let $h: \ u \in \mathbb{R}^j \rightarrow v \in \mathbb{R}^p$, be a NN layer as described in Eq. 5. The* ***reachable set*** *R_h, with input, $I \in R^n$ is defined as*

$$\mathcal{R}_h \triangleq \{v \mid v = h(u), \ u \in \mathcal{I}\} \tag{7}$$

Reachability analysis (or shortly, reach) of a TSRegNN f on Star input set I is similar to the reachable set calculations for CNN [38] or FFNN [39], the only difference being both the previous works had been done for classification networks.

$$Reach(f, I): \ I \rightarrow \mathcal{R}_{ts} \tag{8}$$

We call $\mathcal{R}_{ts}(I)$ the *output reachable set* of the TSRegNN corresponding to the input set I.

For a regression type NN, the output reachable set can be calculated as a step-by-step process of constructing the reachable sets for each network layer.

$$\begin{aligned}
\mathcal{R}_{L_1} &\triangleq \{v_1 \mid v_1 = h_1(x), \ x \in \mathcal{I}\}, \\
\mathcal{R}_{L_2} &\triangleq \{v_2 \mid v_2 = h_2(v_1), \ v_1 \in \mathcal{R}_{L_1}\}, \\
&\vdots \\
\mathcal{R}_{ts} = \mathcal{R}_{L_k} &\triangleq \{v_k \mid v_k = h_k(v_{k-1}), \ v_{k-1} \in \mathcal{R}_{L_{k-1}}\},
\end{aligned}$$

where h_k is the function represented by the kth layer L_k. The reachable set $\mathcal{R}_{L_k}$ contains all outputs of the neural network corresponding to all input vectors x in the input set $\mathcal{I}$.

3 Adversarial Noise

In the case of time series samples, while the sensor transmits the sampled data, sensor noises might get added to the original data. One example of such noise is sensor vibration, but sometimes the actual sources are not even known by the sensor providers [21].

Definition 6. *A* ***noise*** *can be defined as some unintentional, usually small-scaled signal which, when added to the primary signal, can cause malfunctioning of the equipment in an industrial premise. Mathematically, a noisy signal s^{noise} can be produced by a linear parameterized function $g_{\epsilon, s^{noise}}(\cdot)$ that takes an input signal and produces the corresponding noisy signal.*

$$s^{noise} = g_{\epsilon, s^{noise}}(s) = s + \Sigma_{i=1}^{n} \epsilon_i \cdot s_i^{noise} \tag{9}$$

For time series data, we can also assume the noise as a set of unit vectors associated with a coefficient vector ϵ at each time step i, where the value of the coefficient vector ϵ is unknown but bounded within a range $[\underline{\epsilon}, \overline{\epsilon}]$, i.e., $\underline{\epsilon_i} \leq \epsilon_i \leq \overline{\epsilon_i}$.

Types of Possible Noises. For an input sequence with t_s number of time instances and n_f number of features, there can be four types of noises (l_∞ norm)[3], based on its spread on the signal. They can be categorized as below:

1. **Single Feature Single-instance Noise (SFSI)** i.e., perturbing a feature value only at a particular instance (t) by a certain percentage around the actual value.
$$s^{noise} = g_{\epsilon,s^{noise}}(s) = s + \epsilon_t \cdot s_t^{noise} \tag{10}$$
2. **Single Feature All-instances Noise (SFAI)** i.e., perturbing a specific feature throughout all the time instances by a certain percentage around the actual values of a particular feature.
$$s^{noise} = g_{\epsilon,s^{noise}}(s) = s + \Sigma_{i=1}^{n} \epsilon_i \cdot s_i^{noise} \tag{11}$$
3. **Multifeature Single-instance Noise (MFSI)** i.e., perturbing all feature values but only at a particular instance (t), following Eq. 10 for all features.
4. **Multifeature All-instance Noise (MFAI)** i.e., perturbing all feature values throughout all the instances, following Eq. 11 for all features.

4 Verification Properties

Verification properties can be categorized into two types: local properties and global properties. A local property is defined for a specific input x at time-instance t or a set of points X in the input space $R^{n_f \times t_s}$. In other words, a local property must hold for certain specific inputs. On the other hand, a global property [44] is defined over the entire input space $R^{n_f \times t_s}$ of the network model and must hold for all inputs without any exceptions.

Robustness. Robustness refers to the ability of a system or a model to maintain its performance and functionality under various challenging conditions, uncertainties, or perturbations. It is a desirable quality that ensures the system's reliability, resilience, and adaptability in the face of changing or adverse circumstances. For an input perturbation measured by δ and admissible output deviation ϵ, the 'delta-epsilon' formulation for the desired robustness property can be written as:

$$||x' - x||_\infty < \delta \implies ||f(x') - f(x)||_\infty < \epsilon \tag{12}$$

where x is the original input belonging to the input space $R^{n_f \times t_s}$, x' is the noisy input, $f(x')$ and $f(x)$ are NN model outputs for, respectively, x' and x, δ is the max measure of the noise added, ϵ is the max deviation in the output because of the presence of noise ($\delta, \epsilon \in \mathbf{R} > 0$).

Local Robustness. Given a TSRegNN f and an input time series signal S, the network is called **locally robust** to any noise $\mathcal{A}$ if and only if: the estimated

[3] A detailed version of this paper with example plots of noises, sample calculations for the robustness measures and the network architectures used can be found in [25].

output reachable bounds for a particular time-step corresponding to the noisy input lie between predefined allowable bounds w.r.t to the actual signal.

Robustness Value (RV) of a time series signal S is a binary variable, which indicates the local robustness of the system. RV is 1 when the estimated output range for a particular time instance (t) lies within the allowable range, making it locally robust at t; otherwise, RV is 0.

$RV = 1 \iff {LB_t}^{est} \geq {LB_t}^{allow} \wedge {UB_t}^{est} \leq {UB_t}^{allow}$ else, RV = 0

where ${LB_t}^{est}$ and ${UB_t}^{est}$ are estimated bounds and ${LB_t}^{allow}$ and ${UB_t}^{allow}$ are allowable bounds.

Definition 7. ***Percentage Sample Robustness (PR)*** *of a TSRegNN corresponding to any noisy input is defined as*

$$PR = \frac{N_{robust}}{N_{total}} \times 100\%, \tag{13}$$

where N_{robust} is the total number of robust time instances, and N_{total} = the total number of time steps in the time series signal. Percentage robustness can be used as a measure of ***global robustness*** *[44] of a TSRegNN w.r.t any noise.*

In this study, we adapt the concept of Percentage Robustness (PR) previously used in image-based classification or segmentation neural networks [41] to time-series inputs. PR in those cases assessed the network's ability to correctly classify/segment inputs even with input perturbations for a given number of images/pixels. We extend this concept to analyze the robustness of time-series inputs in our research.

Definition 8. ***Percentage Overlap Robustness (POR)*** *of a TSRegNN corresponding to any noisy input is defined as*

$$POR = \frac{\Sigma_{i=1}^{N_{total}}(PO_i)}{N_{total}} \times 100\%, \tag{14}$$

where N_{total} = total number of time instances in the time series signal, and PO_i is the percentage overlap between estimated and allowed ranges at each time step w.r.t the estimated range

$$PO = \frac{Overlapped\ Range}{Estimated\ Range} \tag{15}$$

Here Overlapped Range is the overlap between the estimated range and the allowable range for a particular time step. The Allowable Range indicates the allowable upper and lower bounds, whereas Estimated Range is the output reachable bounds given by the TSRegNN for that time step. Percentage overlap robustness can also be used as a measure of ***global robustness*** *[44] of TSRegNN.*

When selecting robustness properties, it is crucial to consider the specific application area. If the application allows for some flexibility in terms of performance, POR can be utilized. On the other hand, if the application requires a more conservative approach, PR should be considered. An example showing calculations for the robustness measures can be found in [25].

Monotonicity. In PHM applications, the monotonicity property refers to the system's health indicator, i.e., the degradation parameter exhibiting a consistent increase or decrease as the system approaches failure. PHM involves monitoring a system's health condition and predicting its Remaining Useful Life (RUL) to enable informed maintenance decisions and prevent unforeseen failures. For detailed mathematical modeling of the monotonicity property, please refer to [32] and the latest report on formal methods at [9]. In general, for a TSRegNN $f: \mathbf{x} \in \mathbb{R} \rightarrow \mathbf{y} \in \mathbb{R}$ with single-featured input and output spaces, at any time instance t, the property for monotonically decreasing output can be written as:

$$\begin{aligned} \forall x' \exists \delta : x \leq x' \leq x + \delta &\implies f(x') \leq f(x) \\ \forall x' \exists \delta : x - \delta \leq x' \leq x &\implies f(x') \geq f(x) \end{aligned} \tag{16}$$

This is a local monotonicity property. If this holds true for the entire time range, then the property can be considered as a global property [44]. In this paper, the monotonicity property is only valid for the PHM examples for RUL estimation.

5 Robustness Verification Problem Formulation

We consider the verification of the robustness and the monotonicity properties.

Problem 1 ***(Local Robustness Property).*** Given a TSRegNN f, a time series signal S, and a noise $\mathcal{A}$, prove if the network is locally robust or non-robust [Sec. 4] w.r.t the noise $\mathcal{A}$; i.e., if the estimated bounds obtained through the reachability calculations lie within the allowable range of the actual output for the particular time instance.

Problem 2 ***(Global Robustness Property).*** Given a TSRegNN f, a set of N consecutive time-series signal $\mathbf{S} = \{S_1, \ldots, S_N\}$, and a noise $\mathcal{A}$, compute the percentage robustness values (PR [Def. 7] and POR [Def. 8]) corresponding to $\mathcal{A}$.

Problem 3 ***(Local Monotonicity Property).*** Given a TSRegNN f, a set of N consecutive time-series signal $\mathbf{S} = \{S_1, \ldots, S_N\}$, and a noise $\mathcal{A}$, show that both the estimated RUL bounds of the network [Eq. 16] corresponding to noisy input S'_t at any time instance t are monotonically decreasing.

To get an idea of the global performance [44] of the network, local stability properties have been formulated and verified for each point in the test dataset for 100 consecutive time steps.

The core step in solving these problems is to solve the local properties of a TSRegNN f w.r.t a noise $\mathcal{A}$. It can be done using over-approximate reachability analysis, computing the 'output reachable set' $\mathcal{R}_t s = Reach(f, I)$ that provides an upper and lower bound estimation corresponding to the noisy input set I.

In this paper, we propose using percentage values as robustness measures for verifying neural networks (NN). We conduct reachability analysis on the output set to ensure it stays within predefined safe bounds specified by permissible upper-lower bounds. The calculated overlap or sample robustness, expressed as a percentage value, represents the NN's robustness achieved through the verification process under different noise conditions. The proposed solution takes a sound and incomplete approach to verify the robustness of regression neural networks with time series data. The approach over-approximates the reachable set, ensuring that any input point within the set will always have an output point contained within the reachable output set (sound). However, due to the complexities of neural networks and the over-approximation nature of the approach, certain output points within the reachable output set may not directly correspond to specific input points (incomplete). Over-approximation is commonly used in safety verification and robustness analysis of complex systems due to its computational efficiency and reduced time requirements compared to exact methods.

6 Reachability of Specific Layers to Allow Variable-Length Time Series Input

Reachability Of A Fully-connected Layer. We consider a fully-connected layer with the following parameters: the weights $W_{fc} \in R^{op \times ip}$ and the bias $b_{fc} \in R^{op \times 1}$, where op and ip are, respectively, the output and input sizes of the layer. The output of this fully connected layer w.r.t an input $i \in R^{ip \times T_s}$ will be

$$o = W_{fc} \times i + b_{fc}$$
$$\textit{where output } o \in R^{op \times T_s}$$

Thus, we can see that the layer functionality does not alter the output size for a variable length of time sequence, making the functionality of this layer independent of the time series length.
The reachability of a fully-connected layer will be given by the following lemma.

Lemma 1. *The reachable set of a fully-connected layer with a Star input set* $I = \langle c, V, P \rangle$ *is another Star* $I' = \langle c', V', P' \rangle$ *where* $c' = W_{fc} \times c + b_{fc}$*, the matrix multiplication of c with Weight matrix* W_{fc}*,*$V' = \{v_1', ..., v_m'\}$*, where* $v_i' = W_{fc} \times v_i$*, the matrix multiplication of the weight matrix and the* i^{th} *basis vector, and* $P' = P$*.*

Reachability of a 1D Convolutional Layer. We consider a 1d convolution layer with the following parameters: the weights $W_{conv1d} \in R^{w_f \times nc \times fl}$ and the bias $b_{conv1d} \in R^{1 \times fl}$ where $w_f, nc \; and \; fl$ are the filter size, number of channels and number of filters, respectively.

The output of this 1d convolution layer w.r.t an input $i \in R^{ip \times T_s}$ will be

$$o = W'_{conv1d} \cdot i' + b_{conv1d} \;\; \textit{dot product along time dimesion for each filter}$$
$$\textit{where output } o \in R^{fl \times T'_s}$$

where $T_s' = T_s + T_d - T_{fl}$ is the new time series length at the output and T_d, T_{fl} are the time lengths contributed by the dilation factor and the 1d convolution function, respectively. w'_{conv1d} is the modified weight matrix after adding dilation, and i' is the modified input after padding. We can see when T_d becomes equal to T_{fl} for any convolution layer, the layer functionality becomes independent of the length of the time series.

The reachability of a 1d convolution layer will be given by the following lemma.

Lemma 2. *The reachable set of a 1d convolution layer with a Star input set* $I = \langle c, V, P \rangle$ *is another Star* $I' = \langle c', V', P' \rangle$ *where* $c' = W_{conv1d} \cdot c$*, 1d convolution applied to the basis vector c with Weight matrix* $W_{conv1d}, V' = \{v_1', ..., v_m'\}$*, where* $v_i' = W_{conv1d} \cdot v_i$*, is the 1d convolution operation with zero bias applied to the generator vectors, i.e., only using the weights of the layer, and* $P' = P$.

7 Experimental Setup

7.1 Dataset Description

For evaluation, we have considered two different time series datasets for PHM of a Li battery and a turbine.

Battery State-of-Charge Dataset (BSOC) [14]*:* This dataset is derived from a new 3Ah LG HG2 cell tested in an 8 cu.ft. thermal chamber using a 75amp, 5-volt Digatron Firing Circuits Universal Battery Tester with high accuracy (0.1 of full scale) for voltage and current measurements. The main focus is to determine the State of Charge (SOC) of the battery, measured as a percentage, which indicates the charge level relative to its capacity. SOC for a Li-ion battery depends on various features, including voltage, current, temperature, and average voltage and current. The data is obtained from the 'LG_HG2_Prepared_Dataset_McMasterUniversity_Jan_2020', readily available in the dataset folder [14]. The training data consists of a single sequence of experimental data collected while the battery-powered electric vehicle during a driving cycle at an external temperature of 25 °C. The test dataset contains experimental data with an external temperature of -10 °C.

Turbofan Engine Degradation Simulation Data Set (TEDS) [2,30]*:* This dataset is widely used for predicting the Remaining Useful Life (RUL) of turbofan jet engines [2]. Engine degradation simulations are conducted using C-MAPSS (Commercial Modular Aero-Propulsion System Simulation) with four different sets, simulating various operational conditions and fault modes. Each engine has 26 different feature values recorded at different time instances. To streamline computation, features with low variability (similar to Principal Component Analysis [26]) are removed to avoid negative impacts on the training process. The remaining 17 features[4] are then normalized using z-score (mean-standard deviation) for training. The training subset comprises time series data

[4] The detailed version of this paper, available in [25], provides a comprehensive feature extraction method called 'Prognosability' that extracts 17 features out of the total 26 features for the TEDS dataset.

for 100 engines, but for this paper, we focus on data from only one engine (FD001). For evaluation, we randomly selected engine 52 from the test dataset.

7.2 Network Description

The network architecture used for training the BSOC dataset, partially adopted from [1], is a regression CNN(see footnote 3). The network has five input features which correspond to one SOC value. Therefore, the TSRegNN for the BSOC dataset can be represented as:

$$\begin{aligned} f:\ x \in \mathbb{R}^{5\times t_s} &\rightarrow y \in \mathbb{R}^{1\times t_s} \\ \hat{SOC}_{t_s} &= f(t_s) \end{aligned} \tag{17}$$

The network architecture used for training the TEDS dataset is also a regression CNN, adopted from [3](see footnote 3). The input data is preprocessed to focus on 17 features, corresponding to one RUL value for the engine. Therefore, the TSRegNN for the TEDS dataset can be represented as:

$$\begin{aligned} f:\ x \in \mathbb{R}^{17\times t_s} &\rightarrow y \in \mathbb{R}^{1\times t_s} \\ \hat{RUL}_{t_s+1} &= f(t_s) \end{aligned} \tag{18}$$

The output's t_s^{th} value represents the desired estimation of SOC or RUL, with the given series of past t_s values for each feature variable.

8 Experimental Results and Evaluation

The actual experimental results shown in this paper are conducted in a Windows-10 computer with the 64-bit operating system, Intel(R) Core(TM) i7-8850H processor, and 16 GB RAM.

For all four noise scenarios [Sec. 3], local and global (for 100 consecutive time steps) robustness properties are considered for both datasets. The local monotonicity property is only considered for the turbine RUL estimation example.

Battery State-of-Charge Dataset (BSOC): In this dataset, the output value (SOC) is supposed to be any value between 0 and 1 (or 0 and 100%). But, for the instances where the lower bound is negative, we instead treat it as 0 because a negative SOC does not provide any meaningful implications.

For SFSI, for a random (here feature 3) input feature-signal, the noise is added only at the last time step (t_{30}) of the 3rd feature, whereas for SFAI, noise is added throughout all the time instances of the input signal. The effect of four different noise values, 1%, 2.5%, 5% and 10% of the mean(μ), are then evaluated using over-approximate star reachability analysis [Sec. 2.3] on 100 consecutive input signal, each with 30 time instances. We considered ±5% around the actual SOC value as the allowable bounds. For all the noises, 2 different robustness values, PR [Def. 7] and POR [Def. 8] are then calculated, and comparative tables are shown below in Table 1.

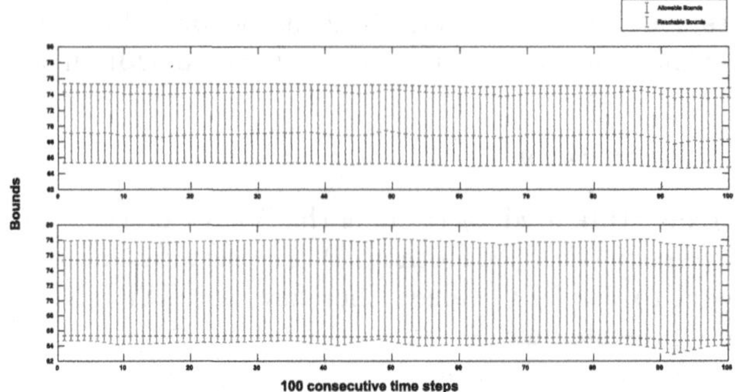

Fig. 2. Allowable (blue) and reachable (red) bounds for battery SOC dataset for 100 consecutive time steps and 2 different SFAI noise values 1% (upper), and 2.5% (lower) respectively (Color figure online)

Table 1. Global Robustness: Percentage Robustness(PR) for noises for 100 consecutive time steps

$noise$	PR_{SFSI}	POR_{SFSI}	$avgRT_{SFSI}(s)$	PR_{SFAI}	POR_{SFAI}	$avgRT_{SFAI}(s)$
1	100	100	0.7080	100	100	20.9268
2.5	100	100	0.7080	100	100	20.9991
5	100	100	0.7116	100	100	21.0729
10	100	100	0.7027	100	100	21.0780

$noise$	PR_{MFSI}	POR_{MFSI}	$avgRT_{MFSI}(s)$	PR_{MFAI}	POR_{MFAI}	$avgRT_{MFAI}(s)$
1	100	100	0.7653	100	100	36.1723
2.5	0	73.87	0.8251	0	73.87	59.0588
5	0	35.95	0.9026	0	35.95	91.6481
10	0	17.89	1.1051	0	17.89	163.7568

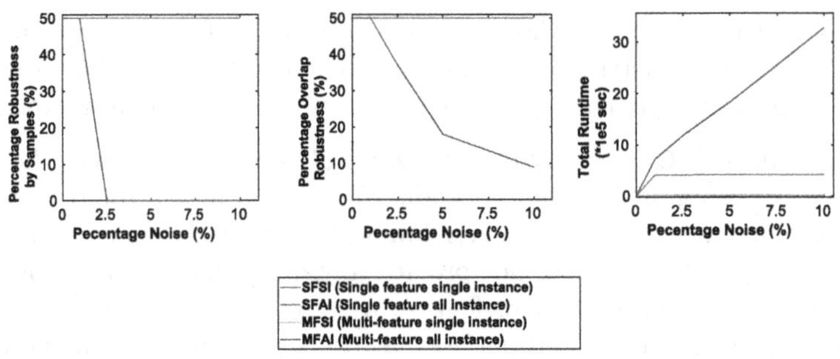

Fig. 3. Percentage Robustness and Runtime plots w.r.t increasing noise

Observation and Analysis: Fig. 2 shows a sample plot for gradually increasing estimation bounds with increasing MFSI noise. We can see from the figure that for each time instance, the system becomes locally non-robust as the noise value increases.

Table 1 presents the network's overall performance, i.e., the percentage robustness measures, PR [Definition 7], POR [Definition 8] and average verification runtime (avgRT), with respect to each noise. The percentage robustness values start decreasing and the average (as well as total) runtime starts increasing as the measure of noise increases for MFAI and MFSI, but for SFSI and SFAI it remains the same for these noise perturbations considered. This is because in the first case, the noise is added to all the features, resulting in increasing the cumulative effect of disturbance on the output estimation. However, in the other case, the noise is attached only to a single feature, assuming that not all features will get polluted by noise simultaneously; and that the reachable bounds are in the acceptable range. A plot of robustness values and the total runtime is shown in Fig. 3.

We can also see that the decrease in POR values for MFSI and MFAI are less compared to the PR values with increasing noise because, for PR calculation, only those time steps are considered where the estimated range falls entirely within the allowed range, whereas for POR calculation even if some part of the estimated range goes outside the allowable range, their fractional contribution is still considered.

Another interesting observation here is the robustness matrices for both SFSI and SFAI are the same; however, the computations for SFAI take almost three times longer than the computations for SFSI. The same analogy is observed for MFSI and MFAI datasets but with an even higher time taken for MFAI. The possible reason for this observation could be that, while the data is subjected to perturbations across all time instances, the noise added to the final time step has the most significant impact on the output.

Turbofan Engine Degradation Simulation Data Set (TEDS): In this dataset, the acceptable RUL bounds are considered to be ± 10 of the actual RUL. For instances where the lower bound is negative, we assume those values to be 0 as well. We then calculate the percentage robustness measures, PR [Definition 7], POR [Definition 8], and average verification runtime (avgRT), for an input set with all 100 consecutive data points, each having 30 time instances. The results for three different noise values, 0.1%, 0.5%, and 1% of the mean (μ), are presented in Table 2. For SFSI and SFAI noises, we randomly choose a feature (feature 7, representing sensor 2) for noise addition. The noise is added to the last time step (t_{30}) of each data sample for SFSI and SFAI noises. The results of the MFAI noise have been omitted due to scalability issues, as it is computationally heavy and time-consuming[5].

For verifying the local monotonicity of the estimated output RUL bounds at a particular time instance, we have fitted the previous RUL bounds along with

[5] The MFAI noise, i.e., adding the L_∞ norm to all feature values across all time instances, significantly increases the input-set size compared to other noise types. This leads to computationally expensive calculations for layer-wise reachability, resulting in longer run times. Moreover, noise in an industrial setting affecting all features over an extended period is unlikely. Considering these factors, we decided to exclude the results of the MFAI noise for the TEDS dataset from our analysis.

the estimated one in a linear equation as shown in Fig. 4. This guarantees the monotonically decreasing nature of the estimated RUL at any time instance.

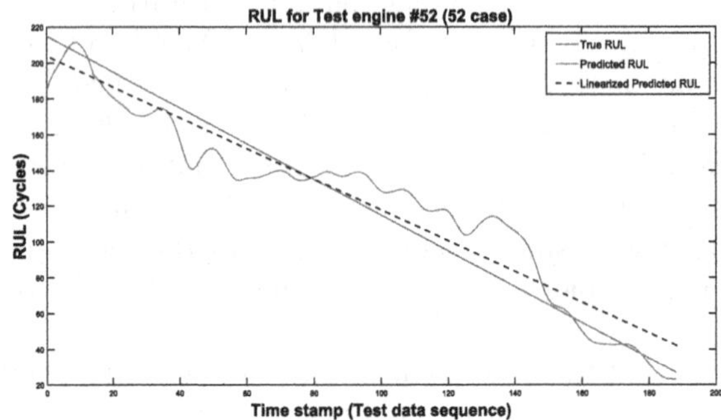

Fig. 4. Percentage Robustness and Runtime plots w.r.t increasing noise

Table 2. Global Robustness: Percentage Robustness(PR) for noises for 100 consecutive time steps

$noise$	PR_{SFSI}	POR_{SFSI}	$avgRT_{SFSI}(s)$	PR_{SFAI}	POR_{SFAI}	$avgRT_{SFAI}(s)$
1	13	13	1.0796	13	13.31	32.8670
2.5	13	13	1.1755	12	13.13	62.1483
5	13	13	1.2908	8	12.64	108.0736

$noise$	PR_{MFSI}	POR_{MFSI}	$avgRT_{MFSI}(s)$
1	13	13	9.6567
2.5	13	13	10.2540
5	13	13	11.2100

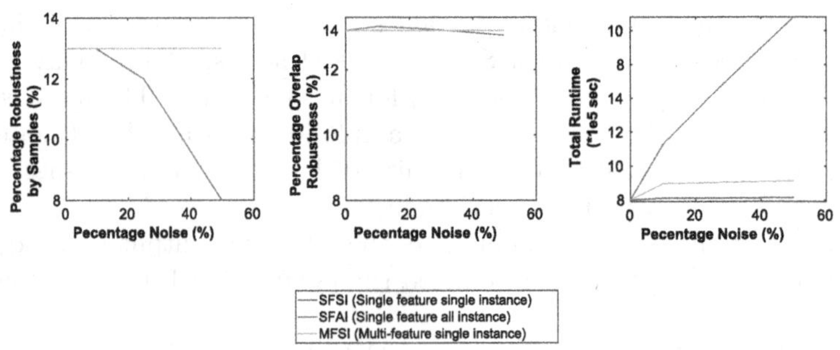

Fig. 5. Percentage Robustness and Runtime plots w.r.t increasing noise

Observation and Analysis: Figure 14 of the detailed version of this paper [25] shows a sample plot for gradually increasing estimation bounds with increasing

SFAI noise. Here we need to notice that the network's performance in terms of following the actual RUL value is not well. However, Table 2 presents the network's overall performance with respect to each noise. Contrary to the other dataset, we see that the percentage robustness measures corresponding to SFAI and SFSI noises differ. Interestingly, while the noise value increases, the PR, and POR for SFSI remain the same, whereas the robustness measures for SFAI decrease. However, the performance matrices for MFSI are the same as the SFSI except for the time. This might be because, for both SFSI and MFSI, the noise is added only at a single time instance, whereas for SFAI, the noise is added to the entire time instances, resulting in an increased cumulative effect of disturbance on the output.

Our results consistently show higher POR values than PR values in Tables [1, 2]. Since we assess output reachable bounds using L_∞ perturbations in the input, we acknowledge the significance of cases where reachable sets overlap with permissible bounds but do not entirely fall within them. In summary, PR measures adopt a more conservative approach, while POR captures the relationship between output reachable bounds and permissible bounds more accurately.

9 Conclusion and Future Work

This paper explores formal method-based reachability analysis of variable-length time series regression neural networks (NNs) using approximate Star methods in the context of predictive maintenance, which is crucial with the rise of Industry 4.0 and the Internet of Things. The analysis considers sensor noise introduced in the data. Evaluation is conducted on two datasets, employing a unified reachability analysis that handles varying features and variable time sequence lengths while analyzing the output with acceptable upper and lower bounds. Robustness and monotonicity properties are verified for the TEDS dataset. Real-world datasets are used, but further research is needed to establish stronger connections between practical industrial problems and performance metrics. The study opens new avenues for exploring perturbation contributions to the output and extending reachability analysis to 3-dimensional time series data like videos. Future work involves verifying global monotonicity properties as well, and including more predictive maintenance and anomaly detection applications as case studies. The study focuses solely on offline data analysis and lacks considerations for real-time stream processing and memory constraints, which present fascinating avenues for future research.

Acknowledgements. The material presented in this paper is based upon work supported by the National Science Foundation (NSF) through grant numbers 1910017, 2028001, 2220426, and 2220401, and the Defense Advanced Research Projects Agency (DARPA) under contract number FA8750-18-C-0089 and FA8750-23-C-0518, and the Air Force Office of Scientific Research (AFOSR) under contract number FA9550-22-1-0019 and FA9550-23-1-0135. Any opinions, findings, conclusions, or recommendations expressed in this paper are those of the authors and do not necessarily reflect the views of AFOSR, DARPA, or NSF. We also want to thank our colleagues, Tianshu and Bernie for their valuable feedback.

References

1. Predict battery state of charge using deep learning - MATLAB & ; Simulink – mathworks.com. https://www.mathworks.com/help/deeplearning/ug/predict-soc-using-deep-learning.html
2. Prognostics center of excellence - data repository. https://ti.arc.nasa.gov/tech/dash/groups/pcoe/prognostic-data-repository/#turbofan
3. Remaining useful life estimation using convolutional neural network - MATLAB & ; Simulink – mathworks.com. https://www.mathworks.com/help/predmaint/ug/remaining-useful-life-estimation-using-convolutional-neural-network.html
4. Anderson, G., Pailoor, S., Dillig, I., Chaudhuri, S.: Optimization and abstraction: a synergistic approach for analyzing neural network robustness. In: Proceedings of the 40th ACM SIGPLAN Conference on Programming Language Design and Implementation, pp. 731–744 (2019)
5. Bogomolov, S., Forets, M., Frehse, G., Potomkin, K., Schilling, C.: JuliaReach: a toolbox for set-based reachability. In: Proceedings of the 22nd ACM International Conference on Hybrid Systems: Computation and Control, pp. 39–44 (2019)
6. Borgi, T., Hidri, A., Neef, B., Naceur, M.S.: Data analytics for predictive maintenance of industrial robots. In: 2017 International Conference on Advanced Systems and Electric Technologies (IC_ASET), pp. 412–417. IEEE (2017)
7. Botoeva, E., Kouvaros, P., Kronqvist, J., Lomuscio, A., Misener, R.: Efficient verification of ReLU-based neural networks via dependency analysis. In: Proceedings of the AAAI Conference on Artificial Intelligence, vol. 34, pp. 3291–3299 (2020)
8. DeLillo, D.: White noise. Penguin (1999)
9. EASA, Aerospace, C.: Formal methods use for learning assurance (formula). Tech. Rep. (2023)
10. Ferguson, C.E.: Time-series production functions and technological progress in American manufacturing industry. J. Polit. Econ. **73**(2), 135–147 (1965)
11. Goodfellow, I.J., Shlens, J., Szegedy, C.: Explaining and harnessing adversarial examples. arXiv preprint arXiv:1412.6572 (2014)
12. Katz, G., et al.: The marabou framework for verification and analysis of deep neural networks. In: Dillig, I., Tasiran, S. (eds.) CAV 2019. LNCS, vol. 11561, pp. 443–452. Springer, Cham (2019). https://doi.org/10.1007/978-3-030-25540-4_26
13. Kauffman, S., Dunne, M., Gracioli, G., Khan, W., Benann, N., Fischmeister, S.: Palisade: a framework for anomaly detection in embedded systems. J. Syst. Archit. **113**, 101876 (2021)
14. Kollmeyer, P., Vidal, C., Naguib, M., Skells, M.: LG 18650hg2 Li-ion battery data and example deep neural network xEV SOC estimator script. Mendeley Data **3**, 2020 (2020)
15. Krizhevsky, A., Sutskever, I., Hinton, G.E.: ImageNet classification with deep convolutional neural networks. Advances in Neural Information Processing Systems, vol. 25 (2012)
16. Lawrence, S., Giles, C.L., Tsoi, A.C., Back, A.D.: Face recognition: a convolutional neural-network approach. IEEE Trans. Neural Netw. **8**(1), 98–113 (1997)
17. LeCun, Y., Bottou, L., Bengio, Y., Haffner, P.: Gradient-based learning applied to document recognition. Proc. IEEE **86**(11), 2278–2324 (1998)
18. Lin, C.Y., Hsieh, Y.M., Cheng, F.T., Huang, H.C., Adnan, M.: Time series prediction algorithm for intelligent predictive maintenance. IEEE Robot. Autom. Lett. **4**(3), 2807–2814 (2019)

19. Lopez, D.M., Choi, S.W., Tran, H.D., Johnson, T.T.: NNV 2.0: the neural network verification tool. In: International Conference on Computer Aided Verification, pp. 397–412. Springer (2023). https://doi.org/10.1007/978-3-031-37703-7_19
20. Lv, F., Wen, C., Liu, M., Bao, Z.: Weighted time series fault diagnosis based on a stacked sparse autoencoder. J. Chemometr. **31**(9), e2912 (2017)
21. Martinez, C.M., Cao, D.: iHorizon-Enabled energy management for electrified vehicles. Butterworth-Heinemann (2018)
22. Mohapatra, J., Weng, T.W., Chen, P.Y., Liu, S., Daniel, L.: Towards verifying robustness of neural networks against a family of semantic perturbations. In: Proceedings of the IEEE/CVF Conference on Computer Vision and Pattern Recognition, pp. 244–252 (2020)
23. Moosavi-Dezfooli, S.M., Fawzi, A., Frossard, P.: DeepFool: a simple and accurate method to fool deep neural networks. In: Proceedings of the IEEE Conference on Computer Vision and Pattern Recognition, pp. 2574–2582 (2016)
24. Müller, M.N., Brix, C., Bak, S., Liu, C., Johnson, T.T.: The third international verification of neural networks competition (VNN-comp 2022): summary and results. arXiv preprint arXiv:2212.10376 (2022)
25. Pal, N., Lopez, D.M., Johnson, T.T.: Robustness verification of deep neural networks using star-based reachability analysis with variable-length time series input. arXiv preprint arXiv:2307.13907 (2023)
26. Pearson, K.: LIII. On lines and planes of closest fit to systems of points in space. The London, Edinburgh, and Dublin philosophical magazine and journal of science **2**(11), 559–572 (1901)
27. Priemer, R.: Introductory signal processing, vol. 6. World Scientific (1991)
28. Priemer, R.: Signals and signal processing. Introductory Signal Processing, pp. 1–9 (1991)
29. de Riberolles, T., Zou, Y., Silvestre, G., Lochin, E., Song, J.: Anomaly detection for ICS based on deep learning: a use case for aeronautical radar data. Ann. Telecommun., pp. 1–13 (2022)
30. Saxena, A., Goebel, K.: Turbofan engine degradation simulation data set. NASA Ames Prognostics Data Repository, pp. 1551–3203 (2008)
31. Semenick Alam, I.M., Sickles, R.C.: Time series analysis of deregulatory dynamics and technical efficiency: the case of the us airline industry. Int. Econ. Rev. **41**(1), 203–218 (2000)
32. Sivaraman, A., Farnadi, G., Millstein, T., Van den Broeck, G.: Counterexample-guided learning of monotonic neural networks. Adv. Neural. Inf. Process. Syst. **33**, 11936–11948 (2020)
33. Soomro, K., Bhutta, M.N.M., Khan, Z., Tahir, M.A.: Smart city big data analytics: an advanced review. Wiley Interdisc. Rev.: Data Min. Knowl. Disc. **9**(5), e1319 (2019)
34. Stübinger, J., Schneider, L.: Understanding smart city-a data-driven literature review. Sustainability **12**(20), 8460 (2020)
35. Susto, G.A., Beghi, A.: Dealing with time-series data in predictive maintenance problems. In: 2016 IEEE 21st International Conference on Emerging Technologies and Factory Automation (ETFA), pp. 1–4. IEEE (2016)
36. Szegedy, C., et al.: Intriguing properties of neural networks. arXiv preprint arXiv:1312.6199 (2013)
37. Touloumi, G., et al.: Analysis of health outcome time series data in epidemiological studies. Environ.: Official J. Int. Environ. Soc. **15**(2), 101–117 (2004)

38. Tran, H.-D., Bak, S., Xiang, W., Johnson, T.T.: Verification of deep convolutional neural networks using ImageStars. In: Lahiri, S.K., Wang, C. (eds.) CAV 2020. LNCS, vol. 12224, pp. 18–42. Springer, Cham (2020). https://doi.org/10.1007/978-3-030-53288-8_2
39. Tran, H.-D., et al.: Star-based reachability analysis of deep neural networks. In: ter Beek, M.H., McIver, A., Oliveira, J.N. (eds.) FM 2019. Star-based reachability analysis of deep neural networks., vol. 11800, pp. 670–686. Springer, Cham (2019). https://doi.org/10.1007/978-3-030-30942-8_39
40. Tran, H.-D., et al.: Star-based reachability analysis of deep neural networks. In: ter Beek, M.H., McIver, A., Oliveira, J.N. (eds.) FM 2019. LNCS, vol. 11800, pp. 670–686. Springer, Cham (2019). https://doi.org/10.1007/978-3-030-30942-8_39
41. Tran, H.-D., et al.: Robustness verification of semantic segmentation neural networks using relaxed reachability. In: Silva, A., Leino, K.R.M. (eds.) CAV 2021. LNCS, vol. 12759, pp. 263–286. Springer, Cham (2021). https://doi.org/10.1007/978-3-030-81685-8_12
42. Tran, H.-D., et al.: NNV: the neural network verification tool for deep neural networks and learning-enabled cyber-physical systems. In: Lahiri, S.K., Wang, C. (eds.) CAV 2020. LNCS, vol. 12224, pp. 3–17. Springer, Cham (2020). https://doi.org/10.1007/978-3-030-53288-8_1
43. Truax, B.: Handbook for acoustic ecology. Cambridge Street Records (1999)
44. Wang, Z., Wang, Y., Fu, F., Jiao, R., Huang, C., Li, W., Zhu, Q.: A tool for neural network global robustness certification and training. arXiv preprint arXiv:2208.07289 (2022)
45. Zeger, S.L., Irizarry, R., Peng, R.D.: On time series analysis of public health and biomedical data. Annu. Rev. Public Health **27**, 57–79 (2006)
46. Zhang, Z., Lai, X., Wu, M., Chen, L., Lu, C., Du, S.: Fault diagnosis based on feature clustering of time series data for loss and kick of drilling process. J. Process Control **102**, 24–33 (2021)

Testing Logical Diagrams in Power Plants: A Tale of LTL Model Checking

Aziz Sfar[1,2(✉)], David Carral[1], Dina Irofti[2], and Madalina Croitoru[1]

[1] LIRMM, Inria, University of Montpellier, CNRS, Montpellier, France
medaziz.sfar@gmail.com
[2] EDF R&D, Paris, France

Abstract. In this paper, we focus on the application of LTL (Linear Temporal Logic) model checking on logical diagrams (LD), which are a type of functional specification used for logical controllers in many nuclear power plants. The goal is to check properties on LDs and to generate counter examples serving as validation tests for logical controllers. We propose a sound and complete LTL encoding framework for LDs allowing the use of model checking (MC) and evaluate different MC techniques on real world LD to efficiently generate counterexamples for verifiable properties.

Keywords: Validation tests · Symbolic Model Checking · Linear Temporal Logic

1 Introduction

We place ourselves in an applicative setting of the EDF company (French Electricity) where the behavior of Programmable Logical Controllers (PLC) used for nuclear power plants is periodically updated and tested manually within expert defined functional validation scenarios. A PLC is a system that embeds a program running control and protection functions. In a critical domain like nuclear energy production, the behavior of PLCs have to satisfy strict performance and safety requirements. Therefore, during the life-cycle of nuclear reactors, several updates are introduced to the PLC programs to keep up with last requirements defined by nuclear authorities. The updated behavior has to be validated by testing it against its functional specifications to ensure that no functional errors were generated following the modification process.

In the case of our application, the functional specifications of the behavior of PLCs are given in the form of Logical Diagrams (LD). These are graphical representations of a number of inputs and outputs connected through different types of logical blocks defining the expected behaviour of the machine (PLC). In a nuclear power plant, the number and size of LDs used as specifications for PLCs is enormous which makes the manual generation of test scenarios, as it is today, a tedious and time consuming task. Moreover, a Logical Diagram may contain feedback connections, i.e. a number of blocks connected to each other

A. Cimatti and L. Titolo (Eds.): FMICS 2023, LNCS 14290, pp. 189–204, 2023.
https://doi.org/10.1007/978-3-031-43681-9_11

in a loop, which could lead to cyclic behavior. This is a situation where one or many outputs keep changing indefinitely without any change on the inputs making the specified behavior divergent.

In this paper, we address the problem of the stability property verification (i.e. absence of cyclic behaviour) on the Logical Diagrams and the generation of validation test cases for PLCs. Several works propose the transformation of the PLC description languages into formal representations like finite state models and timed automata to make use of the already existing tools and methods for test generation. For instance, Provost et al. [11] have proposed a translation of Grafcet specification models into Mealy machines to generate conformance test scenarios. In a previous work [12] inspired from [11], we have introduced a transformation of Logical Diagrams into state/transition graphs. The aim was to make use of the test generation techniques for transition systems as presented in [10,13] as well as the formal verification techniques to prove stability in Logical Diagrams. However, the exponential growth of the size of the generated transition systems makes their generation complicated for the biggest sized LDs. In [8], model-checking techniques were used to generate tests for PLC programs developed in Function Block Diagram (FBD). The paper describes the transformation of FBDs into timed automata and the use of a Model-Checker to generate test sequences. An experimental evaluation of their solution was made for many train control systems programs. However, to the authors knowledge, no similar approach was done for PLCs based on LD specifications used in nuclear power plants. In this paper, we propose to automatise the checking process of PLC behaviour specified in Logical Diagrams using tools from the Model Checking (*MC*) domain. We define a sound and complete transformation of Logical Diagrams into *Linear Temporal Logic (LTL)* formulas. We demonstrate how the stability property can be expressed into *LTL* expressions. We also show how test cases could be generated by formulating properties like the activation and deactivation of the outputs of the system in an LTL encoding and running Model-checkers on them. Finally, we empirically evaluate the efficiency of existing *MC* tools (NuSMV [5] and nuXmv [3]) on EDF logical diagrams. The empirical results obtained show that techniques like *k-MC* [6] is useful for checking the stability property while other techniques (*BDD* [7], *BMC* [1] and *SBMC* [9]) are timing out. The counterexample generation for activation and deactivation of outputs is possible for all techniques except *BDD*. We believe that the overview of the practical usability of *LTL* Model Checking tools for our real world scenario could be of use to researchers undergoing similar tasks (e.g. *LTL* encoding and *LTL* Model Checking for test generation).

This paper is organized as follows. In Sect. 2 we set a formal definition of the Logical Diagram specification and we give an example. Section 3 introduces the *LTL* formalism and presents the *LTL* encoding of the logical diagram and the stability, activation and deactivation properties. Proof of the soundness and completeness of the transformation is given in Sect. 4. Finally, Sect. 5 discusses the application and evaluation of Model-Checking tools and techniques on our Logical Diagrams.

2 Logical Diagram

A *logical diagram* (LD) is a graphical representation of a set of interconnected blocks that perform logical functions. Before running a code implementing the logical diagram on a controller, a few properties of the logical diagram have to be studied. One of these properties is the stability property ensuring that the outputs of the logical diagram converge for some fixed inputs. Moreover, in order to test the implementation of a logical diagram on a controller, we would like to be able to generate input values, that allow to activate or deactivate a chosen output. Thus, we need to define the properties of activation and deactivation of outputs and use these properties in the verification and validation (V&V) process to validate the correct implementation of the logical diagram on the logical controller. In this section, we introduce a formal definition for logical diagrams and the properties of stability, activation and deactivation of outputs, and we illustrate them on the logical diagram in Fig. 1.

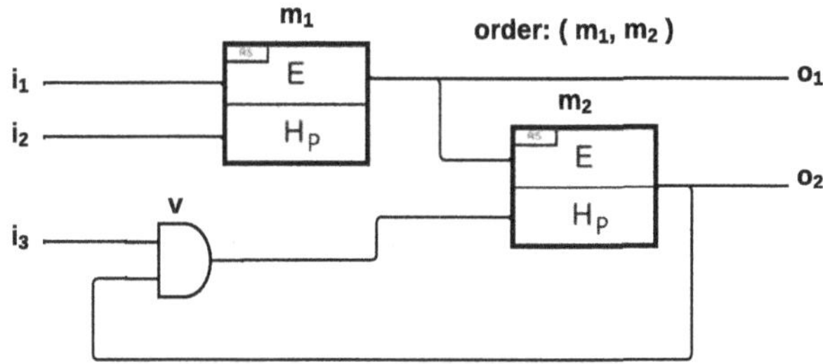

Fig. 1. A logical diagram example $LD = \langle V, E, \mathcal{O}\rangle$: $V(\mathsf{input}) = \{i_1, i_2, i_3\}$, $V(\mathsf{output}) = \{o_1, o_2\}$, $V(\mathsf{M}_E) = \{m_1, m_2\}$, $V(\mathsf{and}) = \{v\}$, $E = \{i_1 \xrightarrow{\mathrm{s}} m_1, i_2 \xrightarrow{\mathrm{r}} m_1, m_1 \xrightarrow{\mathrm{s}} m_2, v \xrightarrow{\mathrm{r}} m_2, i_3 \rightarrow v, m_2 \rightarrow v, m_1 \rightarrow o_1, m_2 \rightarrow o_2\}$, $\mathcal{O}(m_1) = 1$ and $\mathcal{O}(m_2) = 2$.

A logical diagram is formally defined by a set of *vertices* V, and a set of directed edges E connecting these vertices. Every vertex $v \in V$ has a type that defines the number and nature of its incoming and outgoing edges as formally defined in Definition 1. *Output* vertices are denoted by $V(\mathsf{output})$, *input* vertices by $V(\mathsf{input})$, *memory* vertices by $V(\mathsf{M})$ and finally vertices of the type '*and*', '*or*' and '*not*' are denoted $V(\mathsf{and})$, $V(\mathsf{or})$ and $V(\mathsf{not})$, respectively. In a logical diagram, we can find cycles. A cycle is a sequence of edges that starts and finishes at the same vertex v. In the diagrams used by EDF all cycles contain at least one memory vertex within the sequence. Consider the example of Fig. 1: it contains three input vertices i_1, i_2 and i_3, two output vertices o_1 and o_2, two memory vertices m_1 and m_2, one vertex v of type 'and' and one cycle composed of v and m_2. Note that the memory vertices are represented in the diagram by set/reset (RS) blocks that have two inputs: E for set and H for reset. In the case of m_1, the incoming edge corresponding to the set is represented by $i_1 \xrightarrow{\mathrm{s}} m_1$ while $i_2 \xrightarrow{\mathrm{r}} m_1$ represents the reset edge. The incoming edges of the other vertices types is given by a simple arrow as in $i_3 \rightarrow v$. The letter 'p' in 'Hp' indicates that reset has priority over set. Then, we denote M_H as the type of the memory vertex. This is the case for both m_1 and m_2. Otherwise, the memory vertex is of type M_E with the priority expressed by 'Ep' in the set input of the block.

Definition 1 (Vertex type and LD). *The set of* vertex types *is* $\{\mathsf{input}, \mathsf{output}, \mathsf{and}, \mathsf{or}, \mathsf{not}, M_E, M_H\}$. *Henceforth, we associate every vertex* v *with a vertex type* $\mathsf{tp}(v)$. *Given a set* V *of vertices and a vertex type* t, *let* $V(t) = \{v \in V \mid \mathsf{tp}(v) = t\}$. *Moreover, let* $V(\mathsf{M}) = V(M_E) \cup V(M_H)$. *Moreover, a* directed edge *over* V *is an expression of the form* $u \rightarrow v$, $u \xrightarrow{s} v$, *or* $u \xrightarrow{r} v$ *with* $u, v \in V$.

A logical diagram *(LD) is a tuple* $\langle V, E, \mathcal{O} \rangle$ *such that* V *is a set of vertices,* E *is a set of directed edges (over* V*),* $\mathcal{O}$ *is a bijection from* $V(\mathsf{M})$ *to* $\{1, \ldots, |V(\mathsf{M})|\}$, *and all of the following hold:*

1. *If* $u \rightarrow v \in E$ *for some* $u, v \in V$; *then* $\mathsf{tp}(v)$ *is* output, and, or, *or* not.
2. *If* $u \xrightarrow{s} v$ *or* $u \xrightarrow{r} v$ *are in* E *for some* $u, v \in V$, *then* $\mathsf{tp}(v)$ *is* M_E *or* M_H.
3. *For every* $v \in V(\mathsf{not}) \cup V(\mathsf{output})$, *there is exactly one edge of the form* $u \rightarrow v \in E$.
4. *For every* $v \in V(\mathsf{and}) \cup V(\mathsf{or})$, *there are at least two edges of the form* $u \rightarrow v \in E$.
5. *For every* $v \in V(\mathsf{M})$, *there is exactly one edge of the form* $u \xrightarrow{s} v \in E$ *and exactly one edge of the form* $w \xrightarrow{r} v \in E$.
6. *For every* $v_1, \ldots, v_n \in V$, *either* $v_n \rightarrow v_1 \notin E$ *or* $v_{i-1} \rightarrow v_i \notin E$ *for some* $2 \leq i \leq n$. *That is, every cycle have to traverse at least one memory vertex.*

Each vertex in a logical diagram has an associated logical value called the output of the vertex. It takes the value *true* referred to by $\top$ or false referred to by $\bot$. Furthermore, the vertex output is evaluated in accordance to increasing time steps and can vary from a step to another. The time step k starts at zero. Initially, i.e. at $k = 0$, output values of memory and input vertices are given by an *initializing function* f. Then, the output value of every vertex v at a time step $k \geq 0$, is defined by the function $LD_f(v, k)$. Specifically, the output of memory vertices are evaluated one after the other according to an evaluation order specified by the function $\mathcal{O}$. The output value of only one memory vertex can change at each time step if it is its turn, while the others maintain the same value from the previous step. Note that the output of a memory vertex of type M_E (resp. M_H) is evaluated to True, denoted $\top$, (resp. False, denoted $\bot$), when both set and reset inputs are evaluated to True. The complete output evaluation for different vertices types is given by Definition 3.

Definition 2 (ev function). *The set* $\mathcal{B}$ *of Boolean expressions is defined by the grammar* $\mathcal{B} ::= \top \mid \bot \mid \neg\mathcal{B} \mid \mathcal{B} \wedge \mathcal{B} \mid \mathcal{B} \vee \mathcal{B}$. *We define* $\mathsf{ev} : \mathcal{B} \mapsto \{\top, \bot\}$ *such that for every* $a, b \in \mathcal{B}$:

- $\mathsf{ev}(\top) = \top$.
- $\mathsf{ev}(\bot) = \bot$.
- $\mathsf{ev}(\neg a) = \top$ *iff* $\mathsf{ev}(a) = \bot$.

- $\mathsf{ev}(a \vee b) = \top$ *iff* $\mathsf{ev}(a) = \top$ *or* $\mathsf{ev}(b) = \top$.
- $\mathsf{ev}(a \wedge b) = \top$ *iff* $\mathsf{ev}(a) = \top$ *and* $\mathsf{ev}(b) = \top$.

Definition 3 (Output function). *Consider a diagram* $LD = \langle V, E, \mathcal{O} \rangle$ *and an* initializing function f *for LD; that is, a total function from* $V(\mathsf{input}) \cup V(\mathsf{M})$ *to* $\{\top, \bot\}$. *For every vertex* $v \in V(\mathsf{M})$, *let* $\mathsf{turn}_{\mathcal{O}}(v)$ *be the set that contains* $\mathcal{O}(v) + n \cdot |V(\mathsf{M})|$ *for every* $n \geq 0$. *Also, for every* $v \in V$ *and* $k \geq 0$, *we define* $LD_f(v, k) \in \{\top, \bot\}$ *as follows:*

- *If* $v \in V(\mathsf{input})$, *then* $LD_f(v, k) = f(v)$.
- *If* $v \in V(\mathsf{output})$, *then* $LD_f(v, k) = \mathsf{ev}(LD_f(u, k))$ *where* u *is the vertex in* V *with* $u \rightarrow v \in E$.
- *If* $v \in V(\mathsf{not})$, *then* $LD_f(v, k) = \mathsf{ev}(\neg LD_f(u, k))$ *where* u *is the vertex with* $u \rightarrow v \in E$.
- *If* $v \in V(\mathsf{or})$, *then* $LD_f(v, k) = \mathsf{ev}(\bigvee_{u \in P} LD_f(u, k))$ *where* $P = \{u \in V \mid u \rightarrow v \in E\}$.
- *If* $v \in V(\mathsf{and})$, *then* $LD_f(v, k) = \mathsf{ev}(\bigwedge_{u \in P} LD_f(u, k))$ *where* $P = \{u \in V \mid u \rightarrow v \in E\}$.
- *If* $v \in V(\mathsf{M})$ *and* $k = 0$, *then* $LD_f(v, k) = f(v)$.
- *If* $v \in V(\mathsf{M})$, $k \geq 1$, *and* $k \notin \mathsf{turn}_{\mathcal{O}}(v)$ *then* $LD_f(v, k) = LD_f(v, k - 1)$.
- *If* $v \in V(\mathsf{M})$ *and* $k \in \mathsf{turn}_{\mathcal{O}}(v)$, *we consider two cases:*
  - *If* $\mathsf{tp}(v) = M_E$, *then* $LD_f(v, k) = \mathsf{ev}((LD_f(v, k - 1) \wedge \neg LD_f(h, k - 1)) \vee LD_f(e, k - 1))$.
  - *If* $\mathsf{tp}(v) = M_H$, *then* $LD_f(v, k) = \mathsf{ev}(\neg LD_f(h, k - 1) \wedge (LD_f(v, k - 1) \vee LD_f(e, k - 1)))$.

  In the above, $h \in V$ *with* $h \xrightarrow{r} v \in E$ *and* $e \in V$ *with* $e \xrightarrow{s} v \in E$.

In the example of Fig. 1, the evaluation order of LD is $\mathcal{O}(m_1) = 1$ and $\mathcal{O}(m_2) = 2$. The output function LD_f depends on this evaluation order as well as the initializing function as established in Definition 3. Note that input vertices maintain the value given to them in the initial step.

Thus far, we have defined the different elements composing a logical diagram and the output evaluation function. We define in the sequel the properties of stability, activation and deactivation of outputs. For the stability property, we want to make sure that in some future time step k, the output values of vertices converge. In other words, having an initializing function f, the logical output value of every vertex should not oscillate indefinitely between the values true and false, from a step to the next. For this to be avoided, it suffices that the outputs of memory vertices converge as mentioned in Definition 4. In this case, we say that the logical diagram is stable for the initializing function f. We also say that a logical diagram is uniformly stable if it is stable for every possible input scenario, i.e. for every initializing function f.

Definition 4 (stability). *A logical diagram* $LD = \langle V, E, \mathcal{O} \rangle$ *is* stable *for some initializing function* f, *if there exists* $k' \geq 0$ *such that for every* $k \geq k'$ *and* $v \in V(\mathsf{M})$, *we have* $LD_f(v, k) = LD_f(v, k + 1)$. *We say that a logical Diagram LD is* uniformly stable *if it is stable for every initializing function* f.

To illustrate, we consider the initializing function $f(i_1) = \top$, $f(i_2) = \bot$, $f(i_3) = \top$, $f(m_1) = \bot$ and $f(m_2) = \bot$ for the logical diagram of Fig. 1. By applying the evaluation function on the memory vertex m_2, we can see that $LD_f(m_2, k)$ is not equal to $LD_f(m_2, k+2)$ for every $k \geq 0$. Therefore, LD is not stable for f. Hence LD is not uniformly stable.

Once the stability is verified, the next step consists in generating initializing functions that allow to set to true (i.e activate) or set to false (i.e deactivate) an output vertex o. It is also possible to set some initial conditions over the input and output values before generating scenarios. We look to answer questions like: is there an initializing function f that eventually activates an output o, when initially, o is deactivated (i.e. $LD_f(o, 0) = \bot$) and the input i is activated (i.e. $LD_f(i, 0) = \top$). The chosen initial conditions are given by an initial configuration function $\mathsf{conf}_\mathcal{S}$ setting the initial values of a set of vertices $\mathcal{S} \subseteq V(\mathsf{output}) \cup V(\mathsf{input})$. Then, we say that the output o is activated (resp. deactivated) for an initializing function f, if f satisfies the initial configuration $\mathsf{conf}_\mathcal{S}$, and grants the activation (resp. deactivation) of o in some future step k (as per Definition 5).

Definition 5. *Consider a logical diagram $LD = \langle V, E, \mathcal{O} \rangle$ and an* initial configuration *function $\mathsf{conf}_\mathcal{S}$; that is a function from $\mathcal{S} \subseteq V(\mathsf{input}) \cup V(\mathsf{output})$ to $\{\top, \bot\}$. An output vertex $o \in V(\mathsf{output})$ is* activated *(resp.* deactivated *) for some initial configuration $\mathsf{conf}_\mathcal{S}$, if there is an initializing function f and $k' \geq 0$ such that; for every $v \in \mathcal{S}$, $LD_f(v, 0) = \mathsf{conf}_\mathcal{S}(v)$ and for every $k \geq k'$, $LD_f(o, k) = \top$ (resp. $LD_f(o, k) = \bot$).*

Consider for instance the logical diagram of Fig. 1, the set $\mathcal{S} = \{o_1, o_2\}$ and the initial configuration $\mathsf{conf}_\mathcal{S}(o_1) = \bot$ and $\mathsf{conf}_\mathcal{S}(o_2) = \bot$. Let f_1 be an initializing function such that $f_1(i_1) = \top$, $f_1(i_2) = \bot$, $f_1(i_3) = \bot$, $f_1(m_1) = \bot$ and $f_1(m_2) = \bot$. By Definition 3, we have $LD_f(o_1, 0) = \bot$, $LD_f(o_2, 0) = \bot$ and $LD_f(o_2, k) = \top$ for every $k \geq 2$. Therefore, o_2 is activated for f_1.

3 LTL Encoding of Logical Diagrams

In this section, we propose an encoding framework of the logical diagrams and properties into a set of *Linear Temporal Logic* (*LTL*) formulas. An *LTL* formula is built up from a set of *propositional variables AP* and a set of logical and temporal operators. The set $\mathcal{L}$ of *LTL* formulas is defined by the following grammar: $\mathcal{L} ::= p \mid \top \mid \bot \mid \neg\mathcal{L} \mid \mathcal{L} \wedge \mathcal{L} \mid \mathcal{L} \vee \mathcal{L} \mid \mathcal{L} \rightarrow \mathcal{L} \mid \mathcal{L} \leftrightarrow \mathcal{L} \mid \bigcirc\mathcal{L} \mid \Box\mathcal{L} \mid \Diamond\mathcal{L}$ where $p \in AP$. A *word* $\mathcal{W}$ is a sequence $s_0, s_1, \ldots$ of subsets of AP. Each element s_i of the sequence is referred to by $\langle \mathcal{W}, i \rangle$. Given a word $\mathcal{W}$, a propositional variable p, two *LTL* formulas φ and ψ, and some $i \geq 0$; we write:

- $\langle \mathcal{W}, i \rangle \models p$ iff $p \in s_i$.
- $\langle \mathcal{W}, i \rangle \models \top$.
- $\langle \mathcal{W}, i \rangle \not\models \bot$.
- $\langle \mathcal{W}, i \rangle \models \neg\varphi$ iff $\langle \mathcal{W}, i \rangle \not\models \varphi$.
- $\langle \mathcal{W}, i \rangle \models \varphi \wedge \psi$ iff $\langle \mathcal{W}, i \rangle \models \varphi$ and $\langle \mathcal{W}, i \rangle \models \psi$.

- $\langle \mathcal{W}, i\rangle \models \varphi \vee \psi$ iff $\langle \mathcal{W}, i\rangle \models \varphi$ or $\langle \mathcal{W}, i\rangle \models \psi$.
- $\langle \mathcal{W}, i\rangle \models \varphi \rightarrow \psi$ iff $\langle \mathcal{W}, i\rangle \models \neg\varphi \vee \psi$.
- $\langle \mathcal{W}, i\rangle \models \varphi \leftrightarrow \psi$ iff $\langle \mathcal{W}, i\rangle \models (\psi \rightarrow \varphi) \wedge (\varphi \rightarrow \psi)$.
- $\langle \mathcal{W}, i\rangle \models \bigcirc\varphi$ iff $\langle M, i+1\rangle \models \varphi$.
- $\langle \mathcal{W}, i\rangle \models \Diamond\varphi$ iff $\langle M, j\rangle \models \varphi$ for some $j \geq i$.
- $\langle \mathcal{W}, i\rangle \models \Box\varphi$ iff $\langle M, j\rangle \models \varphi$ for every $j \geq i$.

We say that a word $\mathcal{W}$ satisfies an *LTL* formula Φ at a time step i and we write $\langle M, i\rangle \models \Phi$. Moreover, $\mathcal{W}$ is a *model* of Φ ($\mathcal{W} \models \Phi$) if $\mathcal{W}$ satisfies Φ at the time step 0. An *LTL* theory is a defined finite set of *LTL* formulas. A word $\mathcal{W}$ is a model of an *LTL* theory $\mathcal{T}$ if it is a model of every formula $\Phi \in \mathcal{T}$. An *LTL* theory $\mathcal{T}_1$ entails another theory $\mathcal{T}_2$ ($\mathcal{T}_1 \models \mathcal{T}_2$) when every model of $\mathcal{T}_1$ is also a model of $\mathcal{T}_2$.

3.1 LTL Encoding of Logical Diagrams and Initializing Functions

We introduce a sound and complete *LTL* encoding of logical diagrams. The encoding will be given in two *LTL* theories. The first, denoted $\mathcal{T}_{LD}$, encodes the vertices, edges and characteristics of a logical diagram LD; the second $\mathcal{T}_f$ encodes the initial output values given by an initializing function f.

Let $LD = \langle V, E, \mathcal{O}\rangle$ be a logical diagram. We define the *LTL* vocabulary AP_{LD} of propositional variables: we associate to every vertex $v \in V$ a propositional variable t_v and to each number $i \geq 1$ a variable t_i. The set AP_{LD} is composed of these t_v and t_i. Then, the *LTL* theory $\mathcal{T}_{LD}$ contains an *LTL* formula for every vertex $v \in V$. This formula represents the output function of v at every time step. On the logical diagram of Fig. 1, the *LTL* theory $\mathcal{T}_{LD}$ of our example contains the formulas $\{\Box(t_{o_1} \leftrightarrow t_{m_1}), \Box(t_{o_2} \leftrightarrow t_{m_2})\}$ for the vertices o_1 and o_2, the formula $\Box(t_v \leftrightarrow t_{i_3} \wedge t_{m_2})$ for the vertex v, and $\{\Box(\bigcirc t_{m_1} \leftrightarrow ((\neg t_1 \wedge t_{m_1}) \vee (t_1 \wedge \neg t_{i_2} \wedge (t_{m_1} \vee t_{i_1})))), \Box(\bigcirc t_{m_2} \leftrightarrow ((\neg t_2 \wedge t_{m_2}) \vee (t_2 \wedge \neg t_v \wedge (t_{m_2} \vee t_{m_1}))))\}$ for the vertices m_1 and m_2. In the last two formulas, the variable t_1 indicates the evaluation turn of m_1, and likewise with t_2 and m_2. Therefore, we add to $\mathcal{T}_{LD}$ the formulas that translate the ordered evaluation of memory vertices. We construct these formulas in a way that ensures that $t_{\mathcal{O}(v)}$ is exclusively true at the time steps dedicated for the evaluation of the memory vertex v according to $\mathcal{O}(v)$. For the logical diagram LD in Fig. 1, we add to $\mathcal{T}_{LD}$ the set of *LTL* formulas : $\{(t_1 \wedge \neg t_2), \Box(t_1 \leftrightarrow \bigcirc(\neg t_1 \wedge t_2)), \Box(t_2 \leftrightarrow \bigcirc(\neg t_2 \wedge t_1))\}$. Finally, we add to $\mathcal{T}_{LD}$ the set of formulas that translate the fact that input vertices of the logical diagram keep the same values assigned to them in the initial time step. We do this by adding the *LTL* formula $(\Box t_v \vee \Box\neg t_v)$ for every vertex $v \in V(\mathsf{input})$. The formulas $\{(\Box t_{i_1} \vee \Box\neg t_{i_1}), (\Box t_{i_2} \vee \Box\neg t_{i_2}), (\Box t_{i_3} \vee \Box\neg t_{i_3})\}$ belong therefore to the theory $\mathcal{T}_{LD}$ of previous example. The full definition of $\mathcal{T}_{LD}$ is established in Definition 6

Definition 6 ($\mathcal{T}_{LD}$). *The set of propositional variables AP_{LD} contains a variable t_v for every $v \in V$ and a variable t_i for every $i \geq 1$. Consider a logical diagram $LD = \langle V, E, \mathcal{O}\rangle$ and some initializing function f. We define the $\mathcal{T}_{LD}$, the LTL theory over AP_{LD} that contains all the following formulas :*

- $(t_1 \wedge \bigwedge_{i \in \{2,\dots,|V(M)|\}} \neg t_i)$.
- $\bigwedge_{i \in \{1,\dots,|V(M)|-1\}} \Box(t_i \leftrightarrow \bigcirc(\neg t_i \wedge t_{i+1}))$.
- $\Box(t_{|V(M)|} \leftrightarrow \bigcirc(\neg t_{|V(M)|} \wedge t_1))$).
- *For every* $v \in V(\mathsf{input})$, *add* $(\Box t_v \vee \Box \neg t_v)$.
- *For every* $v \in V(\mathsf{output})$, *add* $\Box(t_u \leftrightarrow t_v)$ *where* $u \in V$ *with* $u \to v \in E$.
- *For every* $v \in V(\mathsf{not})$, *add* $\Box(t_u \leftrightarrow \neg t_v)$ *where* $u \in V$ *with* $u \to v \in E$.
- *For every* $v \in V(\mathsf{or})$, *add* $\Box(t_v \leftrightarrow \bigvee_{u \in P} t_u)$ *where* $P = \{u \mid u \to v \in E\}$.
- *For every* $v \in V(\mathsf{and})$, *add* $\Box(t_v \leftrightarrow \bigwedge_{u \in P} t_u)$ *where* $P = \{u \mid u \to v \in E\}$.
- *if* $\mathsf{tp}(v) = M_E$, *then add*

$$\Box\Big(\bigcirc t_v \leftrightarrow ((\neg t_{\mathcal{O}(v)} \wedge t_v) \vee (t_{\mathcal{O}(v)} \wedge ((t_v \wedge \neg t_h) \vee t_e)))\Big)$$

- *if* $\mathsf{tp}(v) = M_H$ *with* $i = \mathcal{O}(v)$, *then:*

$$\Box\Big(\bigcirc t_v \leftrightarrow ((\neg t_{\mathcal{O}(v)} \wedge t_v) \vee (t_{\mathcal{O}(v)} \wedge \neg t_h \wedge (t_v \vee t_e)))\Big)$$

In the above, h *is the vertex with* $h \xrightarrow{r} v \in E$ *and* e *is the vertex with* $e \xrightarrow{s} v \in E$.

Let us now consider some initializing function f. The second *LTL* encoding is given by the *LTL* theory $\mathcal{T}_f$ that contains, for every vertex $v \in V(\mathsf{input}) \cup V(\mathsf{M})$, the *LTL* formula $(t_v \leftrightarrow f(v))$.

Definition 7 ($\mathcal{T}_f$). *Consider some initiliazing function* f *for a logical diagram* $LD = \langle V, E, \mathcal{O} \rangle$. *Then, let* $\mathcal{T}_f$ *be the LTL theory over* AP_{LD} *such that* $(t_v \leftrightarrow f(v)) \in \mathcal{T}_f$ *for every* $v \in V(\mathsf{input}) \cup V(\mathsf{M})$.

Consider a word $\mathcal{W}$ that is a model of the *LTL* encoding $\mathcal{T}_{LD}$ of a logical diagram LD and $\mathcal{T}_f$ of an initializing function f. At each time step k, $\mathcal{W}$ satisfies the variables t_v of the vertices v whose outputs $LD_f(v, k)$ are evaluated to True. In other words, the proposed *LTL* encoding is sound and complete as stated by Theorem 1 proven in Sect. 4.

Theorem 1. *Consider a logical diagram* $LD = \langle V, E, \mathcal{O} \rangle$, *some initializing function* f, *and the LTL theories* $\mathcal{T}_{LD}$ *and* $\mathcal{T}_f$. *Let* $\mathcal{W} \models \mathcal{T}_{LD} \cup \mathcal{T}_f$. *Then for every* $v \in V$ *and* $k \geq 0$, $LD_f(v, k) = \top \Leftrightarrow \langle \mathcal{W}, k \rangle \models t_v$, *where* $t_v \in AP_{LD}$.

3.2 LTL Encoding of Properties

In Sect. 2, three types of properties were defined for logical diagrams. Here, we introduce an *LTL* theory for each different property. We first specify the *LTL* theory $\mathcal{T}_{stable}$ for the stability property. Then, we define the *LTL* theories $\mathcal{T}^o_{act}$ and $\mathcal{T}^o_{deact}$, respectively for the activation and deactivation properties.

Let us consider a logical diagram $LD = \langle V, E, \mathcal{O} \rangle$ and an initializing function f. The stability of LD is satisfied if in some future the output values of all the memory vertices remain unchanged. This can easily be expressed using the temporal operators offered by *LTL*. We encode the stability property of a logical diagram in the *LTL* theory $\mathcal{T}_{stable}$ that contains the formula $\Diamond(\Box t_v \vee \Box\neg t_v)$ for every $v \in V(\mathsf{M})$. Using the *LTL* encoding, we can establish whether or not a logical diagram is stable. In fact, if the model $\mathcal{W}$ of the theories $\mathcal{T}_{LD}$ and $\mathcal{T}_f$ is also a model of $\mathcal{T}_{stable}$, then the logical diagram *LD* is stable for f as stated in Theorem 2. In the case of the logical diagram of Fig. 1, let f_1 be an initializing function such that $f_1(i_1) = \top$, $f_1(i_2) = \bot$, $f_1(i_3) = \top$, $f_1(m_1) = \bot$ and $f_1(m_2) = \bot$. Then, $\mathcal{T}_{f_1} = \{t_{i_1} \leftrightarrow \top, t_{i_2} \leftrightarrow \bot, t_{i_3} \leftrightarrow \top, t_{m_1} \leftrightarrow \bot,\ t_{m_2} \leftrightarrow \bot\}$. The *LTL* encoding of the stability property is $\mathcal{T}_{stable} = \{\Diamond(\Box t_{m_1} \vee \Box\neg t_{m_1}), \Diamond(\Box t_{m_2} \vee \Box\neg t_{m_2})\}$. The *LTL* model checking proves that the satisfaction relation $\mathcal{T}_{LD} \cup \mathcal{T}_{f_1} \models \mathcal{T}_{stable}$ is false. Therefore, we conclude that the logical diagram is not stable for the initializing function f_1. This also means that *LD* is not uniformly stable.

Theorem 2. *Consider a logical diagram* $LD = \langle V, E, \mathcal{O}\rangle$*, some initializing function* f*, and the LTL theories* $\mathcal{T}_{LD}$*,* $\mathcal{T}_f$ *and* $\mathcal{T}_{stable}$*. Then, LD is stable for* f *if* $\mathcal{T}_{LD} \cup \mathcal{T}_f \models \mathcal{T}_{stable}$*. The logical diagram is uniformly stable if* $\mathcal{T}_{LD} \models \mathcal{T}_{stable}$*.*

We next encode the activation and deactivation properties. Let $o \in V(\mathsf{output})$ be an output vertex and $\mathcal{S}$ a subset of vertices. The *LTL* theory $\mathcal{T}^o_{act}$ represents the activation property of o for an initial configuration $\mathsf{conf}_\mathcal{S}$. For every vertex $v \in \mathcal{S}$, it contains the formula $(t_v \leftrightarrow \mathsf{conf}_\mathcal{S}(v))$ which translates the initial configuration. It also contains the formula $(\Diamond\Box t_o)$ that translates the activation of the output o in some future. Likewise, the *LTL* theory $\mathcal{T}^o_{deact}$ that encodes the deactivation property of the output vertex o for the initial configuration $\mathsf{conf}_\mathcal{S}$, contains the formulas $(\Diamond\Box\neg t_o)$ and $(v \leftrightarrow \mathsf{conf}_\mathcal{S}(v))$, for every $v \in \mathcal{S}$. Theorem 3 states that the satisfaction of the *LTL* theory $\mathcal{T}_{LD}$ and the theories of the activation and deactivation properties means that the encoded logical diagram also satisfies these properties. For the illustration example of Fig. 1, consider the subset of vertices $\mathcal{S} = \{o_1, o_2\}$ and the initial configuration $\mathsf{conf}_\mathcal{S}(o_1) = \bot$ and $\mathsf{conf}_\mathcal{S}(o_2) = \bot$. The activation property encoding for the output vertex o_2 is $\mathcal{T}^{o_2}_{act} = \{(t_{o_1} \leftrightarrow \bot), (t_{o_2} \leftrightarrow \bot), \Diamond\Box t_{o_2}\}$. We are looking to find some initializing function f_1 such that $\mathcal{T}_{LD} \cup \mathcal{T}_{f_1} \models \mathcal{T}^{o_2}_{act}$. In order to do so, we run an *LTL* model checking on the formula $\mathcal{T}_{LD} \cup \mathcal{T}^{o_2}_{act} \models \bot$. Using a *BDD* based model checking algorithm [7], the property is declared as false with the counterexample $\mathcal{W} \models \mathcal{T}_{LD} \cup \mathcal{T}_{f_1} \cup \mathcal{T}^{o_2}_{act}$ where $f_1(i_1) = \top$, $f_1(i_2) = \bot$, $f_1(i_3) = \bot$, $f_1(m_1) = \bot$ and $f_1(m_2) = \bot$. The output o_2 is therefore activated for f_1.

Theorem 3. *Consider a logical diagram* $LD = \langle V, E, \mathcal{O}\rangle$ *and the LTL theory* $\mathcal{T}_{LD}$*. An output vertex* $o \in V(\mathsf{output})$ *is activated (resp. deactivated) for some initial configuration* $\mathsf{conf}_\mathcal{S}$*, if there is an initializing function* f *such that* $\mathcal{T}_{LD} \cup \mathcal{T}_f \models \mathcal{T}^o_{act}$ *(resp.* $\mathcal{T}_{LD} \cup \mathcal{T}_f \models \mathcal{T}^o_{deact}$*).*

4 Proofs

In this section we include the proof of Theorem 1. Lines will be enumerated for readability purposes and to make it easier to refer to different elements of the proof. The proof of Theorem 1 is established on three steps (A), (B) and (C).

Moreover, we introduce and prove the following auxiliary lemma, which is later used for the proof of (C).

Lemma 1. *Consider a logical diagram* $LD = \langle V, E, \mathcal{O} \rangle$*, and the LTL theory* $\mathcal{T}_{LD}$*. Let* $\mathcal{W} \models \mathcal{T}_{LD}$ *and* $v \in V(M)$ *then, for every* $k \geq 1$ $\langle \mathcal{W}, k-1 \rangle \models t_{\mathcal{O}(v)}$ *iff* $k \in \mathsf{turn}_{\mathcal{O}}(v)$.

Proof. Proof of Lemma 1.

1. Let $LD = \langle V, E, \mathcal{O} \rangle$ be a logical diagram and $\mathcal{T}_{LD}$ be the corresponding LTL theory over AP_{LD}.
2. Let $\mathcal{W}$ be a word such that $\mathcal{W} \models \mathcal{T}_{LD}$.
3. We prove the following by induction: if $k \in \mathsf{turn}_{\mathcal{O}}(v)$ then $\langle \mathcal{W}, k-1 \rangle \models t_{\mathcal{O}(v)}$ for every $k \geq 1$.
4. We prove the statement for the base case: k = 1.
 4.a By Definition 3, we have $k = 1 \in \mathsf{turn}_{\mathcal{O}}(v)$ where $v \in V(\mathsf{M})$ and $\mathcal{O}(v) = 1$.
 4.b By Definition 6, we have $\langle \mathcal{W}, 0 \rangle \models t_1$.
 4.c Based on 4.a and 4.b, the statement 3 holds for $k = 1$.
5. We assume that the statement in 3 holds for some $k \geq 1$. We then prove that it also holds for $k+1$ and $v \in V(\mathsf{M})$.
6. Let $k \geq 1$ where $k+1 \in \mathsf{turn}_{\mathcal{O}}(v)$. We prove that $\langle \mathcal{W}, k \rangle \models t_{\mathcal{O}(v)}$.
7. If $\mathcal{O}(v) \in \{2 \ldots |V(\mathsf{M})|\}$:
 7.a As established in 6, $k+1 \in \mathsf{turn}_{\mathcal{O}}(v)$. Then by Definition 3, $k \in \mathsf{turn}_{\mathcal{O}}(w)$ where $w \in V(\mathsf{M})$ and $\mathcal{O}(w) = \mathcal{O}(v) - 1$.
 7.b By 5 and 7.a, we conclude that $\langle \mathcal{W}, k-1 \rangle \models t_{\mathcal{O}(v)-1}$.
 7.c By Definition 6 we have $\mathcal{W} \models \bigwedge_{i \in \{1,\ldots,|V(\mathsf{M})|-1\}} \Box(t_i \leftrightarrow \bigcirc(\neg t_i \wedge t_{i+1}))$.
 7.d Based on 7.c, $\langle \mathcal{W}, k-1 \rangle \models (t_{\mathcal{O}(v)-1} \leftrightarrow \bigcirc(\neg t_{\mathcal{O}(v)-1} \wedge t_{\mathcal{O}(v)}))$.
 7.e From 7.b and 7.d we conclude that $\langle \mathcal{W}, k \rangle \models t_{\mathcal{O}(v)}$. Thus, the statement 3 is true for $k+1$.
8. Like in 7, we use 5, Definition 3 and Definition 6 to prove that 3 also holds when $\mathcal{O}(v) = 1$.
9. Based on 7.e and 8, the statement 3 holds for $k+1$. Consequently, for every $k \geq 1$, if $k \in \mathsf{turn}_{\mathcal{O}}(v)$ then $\langle \mathcal{W}, k-1 \rangle \models t_{\mathcal{O}(v)}$.
10. **Next**, we prove the following by induction: for $k \geq 1$, if $\langle \mathcal{W}, k-1 \rangle \models t_{\mathcal{O}(v)}$ then $k \in \mathsf{turn}_{\mathcal{O}}(v)$.
11. We prove the statement 10 for the base case: $k = 1$.
 11.a By Definition 6 we have $\mathcal{W} \models (t_1 \wedge \bigwedge_{i \in \{2,\ldots,|V(\mathsf{M})|\}} \neg t_i)$. Thus, $\langle \mathcal{W}, 0 \rangle \models t_1$.
 11.b By Definition 3, we have $k = 1 \in \mathsf{turn}_{\mathcal{O}}(v)$ where $v \in V(\mathsf{M})$ and $\mathcal{O}(v) = 1$.
 11.c Based on 11.a and 11.b, the statement 10 holds for $k = 1$.
12. We now assume that the statement 10 holds for some $k \geq 1$. We prove that it also holds for $k+1$.
13. Let $v \in V(\mathsf{M})$. Assuming that $\langle M, k \rangle \models t_{\mathcal{O}(v)}$, we prove that $k+1 \in \mathsf{turn}_{\mathcal{O}}(v)$.
14. If $\mathcal{O}(v) \in \{2 \ldots |V(\mathsf{M})| - 1\}$:
 14.a By Definition 6 we have $\mathcal{W} \models \bigwedge_{i \in \{1,\ldots,|V(\mathsf{M})|-1\}} \Box(t_i \leftrightarrow \bigcirc(\neg t_i \wedge t_{i+1}))$.
 14.b Based on 14.a we have: $\langle \mathcal{W}, k \rangle \models (t_{\mathcal{O}(v)} \leftrightarrow \bigcirc(\neg t_{\mathcal{O}(v)} \wedge t_{\mathcal{O}(v)+1}))$.

14.c By 13 we know that $\langle M, k\rangle \models t_{\mathcal{O}(v)}$. Therefore, based on 14.b we have $\langle M, k+1\rangle \models t_{\mathcal{O}(v)+1}$ and $\langle M, k+1\rangle \not\models t_{\mathcal{O}(v)}$.
14.d Based on 14.a, we have $\langle \mathcal{W}, k\rangle \models (t_{\mathcal{O}(v)-1} \leftrightarrow \bigcirc(\neg t_{\mathcal{O}(v)-1} \wedge t_{\mathcal{O}(v)}))$
14.e From 14.c we have $\langle M, k+1\rangle \not\models t_{\mathcal{O}(v)}$. Thus, based on 14.d we conclude that $\langle M, k\rangle \not\models t_{\mathcal{O}(v)-1}$.
14.f Based on 14.a, we have $\langle \mathcal{W}, k-1\rangle \models (t_{\mathcal{O}(v)-1} \leftrightarrow \bigcirc(\neg t_{\mathcal{O}(v)-1} \wedge t_{\mathcal{O}(v)}))$.
14.g From 13 and 14.e we have $\langle M, k\rangle \models t_{\mathcal{O}(v)}$ and $\langle M, k\rangle \not\models t_{\mathcal{O}(v)-1}$. Thus, by 14.f $\langle M, k-1\rangle \models t_{\mathcal{O}(v)-1}$.
14.h As per 12, the statement 10 holds for k. By 14.g, $\langle M, k-1\rangle \models t_{\mathcal{O}(v)-1}$. Thus, $k \in \mathsf{turn}_{\mathcal{O}}(w)$ where $w \in V(\mathsf{M})$ and $\mathcal{O}(w) = \mathcal{O}(v) - 1$.
14.i Based on 14.h and Definition 3 we conclude that $k+1 \in \mathsf{turn}_{\mathcal{O}}(v)$. The statement 10 is therefore true for $k+1$ as per 13.

15. Like in 14, we use 12 and Definition 6 to prove that statement 10 also holds when $\mathcal{O}(v) = 1$ and $\mathcal{O}(v) = |V(\mathsf{M})|$.
16. Based on 14.i and 15, the statement 10 holds for $k+1$. Consequently, for every $k \geq 1$, if $\langle \mathcal{W}, k-1\rangle \models t_{\mathcal{O}(v)}$ then $k \in \mathsf{turn}_{\mathcal{O}}(v)$.
17. **Conclusion:** By 9 and 16 we conclude that Lemma 1 is true.

Next, we give the proof of Theorem 1. Consider a logical diagram $LD = \langle V, E, \mathcal{O}\rangle$, some initializing function f, and a word $\mathcal{W} \models \mathcal{T}_{LD} \cup \mathcal{T}_f$; we prove the following: $LD_f(v, k) = \top \Leftrightarrow \langle \mathcal{W}, k\rangle \models t_v$ where $t_v \in AP_{LD}$

(A) for every $v \in V(\mathsf{input})$ and $k \geq 0$,
(B) for every $v \in V$ and $k = 0$,
(C) for every $v \in V$ and $k \geq 1$.

Proof. Proof of Theorem 1 part (A): $v \in V(\mathsf{input})$ and $k \geq 0$.

18. Consider a logical diagram $LD = \langle V, E, \mathcal{O}\rangle$ and an initializing function f. The *LTL* theories are $\mathcal{T}_{LD}$ and $\mathcal{T}_f$. Let $\mathcal{W} \models \mathcal{T}_{LD} \cup \mathcal{T}_f$. Let $v \in V(\mathsf{input})$.
19. By Definition 3 we have $LD_f(v, k) = \top$ iff $f(v) = \top$ for every $k \geq 0$.
20. By Definition 6 we have $\mathcal{W} \models (\Box t_v \vee \Box \neg t_v)$ and by Definition 7, $\langle M, 0\rangle \models t_v$ iff $f(v) = \top$. Thus, $\langle M, k\rangle \models t_v$ iff $f(v) = \top$ for every $k \geq 0$.
21. By 19 and 20 we conclude that Theorem 1 holds for $v \in V(\mathsf{input})$ and $k \geq 0$.

Proof. Proof of Theorem 1 part (B): $v \in V$ and $k = 0$.

22. Consider a logical diagram $LD = \langle V, E, \mathcal{O}\rangle$ and an initializing function f and the *LTL* theories $\mathcal{T}_{LD}$ and $\mathcal{T}_f$. Let $\mathcal{W} \models \mathcal{T}_{LD} \cup \mathcal{T}_f$ and $v \in V$.
23. We assume that $v \in V(\mathsf{M})$.
24. Based on Definition 3, we have $LD_f(v, 0) = \top$ iff $f(v) = \top$.
25. By Definition 7, $\langle \mathcal{W}, 0\rangle \models t_v \leftrightarrow f(v)$. Consequently, $\langle \mathcal{W}, 0\rangle \models t_v$ iff $f(v) = \top$.
26. Based on 24 and 25 we conclude that $LD_f(v, 0) = \top$ iff $\langle \mathcal{W}, 0\rangle \models t_v$. Thus, the theorem holds for $k = 0$ and for every $v \in V(\mathsf{M})$.
27. Let s be a sequence of vertices $s = v_0, \ldots, v_n \in V$ with $v_i \to v_{i+1} \in E$ for every $i \in 0, \ldots, n-1$ and $u \to v_0 \notin E$ for every $u \in V$. From Definition 1, we prove that $v_0 \in V(\mathsf{input}) \cup V(\mathsf{M})$. We define the position of a vertex v in a logical diagram as follows: if $v \in V(\mathsf{input}) \cup V(\mathsf{M})$ then $\textsc{pos}(v) = 0$. Otherwise, $\textsc{pos}(v) = max(\{pos(u) \mid u \to v \in E\}) + 1$.

28. We prove Theorem 1 for $v \in V(\mathsf{not}) \cup V(\mathsf{or}) \cup V(\mathsf{and}) \cup V(\mathsf{output})$ and $k = 0$.
29. We use the proof by induction. Base case: $\textsc{pos}(v) = 1$.
30. We assume that $v \in V(\mathsf{output})$ and $u \to v \in E$:
  30.a By Definition 3, we have $LD_f(v,0) = ev(LD_f(u,0))$.
  30.b By Definition 6, we have $\mathcal{W} \models \Box(t_u \leftrightarrow t_v)$. Thus, $\langle \mathcal{W}, 0\rangle \models t_v$ iff $\langle \mathcal{W}, 0\rangle \models t_u$.
  30.c As per 27, we have $\textsc{pos}(u) = 0$ and $u \in V(\mathsf{input}) \cup V(\mathsf{M})$.
  30.d As stated in (A) and 26, the theorem is true for $k = 0$ and for every $w \in V(\mathsf{input}) \cup V(\mathsf{M})$.
  30.e By 30.c and 30.d we have $\langle \mathcal{W}, 0\rangle \models t_u$ iff $LD_f(u,0) = \top$.
  30.f From 30.a, 30.b and 30.e we conclude that $\langle \mathcal{W}, 0\rangle \models t_v$ iff $LD_f(v,0) = \top$. Consequently, Theorem 1 holds for $\textsc{pos}(v) = 1$, $k = 0$ and $v \in V(\mathsf{output})$.
31. Similarly, we prove that Theorem 1 holds for $k = 0$ and $\textsc{pos}(v) = 1$ for the vertices $v \in V(\mathsf{not})$, $v \in V(\mathsf{or})$ and $v \in V(\mathsf{and})$.
32. Now, we assume that Theorem 1 holds up to some position $\textsc{pos}(v) = j$ with $v \in V(\mathsf{not}) \cup V(\mathsf{or}) \cup V(\mathsf{and}) \cup V(\mathsf{output})$. We prove that it also holds for the position $j + 1$.
33. We assume that $v \in V(\mathsf{output})$ with $\textsc{pos}(v) = j + 1$ and $u \to v \in E$:
  33.a By Definition 3, we have $LD_f(v,0) = ev(LD_f(u,0))$.
  33.b By Definition 6, we have $\mathcal{W} \models \Box(t_u \leftrightarrow t_v)$. Thus, $\langle \mathcal{W}, 0\rangle \models t_v$ iff $\langle \mathcal{W}, 0\rangle \models t_u$.
  33.c As per 27, we have $\textsc{pos}(u) = j$. Thus, based on 32 we have $\langle M, 0\rangle \models t_u$ iff $LD_f(u,0) = \top$.
  33.d By 33.a, 33.b and 33.c, we conclude that Theorem 1 is true for the position $\textsc{pos}(v) = j + 1$ with $k = 0$ and $v \in V(\mathsf{output})$.
34. Similarly, we prove that the theorem holds for $k = 0$ and $\textsc{pos}(v) = j + 1$ for the vertices $v \in V(\mathsf{not})$, $v \in V(\mathsf{or})$ and $v \in V(\mathsf{and})$.
35. We conclude that Theorem 1 is true for $k = 0$ and $v \in v \in V(\mathsf{not}) \cup V(\mathsf{or}) \cup V(\mathsf{and}) \cup V(\mathsf{output})$.
36. **Conclusion**: by (A), 26 and 35; Theorem 1 holds for $k = 0$ and $v \in V$.

Proof. Proof of Theorem 1 part (C): $v \in V$ and $k \geq 1$.

37. Consider a logical diagram $LD = \langle V, E, \mathcal{O}\rangle$ and an initializing function f. The *LTL* theories are $\mathcal{T}_{LD}$ and $\mathcal{T}_f$. Let $\mathcal{W} \models \mathcal{T}_{LD} \cup \mathcal{T}_f$ and $v \in V$
38. We prove Theorem 1 for $k \geq 1$ by induction. We first prove it holds for the base case $k = 1$ for $v \in V(\mathsf{M}_E)$ then for $v \in V(\mathsf{M}_H)$ and finally for $v \in V(\mathsf{not}) \cup V(\mathsf{or}) \cup V(\mathsf{and}) \cup V(\mathsf{output})$.
39. Let $v \in V(\mathsf{M}_E)$ with $e \xrightarrow{\mathsf{s}} v \in E$, $h \xrightarrow{\mathsf{r}} v \in E$, $e \in V$ and $h \in V$.
40. Let $k = 1$. If $\mathcal{O}(v) = 1$ then $k = 1 \in \mathsf{turn}_{\mathcal{O}}(v)$:
  40.a By Definition 6, $\mathcal{W} \models \Box\Big(\bigcirc t_v \leftrightarrow ((\neg t_{\mathcal{O}(v)} \wedge t_v) \vee (t_{\mathcal{O}(v)} \wedge ((t_v \wedge \neg t_h) \vee t_e)))\Big)$.
  40.b By Lemma 1 we have $\langle \mathcal{W}, 0\rangle \models t_1$.
  40.c By 40.a and 40.b we have $\langle \mathcal{W}, 1\rangle \models t_v$ iff $\langle \mathcal{W}, 0\rangle \models \big((t_v \wedge \neg t_h) \vee t_e\big)$.
  40.d By Definition 3, we have $LD_f(v,1) = \mathsf{ev}((LD_f(v,0) \wedge \neg LD_f(h,0)) \vee LD_f(e,0))$.

40.e By 40.c and 40.d and knowing that Theorem 1 is true for $k = 0$ (proven in (B)), we conclude that $\langle \mathcal{W}, 1\rangle \models t_v$ iff $LD_f(v, 1) = \top$.

41. Let $k = 1$. If $\mathcal{O}(v) \neq 1$ (i.e $k \notin \mathsf{turn}_{\mathcal{O}}(v)$):

41.a By Definition 6, $\mathcal{W} \models \Box\Big(\bigcirc t_v \leftrightarrow ((\neg t_{\mathcal{O}(v)} \wedge t_v) \vee (t_{\mathcal{O}(v)} \wedge ((t_v \wedge \neg t_h) \vee t_e)))\Big)$.

41.b By Lemma 1 we have $\langle \mathcal{W}, 0\rangle \not\models t_1$.

41.c By 41.a and 41.b we have $\langle \mathcal{W}, 1\rangle \models t_v$ iff $\langle \mathcal{W}, 0\rangle \models t_v$.

41.d By Definition 3, we have $LD_f(v, 1) = \mathsf{ev}(LD_f(v, 0))$.

41.e By 41.c and 41.d and knowing that Theorem 1 is true for $k = 0$ (proven in (B)), we conclude that $\langle \mathcal{W}, 1\rangle \models t_v$ iff $LD_f(v, 1) = \top$.

42. By 40.e and 41.e we conclude that Theorem 1 holds for $k = 1$ and $v \in V(\mathsf{M}_E)$.
43. In the same way we prove that Theorem 1 holds for $k = 1$ and $v \in V(\mathsf{M}_H)$.
44. Similarly to (B) from 27 to 35, we have Theorem 1 holds for $k = 1$ and $v \in V(\mathsf{not}) \cup V(\mathsf{or}) \cup V(\mathsf{and}) \cup V(\mathsf{output})$.
45. By (A), 42, 43 and 44, Theorem 1 holds for $k = 1$ and $v \in V$.
46. We assume that Theorem 1 holds for some $k \geq 1$. We prove that it also holds for $k + 1$ for $v \in V(\mathsf{M}_E)$ then for $v \in V(\mathsf{M}_H)$ and finally for $v \in V(\mathsf{not}) \cup V(\mathsf{or}) \cup V(\mathsf{and}) \cup V(\mathsf{output})$.
47. Let $v \in V(\mathsf{M}_E)$ with $e \xrightarrow{\mathrm{s}} v \in E$, $h \xrightarrow{\mathrm{r}} v \in E$, $e \in V$ and $h \in V$.
48. Let $k + 1 \in \mathsf{turn}_{\mathcal{O}}(v)$:

48.a By Definition 6, $\mathcal{W} \models \Box\Big(\bigcirc t_v \leftrightarrow ((\neg t_{\mathcal{O}(v)} \wedge t_v) \vee (t_{\mathcal{O}(v)} \wedge ((t_v \wedge \neg t_h) \vee t_e)))\Big)$.

48.b By Lemma 1 we have $\langle \mathcal{W}, k\rangle \models t_{\mathcal{O}(v)}$.

48.c By 48.a and 48.b we have $\langle \mathcal{W}, k+1\rangle \models t_v$ iff $\langle \mathcal{W}, k\rangle \models \big((t_v \wedge \neg t_h) \vee t_e\big)$.

48.d Based on Definition 3, $LD_f(v, k + 1) = \mathsf{ev}((LD_f(v, k) \wedge \neg LD_f(h, k)) \vee LD_f(e, k))$.

48.e By 48.c and 48.d and knowing that Theorem 1 holds for k as stated in 46, we conclude that $\langle \mathcal{W}, k+1\rangle \models t_v$ iff $LD_f(v, k+1) = \top$.

49. Let $k + 1 \notin \mathsf{turn}_{\mathcal{O}(v)}$:

49.a By Definition 6, $\mathcal{W} \models \Box\Big(\bigcirc t_v \leftrightarrow ((\neg t_{\mathcal{O}(v)} \wedge t_v) \vee (t_{\mathcal{O}(v)} \wedge ((t_v \wedge \neg t_h) \vee t_e)))\Big)$.

49.b By Lemma 1 we have $\langle \mathcal{W}, k\rangle \not\models t_{\mathcal{O}(v)}$.

49.c By 49.a and 49.b we have $\langle \mathcal{W}, k+1\rangle \models t_v$ iff $\langle \mathcal{W}, k\rangle \models t_v$.

49.d Based on Definition 3, we have $LD_f(v, k+1) = \mathsf{ev}(LD_f(v, k))$.

49.e By 49.c and 49.d and knowing that Theorem 1 holds for k as stated in 46, we conclude that $\langle \mathcal{W}, k+1\rangle \models t_v$ iff $LD_f(v, k+1) = \top$.

50. By 48.e and 49.e we conclude that Theorem 1 holds for $k+1$ and $v \in V(\mathsf{M}_E)$.
51. Likewise, Theorem 1 holds for $k + 1$ and $v \in V(\mathsf{M}_H)$.
52. Similarly to (B) from 27 to 35, Theorem 1 holds for $k+1$ and $v \in V(\mathsf{not}) \cup V(\mathsf{or}) \cup V(\mathsf{and}) \cup V(\mathsf{output})$.
53. By (A), 50, 51 and 52, Theorem 1 holds for every $k \geq 1$ and $v \in V$.

Conclusion: theorem 1 holds for every $k \geq 0$ and for every $v \in V$.

Table 1. Evaluation of the *MC* techniques on $\mathcal{P}_{act}$ and $\mathcal{P}_{deact}$ of all the 12 outputs. m: minutes; s: seconds; mean: median time of the 12 outputs; min/max : minimum/maximum time out of the 12 outputs; (n): n is the length of the counterexample.

	BDD	BMC	SBMC	k-MC
$\mathcal{P}_{act}(o)$	timeout	mean: 26 s (33) min: 4.2 s (22) max: 2 m 11 s (57)	mean: 3.4 s (33) min: 1.3 s (22) max: 11.3 s (57)	mean: 6.2 s (33) min: 3.9 s (24) max: 12.9 s (57)
$\mathcal{P}_{deact}(o)$	timeout	mean: 18.2 s (32) min: 4 s (22) max: 35 s (39)	mean: 2.9 s (32) min: 1.3 s (22) max: 4.4 s (39)	mean: 5.3 s (32) min: 3.4 s (22) max: 7.5 s (35)

5 Evaluation and Discussion

In this section, we evaluate different *LTL* model checking *(MC)* techniques on a real world logical diagram used for a logical controller in a nuclear power plant. The goal is to generate scenarios that could be used for validation tests. These scenarios consist in a set of input values and the set of expected output values. In the testing process, the generated inputs are applied on the logical controller in order to observe the real output values and make sure that they are conform to the expected output values of the generated scenario. However, before generating these scenarios it is important to ensure that the logical diagram satisfies the stability property. An unstable behavior is when a value of one or many outputs keep changing indefinitely for fixed inputs. In this case, the logical diagram has to be revised to satisfy the stability. This is because the unstable behavior means that the expected value of the output is not defined and therefore, generating tests for that output becomes meaningless. Verification of the stability and generating test scenarios are the main focus of this evaluation.

The real world logical diagram chosen for the evaluation is representative of many other logical diagrams used by EDF. It contains 16 input vertices, 12 output vertices, 19 memory vertices and 77 vertices of the types $\{\mathsf{and}, \mathsf{or}, \mathsf{not}\}$. First, the satisfaction of the stability property is verified. Then, the purpose is to generate scenarios that set an output to the value true when it is initially set to false (i.e. activation scenarios) and others that put it to false when it is initially set to true (i.e. deactivation scenarios). These scenarios will be generated for each different output. The concerned real world logical diagram will be referred to as LD_R. The results previously established in this paper were implemented to generate the *LTL* theory $\mathcal{T}_{LD_R}$ that encodes the logical diagram LD_R as well as the theory $\mathcal{T}_{stable}$ encoding the stability of LD_R and the theories $\mathcal{T}^{o_i}_{act}$ and $\mathcal{T}^{o_i}_{deact}$ for the activation and deactivation of every output vertex o_i.

The *LTL* theory of stability is $\mathcal{T}_{stable} = \{\Diamond(\Box t_{m_i} \vee \Box\neg t_{m_i}) \mid i \in 1, 2, \ldots, 19\}$. We use the *LTL* model checking techniques to prove the truthfulness of the following *LTL* property: $\mathcal{T}_{LD} \models \mathcal{T}_{stable}$. This property will be referred to as the stability property $\mathcal{P}_{stab}$. If it is proven to be true, then LD_R is uniformly stable. If it is not, then we get a counterexample, i.e. a word $\mathcal{W}$ that is a model of $\mathcal{T}_{LD_R}$ and the theory $\mathcal{T}_f$ of some initializing function f for which LD_R is unstable. The LTL theory that encodes the activation of an output o_i which is initially deactivated is $\mathcal{T}_{act}^{o_i} = \{(t_{o_i} \leftrightarrow \bot), (\Diamond\Box t_{o_i})\}$. Likewise, the LTL theory that encodes the deactivation of an output o_i which is initially activated is $\mathcal{T}_{deact}^{o_i} = \{(t_{o_i} \leftrightarrow \top), (\Diamond\Box\neg t_{o_i})\}$. In order to generate activation and deactivation scenarios for an output o_i, we apply the model checking on the property $\mathcal{T}_{LD} \cup \mathcal{T}_{act}^{o_i} \models \bot$ referred to as $\mathcal{P}_{act}(o_i)$ and the property $\mathcal{T}_{LD} \cup \mathcal{T}_{deact}^{o_i} \models \bot$ referred to as $\mathcal{P}_{deact}(o_i)$. If $\mathcal{P}_{act}(o_i)$ (resp. $\mathcal{P}_{deact}(o_i)$) is true, then no activation (resp. deactivation) scenarios exist. Otherwise, if $\mathcal{P}_{act}(o_i)$ (resp. $\mathcal{P}_{deact}(o_i)$) is not satisfied we get a counterexample, i.e. a word $\mathcal{W}$ that satisfies all the formulae of the LD_R theory $\mathcal{T}_{LD_R}$, the activation theory $\mathcal{T}_{act}^{o_i}$ (resp. the deactivation theory $\mathcal{T}_{deact}^{o_i}$) and the theory $\mathcal{T}_f$ of some initializing function f for which the output o_i is activated (resp. deactivated). The generated word expresses the testing scenario to be applied on the logical controller. We check $\mathcal{P}_{act}(o_i)$ and $\mathcal{P}_{deact}(o_i)$ properties for every output vertex o_i of the 12 outputs in LD_R.

For this evaluation, the verification of each property was done using a well known symbolic model checking tool called *NuSMV* [5]. Different techniques were used for each property. In the following, we list the evaluated *NuSMV LTL* model checking techniques presented in [4]:

- The Binary Decision Diagram (BDD) based *LTL* Model Checking [7].
- Bounded Model Checking (*BMC*) based on SAT solvers as described in [1].
- Simple Bounded Model Checking (SBMC) based on SAT solvers as in [9].

The usage of the *BDD* based technique allows to verify whether an *LTL* property is true or false and to generate a counterexample when it is false. On the other hand, *BMC* based techniques prove that a property is false by increasingly exploring the different lengths of counterexamples starting from zero to a preset upper bound. When the maximum bound is reached and no counterexamples are found, then the truth of the property is not decided. In other words, unlike the *BDD* based technique, the *BMC* based ones are useful only in case the property is false. In this evaluation, the upper bound of the *BMC* based techniques was set to 1000. Another technique tested for the verification of the properties is the *k-liveness* algorithm based model checking technique (*k-MC*) as described in [6]. The technique was introduced in another tool called *nuXmv* [3]: an extension for *NuSMV*. The usage of the technique is presented in [2]. For this evaluation, the timeout delay for each of the mentioned techniques was set to two hours.

The verification of the uniform stability of LD_R was done by checking the property $\mathcal{P}_{stab}$ using the different techniques. The *BDD*, *BMC*, and *SBMC* techniques timed-out. The stability could not therefore be concluded with these techniques. However, the *k-MC* technique terminated successfully in 26 min declaring that the property $\mathcal{P}_{stab}$ is true. Therefore, the logical diagram LD_R is uniformly stable. Each technique was then tested for the activation ($\mathcal{P}_{act}(o_i)$) and deactivation ($\mathcal{P}_{deact}(o_i)$) property for every output o_i. Except for the *BDD* technique which timed-out in every single check, all the other techniques successfully generated counterexamples of the same length for every output of LD_R. The evaluation results are given by table 1. The *SBMC* technique was the fastest to generate the counterexample for every output while *BMC* was considerably slower especially on the longest counterexamples.

This study shows that the proposed *LTL* encoding of the logical diagrams is a good candidate for test generation, as multiple counterexamples can be generated starting from different initial configuration defined by the verification process. We tested the proposed *LTL* encoding on a real, representative logical diagram by comparing different *LTL* model checking techniques. It turns out that *k-MC* and *SBMC* techniques are particularly efficient for checking the properties we defined, allowing us to test the controller's outputs with respect to the LD.

Acknowledgments. David Carral is funded by the ANR project CQFD (ANR-18-CE23-0003).

References

1. Biere, A., Cimatti, A., Clarke, E., Zhu, Y.: Symbolic model checking without BDDs. In: Cleaveland, W.R. (ed.) TACAS 1999. LNCS, vol. 1579, pp. 193–207. Springer, Heidelberg (1999). https://doi.org/10.1007/3-540-49059-0_14
2. Bozzano, M., et al.: nuXmv 2.0. 0 User Manual. Fondazione Bruno Kessler, Technical report, Trento, Italy (2019)
3. Cavada, R., et al.: The NUXMV symbolic model checker. In: Biere, A., Bloem, R. (eds.) CAV 2014. LNCS, vol. 8559, pp. 334–342. Springer, Cham (2014). https://doi.org/10.1007/978-3-319-08867-9_22
4. Cavada, R., et al.: Nusmv 2.4 user manual. CMU and ITC-irst (2005)
5. Cimatti, A., et al.: NuSMV 2: an OpenSource tool for symbolic model checking. In: Brinksma, E., Larsen, K.G. (eds.) CAV 2002. LNCS, vol. 2404, pp. 359–364. Springer, Heidelberg (2002). https://doi.org/10.1007/3-540-45657-0_29
6. Claessen, K., Sörensson, N.: A liveness checking algorithm that counts. In: 2012 Formal Methods in Computer-Aided Design (FMCAD), pp. 52–59. IEEE (2012)
7. Clarke, E.M., Grumberg, O., Hamaguchi, K.: Another look at LTL model checking. Formal Methods Syst. Des. **10**, 47–71 (1997)
8. Enoiu, E.P., Čaušević, A., Ostrand, T.J., Weyuker, E.J., Sundmark, D., Pettersson, P.: Automated test generation using model checking: an industrial evaluation. Int. J. Softw. Tools Technol. Transf. **18**, 335–353 (2016)
9. Latvala, T., Biere, A., Heljanko, K., Junttila, T.: Simple is better: efficient bounded model checking for past LTL. In: Cousot, R. (ed.) VMCAI 2005. LNCS, vol. 3385, pp. 380–395. Springer, Heidelberg (2005). https://doi.org/10.1007/978-3-540-30579-8_25
10. Lee, D., Yannakakis, M.: Principles and methods of testing finite state machines - a survey. Proc. IEEE **84**(8), 1090–1123 (1996)
11. Provost, J., Roussel, J.M., Faure, J.M.: Translating Grafcet specifications into Mealy machines for conformance test purposes. Control. Eng. Pract. **19**(9), 947–957 (2011)
12. Sfar, A., Irofti, D., Croitoru, M.: A graph based semantics for Logical Functional Diagrams in power plant controllers. In: Varzinczak, I. (ed.) FoIKS 2022. LNCS, pp. 55–74. Springer, Cham (2022). https://doi.org/10.1007/978-3-031-11321-5_4
13. Springintveld, J., Vaandrager, F., D'Argenio, P.R.: Testing timed automata. Theor. comput. Sci. **254**(1–2), 225–257 (2001)

Optimal Spare Management via Statistical Model Checking: A Case Study in Research Reactors

Reza Soltani[1(✉)], Matthias Volk[1(✉)], Leonardo Diamonte[2], Milan Lopuhaä-Zwakenberg[1(✉)], and Mariëlle Stoelinga[1,3(✉)]

[1] University of Twente, Enschede, The Netherlands
r.soltani@utwente.nl
[2] INVAP SE, Bariloche, Argentina
[3] Radboud University, Nijmegen, The Netherlands

Abstract. Systematic spare management is important to optimize the twin goals of high reliability and low costs. However, existing approaches to spare management do not incorporate a detailed analysis of the effect on the absence of spares on the system's reliability. In this work, we combine fault tree analysis with statistical model checking to model spare part management as a stochastic priced timed game automaton (SPTGA). We use UPPAAL STRATEGO to find the number of spares that minimizes the total costs due to downtime and spare purchasing; the resulting SPTGA model can then additionally be analyzed according to other metrics like expected availability. We apply these techniques to the emergency shutdown system of a research nuclear reactor. Our methods find the optimal spare management for a subsystem in a matter of minutes, minimizing cost while ensuring an expected availability of 99.96%.

Keywords: Spare management · Fault tree · Statistical model checking · Research reactor · UPPAAL

1 Introduction

Proper spare management is of crucial importance for safety critical systems: when a component breaks, it must be replaced in a timely manner. At the same time spare management is costly: spare parts need not only be purchased, but they must also be maintained and administered. Therefore, spare management policies must carefully trade reliability/availability versus costs.

This work has been partially funded by the NWO grant NWA.1160.18.238 (PrimaVera), by the ERC Consolidator Grant 864075 (*CAESAR*) and by EU Horizon 2020 project MISSION, number 101008233.

Supplementary Information The online version contains supplementary material available at https://doi.org/10.1007/978-3-031-43681-9_12.

A. Cimatti and L. Titolo (Eds.): FMICS 2023, LNCS 14290, pp. 205–223, 2023.
https://doi.org/10.1007/978-3-031-43681-9_12

In practice, spare management is often ad hoc, based on intuitions rather than on systematic analysis. Nevertheless, spare parts optimization is a well-studied topic, especially in optimization research [13]. These approaches use multiobjective optimization to meet the goals of low costs and high reliability; spare management can also be combined with the maintenance policy which also affects these goals [27], to find an optimal joint spare/maintenance policy.

However, in many works reliability is closely linked to the availability of spare parts, rather than based on a detailed analysis of the effect of the absence of spares on the system's reliability. To overcome this shortcoming, this paper aligns spare management with a popular reliability engineering framework, namely fault tree analysis [22]: many companies already use fault trees as a part of their design process. By equipping the fault trees with a minimal amount of additional information (namely, the costs of downtime and spares), we support a more systematic method of studying tradeoffs between costs and reliability [12].

Our Approach. We exploit statistical model checking (SMC) to support spare parts optimization, and especially the tool Uppaal Stratego [9], to automatically synthesize an optimal number of spare parts for a system modelled as a fault tree. Statistical model checking [18] is a state-of-the-art methodology for Monte Carlo simulation. Our key model is a stochastic priced timed game automaton (SPTGA), i.e., a transition system that models the evolution of probability and costs over time. Monte Carlo simulation can estimate (up to a confidence interval) the probability and expected values for a wide variety of random variables. When the model involves decisions, such simulations can also be used to estimate the probability of desirable outcomes for a given strategy. In [12] this is used to find the reliability of a fault tree model given a fixed number of spares.

More recently, however, recent developments in the area of machine learning allow SMC to not only analyze given strategies, but also automatically synthesize optimal strategies [6]. Figure 4. We exploit these techniques in our framework outlined in Fig. 4. We start with a fault tree extended with costs for downtime and spare management, as well as the dependability metric of interest. Via statistical model checking, we synthesize an strategy for spare management that is optimal under the given dependability metric, e.g., the reliability. We further analyze this optimal strategy with respect to other metrics, such as the availability.

The Case Study. We apply our approach to a section of the emergency shutdown system of a research reactor, developed by the company INVAP, Argentina. The section of interest of the system consists of three main subsystems: the reactor protection system, the neutron flux instrumentation, and the temperature difference at the reactor core (DTCore). Each subsystem is implemented in triple modular redundancy. Cost is incurred by buying spares and by suffering downtime due to unreliability; the optimal spare strategy is one that balances these to obtain the lowest total cost.

Results. We determine the optimal spare management of a subsystem by modelling it as a fault tree and translating it into a SPTGA; the optimal spare problem then becomes a strategy synthesis query in Uppaal Stratego. This is solved in 7 min, giving 6 spares as the optimal balance between reliability and spare part costs. Under this strategy, the probability of any downtime during the research reactor's 40-year lifespan is less than 9E−4, with an expected availability of 99.96%.

Contributions. Summarizing, our contributions are a systematic way to find optimal spare management strategies by combining the detailed reliability analysis of fault trees with the strategy synthesis tools of statistical model checking. The resulting timed game automaton allows for a range of queries for further analysis of the optimal strategy. We show the validity of this method on a case study coming from nuclear research reactors.

Artefact. We provide all UPPAAL models, queries and results in a publicly available artefact on Zenodo: https://doi.org/10.5281/zenodo.7970835 [2].

1.1 Related Work

Spare Management. Spare parts management is an active area of research, cf. [24,26] for overviews. Hu et al. [13] surveyed the gap between the theory and practice of spare parts management. According to this work, from a product lifecycle perspective, there are three kinds of forecasting tasks, namely forecasting initial demand, ongoing demand, and demand over the final phase. There are techniques for predicting the need for spare parts based on neural networks [7,11,15,19,25]. The neural network based forecasting is most often used to predict continuing need and demand throughout the final phase. It can rarely be applied in predicting the initial demand since there is limited historical data on the spares' consumption when new equipment is introduced.

[28] considers reordering of spare parts from dual sources, with different lead times and costs. The approach uses Markov decision processes to model the spare management and synthesizes optimal strategies through an exact algorithm. In [12], the impact of different numbers of spares is investigated. Given a dynamic fault tree with spare components, the model is translated into a probabilistic timed automata (PTA). The unavailability is then calculated by analysis of the PTA via UPPAAL. In contrast to our approach, the number of spare parts is manually fixed beforehand, and no automatic synthesis is performed.

Translation from Fault Trees to Timed Automata. Several methods have been developed for fault tree analysis using timed automata.

In [16,17], the authors introduced a framework for converting fault trees and attack trees to timed automata. In [16], the authors translated attack tree gates and leaves into timed automata and defined the properties in weighted CTL queries to perform model checking analysis. They used the UPPAAL CORA model checker to obtain the optimal path of the attacks. In [17], each element of an attack-fault tree is translated into a stochastic timed automaton [10]. As a result, the authors calculated the costliest system failure by equipping the attack-fault tree with stochastic model checking techniques. Ruijters et al. [23] presented a translation from fault maintenance trees—fault trees with maintenance aspects—to priced timed automata, and then applied statistical model

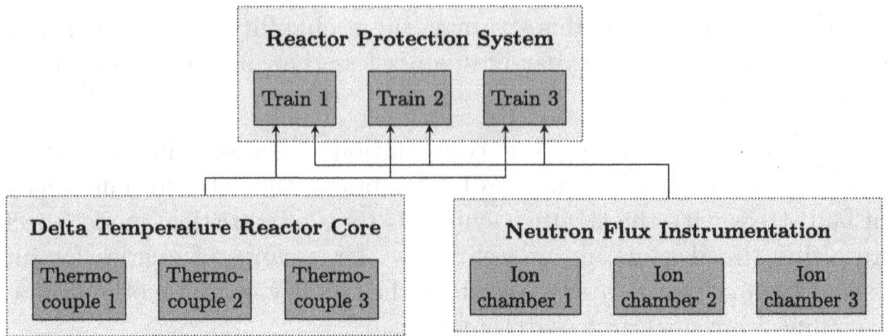

Fig. 1. Schematic of the emergency shutdown system

checking for analysis. In all these papers, the authors only check the dependability metrics, such as system reliability, but do not perform any synthesis on specific parameters. In contrast, our approach allows to automatically synthesize parameters which are optimal under a given dependability metric. Furthermore, these works are less flexible than our model. In previous works, the size of a gate automaton grew linearly with the number of its children. In contrast, the size of our automata is independent of the number of children, and remains constant.

2 Spare Management for a Research Reactor

2.1 Research Reactor

We investigate optimal spare management for research reactors. The case study stems from INVAP S.E. based in Bariloche, Argentina. This high-tech company develops—among others—research reactors, satellites, and radars.

Research reactors are nuclear reactors which are used for research purposes and not for power generation. Application areas of research reactors include research and training, analysis and testing of materials, and the production of radioisotopes used in medical diagnoses and cancer treatment. In contrast to power reactors, research reactors are smaller, operate at lower temperatures, require less fuel and produce less fission products.

Emergency Shutdown System. We consider part of the emergency shutdown system of a research reactor. In case of an emergency, the system automatically stops the nuclear fission chain reaction within the reactor. This process is called "trip" or "scram". The fission reaction is stopped by inserting neutron-absorbing control rods into the reactor core. By absorbing neutrons, the control rods stop the nuclear chain reaction and shut down the reactor. The emergency shutdown system is designed as a *fail-safe* mechanism: if it fails due to internal subsystem failures, operation of the whole research reactor is immediately stopped. In this case study, we focus on the unavailability of the research reactor operation due to the unavailability of the emergency shutdown system caused by internal failures.

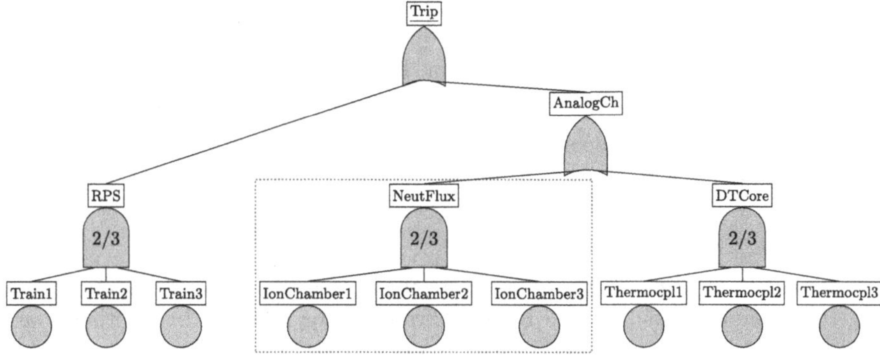

Fig. 2. Fault tree model of the emergency shutdown system (Color figure online)

In particular, we do not consider the trip of the research reactor—through the emergency shutdown system—triggered by the violation of safety thresholds.

The emergency shutdown system (depicted in Fig. 1) consists of three main subsystems: (1) the reactor protection system (RPS), the (2) neutron flux instrumentation and (3) the delta temperature reactor core (DTCore). Both the neutron flex instrumentation and the DTCore feed into the RPS via analog channels. If any of the two inputs or the RPS itself is unavailable, the emergency shutdown system becomes unavailable. The *reactor protection system* consists of three redundant subsystems, also called trains. The RPS signals a trip of the reactor if two out of the three trains are above the safety threshold or if the trains are unavailable due to internal failures. The *neutron flux instrumentation* consists of three ionization chambers. Each ionization chamber measures the neutron flux outside the core and generates an alarm if safety thresholds are violated. The neutron flux instrumentation fails if two of the ionization chambers are failed. The *Delta Temperature Reactor Core (DTCore)* consists of three redundant *thermocouples* which measure temperature differences. DTCore fails if two thermocouples are unavailable.

Figure 2 depicts a fault tree model of the emergency shutdown system. The logical OR-gate *Trip* models that the system fails if any of the three main subsystems fails. Each sub-system is modelled by a 2/3 voting-gate which fails if at least two out of the three inputs fail. The leaves represent the redundant sub-systems which fail according to an associated failure distribution.

In the following, we focus our analysis on the neutron flux subsystem (marked by the box in red), because it has significantly higher costs than the other components. Thus, optimal spare management is most crucial here.

2.2 Optimal Spare Management

Redundancies of the sub-components ensure that the research reactor operates safely and reliably. The safety and reliability of the reactor can be analysed with standard techniques such as fault tree analysis [22]. However, the redundancies

Table 1. Failure rates, replacement rates and costs of components

Component	RPS Train	Ionization chamber	Thermocouple
Failure rate [per hour]	1×10^{-4}	1×10^{-6}	1×10^{-5}
Replacement rate [per hour]	1×10^{-2}	3×10^{-3}	3.5×10^{-3}
Costs [in $ Argentine pesos]	8k	80k	1.2k

do not prevent failures, they only mitigate them. In case of a sub-component failure, the sub-component should be either repaired or replaced by another spare component. It is therefore crucial that enough spare components are available to allow for quick replacement of failed components. On the other hand, ordering and storing a large number of spare components costs a significant amount of money. A pressing question is therefore to find an optimal spare management policy, e.g., "how many spare components should be on stock at a given time?" The number of spares on stock should be small—as to minimize purchasing and storage costs—but sufficiently large such that the research reactor stays operational—especially in case of component failures. The optimal strategy needs to consider various aspects: costs of spare components, warehouse capacity, delivery times for new orders, reliability requirements on the reactors, etc.

Initial Stock. We consider the setting where all necessary spare parts must be initially on stock. Thus, no intermediate ordering is considered. This setting is important in the context of research reactors as ordering additional spare components can take a long time or components may no longer be produced at all. The ordering process involves multiple steps such as (possibly) manufacturing the component on demand, transportation and testing of the component. Thus, the initial stock is crucial to guarantee high availability of the research reactor.

Current Spare Management Strategies. Currently, the number of spare components is often based on experience, such as keeping the square root of used components on stock. For n components which are in use, $\lceil \sqrt{n} \rceil$ components are kept on stock as spare parts. Another approach is manually considering different numbers of spare parts and calculating the system reliability with respect to each configuration. In the end, the best number of spare parts from all considered configurations is selected. However, this approach is very time-consuming as a large number of spare parts need to be considered. Furthermore, if parts of the system change, the whole process has to be performed again.

2.3 System Parameters

We consider a remaining lifetime of 40 years for the research reactor. We assume a gross profit of $1 million Argentine pesos per day of operation for the research reactor. Conversely, this means each day where the research reactor is unavailable, costs of $1 million are accumulated.

Failure Rates and Costs. Component failures occur according to a given failure rate. The failures can be mitigated by replacing the component with a spare one. The replacement time is given by a replacement rate. Table 1 provides the failure rates, replacement rates and the costs for a single component of each type. The values were provided by our industrial partner INVAP S.E.

2.4 Performance Metrics

In our analysis, we are interested in optimizing for two metrics: (1) high availability of the research reactor with (2) minimal cost. The unavailability is calculated for a lifetime of 40 years. As unavailability is also associated with costs—the loss of profit—it suffices to optimize for cost. We therefore want to find the number of initial spares s.t. the costs of the spares plus the costs due to system unavailability is minimal. This yields the metric Q^O we want to optimize for:

$\mathbf{Q^O}$. What number of spare components minimizes total cost?

After finding the optimal number of spares, we further want to analyse the availability of the system under this configuration. To this end, we are also interested in the following metrics:

$\mathbf{Q_1^A}$. What are the costs (costs of spares and costs through unavailability) for a given number of spares?
$\mathbf{Q_2^A}$. Given a number of spares, what is the availability of the system within its lifetime (40 years)?
$\mathbf{Q_3^A}$. Given a number of spares, what is the probability that the system is down for less than a given threshold (e.g., 30 days)?

3 Preliminaries

3.1 Fault Trees

Fault trees (FT) are a common reliability model [22] applied in diverse industries such as automotive, aerospace, and nuclear sectors [14]. A *Fault Tree (FT)* is a directed acyclic graph that serves as a model for determining the causes of system failures. It identifies how failures at lower levels propagate through the system, ultimately leading to a system-level failure. The leaves in a fault tree, called *basic events (BE)*, represent atomic components that fail according to an associated failure rate. Inner nodes, called *gates*, model how failures propagate. The *voting gate* (also known as K/N gate) indicates that the associated event occurs if at least K out of its N input events have failed. The AND gate and OR gate are special cases of the voting gate, corresponding to N/N and $1/N$, respectively. Failure of the root node, called *top event*, represents a system failure.

3.2 Stochastic Priced Timed-Game Automata

A *Stochastic Priced Timed-Game Automaton (SPTGA)* is a Timed Game Automaton (TGA) [20] with probabilities associated to transitions between states. For each state a price is given that represents the cost/benefit of being in that state, as well as there may be a cost for taking a transition. In SPTGA, there are two types of transitions, controllable and uncontrollable. A *controllable* transition refers to a transition that can be controlled or influenced by the system under consideration. The system has control over the timing and occurrence of the transitions, and their execution can impact the outcome of the game or the behavior of the system. Unlike controllable transitions, *uncontrollable* transitions cannot be influenced by the system under consideration. By distinguishing between controllable and uncontrollable transitions, SPTGA provides a framework for analyzing systems where both the player's (system's) decisions and external uncontrollable events play a role in determining the system's behavior and evolution over time. Figure 3 shows an example of SPTGA. In SPTGA, the opponent can be an antagonist, which will be a 2-player game, or stochastic, then the game will be a $1\frac{1}{2}$-player game.

Given an SPTGA, we can split the problems of interest into two different categories. The first category is the *control synthesize problem* whose input is a model of the system $\mathcal{G}$ and a property φ, and its problem is to compute a strategy σ—if such strategy exists—such that $\mathcal{G}|\sigma$ satisfies φ. The second category is the *verification problem* (or model checking problem). Its input is a model of the system $\mathcal{G}$ (or $\mathcal{G}|\sigma$, if subjected to a strategy) and a property φ, and its problem is determining whether $\mathcal{G}$ satisfies φ. While the verification problem is concerned with whether a system meets a set of requirements or not, the control synthesizes problem is concerned with whether the system can be *restricted* to satisfy the requirements.

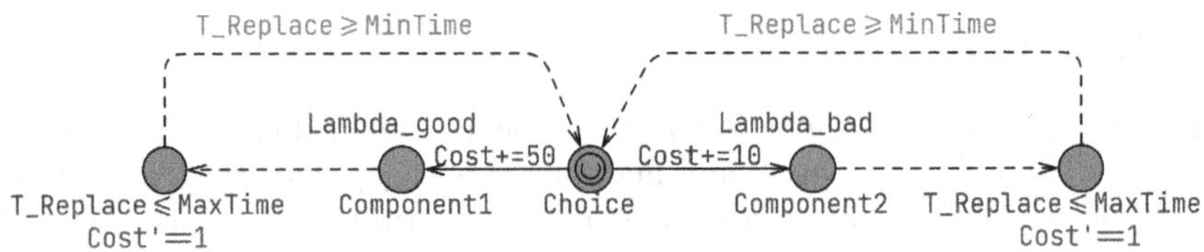

Fig. 3. The SPTGA consists of two controllable transitions (straight arrow) and four uncontrollable transitions (dashed arrow). This example shows a component that needs to be replaced when it fails. When we are in the `Choice` state, we can choose one of the two controllable transitions. One of the transitions is to use a component with a higher cost (50 units) but a lower failure rate. Another choice is a component with a lower cost (10 units) but a higher failure rate ($\lambda_{\text{bad}} > \lambda_{\text{good}}$). When the selected component fails, it will be replaced within `MinTime` and `MaxTime` replacement time based on a uniform distribution, resulting in a cost of 1 per time-unit while the component is being replaced. With the help of SPTGA, we can synthesize a strategy to minimize the expected cost, where the choices are made in such a way that we incur the least cost.

3.3 Uppaal Stratego

Uppaal Stratego [9] is a powerful tool that enables users to generate, optimize, compare, and explore the effect and performance of strategies for stochastic priced timed games. It integrates the various components of Uppaal and its two branches—Uppaal SMC (statistical model checking) [5] and Uppaal Tiga (synthesis for timed games) [3]—as well as the optimization method proposed in [8] (synthesis of near optimal schedulers) into one tool suite. Recently, Uppaal Stratego has become a part of Uppaal 5.0.

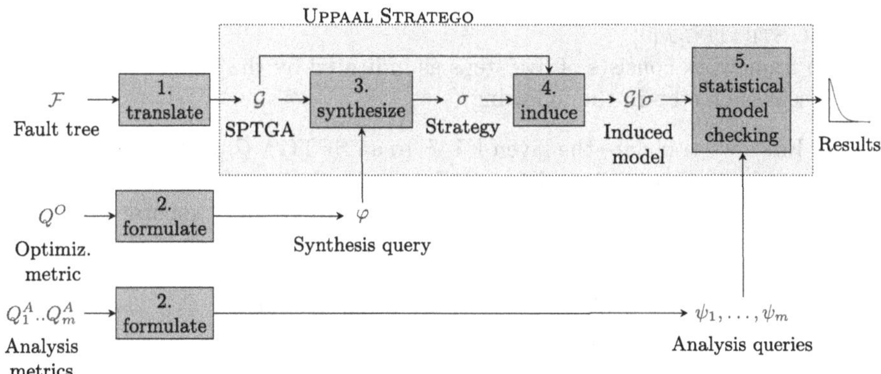

Fig. 4. Overview of the methodology.

In Uppaal Stratego, the query language contains a subset of Time Computational Tree Logic to verify the requirements of the model. We focus on the following two types of queries for a given SPTGA and a strategy. The variable `N` is the number of simulations to be performed and `bound` shows the time bound on the simulations.

1. *Probability Estimation* `Pr[bound]`(ψ) `under Strategy_Name` estimates the probability of a requirement property ψ being satisfied for a given SPTGA and strategy within a time bound.
2. *Expected Value* `E[bound;N]`(ψ) `under Strategy_Name` evaluates the minimum or maximum value of a clock or an integer value while Uppaal Stratego checks the SPTGA w.r.t. a strategy.

In this context, simulations refer to the execution of the model under different conditions and scenarios to observe its behavior and gather information about its properties. Estimation, in this context, refers to the process of determining or approximating numerical values or probabilities associated with specific aspects of the system's behavior or performance.

4 Methodology

Figure 4 outlines our approach for spare parts optimization via statistical model checking. The inputs to the framework are a fault tree $\mathcal{F}$ representing the system under consideration, and the metrics Q^O and $Q_1^A, \ldots, Q_m^A$. The approach returns the number of spare parts which optimizes Q^O, e.g., minimizes cost. Additionally, the framework also outputs the model checking results for $Q_1^A, \ldots, Q_m^A$ when using the optimal number of spares, e.g., the probability of the downtime being less than a defined threshold, the expected cost for having a specific amount of spares, and the system's availability. The synthesis of the optimal number of spares as well as the analysis via statistical model checking are performed using Uppaal Stratego [9].

The framework consists of five steps as indicated by the blue boxes in Fig. 4. We present each step in the following.

Step 1. First, we translate the given FT $\mathcal{F}$ to an SPTGA $\mathcal{G}$. Following [4,23], we employ a compositional translation methodology. That is, we translate each FT element (i.e., basic events and gates) into a separate SPTGA. Then, by combining these different components (automata), we obtain one SPTGA $\mathcal{G}$ capturing the complete FT behaviour. Details on the translation from FT to SPTGA are given in Sect. 5.

Step 2. The optimization metric Q^O as well as the analysis metrics $Q_1^A, \ldots, Q_m^A$ are formalized as temporal logic formulas φ and $\psi_1, \ldots, \psi_m$, respectively.

Step 3. Given the SPTGA $\mathcal{G}$, we use Uppaal Stratego to synthesize a strategy σ that is optimal for the given synthesis query φ, e.g., minimize cost. The synthesized strategy σ then encodes the optimal number of spares to have on stock in the beginning.

Step 4. Applying the synthesized strategy σ on the SPTGA $\mathcal{G}$ yields the induced model $\mathcal{G}|\sigma$ that represents the system's behaviour when using the optimal number of spare parts.

Step 5. Lastly, we use statistical model checking via Uppaal Stratego to calculate the desired analysis queries $\psi_1, \ldots, \psi_m$ on $\mathcal{G}|\sigma$. The analysis yields e.g., the system's availability or the probability of an overall downtime less than a given threshold.

5 INVAP Emergency Shutdown System as an SPTGA

This section presents the SPTGA model for the emergency shutdown system.

Following [4,21], we obtain this SPTGA model from the fault tree in Fig. 2 through a compositional translation methodology. That is, we translate each FT element (i.e., basic event or gate) into a separate SPTGA. Then, by combining these different SPTGA components (automata), we obtain one SPTGA $\mathcal{G}$ capturing the complete FT behaviour. In contrast to previous works, e.g., [23], our translation is agnostic to the number of inputs in the FT. For example, we translate the behavior of a voting gate (K/N gate) to SPTGA regardless of the number of children N or threshold K. These values are dynamically defined in

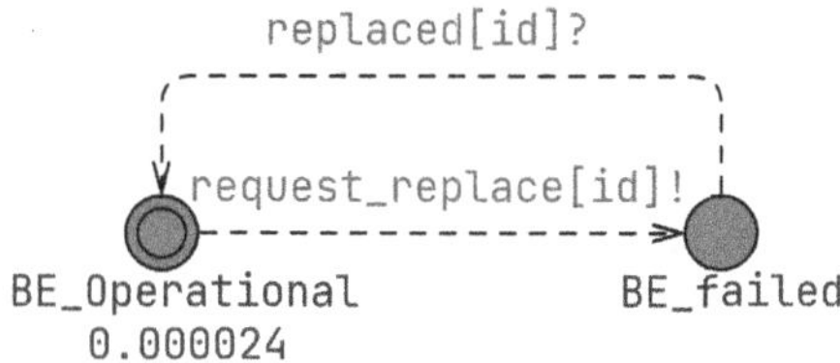

Fig. 5. SPTGA `BE[id]` for basic events, parameterized with their ID `id`. Each BE has an exponential failure rate of 0.000024.

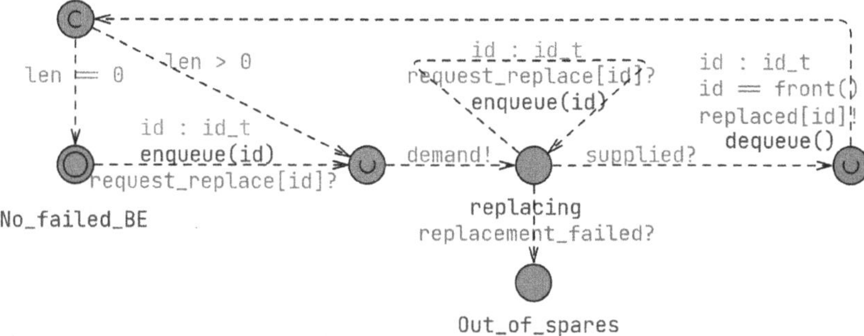

Fig. 6. The automaton for the spare management. Here `request_replace[id]?` and `replaced[id]!` are signals to communicate with the corresponding BE. The `demand!` and `supplied?` are signals to communicate with the warehouse. `len` holds the length of the queue. The `replacement_failed?` signal will be received if no spare is available in the warehouse.

the system declaration without changing the model. A larger FT can be modeled by creating an instance of a translated automaton. For this, the values associated with each gate, e.g., the children's ID, can be specified in the system declaration.

For simplicity, we only present the translation of one component type, marked with dash line in Fig. 2. However, our method can easily be extended for other types and is applicable to fault trees in general. The SPTGA consists of four types of automata, which can be instantiated multiple times: `BE` represents a basic event, `SG` models the spare management, `VOT` represents a voting gate and `W` models the warehouse storing the spares. Each element in the FT can have different states, and in SPTGA, we represent them with locations. For example, BEs are either operational or failed, so we have two different states for the associated `BE`. We use synchronization channels to show the link between different FT elements.

Basic Events. Figure 5 shows the SPTGA model for a BE. This automaton consists of two states: `BE_operational` denotes that the component is operational, whereas `BE_failed` denotes its failure. Since we have several BEs, the SPTGA is parameterized by ID `[id]` with the same failure rate. The BE's failure rate (per day) is an exponential rate of 0.000024 (cf. Table 1 column "Ionization chamber").

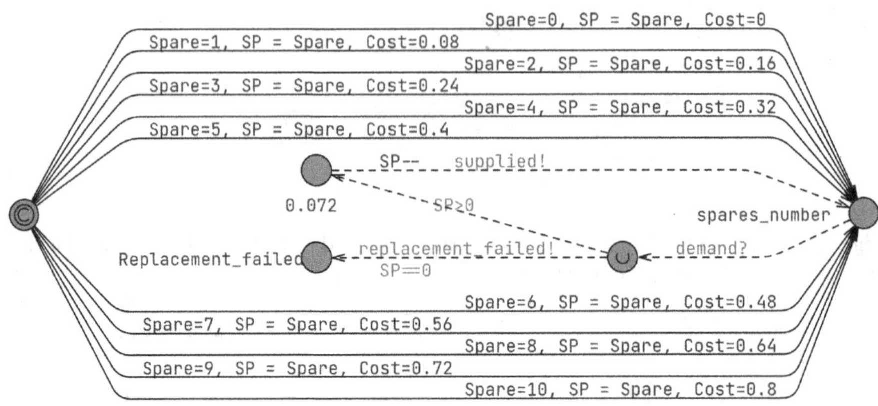

Fig. 7. The automaton for the spare warehouse. The variable `Spare` stores the initial amount of spares in the warehouse, `SP` represents the number of available spares in the warehouse, and `Cost` represents the cost. The `demand?`, `supplied!`, and `replacement_failed!` are signals to communicate with the SG.

In Table 1, failure rates and replacement rates are given per hour, while here, we converted them into per day for convenience. When a BE fails, it communicates with `SG` through the communication channel `request_replace[id]!`. The message `replaced[id]?` is sent by `SG` when the failed BE has been replaced.

Spare Management. Figure 6 shows the SPTGA representing the spare management. When `SG` receives the `request_replace[id]?` message—modeling that `BE[id]` has failed—it stores the ID [id] in the queue, then communicates with the warehouse through the communication channel `demand!`. If there is a spare part in the warehouse, then the replacement will be done, and SG will be informed by the communication channel `supplied?`. If there is no spare in the warehouse, then the `replacement_failed?` message will be sent. The `enqueue()` and `dequeue()` are functions to enqueue the ID of the failed BE or remove the successfully replaced BE from the queue, respectively. The variable `len` holds the length of the queue. If `len` equals zero, no failed BE is waiting to be replaced.

Warehouse. Figure 7 shows the spare warehouse automaton. There are two different types of transitions in this automaton. Solid lines indicate controllable transitions and dashed lines indicate uncontrollable transitions. The spare warehouse is the only automaton with controllable transitions. The initial state in this automaton is a *committed state.* A committed state cannot delay, and the outgoing transition of this state has the highest priority—even higher than the urgent state. As a result, outgoing transitions from this location are the first transitions made in the entire SPTGA, which is the initial decision for the spare quantity in the warehouse. This decision is the only one we can control. Normally, one of these transitions is chosen in a non-deterministic way. But if we synthesize a strategy, we can have control over these transitions (in the next section, we will discuss the strategy synthesis for determining the spare num-

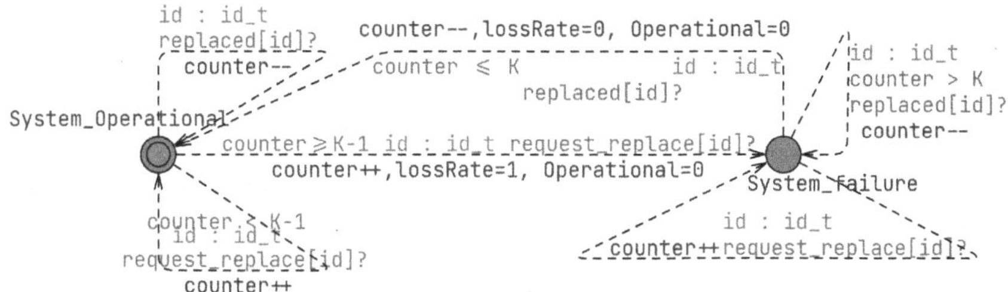

Fig. 8. The `K` out of `N` voting automaton. The **`counter`** keeps track of failed children. Variables **`Operational`** and **`lossRate`** are used only for monitoring and cost calculation purposes. The **`request_replace[id]?`** is the received signal from the corresponding BE. The **`replaced[id]?`** is the received signal from SG.

ber). After deciding on the initial amount of spares `Spare` in the warehouse, this value cannot be changed later on. The variable `SP` represents the number of available spares in the warehouse. In the beginning, `SP`'s value equals `Spare`. The variable `Cost` represents the cost, which is the total cost of buying spares and the cost of system failure. Each spare costs 0.08 units (one unit is equivalent to 1 million Argentine pesos). This cost is stored in the variable `Cost` at the beginning, and the cost of system failure is added later.

During system operations, if a replacement is needed for a failed BE, the warehouse receives the request `demand?` from SG. If a spare is available in the warehouse, the failed BE will be replaced according to an exponential rate of 0.072 per day, and the warehouse sends the `supplied!` signal to SG. Otherwise, the `replacement_failed!` signal will be transmitted.

Voting Gate. Figure 8 shows the SPTGA model for a K/N voting gate. This automaton consists of two states, `System_Operational` and `System_failure`. The `counter` keeps track of failed children.

When BE fails (`request_replace[id]?`), the `counter` value is incremented. If the `counter` value is at least `K`, then the voting gate is failed and the automaton goes into the `System_failure` state. When a failed BE is replaced (`replaced[id]?`), the `counter` value is decremented. If the total number of failed BEs (the `counter` value) is less than `K`, then the automaton goes into the `System_working` state. Variables `Operational` and `lossRate` are used only for monitoring and cost calculation purposes. The monitoring automaton is not shown in this paper since it only has one state to keep track of costs.

6 Analysis and Results

This section presents the statistical model checking results via UPPAAL STRATEGO and its requirement specification language [1].

6.1 Formal Queries

We use two types of queries for statistical model checking to calculate the desired dependability metrics: *strategy queries* and *statistical queries*.

Strategy Queries. By giving them names, strategy queries make it possible to save, load, reuse, and modify the strategies. We use this query in two ways: with the *controller synthesis queries* or *learning queries*.

Strategy as Controller Synthesis Query. Controller synthesis queries synthesize a strategy that makes a given control objective `goal` true, i.e., regardless of the environment choice, the `goal` predicate is always true. If no such strategy exists, then **`false`** is returned. The format of this query for our case is

```
strategy SPCount# = control: A[] NrOfSpares == i
```

This query computes a strategy where, regardless of the environment choice, `goal` predicate—the number of the primary spares must be equal to `i`—is always true. Such a query allows to manually fix the number of spares.

Strategy as a Learning Query. A learning query specifies the objective for which an optimal strategy should be synthesized. We use the following query:

```
strategy MinCost = minE(Cost) [<=lifetime]: <>GlobalTime==lifetime
```

Strategy `MinCost` minimizes the expected `Cost` value within the given `lifetime` (e.g., 40 years which is equivalent to 14 600 days). In order to determine the strategy for exactly the given lifetime, we use the predicate `GlobalTime==lifetime` that stops together with the simulation time bound. `GlobalTime` is a clock that is never reset.

Statistical Queries. We use statistical queries to formally specify the analysis metrics $Q_1^A, \dots, Q_m^A$ from Sect. 2.4.

```
E [<=lifetime;100000] (max: Cost) under Strategy_Name
```

This query estimates the maximal value of `Cost` within the given time span by running 100 000 simulations. The `under Strategy_Name` indicates that the query is subjected to the strategy `Strategy_Name`.

```
E [<=lifetime;100000] (max: ODay/lifetime) under Strategy_Name
```

This query is similar to the previous one, except that the estimated value is the system's availability. Variable `ODay` stores the operational time of the system.

```
Pr[<=lifetime] (<> DTime>0) under Strategy_Name
```

This query estimates the probability that the system is down at all within its lifetime. Variable `DTime` stores the downtime of the system.

6.2 Analysis Results

We limit our following analysis to the neutron flux subsystem. This component type has significantly higher costs than the other ones and thus, optimal spare management is most crucial here.

Table 2. Changed settings in UPPAAL

	Number of successful runs	Maximum number of runs	Number of good runs	Number of runs to evaluate	Probability uncertainty
Default value	200	500	100	100	0.05
Our value	20,000	50,000	10,000	1,000,000	0.01

Table 3. Verification results

Query	Result	Comp. time
`strategy MinCost = minE(Cost) [<=14600]: <> GlobalTime==14600`	✓	411.00 s
`E [<=14600;100000] (min: Spare) under MinCost`	6	0.01 s
`strategy SPCount6 = control: A[] Spare==6`	✓	0.01 s
`E [<=14600;100000] (max: Cost) under SPCount6`	0.488 ± 0.0030	2.46 s
`E [<=14600;100000] (max: ODay/14600) under SPCount6`	0.99965 ± 0.00009	2.45 s
`Pr[<=14600] (<> DTime>0) under SPCount6`	≤ 0.0009	0.02 s

Settings. We run our experiments on a MacBook Air with M1 chip and 16 GB RAM. We use UPPAAL 5.0, which includes UPPAAL STRATEGO. We run the statistical queries with a confidence interval of 95%. We changed some of UPPAAL's default settings to capture rare events and increase accuracy, see Table 2 for the details. Except for the probability uncertainty, which is related to statistical model checking, the other four parameters relate to UPPAAL STRATEGO's learning algorithm.

Results. Table 3 shows the results of the strategy and statistical queries performed on the SPTGA from Sect. 5. First, learning query `MinCost` is used to synthesize the optimal number of spares needed to reduce the cost. The second query then yields this optimal number of spares, which is 6. After finding the optimal number of spares, we use a controller synthesis query to obtain a new strategy `SPCount6` that fixes the spares' number. Afterwards, we analyse this configuration w.r.t. the given statistical queries. The expected cost—the sum of the spares' cost and the cost due to unavailability—with six spares is $488k. Most of the cost stems from the cost of the spares ($480k). The system's availability is 99.96% which corresponds to an expected downtime of 6 days. The probability of encountering a system failure within 40 years is less than 9E−4. This can also be seen in Fig. 9 which shows the probability of having any downtime for different spare numbers.

Figure 10 shows the overall cost (in logarithmic scale) for different number of spares. We see that six spares indeed minimize the cost. For fewer than six spares, the cost due to system failure is too large, whereas for more than six spares, the cost of the spares becomes the major factor. In particular, buying more than six spares incurs more expenses but only marginally decreases downtime.

6.3 Discussion

Rare Events. For six spares, the probability of any downtime within 40 years is less than 9E−4. Thus, a system failure is a rare event and most of the time, the system will not be down at all. However, even one system failure has drastic consequences ($1 million loss per day). It is, therefore, crucial to take these rare events into account. However, statistical model checking has issues with rare events and we had to significantly increase the number of runs in UPPAAL to obtain correct results. With the default settings of UPPAAL STRATEGO, the strategy synthesis returned an incorrect number of spares—due to neglecting rare events. We discovered this issue by performing standard statistical model checking for a fixed number of spares, similar to Fig. 10. By increasing the number of simulation runs (cf. Table 2), we obtained the correct number of spares, again validated by statistical model checking.

Model Flexibility. In our SPTGA model, we use controllable transitions to choose the initial number of spares. This allows to use controller synthesis queries to manually fix the number of spares—instead of creating multiple models for different numbers of spares. This modeling choice also provides flexibility for future extensions where a larger number of configurations need to be considered, such as synthesizing spare numbers for multiple components. Instead of exhaustively checking all possible configurations, this approach allows the use of UPPAAL STRATEGO's optimization algorithms to find the best configuration.

Performance. We started with UPPAAL STRATEGO version 4.1.20 but switched to the recently released UPPAAL 5.0 as the latter performed significantly faster. The `MinCost` strategy synthesis took several days in UPPAAL STRATEGO 4.1.20, but only minutes in UPPAAL 5.0.

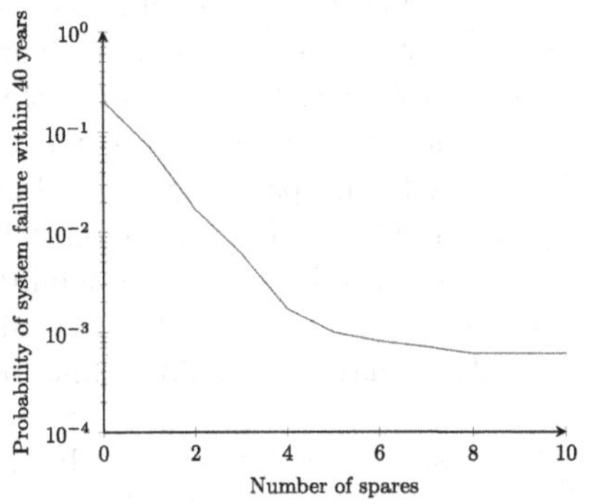

Fig. 9. Probability of any system failure within 40 years

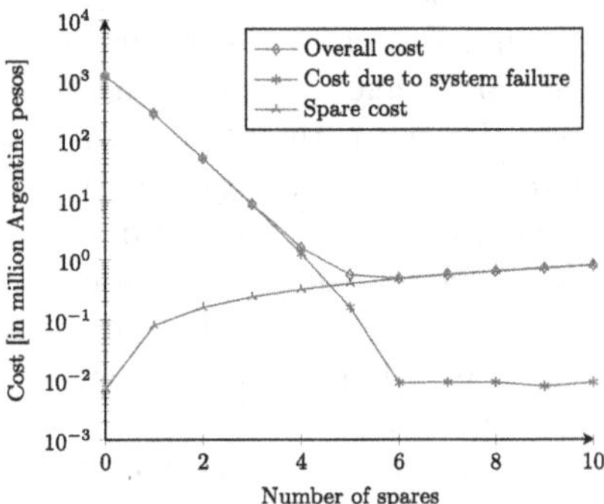

Fig. 10. Costs for different number of spares.

7 Conclusion and Future Work

We presented an approach for optimal spare management by combining fault tree analysis and statistical model checking. Our approach finds the optimal number of spares as a trade-off between costs and reliability. Given fault trees equipped with costs and spares, we translate them into SPTGA and use UPPAAL STRATEGO to synthesize an optimal strategy, i.e., the optimal number of spares. We applied our approach to a section of the emergency shutdown system of a research reactor. Using UPPAAL STRATEGO, we found the optimal number of spares (6 spares) within minutes.

Future work includes extending our approach to larger systems with multiple types of components as well as adding a dynamic warehouse model that includes delivery times, reordering of components, etc.

References

1. UPPAAL requirements specification language. https://docs.uppaal.org/language-reference/requirements-specification/. Accessed 26 May 2023
2. Artefact for "Optimal spare management via statistical model checking: a case study in research reactors. Zenodo, May 2023. https://doi.org/10.5281/zenodo.7970835
3. Behrmann, G., Cougnard, A., David, A., Fleury, E., Larsen, K.G., Lime, D.: UPPAAL-Tiga: time for playing games! In: Damm, W., Hermanns, H. (eds.) CAV 2007. LNCS, vol. 4590, pp. 121–125. Springer, Heidelberg (2007). https://doi.org/10.1007/978-3-540-73368-3_14
4. Boudali, H., Crouzen, P., Stoelinga, M.: Dynamic fault tree analysis using input/output interactive Markov chains. In: DSN, pp. 708–717. IEEE Computer Society (2007). https://doi.org/10.1109/DSN.2007.37
5. Bulychev, P.E., et al.: UPPAAL-SMC: statistical model checking for priced timed automata. In: QAPL. EPTCS, vol. 85, pp. 1–16 (2012). https://doi.org/10.4204/EPTCS.85.1
6. Chatain, T., David, A., Larsen, K.G.: Playing games with timed games. In: ADHS. IFAC Proceedings Volumes, vol. 42, pp. 238–243. Elsevier (2009). https://doi.org/10.3182/20090916-3-ES-3003.00042
7. Chen, F., Chen, Y., Kuo, J.: Applying moving back-propagation neural network and moving fuzzy-neuron network to predict the requirement of critical spare parts. Expert Syst. Appl. **37**(9), 6695–6704 (2010). https://doi.org/10.1016/j.eswa.2010.04.037
8. David, A., et al.: On time with minimal expected cost! In: Cassez, F., Raskin, J.-F. (eds.) ATVA 2014. LNCS, vol. 8837, pp. 129–145. Springer, Cham (2014). https://doi.org/10.1007/978-3-319-11936-6_10
9. David, A., Jensen, P.G., Larsen, K.G., Mikučionis, M., Taankvist, J.H.: UPPAAL STRATEGO. In: Baier, C., Tinelli, C. (eds.) TACAS 2015. LNCS, vol. 9035, pp. 206–211. Springer, Heidelberg (2015). https://doi.org/10.1007/978-3-662-46681-0_16
10. David, A., et al.: Statistical model checking for networks of priced timed automata. In: Fahrenberg, U., Tripakis, S. (eds.) FORMATS 2011. LNCS, vol. 6919, pp. 80–96. Springer, Heidelberg (2011). https://doi.org/10.1007/978-3-642-24310-3_7

11. Gutierrez, R.S., Solis, A.O., Mukhopadhyay, S.: Lumpy demand forecasting using neural networks. Int. J. Prod. Econ. **111**(2), 409–420 (2008). https://doi.org/10.1016/j.ijpe.2007.01.007, special Section on Sustainable Supply Chain
12. Heijblom, R., Postma, W., Natarajan, V., Stoelinga, M.: DFT analysis incorporating spare parts in fault trees. In: 2018 Annual Reliability and Maintainability Symposium (RAMS), pp. 1–7 (2018). https://doi.org/10.1109/RAM.2018.8463074
13. Hu, Q., Boylan, J.E., Chen, H., Labib, A.: OR in spare parts management: a review. Eur. J. Oper. Res. **266**(2), 395–414 (2018). https://doi.org/10.1016/j.ejor.2017.07.058
14. Kabir, S.: An overview of fault tree analysis and its application in model based dependability analysis. Expert Syst. Appl. **77**, 114–135 (2017). https://doi.org/10.1016/j.eswa.2017.01.058
15. Kourentzes, N.: Intermittent demand forecasts with neural networks. Int. J. Prod. Econ. **143**(1), 198–206 (2013). https://doi.org/10.1016/j.ijpe.2013.01.009
16. Kumar, R., Ruijters, E., Stoelinga, M.: Quantitative attack tree analysis via priced timed automata. In: Sankaranarayanan, S., Vicario, E. (eds.) FORMATS 2015. LNCS, vol. 9268, pp. 156–171. Springer, Cham (2015). https://doi.org/10.1007/978-3-319-22975-1_11
17. Kumar, R., Stoelinga, M.: Quantitative security and safety analysis with attack-fault trees. In: HASE, pp. 25–32. IEEE Computer Society (2017). https://doi.org/10.1109/HASE.2017.12
18. Legay, A., Delahaye, B., Bensalem, S.: Statistical model checking: an overview. In: Barringer, H., et al. (eds.) RV 2010. LNCS, vol. 6418, pp. 122–135. Springer, Heidelberg (2010). https://doi.org/10.1007/978-3-642-16612-9_11
19. Li, S.G., Kuo, X.: The inventory management system for automobile spare parts in a central warehouse. Expert Syst. Appl. **34**(2), 1144–1153 (2008). https://doi.org/10.1016/j.eswa.2006.12.003
20. Maler, O., Pnueli, A., Sifakis, J.: On the synthesis of discrete controllers for timed systems. In: Mayr, E.W., Puech, C. (eds.) STACS 1995. LNCS, vol. 900, pp. 229–242. Springer, Heidelberg (1995). https://doi.org/10.1007/3-540-59042-0_76
21. Ruijters, E., Guck, D., van Noort, M., Stoelinga, M.: Reliability-centered maintenance of the electrically insulated railway joint via fault tree analysis: a practical experience report. In: DSN, pp. 662–669. IEEE Computer Society (2016). https://doi.org/10.1109/DSN.2016.67
22. Ruijters, E., Stoelinga, M.: Fault tree analysis: a survey of the state-of-the-art in modeling, analysis and tools. Comput. Sci. Rev. **15**, 29–62 (2015). https://doi.org/10.1016/j.cosrev.2015.03.001
23. Ruijters, E., Stoelinga, M.: Better railway engineering through statistical model checking. In: Margaria, T., Steffen, B. (eds.) ISoLA 2016. LNCS, vol. 9952, pp. 151–165. Springer, Cham (2016). https://doi.org/10.1007/978-3-319-47166-2_10
24. Ţusar, M.I.H., Sarker, B.R.: Spare parts control strategies for offshore wind farms: a critical review and comparative study. Wind Eng. **46**(5), 1629–1656 (2022). https://doi.org/10.1177/0309524X221095258
25. Wu, P., Hung, Y., Lin, Z.: Intelligent forecasting system based on integration of electromagnetism-like mechanism and fuzzy neural network. Expert Syst. Appl. **41**(6), 2660–2677 (2014). https://doi.org/10.1016/j.eswa.2013.11.007
26. Zhang, S., Huang, K., Yuan, Y.: Spare parts inventory management: a literature review. Sustainability **13**(5) (2021). https://doi.org/10.3390/su13052460

27. Zhang, X., Zeng, J.: Joint optimization of condition-based opportunistic maintenance and spare parts provisioning policy in multiunit systems. Eur. J. Oper. Res. **262**(2), 479–498 (2017). https://doi.org/10.1016/j.ejor.2017.03.019
28. Zheng, M., Ye, H., Wang, D., Pan, E.: Joint optimization of condition-based maintenance and spare parts orders for multi-unit systems with dual sourcing. Reliab. Eng. Syst. Saf. **210**, 107512 (2021). https://doi.org/10.1016/j.ress.2021.107512

Applying Rely-Guarantee Reasoning on Concurrent Memory Management and Mailbox in μC/OS-II: A Case Study

Huan Sun, Ziyu Mao, Jingyi Wang(✉), Ziyan Zhao, and Wenhai Wang(✉)

Zhejiang University, Hangzhou, China
{huansun,maoziyu,wangjyee,zhaoziyan,zdzzlab}@zju.edu.cn

Abstract. Real-time operating systems (RTOSs) such as μC/OS-II are critical components of many industrial systems, which makes it of vital importance to verify their correctness. However, earlier specifications for verification of RTOSs often do not explicitly specify the behavior of possible unbounded kernel service invocations. To address the problem, a new event-based modelling approach is recently proposed to treat the operating system as a concurrent reactive system (CRS). Besides, a respective parametric rely-guarantee style reasoning framework called PiCore is developed to verify such systems effectively. Witnessing the advancement, we conduct a case study to investigate the use of PiCore to compositionally verify two important entangled modules of a practical RTOS μC/OS-II, i.e., the memory management module and the mailbox module. Several desirable safety properties regarding the memory pools and mailboxes are formally defined and proved with PiCore ($\approx$ 2500 lines of specifications and proof scripts in Isabelle/HOL) based on a formal execution model considering the two modules simultaneously. We also discuss the shortcomings of PiCore for our case study and present possible improvement directions.

1 Introduction

Real-time operating systems (RTOSs) are the fundamental basis to support real-time applications. They provide a framework for effectively managing the execution of tasks and interrupts, ensuring that critical tasks are given sufficient priority so that timing constraints are met. This is achieved by the cooperation of several important mechanisms integrated within an RTOS: 1) scheduling mechanisms that determine whether and how tasks should execute, 2) mechanisms for managing system resources such as memory and processing power, and 3) inter-process communication (IPC) mechanisms that enable different processes or threads to exchange information and synchronize their activities.

Nowadays, RTOSs are increasingly adopted in various safety-critical industrial control systems, including aerospace, automotive, and medical devices. Every single bug or vulnerability presented in the RTOSs can have far-reaching

A. Cimatti and L. Titolo (Eds.): FMICS 2023, LNCS 14290, pp. 224–241, 2023.
https://doi.org/10.1007/978-3-031-43681-9_13

consequences since it could affect multiple tasks and subsystems within the system, leading to catastrophic failures that result in injuries or even loss of life. Formal verification is a promising approach to ensure that the system behaves as intended, even in complex or unforeseen situations. However, verifying an RTOS is not an easy task, as in principle it requires capturing the interactions of many concurrent kernel services and the possible unbounded sequences of kernel service invocations. There are many verification methods, such as rely-guarantee [19], concurrent separation logic [12], and Owicki-Gries [22], designed for reasoning concurrent imperative programs. However, when attempting to apply these methods to model reactive systems [14], it can lead to unnecessary complications in the verification process.

More recently, a new event-based modelling and verification approach called PiCore [2] has been proposed to treat the operating system as a concurrent reactive system (CRS) that effectively captures the potentially unbounded number of kernel service invocations. At a high level, a CRS [1] can be conceptualized as an ongoing loop that receives input from the environment and executes the relevant event handlers. An RTOS can be modelled as a CRS in the sense that it accepts requests from applications and executes the appropriate kernel services. PiCore introduces an event-based language for defining the behavior of CRSs and a corresponding verification framework that follows the rely-guarantee style. With PiCore, it is possible to perform compositional specification and verification at the low program level for an RTOS. Notably, PiCore has been applied to verify Zephyr's memory management module with success [3].

In this work, we take one step further to investigate the use of PiCore by conducting a case study to compositionally verify two entangled modules: the memory management module and the mailbox module in the context of another widely adopted RTOS in industry, μC/OS-II [21]. μC/OS-II is a portable commercial preemptive real-time multitasking OS kernel intended for microprocessors, microcontrollers, and DSPs. It consists of 6000+ lines of C code and is designed to provide efficient multitasking capabilities in embedded systems. Several desirable safety properties regarding the memory pools and mailboxes are formally defined and proved with PiCore based on a formal execution model considering the two modules simultaneously. What's more, our study highlights some limitations of the existing rely-guarantee style reasoning frameworks, such as PiCore, for the verification system consisting of multiple entangled modules influencing each other: in particular, this may result in unnecessary specifications of irrelevant state space and obvious non-existing environmental interference. The important implication is that, although PiCore is effective, a more convenient modelling and verification approach for CRSs is in need to ease the effort for verifying practical RTOSs with multiple entangled modules in place.

The main contributions of this case study are summarized as follows:

1. We provide a formal execution model considering two important modules in μC/OS-II simultaneously: the memory management module and the mailbox module together with the formal specifications for scheduling, memory allocation/deallocation, and inter-process communication services.

2. We analyze the safety properties of memory pools and mailboxes in μC/OS-II and formally define them as system invariants that should be preserved during the execution of kernel services.
3. We prove the functional correctness and invariant preservation of the two modules mentioned above by using PiCore. The formal specification and correctness proof are developed in Isabelle/HOL using $\approx$ 2500 lines of specifications and proof scripts.
4. Our study shows existing rely-guarantee frameworks like PiCore may lead to certain unnecessary specifications of irrelevant state space and environmental interference when verifying systems with multiple entangled modules.

2 Background

In this section, we give an overview of rely-guarantee reasoning, concurrent reactive system, and semantics of PiCore.

2.1 Rely-Guarantee Reasoning

Rely-guarantee reasoning [19] is a well-known method for the compositional verification of concurrent programs with fine-grained interference. A rely-guarantee specification for a program is typically represented by a quadruple $RGCond = \langle pre, R, G, post \rangle$, where pre and $post$ are sets of states that represent the state before and after system execution, respectively. In this method, each thread perceives the set of all other threads in the system as its environment. The interaction between a thread and its environment is defined using a pair of rely and guarantee conditions. The rely condition denoted as R, describes state transitions caused by the environment, while the guarantee condition, denoted as G, describes state transitions caused by the verified system.

A thread's satisfaction of its rely-guarantee specification is denoted by $\vdash P$ **sat** $\langle pre, R, G, pst \rangle$. It indicates that if the thread is executed from a state $s \in pre$, and the state transitions caused by the environment and the thread itself are included in R and G, respectively, then the resulting state after system execution must be included in $post$.

To compositionally verify the parallel program, e.g., $C_1 \parallel C_2$, we can verify the threads C_1 and C_2 separately and then compose the proof of the individual threads using the PAR rule shown below:

$$\frac{[\textsc{Par}] \quad \vdash C_1 \ \textbf{sat} \ \langle pre, R \vee G_2, G_1, pst_1 \rangle \qquad \vdash C_2 \ \textbf{sat} \ \langle pre, R \vee G_1, G_2, pst_2 \rangle}{\vdash C_1 \parallel C_2 \ \textbf{sat} \ \langle pre, R, G_1 \vee G_2, pst1 \wedge pst_2 \rangle}$$

To ensure successful collaboration between the parallel threads, we need to check that their interfaces are compatible. This means that the rely condition of each thread is implied by the guarantee of the other thread, i.e., $G_1 \subseteq R \vee G_2$ and $G_2 \subseteq R \vee G_1$.

2.2 Concurrent Reactive System and PiCore

Reactive systems are comprised of a set of event handlers that enable the system to respond to environmental stimuli. These stimuli can include various events, such as the clicking of a graphical user interface (GUI) button, the execution of a command at a terminal, the receipt of a network packet, or hardware interruptions in preemptive systems, among others. Essentially, any program that computes in response to events can be considered as a reactive system.

In the concurrent settings, the event handlers within a reactive system have the capability to interact with the execution of other handlers. For example, in multicore architectures, multiple event handlers may run in parallel, allowing them to interact with each other's execution. This concurrent interaction can lead to complex behaviors and coordination challenges, making verifying and synchronizing such systems a crucial aspect of their design and implementation.

Existing rely-guarantee frameworks are typically designed for imperative programs, and when attempting to simulate reactive systems, the complexity of the program and rely-guarantee conditions can increase unnecessarily. To address this issue, PiCore is introduced as a parametric two-level event-based rely-guarantee framework specifically designed for CRSs which is implemented in Isabelle/HOL. The first level of PiCore deals with system behavior, i.e., how and when the event is triggered. The second level deals with the behavior of event handlers which can be instantiated by rely-guarantee frameworks designed for imperative language. In this case study, we instantiated PiCore with Isabelle's built-in rely-guarantee library HOL-Hoare_Parallel [27].

The small-step semantics of PiCore is shown in Fig. 1. At the system reaction level, PiCore considers a CRS as the parallel of reactive systems where each reactive system is a set of event handlers called event systems responding to stimuli from the environment. An example of a typical event is as follows:

$$\textbf{EVENT}\ \mathcal{E}\ [p_1, ..., p_n]@k\ \textbf{WHEN}\ g\ \textbf{THEN}\ P\ \textbf{END}$$

where $\mathcal{E}$ and g define the event's name and trigger conditions respectively. The guard g regulates the context when starting the reaction service, such as parameters of an invocation or occurrence of I/O events. BasicEvt specifies that when the guard of an event holds in the current state, its body starts executing. The execution of an event system concerns the continuous evaluation of guards of the events with their input arguments. From the set of events for which their associated guard condition holds in the current state, one event is non-deterministically selected to be triggered, and its body executed. After the event finishes, the evaluation of guards starts again looking for the next event to be executed. The semantics of the event system are captured by EvtSeq1, EvtSeq2, and EvtSet. The Par rule demonstrates the non-deterministic interleaving of event systems which models different event systems executing concurrently.

$$\text{[InnerEvt]}\ \frac{(P, s) \xrightarrow{c} (P', s')}{(\lfloor P \rfloor, s, x) \xrightarrow{c@k} (\lfloor P' \rfloor, s', x)} \qquad \text{[BasicEvt]}\ \frac{P = body(\alpha) \quad s \in guard(\alpha) \quad x' = x(k \mapsto \textbf{Event}\ \alpha)}{(\textbf{Event}\ \alpha, s, x) \xrightarrow{\textbf{Event}\ \alpha @\kappa} (\lfloor P \rfloor, s, x')}$$

$$\text{[EvtSet]}\ \frac{i \leq n \quad (\mathcal{E}_i, s, x) \xrightarrow{\mathcal{E}_i @\kappa} (\mathcal{E}'_i, s, x')}{(\{\mathcal{E}_0,\ ...,\ \mathcal{E}_n\}, s, x) \xrightarrow{\mathcal{E}_i @\kappa} (\mathcal{E}'_i \oplus \{\mathcal{E}_0,\ ...,\ \mathcal{E}_n\}, s, x')} \qquad \text{[EvtSeq1]}\ \frac{(\mathcal{E}, s, x) \xrightarrow{t@\kappa} (\mathcal{E}', s', x') \quad \mathcal{E}' \neq \lfloor \bot \rfloor}{(\mathcal{E} \oplus \mathcal{S}, s, x) \xrightarrow{t@\kappa} (\mathcal{E}' \oplus \mathcal{S}, s', x')}$$

$$\text{[EvtSeq2]}\ \frac{(\mathcal{E}, s, x) \xrightarrow{t@\kappa} (\lfloor \bot \rfloor, s', x')}{(\mathcal{E} \oplus \mathcal{S}, s, x) \xrightarrow{t@\kappa} (\mathcal{S}, s', x')} \qquad \text{[Par]}\ \frac{(\mathcal{PS}(\kappa), s, x) \xrightarrow{t@\kappa} (\mathcal{S}', s', x') \quad \mathcal{PS}' = \mathcal{PS}(\kappa \mapsto \mathcal{S}')}{(\mathcal{PS}, s, x) \xrightarrow{t@\kappa} (\mathcal{PS}', s', x')}$$

Fig. 1. Operational Semantics of PiCore

3 Kernel Services in μC/OS-II

In this section, we introduce the memory management and mailbox services of μC/OS-II, which are responsible for memory allocation/deallocation and inter-process communication. We begin by discussing the data structures of the memory pool and mailbox. Then we explain the mechanisms of memory management and mailbox modules services. Finally, we define several safety properties to demonstrate the safety invariants that must be maintained throughout the execution of the memory management and mailbox services.

3.1 Data Structure

```
/* MEMORY CONTROL BLOCK */
typedef struct os_mem{
    void    *OSMemAddr;
    void    *OSMemFreeList;
    INT32U  OSMemblkSize;
    INT32U  OSMemNblks;
    INT32U  OSMemNFree;
} OS_MEM;
```

```
/* EVENT CONTROL BLOCK */
typedef struct {
    void     *OSEventPtr;
    INT8U     OSEventType;
    INT16U    OSEventCnt;
    OS_PRIO   OSEventGrp;
    OS_PRIO   OSEventTbl[OS_EVENT_TBL_SIZE];
} OS_EVENT;
```

Fig. 2. The Data Structure of Memory Pool and ECB in μC/OS-II

Memory Pool. μC/OS-II employs a contiguous memory region to provide fixed-size memory chunks. Memory allocation and deallocation operations are deterministic and executed in constant time. Users of μC/OS-II can allocate and deallocate memory blocks of varying sizes at runtime. Figure 2 shows the memory control block. The variable *OSMemAddr* is the starting address of the memory partition. The variable *OSMemFreeList* refers to a list of free memory blocks, with each block's size defined by *OSMemBlkSize*. The total number of memory blocks in the partition is recorded by *OSMemNBlk*, while *OSMemNFree* records the number of free memory blocks in the partition.

Event Control Block. A mailbox in μC/OS-II is an instance of an Event Control Block (ECB), which is a data structure used by μC/OS-II to manage synchronization and communication between tasks in a real-time embedded system. To create a mailbox, one must call OSMboxCreate and successfully allocate an ECB from the free list. The variable *OSEventType* denotes the type of synchronization object associated with the ECB. After successfully creating a Mailbox, the *OSEventType* is set to 0×01, as indicated in the source code [11]. Variables *OSEventGrp* and *OSEventTbl* record the information on tasks that are currently waiting on the synchronization object. Since the initial wait list is empty, *OSEventGrp* and *OSEventTbl* are set to 0×00. The handler of the mailbox is returned as a pointer. The message or resource to be shared is stored in the variable *OSEventPtr*.

3.2 Mechanism of Kernel Services

Memory Management Service. μC/OS-II provides two kernel services for memory management, OSMemGet and OSMemPut, which are responsible for memory allocation and deallocation respectively. μC/OS-II uses an implicitly linked list to connect each memory block which can be accessed by the variable *OSMemFreeList*. Each memory block's starting address is used to store the address of the next free memory block. μC/OS-II constructs the linked list from the memory block itself, significantly improving memory consumption efficiency. Each memory block should be large enough to store at least one pointer. When a user requests a memory block, an element is removed from the linked list's head, and when a user releases a memory block, the memory block is added to the linked list's head. The memory in the memory partition can only be accessed after calling OSMemGet to retrieve the memory, as the initial address of each memory block in the memory partition is used to store a pointer. Directly manipulating memory blocks in the partition is not allowed.

MailBox Service. μC/OS-II mainly provides three kernel services for communication through the mailbox: OSMboxPost, OSMboxAccept, and OSMboxPend, which are responsible for posting messages, getting messages in an unblocking way, and getting messages in a blocking way, respectively.

The OSMboxPost first checks whether the mailbox is available, i.e., it is not currently being used by any other threads, and the message pointer of the mailbox is not NULL. If the mailbox is available and no threads are waiting for the message from the mailbox (i.e., the wait list is empty), the message is stored in the mailbox, then marks the mailbox as full. Once the message is stored successfully, the mailbox allows any thread invoking OSMboxPend to retrieve the message immediately. If there are threads waiting for messages on wait list, the thread with the highest priority is removed from the wait list after receiving

```
/*  MEMORY ALLOCATION  */
void *OSMemGet (OS_MEM *pmem,
    INT8U *perr)
{
    OS_ENTER_CRITICAL();
    if (pmem->OSMemNFree > 0U){
        pblk = pmem->OSMemFreeList;
        pmem->OSMemFreeList =
            *(void **)pblk;
        pmem->OSMemNFree--;
        OS_EXIT_CRITICAL();
        *perr = OS_ERR_NONE;
        return (pblk);
    }
}
```

```
/*  MEMORY RELEASE  */
void *OSMemPut (OS_MEM *pmem, void
    *pblk)
{
    OS_ENTER_CRITICAL();
    if (pmem->OSMemNFree >=
        pmem->OSMemNBlk){
    OS_EXIT_CRITICAL();
    return (OS_ERR_MEM_FULL);
    }
    *(void **)pblk =
        pmem->OSMemFreeList;
    pmem->OSMemFreeList = pblk;
    pmem->OSMemNFree++;
    OS_EXIT_CRITICAL();
    return (OS_ERR_NONE);
}
```

Fig. 3. The C Source Code of Memory Service in μC/OS-II

the message posted to the mailbox. The thread is then set to unblocked (i.e., ready to run), and a context switch is made. However, if the target mailbox does not exist (i.e., the handler is NULL), or the mailbox is full at the point of posting a message, or the posted message is NULL, OSMboxPost will return the corresponding error message.

The OSMboxAccept service enables a thread to get a message from the mailbox in a non-blocking way. If a message is present in the mailbox, OSMboxAccept returns a pointer to the message and marks the mailbox as empty. If the mailbox does not contain any message, OSMboxAccept returns NULL immediately. Unlike the OSMboxPend service, which blocks the calling thread until a message is available, OSMboxAccept does not block the thread. This means that the task can continue executing even if a message is not available in the mailbox.

The OSMboxPend function allows a thread to get a message from the mailbox in a blocking way, i.e., the thread waits for messages until a message is available. It also accepts a parameter timeout, which specifies the duration for which the thread should wait for a message. If there is already a message present in the mailbox, the thread can receive the message and mark the mailbox as empty. Otherwise, if the mailbox is empty, the thread is suspended and added to the mailbox's wait list. The timeout value specifies the maximum waiting time, and if it is set to zero, the thread will wait forever until a message is posted to the mailbox. Otherwise, the threads on the wait list will be blocked until receive messages from the mailbox or the time limit expires. The OSMboxPend function is often used together with the OSMboxPost function. By using message mailboxes and the OSMboxPend/OSMboxPost services, threads can conveniently communicate and synchronize with each other in a multitasking environment.

```
/* EXCERPT OSMboxPend SERVICE */
void *OSMboxPend (OS_EVENT *p,
     INT16U timeout, INT8U *err)
{
    OS_ENTER_CRITICAL();
    msg = p->OSEventPtr;
    if (msg != (void *)0) {
        p->OSEventPtr = (void *)0;
        OS_EXIT_CRITICAL();
        *err = OS_NO_ERR;
        return (msg);
    }
    OSTCBCur->OSTCBStat |=
         OS_STAT_MBOX;
    OSTCBCur->OSTCBDly = timeout;
    OS_EventTaskWait(pevent);
    OS_EXIT_CRITICAL();
    OS_Sched();
    OS_ENTER_CRITICAL();
    msg = OSTCBCur->OSTCBMsg;
    if (msg != (void *)0) {
        OSTCBCur->OSTCBMsg =
             (void *)0;
        OSTCBCur->OSTCBStat =
             OS_STAT_RDY;
        OSTCBCur->OSTCBEventPtr =
             (OS_EVENT *)0;
        OS_EXIT_CRITICAL();
        *err = OS_NO_ERR;
        /*  NO ERROR  */
        return (msg);
    }
    OS_EventTO(p);
    OS_EXIT_CRITICAL();
    *err = OS_TIMEOUT;
    /*    TIMEOUT    */
    return ((void *)0);
}
```

Fig. 4. The Excerpt C Source Code of Mailbox Service in μC/OS-II

3.3 Safety Invariants of Kernel Service

The safety invariants of the system, which must be maintained during execution, are defined in Table 1. The safety invariant is divided into three parts that specify the correctness of data structures for the scheduler, memory pools, and mailboxes, respectively.

For the scheduler, we need to ensure that (1) the currently executing thread is in RUNNING state during the execution of the system.

For memory pools, the critical aspect of the memory service in μC/OS-II is manipulating the free list. Therefore, our invariant focuses on the correctness of the free list in the memory pool structure. We need to ensure (2) the number of blocks ≥ 0 (3) the number of free blocks ≥ 0 (4) the number of blocks $\geq$ the number of free blocks and (5) the number of free blocks = length of the free list.

For mailboxes, we focus on the safety property of the wait list, which can be explained in three aspects: (6) One mailbox can have multiple threads waiting for messages which are set to be BLOCKED; (7) for any mailbox in the mailbox pool, the threads in its wait list are distinct; (8) for different mailboxes in the pool, a thread can occur in at most one wait list (which means that there is no thread waiting for messages from two different mailboxes simultaneously). The threads in the wait list have different levels of priority, and here we assume that the head thread of the wait list has the highest priority to get the message. After a message has been posted to the mailbox, the head thread will be removed from the list.

Then the safety invariant of the entire system executing memory management and mailbox services can be defined by the following equation:

$$inv = inv\_cur \wedge inv\_num\_blks \wedge inv\_free\_blks \wedge inv\_overflow \\ \wedge inv\_len\_list \wedge inv\_blocked \wedge inv\_no\_cross \wedge inv\_no\_dup.$$

Table 1. Invariant Specification of Memory Management and Mailbox Module

Invariant	Description
inv_cur	currently executing thread is in RUNNING state
inv_num_blks	*number of blocks* $\geq$ 0
inv_free_blks	*number of free blocks* $\geq$ 0
inv_overflow	*number of blocks* $\geq$ *number of free blocks*
inv_len_list	*number of free blocks* = *length of free list*
inv_blocked	Any thread in wait list is in a BLOCKED state
inv_no_cross	Threads in wait list are distinct
inv_no_dup	A thread can not appear in two different wait lists

4 Formal Modelling of Kernel Services of μC/OS-II

For system-level modelling, we use PiCore [2], a rely-guarantee reasoning framework for modelling CRSs. PiCore enables the capture of possible unbounded sequences of event handlers and the input arguments passed to event handlers. This feature is useful for modelling the behavior of μC/OS-II where multiple threads constantly invoke kernel services by passing corresponding arguments to kernel functions. For language-level modelling, we utilize Isabelle's built-in library HOL-Hoare_Parallel to specify the C code of kernel functions.

In this section, we present the PiCore model for the execution of μC/OS-II kernel services and introduce the formal specification of kernel services using HOL-Hoare_Parallel.

4.1 Execution Model of μC/OS-II

The execution model of μC/OS-II is shown in Fig. 5. At a high level, the execution of μC/OS-II is modelled as a CRS which receives the invocation of kernel service with parameters from the environment and executes the corresponding kernel functions. Our work mainly focuses on the memory management module and mailbox module. As a result, the entire operating system is modelled as a parallel event system $\mathcal{S} \parallel \mathcal{T}_1 \parallel ... \parallel \mathcal{T}_n$. The parallel event system is composed of an event system $\mathcal{S}$ which determines threads that need to be executed, and multiple event systems $\mathcal{T}_i$ that invoke kernel services constantly. $\mathcal{S}$ is a singleton event system that can execute the event **ScheduleE** to perform the schedule function. $\mathcal{T}_i$ is an event set that can execute five events: **OSMemGetE**, **OSMemPutE**, **OSMboxPostE**, **OSMboxAcceptE**, and **OSMboxPendE**. The scheduler's execution is atomic since no other threads may interrupt it, but the thread's execution may be interrupted by the scheduler. The execution of kernel functions is concurrent so the different event systems may interfere with each other.

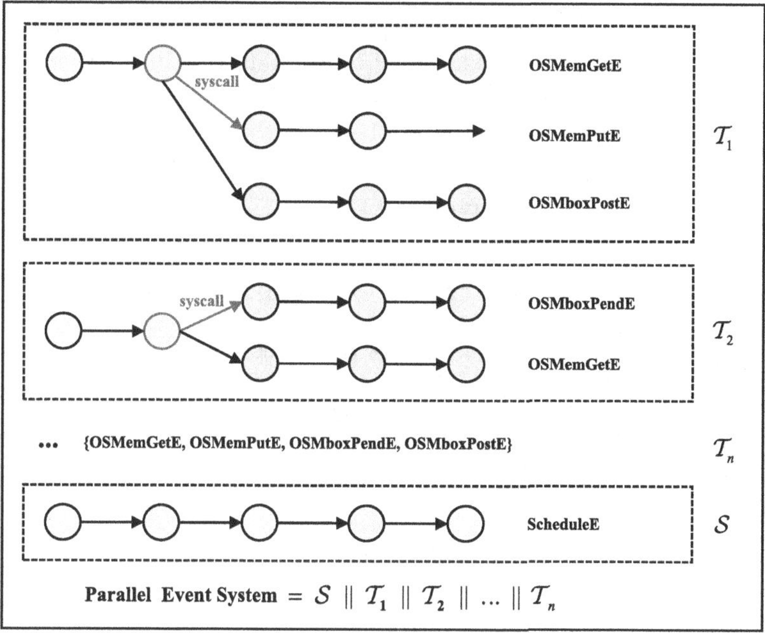

Fig. 5. Execution Model of μC/OS-II

4.2 Formal Specification of Kernel Service of μC/OS-II

The Isabelle/HOL built-in library adopts the "record as state" modelling approach which views the state as functions from variable names to their values to provide a uniform representation of the state space for every program. It also offers standard programming constructs, such as sequential composition, conditional statements, and loops, enabling the simulation of imperative programming languages like C.

State Definition. The record *State* in Isabelle determines how the memory management module and the mailbox are configured. The state is separated into two portions, one representing global variables shared by all threads and the other representing local variables that can only be accessed by one thread. Our program state is defined as follows. The variable *cur* represents the currently executing thread, which could be a specified thread ID or NULL. The variable *tick* records the clock tick of the system which is used to check the timeout in the Mailbox service. The variable *thd_state* records the threads' running state. The memory *OS_MEMs* is depicted as a set of *OS_MEM_ref* that stores all memory pool references. The mapping *OS_MEM_info* allows querying a single memory pool through its reference. The mailbox pool, which contains all accessible mailbox instances, is modelled as a set of *mailbox_ref*. The mapping of *OSMailbox_info* also allows querying a single mailbox through its reference, similar to *OS_MEM* and *OS_MEM_info*. Local variables are depicted as total functions from threads to variable values. As a result, the thread context can be accessed using its corresponding thread Id.

```
record State =
  (* Shared Variables *)
  tick :: nat
  cur :: "Thread Option"
  thd_state :: "Thread ⇒ Thread_State_Type"
  OS_MEMs :: "OS_MEM_ref set"
  OS_MEM_info :: "OS_MEM_ref ⇒ OS_MEM"
  OSMailBoxes :: "mailbox_ref set"
  OSMailbox_info :: "mailbox_ref ⇒ Mail_box"
  (* Thread Local Variables *)
  ret_mem :: "Thread ⇒ mem_ref option"
  ret :: "Thread ⇒ int"
  th :: "Thread ⇒ Thread"
  tmout :: "Thread ⇒ int"
  endt :: "Thread ⇒nat "
  posting_msg ::"Thread ⇒ Message"
  get_msg :: "Thread ⇒ Message option"
  need_resched :: "Thread ⇒ bool"
  statPend :: "Thread ⇒ int"
```

Fig. 6. State of the Operating System

Scheduler events. We highly abstracted the scheduler since our main contribution focuses on kernel services. The scheduled event receives the thread Id t, which represents the thread being scheduled, and if the thread's state is READY, they set the state of the currently running thread to READY and thread t to RUNNING. Finally, the scheduler switches the currently running thread to thread t.

Kernel Services. HOL-Hoare_parallel provides the most basic language characteristics to simulate the C code of kernel services. We use **ATOMIC** to model the critical region which is represented as OS_ENTER_CRITICAL(); $\cdots$

OS_EXIT_CRITICAL(), in C code of μC/OS-II. We use $t \blacktriangleright p$ to represent thread t is currently being scheduled and executed. For system initialization, we use axiomatization in Isabelle to regulate the behavior of the system's initial state which must adhere to the invariant stated in the previous section.

Specifications. We present the PiCore specifications for our case study. For space reasons, we only illustrate some of them in details here as examples and leave the rest to our GitHub page [30]. Figure 7 shows an excerpt from the specification for the message posting service which is invoked to post a message to a target mailbox. The function takes a mailbox handler and a message pointer as parameters and checks whether they are valid (Lines 1–3). Then it checks whether the mailbox is available (Line 5). If not, it just returns an error message. If so, the function enters the critical region to post a message. It first checks whether tasks are waiting for messages from the mailbox (Line 9). If so, it sends the message to the thread with the highest priority and removes the thread from the wait list, then executes the context switch (Lines 10–17). If not, it just drops the message from the message pointer of the mailbox and returns an error message (Lines 19–20).

```
1  EVENT OSMboxPostE [MBRef pevent, Msg msg] ⇛ (𝒯 t)
2  WHEN
3    pevent ∈ OSMailBoxs
4  THEN
5    IF msg = None THEN
6      (t ▶ ret := ret(t := OS_ERR_POST_NULL_PTR))
7    ELSE
8      (t ▶ ATOMIC
9        IF wait_q (OSMailbox_info pevent) ≠ [] THEN
10         tmout := tmout(th t := 0);;
11         get_msg :=get_msg(th t := msg);;
12         statPend := statPend(th t := OS_STAT_PEND_OK);;
13         OSMailbox_info := OSMailbox_info (pevent :=
14         OSMailbox_info pevent
15         ⦇wait_q := tl (wait_q (OSMailbox_info pevent))⦈);;
16         thd_state := thd_state (th t := READY);;
17         /*    CONTEXT SWITCH    */
18       ELSE
19         /*     DROP MESSAGE     */
20         ret := ret(t := OS_ERR_NONE)
21       FI
22     END)
23   FI
24 END
```

Fig. 7. Excerpt Functional Specification of OSMboxPost Service

5 Correctness and Rely-Guarantee Proof

In this section, we formally prove the functional correctness and invariant preservation of the two modules mentioned above by using PiCore. To verify the functional correctness of the system, the pre and post conditions have to be satisfied only before and after the execution of the handler. To verify the invariant preservation, we need to ensure the invariant must be preserved in every step performed by the system. We present the correctness specification and how to use proof rules provided by PiCore to verify the entire system under study.

[BasicEvt]

$$\frac{\vdash body(\alpha)\ \textbf{sat}\ \langle pre \cap guard(\alpha), R, G, pst\rangle \quad stable(pre, R) \quad \forall s.\ (s, s) \in G}{\vdash \textbf{Event}\ \alpha\ \textbf{sat}\ \langle pre, R, G, pst\rangle}$$

[EvtSeq]

$$\frac{\vdash \mathcal{E}\ \textbf{sat}\ \langle pre, R, G, m\rangle \quad \vdash \mathcal{S}\ \textbf{sat}\ \langle m, R, G, pst\rangle}{\vdash (\mathcal{E} \oplus \mathcal{S})\ \textbf{sat}\ \langle pre, R, G, pst\rangle}$$

[EvtSet]

$$\frac{\begin{array}{l}\forall i \le n.\ \vdash \mathcal{E}_i\ \textbf{sat}\ \langle pres_i, Rs_i, Gs_i, psts_i\rangle \\ stable(pre, R) \quad \forall i, j \le n.\ psts_i \subseteq pres_j \\ \forall i \le n.\ pre \subseteq pres_i \quad \forall i \le n.\ psts_i \subseteq pst \\ \forall i \le n.\ R \subseteq Rs_i \quad \forall i \le n.\ Gs_i \subseteq G \quad \forall s.\ (s, s) \in G\end{array}}{\vdash (\{\mathcal{E}_0,\ \ldots,\ \mathcal{E}_n\})\ \textbf{sat}\ \langle pre, R, G, pst\rangle}$$

[Par]

$$\frac{\begin{array}{l}\forall \kappa.\ \vdash \mathcal{PS}(\kappa)\ \textbf{sat}\ \langle pres_\kappa, Rs_\kappa, Gs_\kappa, psts_\kappa\rangle \\ \forall \kappa.\ pre \subseteq pres_\kappa \quad \forall \kappa.\ psts_\kappa \subseteq pst \\ \forall \kappa.\ Gs_\kappa \subseteq G \quad \forall \kappa.\ R \subseteq Rs_\kappa \\ \forall \kappa, \kappa'.\ \kappa \neq \kappa' \longrightarrow Gs_\kappa \subseteq Rs_{\kappa'}\end{array}}{\vdash \mathcal{PS}\ \textbf{sat}\ \langle pre, R, G, pst\rangle}$$

Fig. 8. Important Proof Rules in PiCore

To validate the system within a rely-guarantee framework, we need to provide precondition, postcondition, rely, and guarantee specifications. Similarly, we give an example here and leave the rest to the GitHub page [30] for space reasons. The quadruple for the OSMemGet event, which is invoked by thread t, is shown in Table 2. The precondition specifies that before executing the kernel service, we must ensure that the system invariant is preserved. The rely specification states that (1) the environment will never change the thread's local variables and static settings (e.g. block size) of shared variables, (2) the system invariant is preserved, and (3) if the currently running thread is t, then the environment does not progress, i.e., it does not modify the memory pool or modify thread-local variables. The guarantee specification is similar to the rely specification. The post specification specifies that the system invariant is still preserved after executing the memory allocation service. If the service successfully returns, as indicated by *ret* $t =$ *OS_ERR_NONE*, then the service must return a memory block. Otherwise, it returns an error message and no memory blocks.

To validate the functional correctness of our system, we first apply the proof rule given by the HOL-Hoare_Parallel to prove the satisfaction of the body of each event. After that, we use PiCore's BasicEvt rule to verify the correctness of each event. We use EvtSet rule to establish that event systems meet the rely-guarantee specifications. In the case of thread event systems, as mentioned, an event set $\{\mathcal{E}_0, \mathcal{E}_1, \mathcal{E}_2, \mathcal{E}_3, \mathcal{E}_4\}$ stands for OSMemGetE, OSMemPutE,

OSMboxPostE, OSMboxPendE, and OSMboxAcceptE, respectively. By applying the EVTSET rule, Isabelle/HOL automatically transfers the correctness goal into four subgoals, illustrated as follows.

1) $\forall i \leqslant n.\ \vdash \mathcal{E}_i\ \mathbf{sat}\ \langle pres_i, Rs_i, Gs_i, psts_i\rangle$
2) $stable(pre, R)\quad \forall i, j \leqslant n.\ psts_i \subseteq pres_j$
3) $\forall i \leqslant n.\ pre \subseteq pres_i\quad \forall i \leqslant n.\ psts_i \subseteq pst$
4) $\forall i \leqslant n.\ R \subseteq Rs_i\quad \forall i \leqslant n.\ Gs_i \subseteq G\quad \forall s.\ (s, s) \in G$

Since we have obtained the correctness of every event, we only need to provide proof for the remaining three subgoals. Finally, we use PAR rule to satisfy the rely-guarantee specifications of the whole parallel event system, i.e., $\vdash \mathcal{PS}\ \mathbf{sat}\ \langle pre, R, G, pst\rangle$, which implies the functional correctness of the whole system.

To verify the preservation of system invariant during the execution of the system, we need to prove 3 premises, i.e., (1) the parallel event system satisfies its rely-guarantee specification (2) the initial state s_0 must satisfy the system invariant (3) the system invariant should be stable under the rely condition R and guarantee condition G.

1) $\vdash \mathcal{PS}\ \mathbf{sat}\ \langle pre, R, G, pst\rangle$
2) $pre \subseteq inv$
3) $stable(inv, R)$ and $stable(inv, G)$ is satisfied.

Table 2. Rely-Guarantee Quadruple of OSMemGet Event

Specification	Description
precondition	$inv\ s$
rely	$((lvars\_nochange\_rel\ t \cap gvars\_conf\_stable$ $\cap \{(s,r),\ inv\ s \longrightarrow inv\ r\} \cap \{(s,r),\ (cur\ s = Some\ t$ $\longrightarrow OS\_MEM\_info\ s = OS\_MEM\_info\ r$ $\wedge (\forall t', t' \neq t \longrightarrow lvars\_nochange\ t'\ s\ r))\}) \cup Id$
guarantee	$gvars\_conf\_stable \cap \{(s,r),\ (cur\ s \neq Some\ t$ $\longrightarrow gvars\_nochange\ s\ r \wedge lvars\_nochange\ t\ s\ r)$ $\wedge (cur\ s = Some\ t \longrightarrow inv\ s \longrightarrow inv\ r)$ $\wedge (\forall t', t' \neq t \longrightarrow lvars\_nochange\ t'\ s\ r)\}) \cup Id$
postcondtion	$inv\ s \wedge (ret = OS\_ERR\_NONE \longrightarrow$ $ret\_mem = Some\ blk)$ $\wedge (ret = OS\_ERR\_MEM\_NO\_FREE\_BLK$ $\longrightarrow ret\_mem = NONE)$

Following an approach similar to the one described above, in this case study, we successfully verified the functional correctness and invariant preservation (described in Table 1) of the two modules of μC/OS-II using PiCore. The complete formal specification and correctness proof are developed in Isabelle/HOL using $\approx$ 2500 lines of specifications and proof scripts available at our GitHub page [30].

6 Experience Using PiCore

Lessons. As shown below, when using PiCore to verify the functional correctness and invariant preservation of event OSMemGetE, we need to specify the environmental updates and system progress for all variables, as shown in Eq. (1), (i) the static setting of global variables are unchanged, i.e., both static setting in memory pool and mailbox, and (ii) other threads do not modify the local variables of thread t, (iii) thread t does not modify other threads' local variables and (iv) every step preserves the inv. PiCore may have complicated the proofs in the following aspects. Firstly, we need to write specifications for irrelevant memory, e.g., we need to prove the static setting of the mailbox and local variables only used in mailbox service remain unchanged and preservation of invariant of the mailbox when verifying the memory management services. Secondly, it requires complicated proofs that explicitly specify and rule out the possibility of interference between different modules. Furthermore, as assertions are global in PiCore, every state update must be checked against environmental interference, including updates that cannot interfere with others, such as system-local variable updates. This can result in unnecessarily complex proofs for systems with multiple modules that work on disjoint memory space or systems without complicated interference.

$$\begin{aligned}&\textbf{OSMemGet\_Guar}\ t \equiv \overbrace{gvars\_conf\_stable}^{(i)} \cap \{(s,r).\\&\overbrace{(cur\ s \neq\ Some\ t \longrightarrow lvars\_nochange\ s\ r)}^{(ii)} \wedge \overbrace{(\forall t'.t' \neq t \longrightarrow lvars\_nochange\ t'\ s\ r)}^{(iii)}\\&\wedge \overbrace{(cur\ s = Some\ t \longrightarrow\ inv\ s \longrightarrow inv\ r)}^{(iv)}\} \cup Id\end{aligned} \tag{1}$$

Possible Remedy. Concurrent Separation Logic (CSL) [12] offers a solution to this problem by using frame rules to abstract away irrelevant states from the specification, allowing verification to focus only on the relevant state for a particular system. CSL also records the ownership of resources to avoid interference from different systems and ensures that no more than one program is reading or writing on the same resource simultaneously.

The current semantics of PiCore for the CRS views the entire program state as shared and does not distinguish the resource ownership of different systems. It is possible to develop a new language that can deal with ownership of resources in event systems and a corresponding reasoning framework that embraces CSL in the future to fulfill the gap.

7 Related Work and Conclusion

Related Work. Many studies have been conducted in the area of OS verification, including seL4 [5,6], CertiKOS [7–9], Hyperkernel [10], and PikeOS [23]. [4]

proves the correctness of most kernel services in μC/OS-II except memory management service. The work in [24] proves the microkernel IPC at Meta. Among these, only [4, 7–9, 24] considered concurrency. [4, 7–9] proves the correctness of the system in a refinement way, i.e., providing an abstract interface to simulate the behavior of the concrete execution. [24] treats IPC service as imperative programs and utilizes the state-of the-art CSL framework Iris [25,26] to verify its correctness.

Event-B [28] provides refinement-based verification for reactive systems but lacks support for concurrency. The extension of Event-B for concurrency [29] does not include standard rely-guarantee reasoning. Other works [15–18] study rely-guarantee reasoning for event-based systems, but their semantics differ from PiCore as events are triggered by event handlers, whereas in PiCore events are triggered by the environment.

Conclusion. This paper presents a formal verification effort for the concurrent memory management module and mailbox module of μC/OS-II at the implementation level. By using the rely-guarantee technique in the PiCore framework, we have formally proven series of essential properties for OS kernels. Our study also highlights that when verifying the correctness of a system containing multiple entangled modules, existing rely-guarantee style reasoning frameworks for CRSs, such as PiCore, may result in unnecessary specifications for irrelevant state space and obvious non-existing environmental interference.

Learning from the experience with this case study, we aim to further improve PiCore's ability and reduce the burden of proof to make the verification more practical. In particular, we plan to implement CSL-style reasoning or more advanced techniques such as RGSep [13] and local rely-guarantee [20] for CRSs in the future to deal with local and shared variables separately. Furthermore, we also intend to address program progress issues, such as deadlock freedom or starvation freedom to provide assurance of total correctness and enhance the support for additional event structures to make it more expressive for modelling the system.

Acknowledgement. This work was supported by the National Key R&D Program of China (Grant No. 2020YFB2010900), and Provincial Key R&D Program of Zhejiang (Grant No. 2020C01038 and Grant No. 2021C01032).

References

1. Aceto, L., et al.: Reactive Systems: Modelling, Specification and Verification. Cambridge University Press, Cambridge (2007)
2. Zhao, Y., Sanán, D., Zhang, F., Liu, Y.: A parametric rely-guarantee reasoning framework for concurrent reactive systems. In: ter Beek, M.H., McIver, A., Oliveira, J.N. (eds.) FM 2019. LNCS, vol. 11800, pp. 161–178. Springer, Cham (2019). https://doi.org/10.1007/978-3-030-30942-8_11
3. Zhao, Y., Sanán, D.: Rely-guarantee reasoning about concurrent memory management in Zephyr RTOS. In: Dillig, I., Tasiran, S. (eds.) CAV 2019. LNCS, vol. 11562, pp. 515–533. Springer, Cham (2019). https://doi.org/10.1007/978-3-030-25543-5_29

4. Xu, F., Fu, M., Feng, X., Zhang, X., Zhang, H., Li, Z.: A practical verification framework for preemptive OS kernels. In: Chaudhuri, S., Farzan, A. (eds.) CAV 2016. LNCS, vol. 9780, pp. 59–79. Springer, Cham (2016). https://doi.org/10.1007/978-3-319-41540-6_4
5. Klein, G., et al.: seL4: formal verification of an OS kernel. In: Proceedings of the ACM SIGOPS 22nd Symposium on Operating Systems Principles (2009)
6. Klein, G., Tuch, H.: Towards verified virtual memory in L4. TPHOLs Emerging Trends **4**, 16 (2004)
7. Gu, R., et al.: Deep specifications and certified abstraction layers. ACM SIGPLAN Notices 50.1, 595–608 (2015)
8. Gu, R., et al.: CertiKOS: an extensible architecture for building certified concurrent OS kernels. OSDI, vol. 16 (2016)
9. Chen, H., et al.: Toward compositional verification of interruptible OS kernels and device drivers. In: Proceedings of the 37th ACM SIGPLAN Conference on Programming Language Design and Implementation (2016)
10. Nelson, L., et al.: Hyperkernel: push-button verification of an OS kernel. In: Proceedings of the 26th Symposium on Operating Systems Principles (2017)
11. The μC/OS-II project. https://github.com/weston-embedded/uC-OS2
12. O'hearn, P.W.: Resources, concurrency, and local reasoning. Theoretical Computer Science 375.1-3, 271–307 (2007)
13. Vafeiadis, V., Parkinson, M.: A marriage of rely/guarantee and separation logic. In: Caires, L., Vasconcelos, V.T. (eds.) CONCUR 2007. LNCS, vol. 4703, pp. 256–271. Springer, Heidelberg (2007). https://doi.org/10.1007/978-3-540-74407-8_18
14. Andronick, J., Corey L., Morgan, C.: Controlled Owicki-Gries concurrency: reasoning about the preemptible eChronos embedded operating system. arXiv preprint arXiv:1511.04170 (2015)
15. Dingel, J., et al.: Towards a formal treatment of implicit invocation using rely/guarantee reasoning. Formal Aspects Comput. **10**, 193–213 (1998)
16. Fenkam, P., Gall, H., Jazayeri, M.: Composing specifications of event based applications. In: Pezzè, M. (ed.) FASE 2003. LNCS, vol. 2621, pp. 67–86. Springer, Heidelberg (2003). https://doi.org/10.1007/3-540-36578-8_6
17. Fenkam, P., Gall, H., Jazayeri, M.: Constructing deadlock free event-based applications: a rely/guarantee approach. In: Araki, K., Gnesi, S., Mandrioli, D. (eds.) FME 2003. LNCS, vol. 2805, pp. 636–657. Springer, Heidelberg (2003). https://doi.org/10.1007/978-3-540-45236-2_35
18. Fenkam, P., Gall, H., Jazayeri, M.: Constructing deadlock free event-based applications: a rely/guarantee approach. In: Araki, K., Gnesi, S., Mandrioli, D. (eds.) FME 2003. LNCS, vol. 2805, pp. 636–657. Springer, Heidelberg (2003). https://doi.org/10.1007/978-3-540-45236-2_35
19. Jones, C.B.: Tentative steps toward a development method for interfering programs. ACM Trans. Programm. Lang. Syst. (TOPLAS) 5.4, 596–619 (1983)
20. Feng, X.: Local rely-guarantee reasoning. In: Proceedings of the 36th Annual ACM SIGPLAN-SIGACT Symposium on Principles of Programming Languages (2009)
21. μC/OS-II documentation. https://micrium.atlassian.net/wiki/spaces/osiidoc/overview
22. Owicki, S., Gries, D.: An axiomatic proof technique for parallel programs I. Acta Inform. **6**(4), 319–340 (1976)
23. Verbeek, F., et al.: Formal API specification of the PikeOS separation kernel. In: Havelund, K., Holzmann, G., Joshi, R. (eds.) NFM 2015. LNCS, vol. 9058, pp. 375–389. Springer, Cham (2015). https://doi.org/10.1007/978-3-319-17524-9_26

24. Carbonneaux, Q., et al.: Applying formal verification to microkernel IPC at Meta. In: Proceedings of the 11th ACM SIGPLAN International Conference on Certified Programs and Proofs (2022)
25. Jung, R., et al.: Iris from the ground up: a modular foundation for higher-order concurrent separation logic. J. Functional Programm. **28**, e20 (2018)
26. Jung, R., et al.: Iris: monoids and invariants as an orthogonal basis for concurrent reasoning. ACM SIGPLAN Notices 50.1, 637–650 (2015)
27. Nieto, L.P.: The Rely-Guarantee method in Isabelle/HOL. In: Degano, P. (ed.) ESOP 2003. LNCS, vol. 2618, pp. 348–362. Springer, Heidelberg (2003). https://doi.org/10.1007/3-540-36575-3_24
28. Abrial, J.-R., Hallerstede, S.: Refinement, decomposition and instantiation of discrete models. Abstract State Machines (2005)
29. Hoang, T.S., Abrial, J.-R.: Event-B decomposition for parallel programs. In: Frappier, M., Glässer, U., Khurshid, S., Laleau, R., Reeves, S. (eds.) ABZ 2010. LNCS, vol. 5977, pp. 319–333. Springer, Heidelberg (2010). https://doi.org/10.1007/978-3-642-11811-1_24
30. The μC/OS-II verification project: https://github.com/SunHuan321/uc-OS-verification

Conformance in the Railway Industry: Single-Input-Change Testing a EULYNX Controller

Djurre van der Wal(✉), Marcus Gerhold, and Mariëlle Stoelinga

University of Twente, Enschede, The Netherlands
d.vanderwal-1@utwente.nl

Abstract. We propose a novel framework for model-based testing against specifications from *EULYNX*, a SysML-based standard from the railway industry for the controllers of systems such as points, signals, sensors, and crossings. The main challenge here is the sheer complexity: with state spaces exceeding 10^{10} states, it is hard to derive test suites that achieve a meaningful type of coverage.

We tackle this problem by moving away from the traditional interleaving semantics for SysML. Instead, we propose a synchronous semantics in terms of Finite State Machines (FSMs), leveraging the fact that EULYNX is implemented on Programmable Logic Controllers (PLCs). Then, we deploy Single-Input-Change Deterministic Finite State Machines (SIC-DFSMs), which ensures fully deterministic tests thus minimizing scalability issues.

Our focus lies on the EULYNX specification for *point controllers*. The generated test suite achieves maximal transition coverage, but test execution time remains substantial. We introduce an additional test suite that achieves maximal transition *label* coverage. Remarkably, this smaller suite successfully identifies the same four faults as the larger suite.

Keywords: Conformance testing · Model-based testing · Programmable logic controllers · Railways · Safety-critical systems · Single-Input-Change

1 Introduction

EULYNX [7] is a standard in the railway industry for the controllers of systems such as points, signals, sensors, crossings. The standardization of such systems makes it possible to break away from the monolithic design of railway infrastructure, which has been the norm in the industry for decades. Instead, railway infrastructure becomes more modular, which breaks vendor lock-ins and reduces the amount of time, effort, and money that is required to maintain, upgrade, and expand railway networks. This, in turn, makes it possible to better meet the increasingly high demands that society places on public transportation.

The original version of chapter 14 has been revised: Reference [2] and the publication year in Reference [9] have been corrected. A correction to this chapter can be found at https://doi.org/10.1007/978-3-031-43681-9_15

A. Cimatti and L. Titolo (Eds.): FMICS 2023, LNCS 14290, pp. 242–258, 2023.
https://doi.org/10.1007/978-3-031-43681-9_14

It is crucial that EULYNX controllers are tested thoroughly, firstly because they are safety-critical systems, and secondly because they are intended to be built by a multitude of manufacturers, who may have conflicting interpretations of the specifications. The established approach in the railway industry for conformance testing is (often manual) scenario-based testing, which is laborious, error-prone, and susceptible to bias. To supplement scenario-based testing in the context of EULYNX, we have been researching the application of *model-based testing (MBT)*, which facilitates large-scale testing through automation and provides a way to measure coverage [30,40].

In our earlier work, our focus was on employing MBT on the EULYNX-specified *point controller* [4]. We derived an mCRL2 model from the SysML diagrams that EULYNX provides [6,28], generated test suites from the model, and applied the test suites to a software simulator. This revealed a fault in the simulator. Despite this success two shortcomings became apparent during our study. Firstly, the resulting mCRL2 model proved to be excessively large, with a state space ranging from 10^{10} to 10^{18} states, leading to significant computational inefficiencies and limited model coverage. Secondly, we encountered discrepancies between the model and the simulator that were greater than anticipated, specifically related to the ordering of inputs and outputs. Developing a reliable interface adapter to appropriately match inputs and outputs presented a non-trivial challenge. These two issues can be addressed independently, e.g., by employing compositional MBT to tackle the large state space, and devising a custom conformance relation to overcome semantic differences between the model and the system-under-test. However, the substantial disparity between the model's size and the functionality of a point controller, as well as the quick acceptance by EULYNX developers of the behavior of the simulator, suggest that our generic interpretation of SysML does not align with its intended meaning.

In this paper, we present a novel framework for model-based testing against EULYNX specifications. The framework is founded on two propositions. First, we propose that SysML should be interpreted in the context of EULYNX in a way that aligns more strongly with the cyclic behavior of *Programmable Logic Controllers (PLCs)*, the preferred implementation platform for EULYNX controllers. This implies a semantics for EULYNX specifications that is synchronous and based on a *Finite State Machine (FSM)*, rather than a semantics that is asynchronous and based on a *Labeled Transition System (LTS)*, like the semantics of our mCRL2 model. Second, we propose to adopt a methodology from the field of hardware/PLC testing, namely *Single-Input-Change (SIC) testing.* SIC testing avoids inputs that cause non-deterministic outputs when the communication with a system-under-test is asynchronous. In general, SIC testing does not cover all behavior of a model, but it often achieves better fault coverage in practice [44]. To our knowledge, SIC testing has not been applied to a EULYNX system before, nor has the semantics of a EULYNX specification been expressed with an FSM in the past.

Approach. We use again the EULYNX point controller as the target of our work (entirely for practical reasons: it has a specification that is balanced in terms of size and complexity; it has a readily available system-under-test, namely the software simulator; and it is easy to modify our existing interface adapter very quickly). Utilizing the SysML diagrams provided in the specification, we derived a non-deterministic FSM. From this FSM, we extracted a *SIC-DFSM*, which contains all SIC-testable behavior from the FSM. We reduced the SIC-DFSM based on bisimulation.

We employed a random greedy exploration method to generate test suites from the SIC-DFSM, achieving maximal transition (label) coverage. Remarkably, this feat was not successfully achieved by any other test suite for EULYNX systems. We applied our generated test suites to the software simulator, leading to the discovery of four distinct faults. Among them were the previously identified fault, a fault uncovered through manual scenario-based testing, and two previously unknown faults.

Contributions. In summary, our efforts have resulted in

- an alternative interpretation of EULYNX specifications;
- automated pipelines for EULYNX specifications from SysML to FSMs/SIC-DFSMs/test suites;
- test suites for EULYNX point controllers that achieve maximal transition (label) coverage of a SIC-DFSM; and
- the discovery of four faults in a software simulator of a EULYNX point controller, three more than were discovered with scenario-based testing.

Paper Organization. We write about the background on EULYNX point controllers and SIC testing in Sect. 2; our proposed FSM-based semantics for EULYNX specifications in Sect. 3; the formalized derivation of a SIC-DFSM in Sect. 4; and our experiments with the software simulator in Sect. 5. Section 6 provides related work. Final remarks (conclusion, discussion, and future work) can be found in Sect. 7.

Data Sources. The source code and software that corresponds with this paper can be found at https://doi.org/10.4121/237905e5-54cc-4a98-abf3-38324d516bf3.

2 Background

We describe two aspects of EULYNX point controllers in this section: the architecture of their specification, and the characteristics of their implementation platform (Programmable Logic Controllers). We end the section with an explanation of Single-Input-Change testing (see Sect. 2.3).

2.1 Point Architecture in EULYNX

Points (also known as 'turnouts' or 'switches') are mechanical installations that can guide a train from one set of rails to another. At their simplest, points have two 'end positions', i.e. 'left' and 'right', which correspond with the set of rails toward which a train is to be guided. A point has sensors that detect if the point is in one end position or in the other, or if the point is currently in between the two end positions. The latter happens when a point is changing from one end position to the other, which it achieved with motors.

Traditionally, the sensors and motors of a point are directly connected to the control system of all railway equipment in the area – the so-called 'interlocking'. Consequently, the implementation of a point is often intertwined with the implementation of the interlocking: for example, it is not straightforward to replace a point with one motor and two sensors with a point with two motors and one sensor. This is different under the paradigm of EULYNX, where sensors and motors of a point are managed on-site by a controller, which exchanges standardized messages with the interlocking via an IP network. This means that, in principle, the communication between a point and an interlocking occurs always in the same way, independent of the underlying implementation of the point.

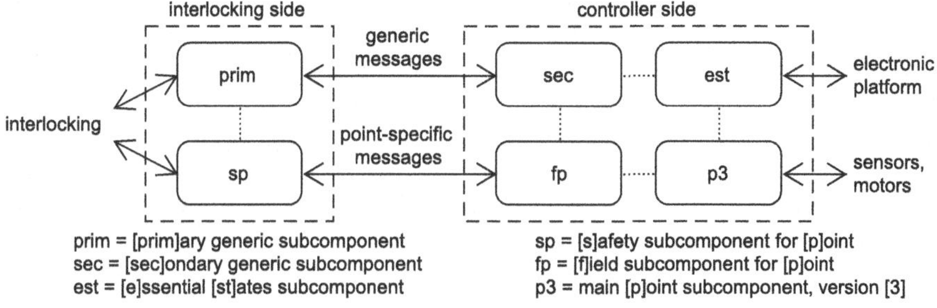

Fig. 1. The architecture of EULYNX point controllers.

The EULYNX specification for point controllers defines six subcomponents, which can be grouped into two layers: a generic layer and a point-specific layer. The subcomponents 'prim', 'sec', and 'est' are part of the generic layer, and provide functionality that is also used by other EULYNX controller types: 'prim' and 'sec' have as their main task to establish/restore the connection between the controller and the interlocking when needed, and 'est' will restart the system after a power failure. The subcomponents 'sp', 'fp', and 'p3' are in the point-specific layer, and perform point-specific functions: 'sp' and 'fp' send/receive commands to change the end position of the point, as well as reports of what the current end position is; and 'p3' is there to electronically manage the sensors and motors. See Fig. 1 for an overview.

Strictly speaking, 'prim' and 'sec' are located "on the interlocking side", and do not specify the point controller. Their purpose is to specify how the interlocking is expected to behave in its interaction with the point controller.

EULYNX specifications are described in SysML [28], a popular system engineering modeling language that is related to UML [27]: *Internal Block Diagrams (IBDs)* define how the various subcomponents of a controller are interconnected, and *State Machine Diagrams (SMDs)* define the behavior of a specific subcomponent. To save space, we do not discuss the SysML aspects of EULYNX in this paper, except for mentioning that SMDs follow a so-called *run-to-completion*

(RTC) semantics. The RTC semantics specify that the processing of an event, once started, is completed before the processing of another event is begun. The RTC semantics make it more straightforward to define *invariants* for an SMD, which only have to hold when no event is being processed. The RTC semantics only affect SMDs that distribute behavior over *orthogonal regions* (i.e. the behavior of one region cannot interleave the behavior of another region).

2.2 Programmable Logic Controllers

The EULYNX point controller is implemented as a Programmable Logic Controller (PLC). PLCs are ruggedized computers for the purpose of managing industrial processes in real-time [37]. They are expected to be highly reliable, easy to program, and easy to diagnose, and they come in a large variety of types and sizes. Interoperability between PLCs, actuators, and sensors is facilitated through PLC standards, of which IEC 61131 [14] is the most prominent.

Although demands on PLCs have increased over the decades, the basics of their operation have largely remained the same. A PLC continuously goes through a *read-execute-write* (or *scanning*) *cycle.* At the start of the cycle, the PLC samples the signals received on its *input ports* and writes them as data to its internal state. It then executes its tasks (called *functions*), which modify the internal state and plan modifications to values of the PLC's *output ports.* At the end of the cycle, the modifications of the values of the PLC's output ports are executed. Often, the duration of the execution phase of a cycle is padded such that the total duration of each cycle is always the same.

A typical way to model the behavior of a PLC is as a deterministic finite state machine (DFSM) that converts bit inputs into bit outputs [33]. Let $\mathbb{V} = \{0, 1\}$:

Definition 1 (DFSM). *We define a Moore-style deterministic finite state machine (DFSM) as the tuple* $\langle S, I, O, \delta, G, s_0 \rangle$, *where*

- S *is the set of states;*
- I *and* O *are the sets of inputs ports and outputs ports of the PLC, respectively, such that* $I \cap O = \emptyset$;
- $\delta : S \times \mathbb{V}^I \mapsto S$ *is the transition function;*
- $G : S \mapsto \mathbb{V}^O$ *is the state output function; and*
- $s_0 \in S$ *is the initial state.*

Non-bit data values can be encoded with a combination of ports. Transitions (δ) are labeled with an input valuation ($\mathbb{V}^I$), which represents the input port values read at the start of a read-execute-write cycle. Similarly, G relates states with an output valuation ($\mathbb{V}^O$), which represents the output port values set by the PLC at the end of a read-execute-write cycle. The transition function δ is deterministic *and* total, i.e. for every state and input valuation we define exactly one successor state.

DFSMs do not allow for the *transient evolution* of states, meaning that the repeated application of an input valuation $\zeta \in \mathbb{V}^I$ never causes more than one change of states. Formally, $\forall s, t \in S, \zeta \in \mathbb{V}^I \,.\, \delta(s, \zeta) = t \implies \delta(t, \zeta) = t$.

2.3 Single-Input-Change Testing

A well-known issue with testing PLCs is that, due to the periodic sampling of input values, simultaneous input changes may be perceived as sequential, and sequential input changes may be perceived as simultaneous [32]. As an example, consider the situation modeled by the partial FSM ($I = \{p, q\}$ and $O = \{x, y\}$) in Fig. 2, in which a PLC has just moved to state s using input valuation $\{p \mapsto 0, q \mapsto 0\}$. To go from s to v, the PLC must receive two input changes, $p \mapsto 1$ and $q \mapsto 1$. However, despite these input changes being sent simultaneously, they may arrive during different cycles of the PLC (e.g., due to a delay in a communication buffer), and thus be perceived by the PLC as sequential. In other words, the PLC could move to u instead. The opposite can also happen: sending $p \mapsto 1$ and $q \mapsto 1$ sequentially may not lead from s to u, because they may still arrive during the same cycle of the PLC, be perceived simultaneously, and make the PLC move to v instead. At the same time, the interval between sending the two input changes cannot be too long, or the PLC moves from t to w.

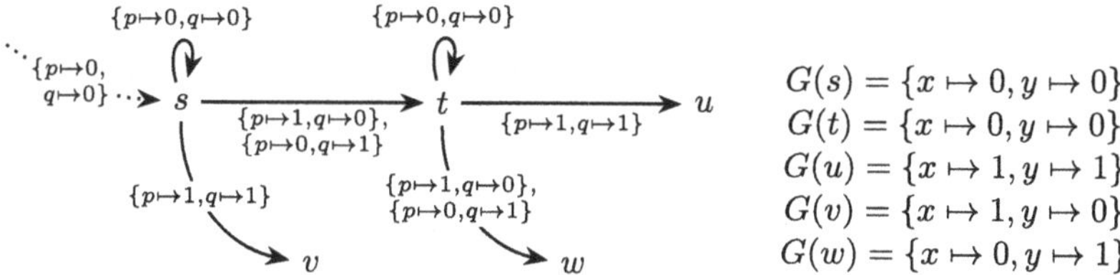

Fig. 2. Partial FSM of a PLC. State s has timing-sensitive inputs.

In the example, s and t have outgoing transitions that cannot be triggered reliably because all possible sequences of input changes potentially trigger another outgoing transition. We say that s and t have *timing-sensitive inputs*.

Timing-sensitive inputs make it so that test sequences that are derived from a deterministic model must take non-deterministic responses into account. There is another approach, namely to derive only test sequences that do not include timing-sensitive inputs. *Single-Input-Change (SIC) sequences* satisfy this criterion [33]. SIC sequences are a concept from testing integrated circuits, and have been shown in this field to achieve better fault coverage than *Multiple-Input-Change (MIC) sequences* [44], as well as to demand less power [42]. SIC sequences are obtained by repeating the following: (i) change the value of a single input of the SUT; (ii) wait until the internal state of the SUT no longer changes; and (iii) validate the output values of the SUT. The second step is called *stabilization*. In practice, stabilization is achieved by waiting a certain amount of time. It is assumed that the SUT never needs more time to finish its computations.

It is not always the case that all behavior of a model can be traversed with a set of SIC sequences. As we saw before in the example of Fig. 2, u and v cannot be reached via a SIC sequence.

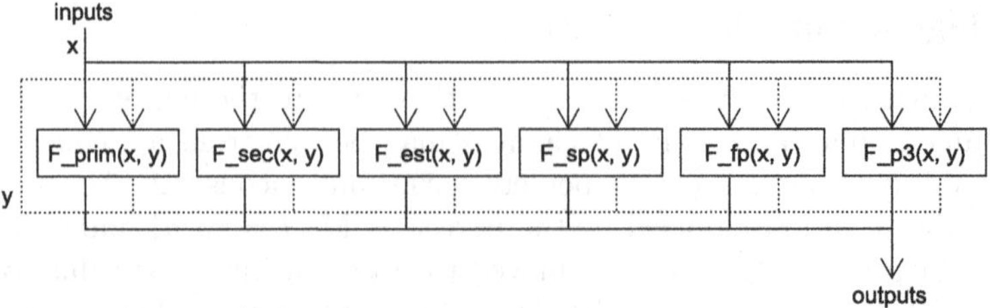

Fig. 3. Subcomponents perform one run-to-completion per cycle, if possible. 'x' are inputs from the environment, 'y' are outputs from the previous cycle that have become inputs.

3 Interpretation of EULYNX Specifications

A common, generic interpretation of communicating SysML SMDs is one where the SMDs are scheduled arbitrarily, and where they communicate asynchronously via non-blocking communication buffers [21,29]. Under this interpretation, the size of the resulting models increases exponentially with the capacity of the communication buffers, and at-capacity communication buffers can lead to unsound deadlocks. This complicates deploying MBT that is thorough, feasible, and appropriately sensitive.

In the case of EULYNX specifications, we believe that the generic interpretation of SMDs is extravagant, and that EULYNX subcomponents and their SMDs are intended to specify PLC *functions* (as described in Sect. 2.2) that are scheduled to be executed once per cycle. In this section, we provide our proposed alternative interpretation of SMDs in the context of EULYNX, and a modified finite state machine definition that we use to express it.

3.1 Proposed Interpretation

We interpret the subcomponents from a EULYNX specification and their SMDs as a finite state machine – as per Definition 1, with some modifications – based on the following assumptions:

Assumption 1: Subcomponents do one run-to-completion per cycle.
As stated, a subcomponent specifies a *function* of the EULYNX controller. Each function receives an opportunity to perform computations once per read-execute-write cycle. A function executes one run-to-completion per cycle, if possible; as a result, each transition of the FSM represents one run-to-completion *or* one idle step per function. Functions perform their computations independently, i.e. the order in which functions are scheduled does not affect the outcome.
Figure 3 depicts this aspect of our interpretation. Inputs from the environment ('x') and outputs of subcomponents from the previous cycle are fed into the subcomponent functions, which produce new outputs for the environment and for the next cycle.

Assumption 2: There can be a transient evolution of states.
The stabilization of a PLC's behavior can require multiple cycles, as functions within the system may initiate computations in subsequent cycles. To accurately represent this phenomenon, our modeling approach incorporates a transient evolution of states, deviating from the restriction in the literature [33].
A transient evolution of states can result in *output evolutions*, i.e. an output port that changes in value over time. We capture a chronologically ordered sequence of output values with $\mathbb{V}^*$.

Assumption 3: Subcomponents can behave non-deterministically.
EULYNX specifications do not specify which event should be prioritized by a subcomponent when it has multiple events to process during a cycle. We preserve this under-specification, and modify the transition function δ such that it returns a non-empty set of successor states.

Assumption 4: Non-bit data values are set atomically.
PLCs almost certainly have functionality that ensures that data values are received atomically on their input ports. We therefore do not retain the abstraction of data values with a bit encoding, and say that $\mathbb{V}$ is an abstracted set of all data values.

Assumption 5: Pulse ports are 1 for one cycle.
Some of the ports that EULYNX specifications contain are *pulse ports*, a special type of port that can be used to avoid the transition evolution of states. Pulse ports can have the value 0 or 1, and they automatically change from 1 to 0 after one cycle. Because of this behavior, subcomponents can respond at most one time to an input pulse port being set to 1. It also means that subcomponents may discard an incoming pulse if they are not ready for it, or if they have alternative inputs to which they can respond instead.

3.2 Formal Model

To capture EULYNX specifications under our proposed interpretation, we modify Definition 1 to:

Definition 2 (FSM). *We define a non-deterministic Moore-style finite state machine (FSM) as the tuple* $\langle S, I, O, \delta, G, s_0 \rangle$, *where*

- S *is the set of states;*
- I *and* O *are the sets of input ports and output ports;*
- $\delta : S \times \mathbb{V}^I \mapsto 2^S$ *is the transition function;*
- $G : S \mapsto \mathbb{V}^O$ *is the state output function; and*
- $s_0 \in S$ *is the initial state;*

such that $\forall s \in S, \zeta \in \mathbb{V}^I \,.\, \delta(s, \zeta) \neq \emptyset$.

As stated in the explanation of Assumption 3, the transition function (δ) has changed, now yielding non-empty sets of potential successor states; and $\mathbb{V}$ is now an abstracted set of data values, as per Assumption 4. To identify pulse ports (see Assumption 5), we define the auxiliary abstract function $pulses : \mathcal{P}(I \cup O) \mapsto \mathcal{P}(I \cup O)$, which filters all pulse ports from a set of ports.

4 From FSM to SIC-DFSM

4.1 SIC-DFSM

We use a SIC-DFSM to express the part of an FSM that is reachable with deterministic SIC sequences. We use two auxiliary definitions. First, we formally express the changes in input valuation $\zeta' \in \mathbb{V}^I$ relative to the (preceding) input valuation $\zeta \in \mathbb{V}^I$ with $dI : \mathbb{V}^I \times \mathbb{V}^I \mapsto 2^I$:

$$dI(\zeta, \zeta') = \{\, i \in I \setminus \mathit{pulses}(I) \mid \zeta'(i) \neq \zeta(i) \,\} \cup \{\, i \in \mathit{pulses}(I) \mid \zeta'(i) \neq 0 \,\}$$

The second is the function $\downarrow : \mathbb{V}^I \mapsto \mathbb{V}^I$, which "turns off" all pulses in an input valuation: $\downarrow\zeta = \{\, i \mapsto \zeta(i) \mid i \in I \setminus \mathit{pulses}(I) \,\} \cup \{\, i \mapsto 0 \mid i \in \mathit{pulses}(I) \,\}$.

We can now define SIC-DFSMs formally. Note that we require the FSM to stabilize upon initialization:

Definition 3 (SIC-DFSM).
A Single-Input-Change deterministic Mealy-style finite state machine (SIC-DFSM) is defined as the tuple $\langle S, I, O, T, \zeta_0, \Omega_0, s_0 \rangle$, where:

- *S is the set of states;*
- *I and O are the sets of input ports and output ports;*
- *$T \subseteq S \times \mathbb{V}^I \times (\mathbb{V}^*)^O \times S$ is the transition relation;*
- *$\zeta_0 \in \mathbb{V}^I$ is the input valuation before the initial stabilization;*
- *$\Omega_0 : (\mathbb{V}^*)^O$ are the output evolutions during the initial stabilization; and*
- *$s_0 \in S$ is the state after the initial stabilization;*

such that for all $(s_1, \zeta_1, \Omega_1, t_1), (s_2, \zeta_2, \Omega_2, t_2) \in T$ it holds that

$$s_2 = t_1 \implies |dI(\downarrow\zeta_1, \zeta_2)| = 1 \ \textit{and}\ \langle s_1, \zeta_1 \rangle = \langle s_2, \zeta_2 \rangle \implies \langle \Omega_1, t_1 \rangle = \langle \Omega_2, t_2 \rangle.$$

Informally, the restrictions specify that there must be exactly one Single-Input-Change in the input valuation of a transition relative to the input valuations of its successor transitions; and that in any state an input valuation must always produce the same output evolutions *and* lead to the same successor state.

4.2 SIC-DFSM Derivation

We formalize the derivation of a SIC-DFSM $\langle \hat{S}, I, O, \hat{T}, \zeta_0, \Omega_0, \hat{s}_0 \rangle$ from an FSM $\langle S, I, O, \delta, G, s_0 \rangle$ for a chosen $\zeta_0 \in \mathbb{V}^I$. We use various auxiliary denotations. First of all, for all $s, t \in S$ we use $s \xrightarrow{\zeta} t$ and $s \xRightarrow{\zeta} t$ to denote $t \in \delta(s, \zeta)$ and $\exists c_1, \cdots, c_n \in S \,.\, s \xrightarrow{\zeta} c_1 \xrightarrow{\zeta} \cdots \xrightarrow{\zeta} c_n \xrightarrow{\zeta} t$, respectively.

Next, we define two functions that collect states in S that can be reached from a state $s \in S$ with transitions that use a specific input valuation $\zeta \in \mathbb{V}^I$. The function $\mathit{stable} - \mathit{succs}(s, \zeta)$ yields all reachable states that use ζ for a self-loop, whereas the function $\mathit{cycle} - \mathit{succs}(s, \zeta)$ yields all reachable states that could prevent stabilization:

$$\mathit{stable} - \mathit{succs}(s, \zeta) = \left\{ t \in S \;\middle|\; s \xRightarrow{\zeta} t \wedge \delta(t, \zeta) = \{t\} \right\}$$

$$\mathit{cycle} - \mathit{succs}(s, \zeta) = \left\{ t \in S \;\middle|\; s \xRightarrow{\zeta} t \wedge t \xRightarrow{\zeta} t \wedge \delta(t, \zeta) \neq \{t\} \right\}$$

The possible evolutions of an output port $o \in O$ can be computed with

$$evos_o(s,\zeta,\zeta') = \left\{ G(s)(o) +\!\!+\, \sigma \;\middle|\; s \xrightarrow{\zeta} t \,\wedge\, t \neq s \,\wedge\, \sigma \in evos_o(t,\zeta',\zeta') \right\} \cup \left\{ G(s)(o) \;\middle|\; s \xrightarrow{\zeta} s \right\}$$

where $+\!\!+ : \mathbb{V} \times \mathbb{V}^* \rightarrow \mathbb{V}^*$ constructs a sequence of values in which the same value cannot occur consecutively. Formally, for $v, w \in \mathbb{V}$ and $\sigma \in \mathbb{V}^*$, we define $v +\!\!+\, w\,\sigma = v\,w\,\sigma$ if $w \neq v$ and $v +\!\!+\, w\,\sigma = v\,\sigma$ if $w = v$.

Finally, let $s, t \in S$, $\zeta \in \mathbb{V}^I$, and $\Omega : (\mathbb{V}^*)^O$. We use $s \overset{\zeta/\Omega}{\Longrightarrow} t$ to denote a situation where the state s under the input valuation ζ is guaranteed to stabilize into the state t, and to produce the output evolutions in Ω along the way. This is the case iff all of the following conditions hold:

1. $\bigcup_{x \in \delta(s,\zeta)} cycle - succs(x, \downarrow \zeta) = \emptyset$
2. $\bigcup_{x \in \delta(s,\zeta)} stable - succs(x, \downarrow \zeta) = \{t\}$
3. $\forall o \in O \,.\, evos_o(s, \zeta, \downarrow \zeta) = \{\Omega(o)\}$

To construct the SIC-DFSM, we require that there exists a state $t \in S$ and a set of initial output evolutions Ω_0 such that $s_0 \overset{\zeta_0/\Omega_0}{\Longrightarrow} t$; in other words, the initial state of the FSM s_0 should stabilize in a deterministic manner. The initial state of the SIC-DFSM can be expressed as $\hat{s}_0 = \langle t, \downarrow \zeta_0 \rangle$.

Intuitively, a state $\langle s, \alpha \rangle \in \hat{S}$ is a state from the FSM s in combination with the input valuation with which we arrived at the state α. We move to new states by making Single-Input-Changes to α; we express this with the relation

$$\hat{R} = \left\{ (\langle s, \alpha \rangle, \langle t, \downarrow \zeta \rangle) \;\middle|\; \alpha, \zeta \in \mathbb{V}^I; \Omega : (\mathbb{V}^*)^O; s, t \in S; |dI(\alpha, \zeta)| = 1; s \overset{\zeta/\Omega}{\Longrightarrow} t \right\}$$

$\hat{S}$ is the transitive closure of $\hat{s}_0$ under $\hat{R}$ (i.e. all states that are reachable from the initial state). We write

$$\hat{S} = \left\{ s \in S \times \mathbb{V}^I \mid \exists c_1, \cdots, c_n \in S \times \mathbb{V}^I \,.\, \hat{s}_0 \Rrightarrow c_1 \Rrightarrow \cdots \Rrightarrow c_n \Rrightarrow s \right\}$$

where $p \Rrightarrow q$ denotes $\langle p, q \rangle \in \hat{R}$ for $p, q \in S \times \mathbb{V}^I$.

Finally, we define the transition relation $\hat{T}$, which is similar to $\hat{R}$ but with two additional transition labels (an input valuation and a set of output evolutions) and restricted to states in $\hat{S}$:

$$\hat{T} = \left\{ (\langle s, \alpha \rangle, \zeta, \Omega, \langle t, \downarrow \zeta \rangle) \;\middle|\; \begin{array}{c} \zeta \in \mathbb{V}^I; \Omega : (\mathbb{V}^*)^O \\ \langle s, \alpha \rangle, \langle t, \downarrow \zeta \rangle \in \hat{S} \\ |dI(\alpha, \zeta)| = 1; s \overset{\zeta/\Omega}{\Longrightarrow} t \end{array} \right\}$$

In other words, if $(s, \alpha, \Omega, t) \in \hat{T}$, then there is an input valuation $\alpha \in \mathbb{V}^I$ that causes movement from the (stable) state $s \in \hat{S}$ to the (stable) state $t \in \hat{S}$, producing the output evolutions $\Omega \in (\mathbb{V}^*)^O$.

5 Case Study

To evaluate the design of our MBT framework, we applied it to the EULYNX specification for point controllers. To this end, we extended the software from our previous work [4] with two pipelines, one to compute an FSM and one to compute a SIC-DFSM, cf. Fig. 4.

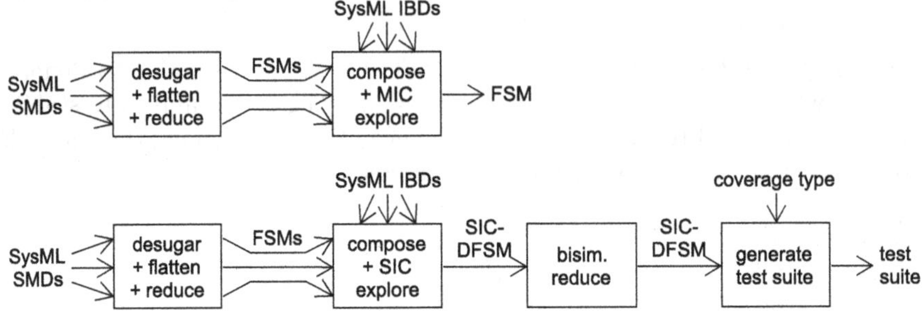

Fig. 4. The two pipelines implemented in our software framework.

5.1 Pipelines

The beginning of the two pipelines is the same. Our framework uses an embedded domain specific language (DSL) for capturing the IBDs and SMDs. It desugars, flattens, and reduces each SMD, producing one component FSM per SMD.

To compute the FSM, we apply multi-threaded breadth-first exploration, starting at the initial state. We combine the component FSMs on-demand, based on information from the IBDs. We explore all possible input valuations; that is, we use Multiple-Input-Changes. To handle this efficiently, we merge input valuations into equivalence classes first.

To compute the SIC-DFSM, we do the same, except that we only allow Single-Input-Changes. Afterwards, we reduce the resulting SIC-DFSM based on bisimulation with a Kanellakis-Smolka-style partition refinement algorithm [17]. We generate test suites from the reduced SIC-DFSM with a random greedy exploration algorithm. The algorithm is "greedy" in the sense that it navigates to untested transitions that require the smallest number of transitions to reach, either from the most recently tested state or from the initial state.

5.2 Results

We derived the FSM and SIC-DFSM for the EULYNX point controller. Table 1 presents sizes and computation times.

We generated two test suites for the EULYNX point controller: the first test suite achieves maximal transition coverage (that is, it covers all transitions of the SIC-DFSM) and the second test suite achieves maximal transition *label* coverage (where a label is an element in $\mathbb{V}^I \times (\mathbb{V}^*)^O$; 572 such labels occur in the SIC-DFSM). See Table 2.

The first test suite is dramatically larger than the second test suite; yet, when applying the test suites to the software simulator, both test suites revealed the same faults. The revealed faults are the following:

Fault 1. The simulator includes an unspecified timer that automatically moves the 'est' subcomponent from its 'BOOTING' state to its 'INITIALIZED' state. This discrepancy is a fault in the simulator.

Fault 2. This fault concerns the 'p3' subcomponent of the simulator. When 'p3' is in the state 'MOVING_LEFT' *and* 'p3' is currently detected the end position 'RIGHT' *and* 'p3' receives a command to move to the end position 'RIGHT', 'p3' moves to the state 'MOVING_RIGHT' and stays there. The intended behavior is that 'p3' moves to the 'STOPPED' state, instead. An analogous discrepancy exists for the reverse situation, i.e. in the state 'MOVING_RIGHT' while detecting the end position 'LEFT'.

Fault 3. When the simulator has achieved an end position *and* it has reported this to the interlocking *and* it is subsequently commanded by the interlocking to move to its current end position, then the simulator does not respond with reporting the current end position a second time (as specified).

Fault 4. The 'p3' subcomponent of the simulator can move from the 'NO_END_POSITION' state to the 'TRAILED' state. By allowing this behavior, the simulator corrects the accidental omission of a transition between two states from the specification (i.e. EULYNX developers confirmed that the transition should have been specified).

Table 1. States/Transitions and computation time per FSM/SIC-DFSM.

Model	#States	#Transitions	Computation time
FSM	13.322.223	$3 \cdot 10^9$	4 h 34 m
SIC-DFSM	134.490	3.362.250	1 h 35 m
SIC-DFSM (bisim. reduced)	70.428	1.760.700	1 h 36 m

Table 2. Tests/Steps and generation/execution time per test suite.

Coverage type	#Tests	#Steps	Generation time	Execution time
Transitions	48.738	4.847.018	18 m 25 s	13 h
Transition labels	48	3167	30 s	52 s

5.3 Validation

The correct derivation of the SIC-DFSM is confirmed to a great extent by the passing of the software simulator of the vast majority of the tests. Note that our tests are permissive in two ways: they do not include state verification (i.e. the application of inputs to confirm that transitions reached their target state), and they do not check how output evolutions interleave.

We validated that the FSM and SIC-DFSM for the EULYNX point controller contain the behavior that we expect by analyzing their coverage of SMD states/transitions. Tracing back with our software framework the SMD states from which the states of the FSM and SIC-DFSM originate, we found that the FSM and the SIC-DFSM both cover 39 SMD states. Similarly, we traced back transitions of the FSM and SIC-DFSM to SMD transitions, and found that the FSM covers 98 SMD transitions, and that the SIC-DFSM covers 95 SMD transitions. We confirmed by hand that the transitions not covered by the SIC-DFSM are enabled only by Multiple-Input-Changes.

The fact that we found all faults that were known beforehand (Faults 1 and 2) as well as two additional faults (Faults 3 and 4) supports the claim that our approach produces comprehensive test suites. Of course, it is remarkable that the second test suite reveals the same faults in a fraction of the time. This could be because all revealed faults are located at the subcomponent level (the faults do not require multiple components to be in specific states). A concern that occurs to us is that a fault that is located at the system level may be unlikely to be revealed through SIC testing.

6 Related Work

Testing EULYNX Controllers. As stated, this paper is an extension of previous work on the EULYNX point controller specification and its software simulator [4]. In that work, we used a highly concurrent and fine-grained mCRL2 model for both formal verification and MBT. MBT of the software simulator achieved very limited coverage, revealing only Fault 1. We also encountered erroneous test verdicts, which were caused by timing-sensitive inputs or by unexpected orderings of output values.

The software simulator of the EULYNX point controller has been tested partially with the Axini Modeling Platform [1]. This achieved symbolic transition coverage of the 'sp', 'fp', and 'p3' subcomponents; the methodology did not scale to more subcomponents. Also in this work problems were encountered due to unexpected orderings/interleavings of output values.

Verification with Event-B has been performed of individual SMDs of the EULYNX point controller [34]. There is also research into the development of a test setup for physical EULYNX controllers [31].

MBT in Railways. MBT has also been applied to other railway systems, ranging from on-board speed controllers [5,43] to interlockings [16,36,38]. MBT has been applied online [36,43] and offline [3,22,35], using a variety of MBT software tools, such as RT-Tester [30] and UPPAAL-TRON [36]. For overviews on MBT in railway industry, see [2,8,9,12].

Single-Input-Change Testing. The use of SIC sequences has gained traction in the field of testing integrated circuits because of the improved fault coverage [42] and reduced power consumption relative to Multiple-Input-Testing (MIC) sequences [44]. The idea to test PLCs with SIC sequences was conceived when testing PLCs with minimum-length test sequences resulted in erroneous test verdicts [32]. However, it was shown that a SIC sequence to a given location in a model does not necessarily exist [33]. This inspired a Design-To-Test (DTT) approach [23–25], in which minimal changes are made to a specification FSM to ensure SIC-testability and the existence of short state verification sequences.

Testing Asynchronous Systems. The most intuitive approach of asynchronous MBT is to add an input queue and an output queue to the model, and to consider them together to be a single system [41]. However, this comes with scalability issues, and therefore tests have instead been generated directly from the specification model [13] or from a model combined with a single input action context [11].

An often used conformance relation in MBT is *input-output conformance*, or *ioco* [39], which is based on LTSs and which facilitates non-determinism and under-specification. A method for ioco-based test generation exists where inputs are applied only if *quiescence* is observed, i.e. no output from the SUT [26]. This is essentially the ioco-equivalent of SIC testing, and the method could be applied to the mCRL2 model from our previous work to see if MBT is feasible *without* interpreting subcomponents as cyclically executed PLC functions. Note that computing all behavior of controller (which we can do) would again be daunting, and making a comparison of SIC-testable behavior and all behavior would not be straightforward.

7 Final Remarks

Conclusion. Our proposed interpretation of EULYNX specifications – of the SMDs in particular – leads to FSMs that (i) capture all specified behavior and (ii) have a manageable size. By using SIC testing, a meaningful type of coverage (e.g. transition coverage) can be achieved. We have shown this experimentally for the EULYNX point controller, with results that are superior to those from our previous MBT activities [4].

Discussion & Future work. With our approach, we aimed to maximize coverage of a meaningful type, and we found that this improved fault coverage (revealing three discrepancies that were not revealed through scenario-based testing, namely Faults 1, 2, and 3). It should be noted, however, that coverage-guided testing does not improve fault coverage in general [10]. Mutation testing [15] could lead to a better picture of the fault coverage of our approach.

We expect that our approach scales to the larger EULYNX specifications. This may require optimizations of our software framework.

Our approach uses a specific interpretation of SysML state machine diagrams; consequently, an implementation that follows a different, yet also reasonable interpretation may fail a test suite that we generate. By analyzing the reason for such a failure, the semantics of EULYNX specifications can be refined. In our case study, none of the failures were the result of our alternative interpretation. This may be because behavioral differences are not exposed by SIC-testing.

Since EULYNX does not specify in which order simultaneously arriving events should be processed, we model this with non-determinism. Input events can originate from the environment or from another subcomponent. We believe that non-deterministic behavior that results from inputs that originate from other subcomponents only (i.e. non-deterministic behavior that results from internal communication) is not intended by EULYNX developers, and undesirable in particular for a safety-critical systems. This type of non-determinism can be avoided through the addition of priority values to certain transitions of an SMD, or by ensuring that the events that trigger transitions are mutually exclusive.

Our test suite generation algorithm does not compute *state verification sequences* [20]. State verification sequences are not guaranteed to exist for all states, and if they exist, their length can be exponential in the number of states of the model. The existence of short state verification sequences can be guaranteed with a DTT approach [25], which we highly recommend in the context of safety-critical systems. DTT could also ensure that all behavior in a specification is SIC-testable. Otherwise, a strategy that involves test suite optimization and/or reduction may need to be developed [18,19].

Acknowledgements. This paper is a product of the FormaSig project, fully funded by DB Netz AG and ProRail. The vision illustrated in this article reflects the personal views of the authors, and is not part of the strategy of DB Netz AG or ProRail. We thank the SIGNON Group (https://signon-group.com/) for providing access to the source code of the software simulator.

References

1. Bachmann, T., van der Wal, D., van der Bijl, M., van der Meij, D., Oprescu, A.: Translating EULYNX SysML models into symbolic transition systems for model-based testing of railway signaling systems. 2022 IEEE Conference on Software Testing, Verification and Validation (ICST), pp. 355–364 (2022)
2. Basile, D., et al.: On the industrial uptake of formal methods in the railway domain. In: Furia, C., Winter, K. (eds.) IFM 2018. LNCS, vol. 11023, pp. 20–29. Springer, Cham (2018). https://doi.org/10.1007/978-3-319-98938-9_2
3. Bonacchi, A., Fantechi, A., Bacherini, S., Tempestini, M.: Validation process for railway interlocking systems. Sci. Comput. Program. **128**, 2–21 (2016)
4. Bouwman, M., van der Wal, D., Luttik, B., Stoelinga, M., Rensink, A.: A case in point: verification and testing of a EULYNX interface. Formal Aspects Comput. **35**, 1–38 (2022)

5. Braunstein, C., et al.: Complete model-based equivalence class testing for the ETCS ceiling speed monitor. In: Merz, S., Pang, J. (eds.) ICFEM 2014. LNCS, vol. 8829, pp. 380–395. Springer, Cham (2014). https://doi.org/10.1007/978-3-319-11737-9_25
6. Bunte, O., et al.: The mCRL2 toolset for analysing concurrent systems - improvements in expressivity and usability. In: International Conference on Tools and Algorithms for Construction and Analysis of Systems (2019)
7. EULYNX website. http://eulynx.eu. Accessed 18 Jan 2023
8. Fantechi, A.: Twenty-five years of formal methods and railways: what next? In: SEFM Workshops (2013)
9. Ferrari, A., ter Beek, M.H.: Formal methods in railways: a systematic mapping study. ACM Comput. Surv. **55**, 1–37 (2022). https://doi.org/10.1145/3520480
10. Gay, G., Staats, M., Whalen, M.W., Heimdahl, M.P.E.: The risks of coverage-directed test case generation. IEEE Trans. Software Eng. **41**, 803–819 (2015)
11. Graf-Brill, A., Hermanns, H.: Model-based testing for asynchronous systems. In: FMICS-AVoCS (2017)
12. Haxthausen, A.E., Peleska, J.: model checking and model-based testing in the railway domain. In: SyDe Summer School (2015)
13. Huo, J., Petrenko, A.: Transition covering tests for systems with queues. Softw. Testing **19**, 55–83 (2009)
14. International Electrotechnical Commission: International Standard IEC 61131: Programmable Controllers (2017)
15. Jia, Y., Harman, M.: An analysis and survey of the development of mutation testing. IEEE Trans. Software Eng. **37**, 649–678 (2011)
16. Kadakolmath, L., Ramu, U.D.: Model-checking-based automated test case generation for Z formal specification of an urban railway interlocking system. In: 2022 Fourth International Conference on Emerging Research in Electronics, Computer Science and Technology (ICERECT), pp. 1–8 (2022)
17. Kanellakis, P.C., Smolka, S.A.: CCS expressions, finite state processes, and three problems of equivalence. Inf. Comput. **86**, 43–68 (1983)
18. Khan, S.U.R., Lee, S.P., Javaid, N., Abdul, W.: A systematic review on test suite reduction: approaches, experiment's quality evaluation, and guidelines. IEEE Access **6**, 11816–11841 (2018)
19. Kiran, A., Butt, W.H., Anwar, M.W., Azam, F., Maqbool, B.: A comprehensive investigation of modern test suite optimization trends, Tools and Techniques. IEEE Access **7**, 89093–89117 (2019)
20. Lee, D., Yannakakis, M.: Principles and methods of testing finite state machines-a survey. Proc. IEEE **84**, 1090–1123 (1996)
21. Liu, S., et al.: A formal semantics for complete UML state machines with communications. In: Johnsen, E.B., Petre, L. (eds.) IFM 2013. LNCS, vol. 7940, pp. 331–346. Springer, Heidelberg (2013). https://doi.org/10.1007/978-3-642-38613-8_23
22. Lv, J., Wang, H., Liu, H., Zhang, L., Tang, T.: A model-based test case generation method for function testing of train control systems. In: 2016 IEEE International Conference on Intelligent Rail Transportation (ICIRT), pp. 334–346 (2016)
23. Ma, C., Jordan, C.V., Provost, J.: SATE: model-based testing with design-to-test and plant features. IFAC-PapersOnLine **51**, 310–315 (2018)
24. Ma, C., Provost, J.: Design-to-test: an approach to enhance testability of programmable controllers for critical systems-two case studies (2016)
25. Ma, C., Provost, J.: Design-to-test approach for programmable controllers in safety-critical automation systems. IEEE Trans. Industr. Inf. **16**, 6499–6508 (2020)

26. Noroozi, N., Khosravi, R., Mousavi, M.R., Willemse, T.A.C.: Synchronizing asynchronous conformance testing. In: Barthe, G., Pardo, A., Schneider, G. (eds.) SEFM 2011. LNCS, vol. 7041, pp. 334–349. Springer, Heidelberg (2011). https://doi.org/10.1007/978-3-642-24690-6_23
27. Object Management Group: OMG Unified Modeling Language, Version 2.5.1 (2017). https://www.omg.org/spec/UML/
28. Object Management Group: OMG Systems Modeling Language, Version 1.6 (2019). https://www.omg.org/spec/SysML/
29. Paltor, I.: The Semantics of UML State Machines (1999)
30. Peleska, J.: Industrial-strength model-based testing - state of the art and current challenges. In: MBT (2013)
31. Polze, A.: EULYNX-Live: a methodology for validating system specifications in hybrid field tests EULYNX-Live: Eine Methodik zum Validieren von Systemspezifikationen in hybriden Feldtests (2021)
32. Provost, J., Roussel, J.M., Faure, J.M.: Testing programmable logic controllers from finite state machines specification. In: 2011 3rd International Workshop on Dependable Control of Discrete Systems, pp. 1–6 (2011)
33. Provost, J., Roussel, J.M., Faure, J.M.: Generation of single input change test sequences for conformance test of programmable logic controllers. IEEE Trans. Industr. Inf. **10**, 1696–1704 (2014)
34. Salunkhe, S., Berglehner, R., Rasheeq, A.: Automatic transformation of SysML model to event-B model for railway CCS application. In: International Conference on Abstract State Machines, Alloy, B, TLA, VDM, and Z (2021)
35. Sánchez, C., Cavalli, A.R., Yevtushenko, N.V., Santos, J., Abreu, R.: On modeling and testing components of the European train control system (2014)
36. Scippacercola, F., Pietrantuono, R., Russo, S., Zentai, A.: Model-in-the-loop testing of a railway interlocking system. In: Desfray, P., Filipe, J., Hammoudi, S., Pires, L.F. (eds.) MODELSWARD 2015. CCIS, vol. 580, pp. 375–389. Springer, Cham (2015). https://doi.org/10.1007/978-3-319-27869-8_22
37. Sehr, M.A., et al.: programmable logic controllers in the context of industry 4.0. IEEE Trans. Industr. Inf. **17**, 3523–3533 (2021)
38. Su, H., Chai, M., Liu, H., Chai, J., Yue, C.: A model-based testing system for safety of railway interlocking. 2022 IEEE 25th International Conference on Intelligent Transportation Systems (ITSC), pp. 335–340 (2022)
39. Tretmans, J.: Model based testing with labelled transition systems. In: Formal Methods and Testing (2008)
40. Utting, M., Pretschner, A., Legeard, B.: A taxonomy of model-based testing approaches. Softw. Testing **22**, 297–312 (2012)
41. Verhaard, L., Tretmans, J., Kars, P., Brinksma, E.: On asynchronous testing. In: Protocol Test Systems (1992)
42. Virazel, A., David, R., Girard, P., Landrault, C., Pravossoudovitch, S.: Delay fault testing: choosing between random SIC and random MIC test sequences. J. Electron. Test. **17**, 233–241 (2000)
43. Wang, Y., Chen, L., Kirkwood, D., Fu, P., Lv, J., Roberts, C.: Hybrid online model-based testing for communication-based train control systems. IEEE Intell. Transp. Syst. Mag. **10**, 35–47 (2018)
44. Yi, W., Xing-hua, F., Dai-qiang, W.: An implementation of random single input change technique for low-power test. In: 2008 2nd International Conference on Anti-counterfeiting, Security and Identification, pp. 352–355 (2008)

Correction to: Formal Methods for Industrial Critical Systems

Alessandro Cimatti and Laura Titolo

Correction to: A. Cimatti and L. Titolo (Eds.): *Formal Methods for Industrial Critical Systems*, LNCS 14290, https://doi.org/10.1007/978-3-031-43681-9

The original version of the book was inadvertently published with an incorrect form of reference [36] in Chapter 1. Two authors' names were not published correctly in this reference.

The correct citation of the authors' names should be: "Garavel, H., ter Beek, M.H., van de Pol, J." and in the Reference 31 the publication year should be 2022. This has been corrected.

The original version of the book was inadvertently published with an incomplete reference [2] in Chapter 14. The correct citation of this reference should be: "Basile, D., Mazzanti F., Ferrari, A.: On the Industrial Uptake of Formal Methods in the Railway Domain. In: Furia, C., Winter, K. (eds.) IFM 2018. LNCS, vol. 11023, pp. 20–29. Springer, Cham (2018). https://doi.org/10.1007/978-3-319-98938-9_2." and in the Reference 9 the publication year should be 2022. This has been corrected.

The updated version of these chapters can be found at
https://doi.org/10.1007/978-3-031-43681-9_1
https://doi.org/10.1007/978-3-031-43681-9_14

A. Cimatti and L. Titolo (Eds.): FMICS 2023, LNCS 14290, p. C1, 2024.
https://doi.org/10.1007/978-3-031-43681-9_15

Author Index

A. Cimatti and L. Titolo (Eds.): FMICS 2023, LNCS 14290, pp. 259–260, 2023.
https://doi.org/10.1007/978-3-031-43681-9

Printed in the United States
by Baker & Taylor Publisher Services